Global Information Society Watch

2011

APC Hivos

This edition of Global Information Society Watch is dedicated to the people of the Arab revolutions whose courage in the face of violence and repression reminded the world that people working together for change have the power to claim the rights they are entitled to.

Steering committee
Anriette Esterhuysen (APC)
Loe Schout (Hivos)

Coordinating committee
Karen Banks (APC)
Monique Doppert (Hivos)
Karen Higgs (APC)
Marjan Besuijen (Hivos)
Joy Liddicoat (APC)
Pablo Accuosto (APC)
Valeria Betancourt (APC)

Project coordinator
Karen Banks

Editor
Alan Finlay

Assistant editor
Lori Nordstrom

Publication production
Karen Higgs, Analía Lavin and Flavia Fascendini

Graphic design
MONOCROMO
info@monocromo.com.uy
Phone: +598 2 400 1685

Cover illustration
Matías Bervejillo

Proofreading
Stephanie Biscomb, Valerie Dee and Lori Nordstrom

Financial partners
Humanist Institute for Cooperation with Developing Countries (Hivos)
Swedish International Development Cooperation Agency (Sida)

The views expressed in this publication are those of the individual authors and not necessarily those of APC or Hivos

Printed in Goa, India
by Dog Ears Books & Printing

Global Information Society Watch
Published by APC and Hivos
South Africa
2011

ISSN: 2224-5162
APC-201111-CIPP-R-EN-P-0104
ISBN: 978-92-95096-13-4

APC and Hivos would like to thank the Swedish International Cooperation Agency (Sida) for its support for Global Information Society Watch 2011.

Sida

Table of contents

Thematic reports

Internet charters and principles

Mapping rights

Country reports

Preface

Unlike any other medium, the internet enables individuals to seek, receive and impart information and ideas of all kinds instantaneously and inexpensively across national borders. Unlike any other technological development, it has created an interactive form of communication, which not only allows you to send information in one direction, but also to send information in many directions and receive an immediate response. The internet vastly increases the capacity of individuals to enjoy their right to freedom of opinion and expression, including access to information, which facilitates the exercise of other human rights, such as the right to education and research, the right to freedom of association and assembly, and the right to development and to protect the environment. The internet boosts economic, social and political development, and contributes to the progress of humankind as a whole; but it is especially an instrument that strengthens democracy by facilitating citizen participation and transparency. The internet is a "plaza pública" – a public place where we can all participate.

The past year has been a difficult time globally: whether the aftermath of the tsunami in Japan, unsteady global markets, post-election riots in Nigeria, civil war in Libya and a military clampdown in Syria. But there have been positive, and equally challenging, developments in countries such as Tunisia and Egypt. Throughout the year people around the world have increasingly used the internet to build support for human rights and social movements. This edition of Global Information Society Watch (GISWatch) offers timely commentary on the future of the internet as an open and shared platform that everyone has the right to access – to access content and to have access to connectivity and infrastructure.

Through the lens of freedom of expression, freedom of association and democracy, the thematic reports included here go to the heart of the debates that will shape the future of the internet and its impact on human rights. They offer, amongst other things, an analysis of how human rights are framed in the context of the internet, the progressive use of criminal law to intimidate or censor the use of the internet, the difficult role of intermediaries facing increasing pressure to control content, and the importance of the internet to workers in the support of global rights in the workplace. Some call for a change of perspective, as in the report on cyber security, where the necessity of civil society developing a security advocacy strategy for the internet is argued. Without it, the levels of systems and controls, whether emanating from government or military superpowers, threaten to overwhelm what has over the years become the vanguard of freedom of expression and offered new forms of free association between people across the globe.

Many of these issues are pulled sharply into focus at the country level in the country reports that follow the thematic considerations. Each of these country reports takes a particular "story" or event that illustrates the role of the internet in social rights and civil resistance – whether positive or negative, or both. Amongst other things, they document torture in Indonesia, candlelight vigils in South Korea, internet activism against forgetting human rights atrocities in Peru, and the rights of prisoners accessing the internet in Argentina. While the function and role of the internet in society remains debated, and necessarily so, in many contexts these stories show that to limit it unfairly will have a harmful impact on the rights of people. These stories show that the internet has become pivotal in actions aimed at the protection of human rights.

GISWatch makes a valuable contribution to dialogue on freedom of expression, freedom of association and democratisation and seeks to inspire and support collaborative approaches. ■

Frank La Rue

UNITED NATIONS SPECIAL RAPPORTEUR ON THE PROMOTION AND PROTECTION OF THE RIGHT TO FREEDOM OF OPINION AND EXPRESSION

Introduction

Jillian C. York
Electronic Frontier Foundation
eff.org

Early visionaries imagined the internet as a borderless world where the rule of law and the norms of the so-called physical world did not apply. Free expression and free association were envisioned as entitlements, a feature of cyberspace rather than rights to be asserted.

These early conceptions quickly gave way to the realisation that, just as the internet was embraced by people, so would it be controlled: by corporations, by policy makers, by governments, the latter of which began asserting control over the internet early on, enacting borders to cyberspace and preventing the free flow of information, not unlike the physical borders that prevent free movement between nations.

For more than a decade, academics and activists have dissected and debated the various challenges to a free and open net. But the use of digital tools in the uprisings in the Middle East and North Africa, as well as the subsequent restrictions placed on them by governments, have inspired new public discourse on the subject, bringing to light the importance of and highlighting new challenges to internet freedom.

In Tunisia and in Egypt, the ability to organise and share information online proved vital to many in organising the revolutions that eventually led to the downfall of both countries' regimes. There, and in Syria, Viet Nam, Iran, the Occupied Palestinian Territories, and beyond, the videos and images disseminated from protests have demonstrated precisely why online freedom must be a policy imperative.

The Charter of Human Rights and Principles for the Internet,[1] developed by the Internet Rights and Principles Coalition, defines online freedom of expression to include the freedom to protest, freedom from censorship, the right to information, the freedom of the media, and the freedom *from* hate speech. Framed by Article 19 of the Universal Declaration of Human Rights (UDHR), the Charter recognises certain legal restrictions placed on such rights (such as the necessity to keep public order). Similarly, the Charter also frames the freedom of assembly or association online within the space of the UDHR, including in its definition the right to "form, join, meet or visit the website or network of an assembly, group, or association for any reason" and noting that "access to assemblies and associations using ICTs [information and communications technologies] must not be blocked or filtered." The two aforementioned definitions comprehensively address online rights as defined within the framework of the UDHR.

But while the freedoms of expression and association are guaranteed by Articles 19 and 20 of the UDHR, and by the individual constitutions of many of the world's nation-states, their application online has proved troublesome for even the most democratic of governments.

The internet is unique, both structurally and practically. A medium unlike any other, it enables individuals to cross borders in an instant, to seek and share information rapidly and at little cost. But just as it provides a unique means of communication, so too does it present unique challenges for regulators who, so far, have relied upon outmoded legislation to regulate the digital space.

For example, defamation laws in Turkey have led to an environment where any individual or organisation can all too easily petition a judge to block an allegedly defamatory website, thereby silencing what may very well be legitimate criticism. Similarly, in Tunisia, not long after the country's decade-long censorship of the internet ended, a group of judges successfully petitioned the court to order the Tunisian Internet Agency to block access to a large swath of pornographic websites in the interest of "morality".

The desire to restrict access to "adult content" exemplifies the challenges of enforcing existing age restrictions on online content. Where a magazine can be restricted for sale to minors or hidden in opaque packaging, and a television programme or film can come with age-appropriate warnings, online content is not so easily restricted. Instead, the most oft-used method of restriction, technical filtering, cannot differentiate between the adult and child user and therefore blocks access to content from all. In any scenario, filtering tends to be overbroad and expensive, but is also fallible, and

1 internetrightsandprinciples.org/node/367

in most cases easily circumvented by commercially available tools.

Blocking websites is not the only means of restricting access: in Iran and in Syria, for example, authorities have slowed bandwidth to a crawl, limiting the ability of users to upload or download content such as videos or images. Several countries, including South Korea, have attempted to control access to certain content, or to track users by requiring government identification to use certain websites or to enter cybercafés. Government-enabled or sponsored attacks on infrastructure or individual websites have become increasingly common. And more recently, governments aware of the internet's organising potential have taken to implementing "just-in-time" blocking – limiting access to sites during specific periods of election or protest, or worse, arresting bloggers and social media users or shutting down the internet entirely as has occurred in Egypt, Libya and Syria.

These various forms of restriction leverage the ability of governments to censor and discredit unwanted speech, while fears of "cyberwar" make it easy for governments to justify political repression, blocking access to opposition content or arresting bloggers under terrorism legislation. A genuine need for digital security has pushed governments to develop strategies to identify and track down actual criminals; these methods are in turn used to crack down on political dissidents and others. Similarly, efforts to enforce copyright have led to chilling effects, such as in the United States (US) where, in an effort to crack down on copyright infringement, the intellectual property wing of the Immigrations and Customs Enforcement seized dozens of domain names under the guise of "consumer protection". Similarly, proposals such as France's HADOPI – which would terminate the internet access of subscribers accused three times of (illegal) file sharing – silence speech while doing little to solve the problem they are intended to combat.

Lawmakers have also found ways to restrict access to certain content from users *outside* of their countries using what is known as geolocational IP blocking. This tactic has a variety of uses, from media content hosts like Netflix and Hulu blocking users outside of the US in compliance with copyright schemes, to US companies blocking access to users in sanctioned countries like Syria and Iran.

Free expression online is challenged not only by governments, but also by private entities. Though censorship is, by definition, the suppression of *public* communications, the right to free expression is increasingly challenged by intermediaries, whether by their own volition or at the behest of governments. States have on numerous occasions relied upon intermediaries to undertake censorship on their behalf, such as in the case of South Korea, where the Korea Communications Standard Commission – a semi-private initiative – has been developed to regulate online content, or in the United Kingdom (UK), where the Internet Watch Foundation, an opaque non-governmental agency, determines a blacklist of child sexual abuse websites, which is in turn used by internet service providers (ISPs) and governmental regulators (as was the case with Australia's proposed filtering scheme). Currently, several Australian ISPs have agreed to voluntarily filter illegal content in lieu of filtering legislation, raising questions about the role of ISPs in moderating content. These issues are at the core of the debate around network neutrality, a policy framework which has yet to be widely adopted.

Companies that operate in foreign countries can impose or be complicit in limits to free expression. Companies are obliged to abide by the rules of their host country, which, in countries where restrictions to online content are the norm, results in aiding that country's censorship. Between 2006 and 2010, Google censored its search results at the behest of the Chinese government, while Microsoft continues to do so. And several companies – including US companies Cisco and SmartFilter, and Canadian company Netsweeper – allow their filtering software to be used by foreign governments.

These concerns also extend to platforms that host user-generated content. Across the Arab world and beyond, the use of social platforms to organise and disseminate information has garnered praise for sites like Facebook and Twitter. But while these platforms offer seemingly open spaces for discourse, the policies and practices of these privately owned platforms often result in content restrictions stricter than those applied by government censors, presenting a very real threat to free expression. Take, for example, the case of Wael Ghonim, the Egyptian Google executive who created the "We Are All Khaled Said" Facebook page, a core site for organising the protests. Several months prior to the uprising, the page was taken down, a result of Facebook policies that require users to utilise a real name on the service, and was only reinstated when another, identified, user stepped in to take Ghonim's place. Similarly, Facebook recently removed a page calling for a third intifada in Palestine, following public objections and numerous user reports. Other platforms have acted similarly, removing content when it violates their proprietary terms of use.

While filtering and other means of restriction affect the ability to access *content*, access to the physical and technical infrastructure required to connect to the internet can also be used by governments as a means of restricting the free flow of information and limiting individuals' ability to associate and organise. While in many cases, low internet penetration is a sign of economic or infrastructural challenges, it can also be an intentional strategy by governments attempting to restrict citizens from accessing information or developing civil society. Though this strategy is best exemplified by Cuba and North Korea – where the majority of citizens are barred entirely from accessing the internet – dozens of countries with the capability to do so have slowed or stifled the infrastructural development necessary to expand access.

These various forms of control have led to what scholars have referred to as the "Balkanisation" of the internet, whereby national boundaries are applied to the internet through these various means of control. In 2010, the OpenNet Initiative estimated that more than half a billion (or about 32%) of the world's internet users experience some form of national-level content restriction online. That number is undoubtedly increasing: in recent months, various governments across the globe have taken new steps to restrict access to content. Egypt, which had blocked websites minimally and only sporadically, took an enormous step backward when it shut down the internet for a week during the protests. Libya, which prior to 2011 filtered only selectively, has barred access for most of its population since February. Iran has recently announced plans to withdraw from the global internet, creating essentially an intranet inside the country. And even in states where access remains low – such as in Ethiopia, where internet penetration hovers around 0.5% – governments fearing the democratising power of the internet are preemptively putting additional restrictions in place. As of 2011, more than 45 states have placed restrictions on online content.

When a country restricts the free flow of information online, it impacts not only the citizens of that country, but reduces the value of the internet for all of its users and stakeholders. Just as China's extensive filtering of online content prevents Chinese users from reaching the BBC, the BBC is prevented from doing business in China; and just as Chinese users cannot access Facebook, Facebook users from across the world cannot interact with the Chinese populace.

The challenges to an open internet are decidedly complex. And with the fragmentation of the internet aided not only by authoritarian regimes, but also democratically elected governments, ISPs, user-generated content platforms, and other corporate entities, the solutions to creating an open internet are equally, if not more, complex than the problems.

Censorship does not exist in a vacuum; for every step closer to freedom, there is another step back, as governments learn from one another and implement new "solutions" for limiting free expression.

At the top level lies the simplest yet most difficult solution: convincing governments of the value of a free internet. The ideals of an open internet are often in direct conflict with the interests of policy makers, whether in debating network neutrality in the US or in the current proposal to erect a China-style firewall in Iran.

Solutions to the latter problem abound, but often act as mere bandages, offering a fallible solution to a vast and ever-developing problem. The US and other governments have poured money into circumvention technology, which can be effective in getting around internet censorship, but simply furthers the cat-and-mouse game between governments and tool developers, the former blocking the latter as the developers attempt to keep up. Mesh networking has, of late, also become a strong contender for solving the dual problems of censorship and access, with several nascent projects receiving attention – and funding – from government entities.

Trade restrictions have been proposed to curb internet censorship; notably, in 2010, Google proposed the idea of stricter trade governance as a means to prevent or lessen restrictions placed by governments on internet access. At the same time, the Global Network Initiative, a multi-stakeholder organisation comprised of academics, activists, corporations and NGOs, is working with companies to guide them toward better policies around privacy and free expression online.

But while attainment of these ideals may at times seem nearly impossible, the costs of *not* fighting for them are too great. It is therefore imperative that we – the users, the citizens – continue to push for better choices at the hands of governments and corporations, and keep fighting for the equally necessary freedoms of expression and association in this most unique of spaces. ■

Thematic reports

Conceptualising accountability and recourse

Joy Liddicoat
Association for Progressive Communications (APC)
www.apc.org

Introduction

The modern foundations of international human rights rest on the Universal Declaration of Human Rights (UDHR) and the Charter of the United Nations (UN).[1] The UDHR affirmed human rights are universal, inalienable and interconnected. The human rights framework recognises both the right of states to govern and the duty of states to respect, protect and promote human rights. The global transformation of human rights from moral or philosophical imperatives into a framework of rights that are legally recognised between nations continued into the 21st century, but this basic framework has been reaffirmed by UN member states and remains the foundation of human rights today.[2] The internet has been used to create new spaces in which human rights can be exercised and new spaces in which rights violations can take place. This report looks at human rights concepts, the internet and accountability mechanisms for internet-related human rights violations.[3]

The human rights framework

The UDHR is not legally binding but has a powerful moral force among UN member states. Binding standards have been developed, including the International Covenant on Civil and Political Rights (ICCPR)[4] and the International Covenant on Economic, Social and Cultural Rights (ICESCR).[5] Together with the UDHR, these two standards have become known as the International Bill of Human Rights.[6] Other international human rights standards followed, including the Convention against Torture and Other Cruel, Inhuman or Degrading Treatment or Punishment.[7]

Accountability and remedies

When the UDHR was being negotiated, litigation was not seen as the appropriate way to seek remedies or accountability between nations (nor was there an international court system). New forums were established, including the Security Council, the Human Rights Committee and, more recently, the Human Rights Council. Accountability to these forums was primarily by way of periodic reporting. Once a state had ratified a treaty (such as the ICCPR) it agreed to periodically report on implementation, but ratification was also permitted with reservations. Some treaties adopted complaint procedures for individual complaints (which are known as optional protocols), but states are not obliged to submit to these. Each treaty has different standards for accountability. For example, states are obliged to implement economic, cultural and social rights as resources allow, through a system known as "progressive realisation". Civil and political rights, on the other hand, must be implemented immediately and some, such as freedom from torture, can never be suspended or limited, even in emergency situations.

The premise underlying these forms of accountability is that states, as equal members of the international community of nations, will subject their conduct to the scrutiny of other states. In doing so states also agree to abide by recommendations or take into account observations made about matters within their own borders. States therefore agree to be publicly accountable for their human rights performance. This was a major transformation in the international community of states.

1 The United Nations officially came into existence after ratification of the Charter on 24 October 1945.

2 The 1993 Vienna World Conference on Human Rights reaffirmed that human rights are indivisible and interrelated and that no right is superior to another. UN General Assembly (1993) *Vienna Declaration and Programme of Action*, Article 5. www.unhchr.ch/huridocda/huridoca.nsf/(symbol)/a.conf.157.23.en

3 "Accountability mechanisms" range from international mechanisms, to litigation, to community action and lawful forms of protest.

4 The ICCPR includes rights related to the right to vote, freedom of expression, freedom of association, and the rights to a fair trial and due process.

5 The ICESCR includes rights related to the right to health, the right to education, the right to an adequate standard of living, and the right to social security.

6 Office of the High Commissioner for Human Rights (1996) *Fact Sheet No. 2 (Rev. 1) The International Bill of Human Rights*, United Nations, Geneva. www.ohchr.org/Documents/Publications/FactSheet2Rev.1en.pdf

7 Others include the International Convention on the Elimination of All Forms of Racial Discrimination (ICERD), the Convention on the Elimination of All Forms of Discrimination Against Women (CEDAW), the Convention on the Rights of the Child (UNCROC), and the Convention on the Rights of Persons with Disabilities (CRPD).

In practice, the effectiveness of these accountability mechanisms varies widely. Some treaty body processes[8] are seen as very ineffective: the reporting processes are cumbersome, lengthy and time consuming for states and civil society groups alike. Some states simply do not file their periodic reports. For these and other reasons the treaty body processes are currently being reviewed.[9] Other mechanisms, such as the Universal Periodic Review, are seen as much more effective.

This variability has implications for civil society groups, which must strategise carefully about the use of different or multiple mechanisms depending on a number of factors, including the issue, and whether the context is national or local. Multiple mechanisms might be used at the same time, over time, or not at all, depending on the particular issues and context.

The human rights framework also has limitations. As a forum of governments the UN is necessarily infused with politics. Agreed human rights standards are, generally, the product of the best possible political consensus. The result is often a minimum standard: the lowest common denominator of agreement. The international human rights system is still evolving, with the UN's mandate under constant scrutiny, and its utility questioned in the face of the modern horrors of human rights violations. In addition, the framework itself is not static. The UN system is evolving with new processes such as the Universal Periodic Review providing new opportunities for scrutiny and leadership. While changes may be positive, these take time to implement, requiring civil society organisations (CSOs) to develop or enhance capacity to engage and use them effectively while also trying to advance their issues and concerns.

Yet the UN – and the Human Rights Council in particular – remains the central global human rights forum. Opportunities for recourse against states, as ways to hold them accountable for human rights violations, must be considered taking into account both strengths and limitations of the international human rights framework. And today there are more processes for state accountability for human rights violations than have ever existed. These include:

- Scrutiny by treaty bodies
- Complaints to UN bodies under optional protocols
- Engagement with special procedures of the UN (for example, the Special Rapporteurs on Freedom of Opinion and Expression, Freedom of Association and Human Rights Defenders)
- State peer review in the Universal Periodic Review process
- Formal complaints to regional mechanisms, for example, the European Court of Human Rights, the Inter-American Court of Human Rights or the African Court on Human and People's Rights
- Complaints to or investigations by ombudspersons or national human rights institutions
- Litigation (where national constitutions allow for this or where international standards have been incorporated into domestic law).

As human rights violations in relation to the internet increase,[10] questions arise about accountability and remedies. The implications for internet-related human rights violations cannot be considered without first looking at the internet-related forums in the UN.

Human rights and the internet at the UN

Despite the centrality of human rights to the creation of the UN, the World Summit on the Information Society (WSIS),[11] the WSIS Geneva Declaration of Principles[12] and the Internet Governance Forum (IGF),[13] discussions about accountability for human rights violations remain limited. Tensions have emerged given the openness of the internet, which has been both a factor in its success and a point of political contention in debates about internet governance.[14] Early adopters of the internet and information and communications technologies (ICTs) reached for rights as a way to navigate these tensions by articulating their freedom to use and create online spaces, to assert their rights to communicate and share information, and to resist state or government interference with rights to privacy.[15] The simple application of existing human rights standards was the

8 Treaty body processes refers to the various mechanisms for oversight of implementation of treaties; for example, the Committee for the Elimination of All Forms of Discrimination Against Women oversees the CEDAW convention and the Human Rights Committee oversees the ICCPR.

9 www2.ohchr.org/english/bodies/HRTD/index.htm

10 La Rue, F. (2011) *Report of the Special Rapporteur on the promotion and protection of the right to freedom of opinion and expression*, 26 April, A/HRC/17/27, p. 8-15.

11 World Summit on the Information Society, United Nations and International Telecommunication Union (2005) WSIS Outcome Documents. www.itu.int/wsis/documents/doc_multi.asp?lang=en&id=2316lo

12 Article 19 of the UDHR is cited in paragraph 4 of the Geneva Declaration of Principles (2003).

13 www.intgovforum.org

14 Cavalli, O. (2010) Openness: Protecting Internet Freedoms, in Drake, W. J. (ed) *Internet Governance: Creating Opportunities for All*, United Nations, New York, p. 15.

15 One of the more famous examples was John Perry Barlow's Declaration of the Independence of Cyberspace (February 1996). projects.eff.org/~barlow/Declaration-Final.html

starting point for civil society groups and, building on the work of the People's Communication Charter, the Association for Progressive Communications (APC) developed the first Internet Rights Charter in 2001-2002 (subsequently updated in 2006).[16] In 2010, the Dynamic Coalition on Internet Rights and Principles released a Charter of Internet Rights and Principles and, in 2011, a more condensed set of ten principles.[17]

But further elaboration and clear explanation of how existing human rights standards apply seemed necessary. New charters and statements of principles have emerged in regional bodies (such as the Council of Europe) and nationally (for example, in Estonia and Finland).[18] It is not yet clear if a new "Super Charter" will emerge or if a new model national law will be developed.

The internet-related aspects of freedom of expression and freedom of association have received some scrutiny in UN human rights mechanisms. The 2011 annual report of the Special Rapporteur on Freedom of Opinion and Expression[19] was the first time the Human Rights Council had considered a report specifically focused on human rights and the internet. In 2010, the Human Rights Committee began a review of General Comment 34 (a key document which the Committee uses to interpret Article 19 of the ICCPR) and released its preliminary report in May 2011.[20] The new general comment includes specific reference to "electronic and internet-based modes of expression".[21] This will strengthen the mechanisms for recourse and reporting internet-related violations of freedom of expression under Article 19 by requiring states to include these in their reports. The final revised comment was released in June 2011 and should be available for use in periodic reporting and other accountability mechanisms by early 2012.

These various initiatives are welcome, but more work needs to be done to ensure the internet is a cross-cutting issue within all treaty bodies and human rights mechanisms. The topic of human rights, the internet and accountability mechanisms remains complex for a variety of reasons, including:

- The complexity of the internet ecosystem (for example, no single point of governance and network operation, diverse standard-setting systems, the role of internet intermediaries and platform providers, and so on) and the various connection points of that ecosystem with the human rights ecosystem (or lack of connection points).
- While there may be a single international human rights standard (for example, on freedom of expression) there is no single way and no single correct way to give effect to that standard.
- The diverse ways that human rights issues arise; for example, from privacy and surveillance, to the ICT production line (conflict minerals, the rights of workers), to content filtering, content blocking and harassment, arrest and detention of online human rights activists.
- Human rights violations may involve multiple and intersecting rights across different treaties and affect groups differently (such as women, sexual and gender minorities, people with disabilities, or racial and cultural minorities).
- The application of human rights standards to the fast-changing forms of connectivity (mobile is outpacing other forms of connectivity, for instance).[22]
- The nebulous legal environments of many countries, including absence of the rule of law (or ineffective legal systems), lack of legislation and constitutional protections or, conversely, over-regulation and extensive direct or indirect censorship.[23]
- The diverse human rights situations in diverse countries, especially within and between developed and developing countries.
- The actual and perceived limitations of human rights remedies where the state violates human rights or where non-state actors can act with impunity.
- The frequent need to obtain remedy or recourse quickly and the slow and cumbersome nature of most legal processes.

16 www.apc.org/en/node/5677

17 www.internetrightsandprinciples.org

18 In relation to Estonia, see Woodard, C. (2003) Estonia, where being wired is a human right, *Christian Science Monitor*, 1 July. In relation to Finland, see Ministry of Transport and Communications (2009) *732/2009, Decree of the Ministry of Transport and Communications on the minimum rate of a functional Internet access as a universal service*. www.finlex.fi/en/laki/kaannokset/2009/en20090732

19 La Rue (2011) op. cit.

20 Human Rights Committee (2011) *Draft General Comment No. 34 (upon completion of the first reading by the Human Rights Council*, 3 May, CCPR/C/GC/34/CRP.6.

21 Ibid., para 11.

22 See, for example, Southwood, R. (2011) *Policy and regulatory issues in the mobile internet*, APC. www.apc.org/en/node/12433; Horner, L. (2011) *A human rights approach to the mobile internet*, APC. www.apc.org/en/node/12431; and Comninos, A. (2011) *Twitter revolutions and cyber-crackdowns: User-generated content and social networking in the Arab Spring and beyond*, APC. www.apc.org/en/node/12432

23 For example, in relation to Turkey, see Johnson, G. (2011) *Censorship Threatens Turkey's Accession to EU*, unpublished research paper.

- The cost of litigation and the lack of access to this remedy for many individuals and groups.
- The geopolitics and how these play out in various forums.
- The multiple and sometimes conflicting mechanisms for remedy within countries (for example, in relation to content censorship, the intersections of defamation law, constitutional protections where these exist, and criminal or civil legislation for different types of material).

What future for accountability mechanisms?

Given these complexities it is perhaps no surprise that those discussing internet rights charters and principles have steered away from creating new accountability mechanisms – none appear to contain new complaints procedures. The question is, can the existing human rights framework provide adequate accountability mechanisms for internet-related human rights violations?

The answer is unclear. A mixed picture emerges from current practice. Some CSOs have been active in the Universal Periodic Review process.[24] Regional human rights mechanisms (such as the European Court of Human Rights) are receiving increasing numbers of complaints[25] together with strategic interventions in litigation by CSOs.[26] But no complaints have been received by the African Special Rapporteur on Freedom of Expression in relation to freedom of expression and the internet.[27] There have been few complaints to national human rights institutions, possibly because these have not yet adequately considered how to deal with internet-related complaints.[28] Civil litigation remains a primary way to gain recourse in many countries.[29]

More research is needed to develop a better global picture of the use of these various mechanisms and monitor change. For example, some mechanisms may be best suited to certain types of complaints and offer different remedies. Capacity building also may be needed to support civil society advocacy and strengthen the mechanisms to ensure judicial and other officers adequately understand internet-related human rights issues.

New avenues for global recourse and accountability mechanisms are emerging. The Special Rapporteur on Freedom of Expression has emphasised the need for effective remedies, including rights of appeal.[30] In addition, he noted that the internet has created more avenues for use of traditional remedies including the right of reply, publishing corrections and issuing public apologies.[31] In one defamation case, for example, the settlement agreement included the defendant apologising 100 times, every half hour over three days, to more than 4,200 followers of his Twitter account.[32]

A rights-based approach to the internet and human rights

The rights-based approach, or human rights approach as it is also known, was developed as a practical way to implement human rights standards. The rights-based approach was first articulated in the UN in 2002, when the Office of the UN High Commissioner for Human Rights convened an ad hoc expert committee on biotechnology. The committee noted this was a new and emerging area of human rights, with no specific human rights standards. To overcome this difficulty the committee decided to rely on a "rights-based approach" for its task, indicating that such an approach should:[33]

- Emphasise the *participation* of individuals in decision making
- Introduce *accountability* for actions and decisions, which can allow individuals to complain about decisions affecting them adversely
- Seek *non-discrimination* of all individuals through the equal application of rights and obligations to all individuals
- *Empower* individuals by allowing them to use rights as a leverage for action and legitimise their voice in decision making
- Link decision making at every level to the *agreed human rights norms* at the international level as set out in the various human rights covenants and treaties.

24 Universal Periodic Review (UPR), Thailand: Joint CSO Submission to the Office of the High Commissioner for Human Rights (March 2010), endorsed in whole or in part by 92 Thai organisations.

25 For a summary of recent European Court of Human Rights cases in relation to the internet and human rights see the European Court of Human Rights "New Technologies Fact Sheet" (May 2011).

26 For example, the Electronic Frontier Foundation and Privacy International.

27 Advocate Pansy Tsakula, personal communication to APC, 2011.

28 See, for example, New Zealand Human Rights Commission (2010) *Roundtable on Human Rights and the Internet.* www.hrc.co.nz

29 Kelly, S. and Cook, S. (eds) (2011) *Freedom on the Net 2011: A global assessment of the internet and digital media*, Freedom House, Washington.

30 La Rue (2011) op. cit., para 47.

31 Ibid., para 27.

32 www.thejournal.ie/malaysian-man-apologises-via-100-tweets-in-defamation-settlement-147842-Jun2011

33 High Commissioner for Human Rights (2002) *Report of the High Commissioner's Expert Group on Human Rights and Biotechnology: Conclusions*, OHCHR, Geneva, para 21.

This approach has been extended into a wide range of areas, particulary those where no specific human rights standards seem to apply. The approach is increasingly being used to critique internet regulations on access to the internet, privacy, filtering[34] and the mobile internet.[35] The UN Special Representative on Business and Human Rights has also drawn on the rights-based approach to consider liability of transnational corporations for human rights violations. The resulting framework highlights the need for access to effective remedies, both judicial and non-judicial.[36]

There is scope to use this approach in other areas, for example, with the mandates of various UN forums that focus on the internet. The recent appointment of a Special Rapporteur on Freedom of Association provides an opportunity to explore such an approach taking account of modern human rights movements, the use of the internet and ICTs to mobilise, and the special situation of human rights defenders seeking to improve democratic participation. New forms of accountability may yet emerge, as well as new remedies that relate specifically to the internet.

Conclusion

There are more opportunities at global levels for recourse for human rights violations than ever before. Yet these appear largely underutilised in relation to the internet and human rights. Diverse and complex factors interact to create this situation and it is difficult for CSOs to develop effective strategies. At the same time, new human rights standards and mechanisms are emerging in relation to freedom of expression and freedom of association, creating new opportunities for recourse. Taking a rights-based approach to the internet and human rights may provide a way to negotiate these complex issues, to build broad consensus on the application of human rights standards, and provide greater access to, and measurement of, accountability mechanisms. ■

34 Access (2011) To Regulate or Not to Regulate, Is That the Question? A Roadmap to Smart Regulation of the Internet, discussion paper released ahead of the OECD High-Level Meeting on the Internet Economy on 28-29 June 2011. www.accessnow.org/policy-activism/docs

35 See footnote 22.

36 Ruggie, J. (2011) *Report of the Special Representative of the Secretary-General on the issue of human rights and transnational corporations and other business enterprises. Guiding Principles on Business and Human Rights: Implementing the United Nations "Protect, Respect and Remedy" Framework*, 21 March, A/HRC/17/31, para. 26-31.

Freedom of expression on the internet: Implications for foreign policy

Ben Wagner
European University Institute, Department of Political and Social Sciences
www.eui.eu

Introduction

Since the birth of the public internet, questions of global internet governance have also been questions of international affairs.[1] However, while internet security has historically been heavily politicised at an international level, it is only more recently that the questions of internet expression and free speech have been perceived as a foreign policy issue. The following analysis will provide an overview of the two key foreign policy debates on free expression on the internet, before suggesting paths for the development of future internet foreign policy and what consequences these paths are likely to have for freedom of expression on the internet.

Internet freedom as foreign policy

The "internet freedom debate" has become one of the most important international debates on international freedom of expression and foreign policy.[2] One of the most important public statements of such a foreign policy initiative was United States (US) Secretary of State Hillary Clinton's "Remarks on Internet Freedom"[3] made on 21 January 2010. Despite including other countries, the obvious focus of her statement was China and Iran, which are both mentioned more than any other country. Moreover, within this foundational statement on internet freedom as foreign policy, two key aspects stand out: the assumption that ensuring freedom of expression might serve to foment "US friendly revolutions"[4] and the highly ambiguous role of the corporate sector in securing free expression.[5]

Following Clinton's remarks, several European countries began to develop internet freedom initiatives, which were generally understood to be a response to the suppression of mass public protests in Iran in 2009. Perhaps the best known of these is the Franco-Dutch initiative which was launched in a joint communiqué by Bernard Kouchner and Maxime Verhagen, then French and Dutch foreign ministers, in May 2010. The initiative culminated in a meeting at ministerial level on "The Internet and Freedom of Expression" in July 2010.[6] Here too the key aspects of the meeting agenda were the support of the supposed revolutionary activities of "cyber dissidents" and the ambiguous role of the corporate sector. However, the Franco-Dutch initiative includes significantly stronger references to a human rights framework to guarantee freedom of expression, compared to the US State Department's internet freedom initiative.

Since the Franco-Dutch initiative, however, it appears that the two countries have taken divergent paths in their approach to internet freedom. This can be attributed in significant part to cabinet reshuffles and shifting balances of power within the respective governments. The French foreign ministry has been hit by a turbulent period following the resignation of Bernard Kouchner. In this period the presidential palace increasingly came to dominate internet foreign policy following President Nicolas Sarkozy's call for a "civilised internet", with the state acting as a civilising force.[7] In the Netherlands, parliamentary elections in 2010 and the resulting cabinet reshuffle has also led to the appointment of a new foreign minister, Uriel Rosenthal. In contrast to France, he recently stated his interest to go *beyond* existing internet freedom initiatives, suggesting that industry self-regulation is insufficient and that additional governmental regulation is necessary.[8]

1 Tallo, I. (2011) eGovernment and eParticipation, paper presented at the European University Institute workshop Government and the Internet: Participation, Expression and Control, Florence, Italy, 8-9 March.

2 Ross, A. (2010) Internet Freedom: Historic Roots and the Road Forward, *SAIS Review*, 30 (2), p. 3-15; McCarthy, D. R. (2011) Open Networks and the Open Door: American Foreign Policy and the Narration of the Internet, *Foreign Policy Analysis*, January.

3 Clinton, H. (2010) Remarks on Internet Freedom. www.state.gov/secretary/rm/2010/01/135519.htm

4 Nye, J. S. J. (2009) Get Smart: Combining Hard and Soft Power, *Foreign Affairs*, 88 (4).

5 Human Rights Watch (2006) *"Race to the bottom": Corporate complicity in Chinese internet censorship*, Human Rights Watch, New York.

6 de la Chapelle, B. (2010) Remarks by Bertrand de la Chapelle during the Dynamic Coalition on Freedom of Expression and Freedom of the Media on the Internet Coalition Meeting, at the 5th Internet Governance Forum, Vilnius, Estonia, 14-17 September. webcast. intgovforum.org/ondemand/?media=workshops

7 Woitier, C. (2011) Sarkozy préfère «l'internet civilisé» aux cyberdissidents, *Le Figaro*, 20 May. www.lefigaro.fr/politique/2011/05/20/01002-20110520ARTFIG00584-sarkozy-prefere-l-internet-civilise-aux-cyberdissidents.php

8 Rosenthal, U. (2011) Speech by Dutch Foreign Minister Uri Rosenthal at the International Digital Economy Accords (IDEA) Brussels Meeting, Brussels, Belgium, 23-24 March. www.rijksoverheid.nl/documenten-en-publicaties/toespraken/2011/03/24/speech-by-pieter-de-gooijer-at-the-international-digital-economy-accords-idea-brussels-meeting.html

The internet freedom debate has also reached the German foreign ministry. Despite widespread public debates about national internet governance and regulation within Germany, these debates have had a limited impact on German foreign policy outside of Europe until relatively recently. Following this model, the first statement on internet freedom made by the German Foreign Minister Guido Westerwelle in May 2011 draws significantly more on international discourses on internet freedom than national debates about internet governance and regulation.[9]

Consequently, the challenge facing the German, French, Dutch and US foreign ministries is to create a coherent overall frame for internet governance that considers both national and international debates. It is important to note that the US, Dutch, French and German foreign ministries have all created internal structures that are explicitly tasked with pursuing internet freedom policies which promote freedom of expression internationally. This should in the medium and long term lead to noticeable development of internet foreign policy initiatives. However, as was previously noted, their ability to effect meaningful change on government policy depends heavily on dynamics within the respective ministries and governments.

Equally, there are signs that the internet freedom debate is maturing, both in regard to the development of substantive policy initiatives on internet freedom and a greater coherence between national and international policy. A recent report by the Washington think tank Center for New American Security, entitled "Internet Freedom: A Foreign Policy Imperative in the Digital Age",[10] proposes eight "principles" which should guide internet freedom policies in the US, many of which involve substantive policy initiatives for promoting freedom of expression such as reforming export controls, creating economic incentives for corporations to support freedom of expression, and an attempt to create international norms.

Internet human rights as foreign policy

While the internet freedom debate continues, another strand of the international debate on freedom of expression on the internet is noticeably distinct and could be termed the "human rights-based approach". This strategy has specifically been pursued by a number of states, particularly Sweden and Brazil, as well as a variety of international organisations and civil society actors. This discourse seeks to situate the debate on freedom of expression on the internet within existing human rights law, looking for ways of applying existing norms and developing "new rights" for the internet.[11] This strategy is typically pursued in co-operation with existing international institutions which promote human rights and freedom of expression, including the United Nations (UN).

A recent report by UN Special Rapporteur Frank La Rue entitled "Report on the promotion and protection of the right to freedom of opinion and expression" is primarily devoted to developing "general principles on the right to freedom of opinion and expression and the internet"[12] as well as a framework within which internet content can reasonably be restricted. This report was based on an extensive consultation process with governments, civil society, international corporations and experts. Consequently, it represents probably the single most well-developed framework for applying human rights norms to freedom of expression on the internet.

The Swedish foreign ministry has been particularly actively following this strategy at various different levels, most notably through consistent support of the Special Rapporteur.[13] Its long-standing support of human rights frameworks on the internet gives the foreign ministry a considerable level of international credibility when it comes to free expression on the internet, as does its ability to organise statements on freedom of expression on the internet representing a broad international coalition at the UN Human Rights Council.[14]

The pursuit of a human rights-based approach has also led to the development of a wide variety of declarations, principles and charters of rights on the internet. These are typically developed within international organisations or multi-stakeholder coalitions and attempt to develop human rights frameworks which also apply to freedom of expression on the internet.[15] The content of these documents is extremely diverse and ranges from an elaboration of basic principles such as the Brazilian Principles for the Governance and Use of the Internet (2009), the Global Network Initiative Principles (2008) or the Council of Europe's Internet Governance Principles (2011), to more extensive documents which seek to elaborate and apply rights such as the Association for

9 Westerwelle, G. (2011) Gastbeitrag von Guido Westerwelle: Die Freiheit im Netz, *Frankfurter Rundschau*, 27 May. www.fr-online.de/politik/meinung/die-freiheit-im-netz/-/1472602/8496970/-/index.html

10 Fontaine, R. and Rogers, W. (2011) *Internet Freedom: A Foreign Policy Imperative in the Digital Age*, Center for a New American Security, Washington, D.C.

11 Benedek, W., Kettemann, M. C. and Senges, M. (2008) *The Humanization of Internet Governance: A roadmap towards a comprehensive global (human) rights architecture for the Internet.* www.worldcat.org/title/humanization-of-internet-governance-a-roadmap-towards-a-comprehensive-global-human-rights-architecture-for-the-internet/oclc/619152167&referer=brief_results

12 La Rue, F. (2011) *Report of the Special Rapporteur on the promotion and protection of the right to freedom of opinion and expression*, UN Human Rights Council, Geneva, p. 6.

13 Bildt, C. (2011) Carl Bildt's remarks on Digital Authoritarianism. www.sweden.gov.se/sb/d/14194/a/169246

14 Knutsson, J. (n.d.) Freedom of Expression on the Internet Cross-regional Statement. www.sweden.gov.se/sb/d/14194/a/170566

15 Benedek, Kettemann and Senges (2008) op. cit.

Progressive Communications (APC) Internet Rights Charter (2006)[16] or the Charter of Human Rights and Principles for the Internet (2010).

Common to all these documents is their reference to international human rights law, most frequently to the Universal Declaration of Human Rights (1948). Moreover, they are typically developed by a wide range of stakeholders from various institutional backgrounds, including civil society, the private sector, and the academic and technical communities. Foreign ministries, while often directly involved in the drafting process, have not typically taken leadership in the drafting of such documents.

One of the most interesting examples of such collaborative efforts is the Charter of Human Rights and Principles for the Internet,[17] which was developed by the Internet Rights and Principles Dynamic Coalition of the Internet Governance Forum. To give some idea of the diversity involved in the drafting process, the Steering Committee of the Coalition is composed of academics from Japan, Brazil, the UK and the US, Indian, US and Brazilian civil society representatives, German, US and UK private sector actors, representatives of the Council of Europe and UNESCO, and a Swedish diplomat.

Fundamental to all of these documents is the belief that human rights are a relevant frame for promoting the rights of individuals on the internet. Consequently, this approach stands and falls with the acknowledgement of "internet human rights" within the wider human rights community and international human rights law. It would seem that with the report by La Rue, which was presented to the Human Rights Council, a significant step in this direction has been taken, but it remains to be seen how the report itself is received.

The paths ahead? Internet policy coherence...

While many states are prepared to affirm the importance of human rights and rights to freedom of expression on the internet, as mentioned, relatively few have been actively involved in the process of developing the charters and principles which have proliferated over the last five years. Although these processes do not necessarily have to lead to international treaties like the Council of Europe Cybercrime Convention (2001), they do provide a space for defining and elaborating concepts and principles on freedom of expression on the internet.

Increasingly, foreign ministries have to wrestle with translating initiatives related to freedom of expression into foreign policy. The three key aspects that are persistently mentioned in this regard are (1) a linkage to existing human rights frameworks, (2) the perceived role of the internet in enabling or fuelling revolutions, and (3) the questionable role of the private sector. However, these aspects are developed in very different policy contexts. "Internet freedom strategies" focus more on specific foreign policy goals and specific events which are perceived to be causally linked to freedom of expression, typically protest events and revolutions. In contrast, "internet human rights strategies" focus more on developing and embedding aspects of freedom on the internet into existing human rights frameworks.

In the case of internet freedom-based strategies, overall government internet policy coherence is particularly important. This stems from very different international and national policy strategies on the internet, leading to value conflicts which may be particularly harmful for foreign policy. The tension between internet policies at a national level – WikiLeaks in the US or the HADOPI law in France – and a foreign policy which promotes internet freedom is by no means lost on those addressed by these policies. The challenge here is not just to bring the relevant policy areas together in one document, as was the case in the US International Strategy for Cyberspace,[18] but to develop a coherent framework with principles that can be applied across ministries and policy areas.

Here internet human rights strategies are at an advantage, as they already have a clear set of principles, but are dependent on the acknowledgement of "internet rights as human rights".[19] They also profit from a wide base of stakeholders who are involved in the drafting process. Considering the number of charters and principles currently circulating, it remains to be seen whether a coherent overall internet human rights framework can be developed.

Finally, as internet freedom policies mature and internet human rights frameworks develop, there is likely to be an increasing overlap between both internet freedom and human rights-based strategies.

While the divide between states pursuing separate foreign policy strategies on these issues is likely to remain, due to differing strategic interests and foreign policy objectives, there is reason to suggest that there might be space for greater cooperation between states in developing policies which pursue greater freedom of expression on the internet. ■

16 Association for Progressive Communications (2006) *APC Internet Rights Charter*. www.apc.org/en/node/5677

17 Internet Rights and Principles Dynamic Coalition (2010) *Charter of Human Rights and Principles for the Internet: Beta Version 1.1.* internetrightsandprinciples.org/node/367

18 US National Security Council (2011) *International Strategy for Cyberspace: Prosperity, Security, and Openness in a Networked World,* Executive Office of the President of the United States, National Security Council, Washington, D.C.

19 Association for Progressive Communications (2011) *Internet Rights Are Human Rights.* www.apc.org/en/pubs/briefs/internet-rights-are-human-rights-claims-apc-human-

Towards a cyber security strategy for global civil society?

Ron Deibert
The Canada Centre for Global Security Studies
and the Citizen Lab, Munk School of Global Affairs,
University of Toronto
www.citizenlab.org

Cyberspace is at a watershed moment. Technological transformations have brought about an architectonic change in the communications ecosystem. Cyber crime has exploded to the point of becoming more than a nuisance, but a national security concern. There is a seriously escalating arms race in cyberspace as governments scale up capabilities in their armed forces to fight and win wars in this domain. Telecommunication companies, internet service providers (ISPs) and other private sector actors now actively police the internet. Pressures to regulate the global network of information and communications have never been greater.

Although states were once thought to be powerless in the face of the internet, the giants have been woken from their slumber. How exactly governments react to these problems will determine the future of cyberspace – and by extension the communications platforms upon which global civic networks depend.

Global civil society, now increasingly recognised as an important stakeholder in cyberspace governance, needs to step up to the challenge. A constitutive moment awaits. What is required is nothing less than a serious and comprehensive *security* strategy for cyberspace that addresses the very real threats that plague governments and corporations, addresses national and other security concerns in a forthright manner, while protecting and preserving open networks of information and communication. It is an enormous challenge but also a great opportunity that, if not handled well, could end up having major detrimental consequences for human rights online. Of course, "global civil society" is not an undifferentiated whole, but an amalgam of multiple and diverse local networks. Regardless of their differences, citizens who share an interest in democracy and human rights also share common interests in a secure but open global communications space. Those common interests can lay the basis for a civil society cyber security strategy.

Prior to laying out the elements of such a strategy, it is useful to take a step back and look at some major social forces that are shaping the domain of global communications. The internet's de facto and distributed regime of governance – largely informal and driven up to now by decisions of like-minded engineers – has come under massive stress as a function of the internet's continuing rapid growth. Not only have there been continuing exponential increases in users and deeper penetration into everyday life (a recent Cisco report[1] said that by 2020, there will be 50 billion "things", meaning devices, connected to the internet), but there has been a vast growth in the developing world, as millions of new digital natives come online. With these new digital natives come new values and interests that in turn are affecting internet governance, as governments like China, Russia and India exercise their influence. The latter are now key players in several internet governance forums, and have been collectively pushing for the legitimisation of nationalised controls, such as those over the domain naming system. They also have a shared interest in limiting the voices of civil society in these decision-making forums, an interest exemplified by the push to have the United Nations and the International Telecommunication Union (a state-based organisation) take the lead on internet governance. Civic networks need to be vigilant that such a strategy does not succeed.

Another major force shaping cyberspace arises out of technological innovation and economic factors that have created the architectonic shifts in the nature of the ecosystem of global communications. Whereas before the internet was largely a self-segmented and isolated network generally separate from other means of communication, such as television, telephony and radio, all of these media have integrated into a single system of planetary communications, which we call cyberspace. The integration of these media into a common space has happened at the same time that business models and service delivery mechanisms for information and communications have changed fundamentally, with the rise of social networking, cloud computing, and mobile forms of connectivity. This paradigm shift has upset

1 www.readwriteweb.com/archives/cisco_50_billion_things_on_the_internet_by_2020.php

the principles, norms and rules of what used to be just the "internet", with implications for freedom of speech and access to information. Today, our data is entrusted to vast transnational information empires who act as gatekeepers and increasingly arbiters of what gets communicated, and what information is accessible or not. Market considerations can easily outweigh privacy and other rights concerns, and have already made largely irrelevant so-called "end-to-end" principles that once ensured network neutrality. Even something as benign as a spam filter gone wild can end up unintentionally disrupting political communications, as our research on Apple's MobileMe filtering system[2] has shown.

More serious, however, are the ways in which the private sector is being pressured, compelled, and even *incentivised* to "police the internet" by governments looking to download their growing cyberspace controls. For example, in Canada, the Stephen Harper government is introducing an Omnibus Crime Bill[3] through parliament that would require ISPs and telecommunications companies to retain user data, process the data in ways that make it amenable to law enforcement and intelligence, and then share that data with law enforcement representatives – all without judicial oversight. Arrangements like these are not uncommon. Privacy researcher Chris Soghoian has made a career documenting[4] how private sector actors not only facilitate access to information for law enforcement, but actually derive revenues from doing so. He has also documented extensive variation among these actors on the specifics of their data retention and privacy policies. As a result, citizens using different communications services can live in entirely different universes of rights.

The downloading of policing functions to the private sector – a phenomenon known as "intermediary liability" – extends to the protection of intellectual property. At a recent meeting[5] on the internet economy organised by the Organisation for Economic Co-operation and Development (OECD) in Paris, the final communiqué argued that ISPs should take on more expansive roles chasing down copyright violators using their networks. Civil society stakeholders refused to sign on to the final communiqué largely in objection to this component. The OECD communiqué is but a reflection of a larger trend. In the United States (US), several ISPs and carriers have already taken on this responsibility as a voluntary arrangement. Across the industrialised world, it is considered standard practice for large carriers to "clean their pipes" of malicious networks and traffic that is associated with file sharing or similar "undesirable" activities. The bottom line of business now demands it.

Of course what is considered "intermediary liability" or a market imperative in Canada and the US differs quite fundamentally from Belarus, Iran, Viet Nam or China. In non-democratic countries, ISPs, telecom carriers and mobile operators are being asked to police political content, track dissidents, identify protesters, send threatening messages over their networks, and disable certain protocols used by adversaries – all as part of what my colleague Rafal Rohozinski[6] and I have dubbed "next-generation controls"[7] that we see emerging throughout the developing world. During the Arab Spring, for example, the Egyptian government took the drastic step of forcing ISPs to shutter the internet, and required the country's main mobile phone operator, Vodafone, to send mass text messages encouraging pro-regime sympathisers to take to the streets to counter the protesters. This shift towards intermediary liability is perhaps one of the greatest practical changes around internet governance in the last decade, particularly when considered in the context of growing cyberspace securitisation, of which it is a part.

The *securitisation* of cyberspace – a transformation of the domain into a matter of national security – is perhaps the most important factor shaping the global communications ecosystem today. Faced with the combined pressures above, and seemingly incessant and embarrassing large-scale data breaches, policy makers around the world are racing to develop cyber security strategies. Some are following the lead of the US, standing up within their armed forces dedicated cyber commands and laying out formal doctrines for cyberspace. Others are adopting less conventional means, including providing tacit support for pro-patriotic groups to engage in offensive cyber attacks in defence of their country, as seems to be the case in Iran, Syria, Russia, Burma and China.

Cyberspace securitisation includes a political economy dimension: there is a growing cyber industrial complex[8] around security products and services that both responds to, but also shapes the policy

2 opennet.net/apple-mobileme-brief

3 www.michaelgeist.ca/content/view/5808/135

4 www.dubfire.net/#pubs

5 www.oecd.org/document/59/0,3746,en_21571361_44315115_48173819_1_1_1_1,00.html

6 Rafal Rohozinski is a Senior Scholar at the Canada Centre for Global Security Studies at the Munk School of Global Affairs, University of Toronto. He is a co-principal investigator of the OpenNet Initiative and Information Warfare Monitor projects.

7 www.access-controlled.net/wp-content/PDFs/chapter-1.pdf

8 www.theglobeandmail.com/news/opinions/opinion/the-new-cyber-military-industrial-complex/article1957159

marketplace. Corporate giants of the Cold War, like Northrup Grunman, Boeing and General Dynamics, are repositioning themselves for lucrative defence contracts, alongside an array of subterranean niche companies that offer computer network exploitation products and services. The global cyber arms trade[9] now includes malicious viruses, zero-day exploits and massive botnets. An arms race in cyberspace has been unleashed, with international implications. For every US Cyber Command, there is now a Syrian or Iranian cyber army equivalent. For every "Internet Freedom in a Suitcase",[10] there is justification for greater territorialisation of cyberspace controls.

Cyberspace securitisation has also effectively *normalised* internet censorship. What was once the province of pariah states, like China and Saudi Arabia, is now quickly becoming the norm among liberal democracies and authoritarian regimes alike. Our OpenNet Initiative[11] project tracks internet filtering and information controls in more than 40 countries worldwide. But perhaps the best insight on the normalisation of internet restrictions comes from data provided by Google. As part of its Transparency Report,[12] Google now discloses requests from governments for user data or the removal of information on its websites and services, like YouTube. The data it released for the July-December 2010 period was perhaps most remarkable not so much for confirming the usual suspects, but rather for the way it revealed that censorship is now normal among democratic countries. The governments of Germany, the United Kingdom, Brazil, Italy and others make thousands of take-down requests every year.[13] Here too, as a complement to these new developments, internet censorship services – produced primarily in the West[14] – have become a major commercial sector. When Canadian filtering software companies who provide services and products to Yemen, Kuwait and the United Arab Emirates are actually applauded[15] for their efforts by the Canadian government, we can safely say that internet censorship has become a global norm.

9 www.businessweek.com/magazine/cyber-weapons-the-new-arms-race-07212011.html

10 www.nytimes.com/2011/06/12/world/12internet.html?_r=1&pagewanted=all

11 map.opennet.net

12 www.google.com/transparencyreport

13 www.washingtonpost.com/blogs/blogpost/post/web-censorship-moves-to-democracies-the-west/2011/06/27/AGPi4xnH_blog.html

14 opennet.net/west-censoring-east-the-use-western-technologies-middle-east-censors-2010-2011

15 opennet.net/blog/2011/07/canadian-government-lauds-uae-internet-service-provider-pervasively-censors-political-r

Rohozinski and I have summed up these cumulative forces as the coming "perfect storm" in cyberspace. With threats seemingly multiplying, and mutually reinforcing tendencies like those above growing, the prospects of extreme solutions finding widespread acceptance are high. Whether it is a proposal for an entirely new internet (as former CIA director Michael Hayden recently argued)[16] or the gradual metamorphosis of the existing open communications space into sovereign-controlled national internets, the securitisation wave is going to have major and potentially damaging consequences for civic networks. What is to be done?

First, as argued, there is an urgent need for the articulation of a cyber security strategy for civic networks. For many who would characterise themselves as part of global civil society, "security" is seen as anathema. In today's world of exaggerated threats and self-serving hyperbole from the computer security industry, it is easy to dismiss security as a myth to be demolished, rather than engaged. Securitisation is associated with the defence industry, Pentagon strategists, and the cyber security military industrial complex. Many might question whether employing the language of security only plays into this complex and the growing might of cyberspace controls.

But the vulnerabilities of cyberspace are very real, the underbelly of cyber crime is undeniably huge and growing, an arms race in cyberspace is escalating, and major governments are poised to set the rules of the road[17] that may impose top-down solutions that subvert the domain as we know it. Dismissing these as manufactured myths propagated by the power elite will only marginalise civic networks from the conversations where policies are being forged.

Civic networks need to be at the forefront of security solutions that preserve cyberspace as an open commons of information, protect privacy by design, and shore up access to information and freedom of speech, while at the same time address the growing vulnerabilities that have produced a massive explosion in cyber crime and security breaches. How can security and openness be reconciled? Aren't the two contradictory? Not at all. The answer lies in the internet itself. As my colleague Jonathan Zittrain has forcefully argued, there are open and generative self-healing and protective mechanisms that are a part of the everyday functioning of the internet itself. Zittrain's views are backed up by a recent European

16 www.nextgov.com/nextgov/ng_20110706_1137.php

17 arstechnica.com/tech-policy/news/2011/05/france-attempts-to-civilize-the-internet-internet-fights-back.ars

security study which explained how the open and decentralised organisation that is the very essence of the ecosystem is essential to the success and resilience of the internet.[18] What is remarkable, in other words, is that the internet functions precisely in the *absence* of centralised control and *because* of the thousands of distributed, loosely coordinated monitoring mechanisms. While these decentralised mechanisms are not perfect and can occasionally fail, they should be bolstered and enhanced as part of a coherent distributed security strategy. Bottom-up, "grassroots" solutions to the internet's security problems are consistent with principles of openness, avoid heavy-handed centralised controls, and provide checks and balances against the concentration of power in cyberspace. Part of a civil society security strategy should be to find ways to facilitate cooperation among the existing, largely scattered security networks while simultaneously making their actions more transparent and accountable.

Part of the civic strategy must also include a serious engagement with law enforcement – another traditional anathema for civil society. Law enforcement agencies are often stigmatised as the Orwellian bogeymen of internet freedom (and in places like Belarus, Uzbekistan and Burma, they are), but the reality in the liberal democratic world is more complex. Many law enforcement agencies are overwhelmed with cyber crime, are understaffed, lack proper equipment and training, and have no incentives or structures to cooperate across borders. Instead of dealing with these shortcomings head on, politicians are opting for new "Patriot Act" powers that dilute civil liberties, place burdens on the private sector, and conjure up fears of a surveillance society. What law enforcement needs is not new powers, it needs new resources, capabilities, proper training and equipment. But alongside those new resources should be the highest standards of judicial oversight and public accountability. Civic networks can articulate the differences between powers and resources, and highlight the importance of public accountability to liberal democracy as an example to the rest of the world without alienating what could be an important natural ally.

The same basic premise of oversight and accountability must extend to the private sector as well. Civic networks are inherently transnational and are because of this best equipped to monitor globe-spanning corporations who own and operate cyberspace. Persistent public pressure, backed up by credible evidence-based research and campaigns – like the Electronic Frontier Foundation's (EFF) privacy scorecard[19] – are the best means to ensure the private sector complies with human rights standards worldwide. Going further, however, civic networks should make the case that government pressures to police the internet impose costly burdens on businesses that should be conceded only with the greatest reservations and proper oversight. Such self-interest-based arguments will have much greater traction with the private sector than either pleas for magnanimity or pressures of naming and shaming ever will.

Lastly, civic networks need to be players in the rule-making forums where cyberspace rules of the road are implemented. This is not an easy task. There is no one single forum of cyberspace governance; instead, governance is diffuse and distributed across multiple forums, meetings and standard-setting bodies at local, national, regional and global levels. The idea of civil society participation in these centres of cyberspace governance varies widely, and is alien to some. Civic networks will need to monitor all of these centres of governance, open the doors to participation in those venues that are now closed shops, and make sure that "multi-stakeholder participation" is not just something paid lip service to by politicians, but something meaningfully exercised by networks of citizens. The civil society rejection of the OECD final communiqué is a model in this regard.

The idea of *security* is most closely associated with the tradition of *realpolitik*, and the denizens of the national security apparatus. Global civil society, on the other hand, is most often associated with respect for rights, democracy, diversity and openness. As the securitisation of cyberspace builds momentum, it may be tempting for civic networks to either concede the terms of the security debate to the national security community, or resist it altogether. That would be a mistake. There is a long-standing and very powerful tradition of *liberal security*, associated with distributed checks and balances, respect for individual rights, and decentralisation. What is urgently required now is the translation of that tradition to the domain of cyberspace, and the practical application of its principles by citizens worldwide. Otherwise, the great gains in networking that have produced an explosion in global civil society over the last decades could gradually evaporate. ■

18 www.lightbluetouchpaper.org/2011/04/12/resilience-of-the-internet-interconnection-ecosystem

19 www.eff.org/pages/when-government-comes-knocking-who-has-your-back

Internet intermediaries: The new cyber police?

Joe McNamee
European Digital Rights
www.edri.org

Introduction

The purpose of this report is to look at the increasing trend for internet intermediaries to be used to police and enforce the law on the internet and even to mete out punishments. As well as undermining the fundamental rights of freedom of communication, privacy and right to a fair trial, this approach is serving to create borders in the online world, undermining the very openness that gives the internet its value for democracy and, indeed, for the economy.

This issue is becoming increasingly important due to four different trends, which are developing simultaneously and synergetically. These are:

- The increased technical possibilities for online surveillance by internet access providers. The use of some of these possibilities is required by legal obligations such as the 2004 Communications and Law Enforcement Act (CALEA)[1] in the United States (US) and the European Union's (EU) Data Retention Directive.[2]
- The increased business interest that larger access providers see in blocking or limiting access to certain online content, as illustrated by recent discussions in both the US and Europe on "net neutrality".
- A concerted push at an intergovernmental level to legitimise and spread privatised enforcement measures.[3]
- Mergers of access providers and media companies, and distribution agreements between content providers and intermediaries where the contract includes obligations for the intermediary to undertake policing/punishment measures.[4]

Limitations of intermediary liability

The need for an open internet was recognised by both the US and the EU at the end of the 1990s. The US adopted the Digital Millennium Copyright Act (DMCA) in 1998, offering significant "safe harbours" to internet intermediaries for unauthorised content on their networks, while the EU adopted the E-Commerce Directive in 2000, which took a horizontal approach to safe harbours for all forms of illegal and unauthorised content. The public policy objectives on both sides of the Atlantic were clear, namely to maintain an open internet. This was seen as necessary to allow the economy to take full advantage of the internet and, as a collateral benefit, freedom of expression and almost unrestricted access to information. The benefits of such an approach can be seen in the economy[5] and in the effect of the internet in opening closed societies right around the world.

Nonetheless, despite this comparatively robust legal framework, weaknesses appeared almost from the start. This occurred particularly in Europe, where the wording of the E-Commerce Directive is too vague (due to the political compromises that were made during the adoption process) to allow intermediaries to feel completely secure, resulting in significant infringements of the right to communication. In 2004, a study by the Dutch NGO Bits of Freedom tested twelve hosting providers, nine of which deleted innocent material as a result of an obviously bogus "notice" sent from a Hotmail account set up solely for that purpose. This experience was duplicated by a team of United Kingdom (UK) academics,[6] also in 2004 (although it should be pointed out that this project did find the DMCA's process comparatively robust), and Dutch firm ICTRecht in 2009. Unilateral actions by internet providers have now effectively shifted their core activities from hosting providers to internet access providers, who have started "blocking" content, very often outside the rule of law. This started in the UK in 2004, supported by the Internet Watch Foundation, and spread to Denmark, Sweden and Finland in the ensuing years, as well as into the

1 en.wikipedia.org/wiki/Communications_Assistance_for_Law_Enforcement_Act

2 eur-lex.europa.eu/LexUriServ/LexUriServ.do?uri=OJ:L:2006:105:0054:0063:EN:PDF

3 See, for example, article 5.3 of the Anti-Counterfeiting Trade Agreement at www.ustr.gov/webfm_send/2379

4 www.bof.nl/2011/01/04/vrije-internettoegang-ook-in-nederland-onder-vuur

5 eur-lex.europa.eu/LexUriServ/LexUriServ.do?uri=OJ:L:2006:105:0054:0063:EN:PDF

6 pcmlp.socleg.ox.ac.uk/sites/pcmlp.socleg.ox.ac.uk/files/liberty.pdf

mobile environment, thanks to an agreement brokered by the European Commission.[7] It is worth noting the heavy overlap between parts of the internet access market most opposed to net neutrality and the parts most favourable to voluntary internet blocking.

Operators that have been at the forefront of "voluntary" internet blocking – such as British Telecom, Telenor, Virgin and the mobile industry in general – have also been the loudest voices opposed to net neutrality. In January 2011, British Telecom announced plans to charge certain online video providers more for prioritised traffic,[8] as did Telenor,[9] while Virgin Media announced plans to launch a deep packet inspection of the traffic of 40% of its customers in 2010.[10] Similarly, there have been multiple examples of mobile industry efforts seeking to exploit and reinforce their control over access to their clients, such as the blocking of voice over internet protocol (VoIP) applications.[11] This creates a situation where these providers are eager to accept demands from regulators for so-called "self-regulatory" blocking measures as, in the long term, it will be difficult for regulators to sustainably argue that access providers should be voluntarily interfering in traffic for public policy reasons but not for business reasons.

The beginning of large-scale privatised enforcement

At the moment there appears to be a "tipping point", with governments apparently feeling that the openness that gives the internet its economic value is now so unbreakable that unfettered meddling by intermediaries for the protection of (mainly) intellectual property can be actively promoted.[12] They are not only promoting this approach internally, and not only in countries with strong democratic traditions, but across the globe, potentially blocking off markets and legitimising privatised surveillance and control on communication in totalitarian and highly controlled regimes. As a result, there has been a veritable rash of international-level measures which seek to encourage or coerce intermediaries – many with their own long-term vested interests in this – to filter, block and punish alleged online infringements.

In November 2010, the negotiating parties published the final text of the Anti-Counterfeiting Trade Agreement (ACTA). Although significantly improved from earlier versions, the section of the agreement on intellectual property enforcement circuitously talks about maintaining an internet service provider (ISP) liability regime which preserves "the legitimate interests of rights holders" and obliges parties to "endeavor to promote cooperative efforts within the business community to effectively address trademark and copyright or related rights infringement"[13] – a footnote in a leaked draft explaining that "an example of such a policy is providing for the termination in appropriate circumstances of subscriptions and accounts in the service provider's system or network of repeat [alleged, presumably] infringers."

In February 2011, the World Intellectual Property Organization (WIPO) tried and failed[14] to launch a discussion[15] on internet intermediary liability for trademark infringements. This was followed in June 2011 by a side-event at a WIPO event in Geneva on the "role and responsibility of internet intermediaries in the field of copyright" which, interestingly, included no internet intermediaries at all! WIPO has also recently commissioned and published two independent studies on intermediary liability.[16] It has successfully tabled a workshop proposal for the Internet Governance Forum in Nairobi in September 2011 to discuss "thought-provoking ideas" such as in ACTA, the US Combating Online Infringements and Counterfeits Act (COICA) (which requires "blocking" by internet intermediaries) and the EU Intellectual Property Rights Enforcement Directive (whose use for mandatory internet blocking and surveillance is currently being assessed by the European Court of Justice).[17]

In June 2011, the Organisation for Economic Co-operation and Development (OECD) adopted its Communiqué on Principles for Internet Policy Making.[18] Under the heading "limit internet intermediary liability" it calls for states to undertake multi-stakeholder processes to "identify the

7 ec.europa.eu/information_society/newsroom/cf/itemlongdetail.cfm?item_id=3153

8 www.wired.com/epicenter/2011/01/bt-rejects-accusations-of-net-neutrality-breach-sort-of

9 www.dn.no/forsiden/etterBors/article2067200.ece

10 technology.timesonline.co.uk/tol/news/tech_and_web/the_web/article6989510.ece

11 www.ft.com/cms/s/0/1ce4e1c8-1fd7-11de-a1df-00144feabdc0.html#axzz1STK17d9n

12 The draft PROTECT IP Act in the US was accused of allowing "the government to break the Internet addressing system" and "breaking the Internet's infrastructure" by a group of 108 professors in a recent public letter on this proposed legislation. blogs.law.stanford.edu/newsfeed/files/2011/07/PROTECT-IP-letter-final.pdf

13 www.ustr.gov/webfm_send/2379

14 www.ccianet.org/index.asp%3Fsid=5%26artid=213%26evtflg=False

15 www.wipo.int/edocs/mdocs/sct/en/sct_25/sct_25_3.pdf

16 www.wipo.int/copyright/en/internet_intermediaries/index.html

17 European Court of Justice Case C70/10

18 www.oecd.org/dataoecd/40/21/48289796.pdf

appropriate circumstances under which internet intermediaries could take steps to educate users, assist rights holders in enforcing their rights or reduce illegal content" (this communiqué itself was the subject of a multi-stakeholder process that civil society rejected).[19] The text avoids supporting network neutrality and instead meaninglessly refers to maintaining "appropriate" quality. It also pointedly avoids even a single reference to "due process", opting for the less restrictive and legally meaningless "fair process" instead.

Privatised policing in practice

So what does all of this mean on a practical level? As this approach is generally outside the rule of law, implementations tend to be very ad hoc. Across Europe, internet hosting providers and social networks delete material which they fear could result in them being liable, based on random criteria. As seen in the 2004 Bits of Freedom study, the same content will be deleted or left online depending on the unpredictable internal practices of the companies in question. Dutch social networking site Hyves will automatically delete anything if users with ten different IP addresses click the "report material" button. Remarkably, the European Commission has actively encouraged hosting providers to change their terms of service to give them an unfettered ability to delete anything they want.[20] Similarly, internet providers who started "blocking" websites accused of containing child abuse material are now being asked and sometimes required to introduce blocking measures for other content.

In Ireland, the former monopoly internet provider Eircom has agreed to become judge, jury and executioner on accusations of illegal downloading – cutting off consumers repeatedly accused of infringements[21] and blocking websites[22] accused by music industry interests of facilitating infringements. The Spanish "Sinde" law offers an interesting mix of rule of law and extra-judicial coercion. Under that approach, the plaintiff requests extra-judicial action from the internet provider first and, afterwards, if the internet provider wants to incur the expense of pursuing a court case, a judicial procedure is foreseen. In the US, the large ISPs that have been lobbying hard for the right to throttle bandwidth for their own commercial benefit have kindly offered to throttle bandwidth to users who have been repeatedly accused of copyright violations.

In addition to their business interest in this anti-net neutrality approach, the changing nature of the business (demonstrated *inter alia* by Comcast's purchase of NBC and Verizon's recent move to movie distribution)[23] creates new incentives for this approach. Smaller access providers will be increasingly "squeezed" – they are obliged to incur the cost of implementing technologies to be able to interfere with internet traffic in the absence of the economies of scale that would permit this to be done in a cost-effective way, or in a way which could be used for non-net neutral purposes.

In addition to the threats to citizens' ability to access the internet at all, to access an open and neutral internet, and to access material "voluntarily" or accidentally blocked by their ISP, there are also increasing efforts to use the structure of the internet itself as a law enforcement tool. The EU and the US, for example, have an ongoing project to discuss the revocation of domain names (on which the US claims wide-ranging jurisdiction)[24] and IP addresses[25] (the regional registry for Europe, the Middle East and parts of central Asia is located in the Netherlands). While the US approach is partly based on law, with COICA and the PROTECT IP (Preventing Real Online Threats to Economic Creativity and Theft of Intellectual Property) Act[26] planned to regulate the blocking and revocation of domain names, a non-legislative approach is also followed in some circumstances, such as regarding unlicensed online pharmacies. In the EU, blocking is regulated by law in some countries (France and Italy, for example), without law in others (the UK and Sweden) and with and without law in others, depending on the subject (such as in Denmark and, possibly in the future, the UK). Revocation of domain names, on the other hand, is generally without a legal framework.[27]

Conclusion

The promotion of a closed internet regulated outside the rule of law undermines efforts of Western governments to support the democratising potential of the internet in closed and totalitarian regimes. The

19 www.edri.org/files/CSISAC_Press_Release%20_0628011_FINAL.pdf

20 www.edri.org/edrigram/number8.15/edri-euroispa-notice-takedown-comission

21 www.theregister.co.uk/2009/02/03/eircom_agrees_to_three_strikes_enforcement

22 www.theregister.co.uk/2009/02/23/irma_demands_irish_isps_block_access_to_piracy_sites

23 www.nytimes.com/2011/07/17/opinion/sunday/17sun3.html?partner=rssnyt&emc=rss

24 digitizor.com/2011/07/06/us-jurisdiction-com-net-websites

25 www.theregister.co.uk/2010/04/27/eu_cybercrime

26 en.wikipedia.org/wiki/Protect_IP_Act

27 www.theregister.co.uk/2011/05/18/nominet_wrestles_with_net_cop_role

imposition of unreasonable jurisdiction claims over parts or all of the IP address allocation and domain name systems creates dangers for the integrity of the global internet. The outsourcing of policing of the internet and imposition of punishments by internet intermediaries contradicts basic democratic values and our democratic societies' view of the rule of law. The outsourcing of these activities to large corporations who have a publicly stated vested interest in the development and imposition of a non-neutral internet creates an online environment which is diametrically opposed to the openness of the internet. This openness gives us the democratic – and the economic – value of the internet and is too important for governments to simply take for granted and to experiment with as if it were insignificant. Our social interaction is increasingly online and freedoms which were previously unquestioned are now increasingly at the whim of private companies: our freedom of expression, our freedom of assembly, our privacy and our right to due process and presumption of innocence.

Next steps

- Activists should demand that the spirit and the letter of constitutional[28] and human rights[29] be respected
- The dangers of pushing world regions or individual countries into developing "splinternets" to avoid EU/US jurisdiction should be recognised.
- Positive positions of international organisations should be publicised as much as possible.[30]
- Positive political statements on the need to keep the internet open should be publicised and promoted.[31]
- The contradictions between calls for an open internet in certain countries and support for a privately regulated and closed internet domestically should be highlighted.
- More attention should be given to the economic damage of moving from an innovative, competitive and open internet to a closed non-neutral internet.

28 Such as the US First Amendment.

29 Such as Articles 8 and 10 of the European Convention on Human Rights and Article 19 of the International Covenant on Civil and Political Rights.

30 www2.ohchr.org/english/bodies/hrcouncil/docs/17session/A.HRC.17.27_en.pdf

31 www.physorg.com/news/2011-02-clinton-renews-internet-access.html

E-revolutions and cyber crackdowns: User-generated content and social networking in protests in MENA and beyond

Alex Comninos
Doctoral candidate, Department of Geography, Justus Liebig University Giessen
www.comninos.org, www.uni-giessen.de/cms/faculties/f07/07/geography/depart-geo

Introduction

The recent protests and uprisings in Tunisia and Egypt have both been called "Twitter revolutions" and "Facebook revolutions" due to the widespread use of user-generated content (UGC) disseminated over social networks like Facebook and Twitter by protesters, activists and supporters of the protests, as well as by those following the events around the globe. This report investigates the usage and role of UGC and social networking websites in the recent protests and uprisings in the Middle East and North Africa (MENA), as well as other cases outside of the region.

In addition to being effective tools for communication and coordination by protesters, UGC and social networking have also been used by governments in response to these protests, often to crack down on protesters. Content and social networking platforms are areas of contestation between protesters and governments not necessarily balanced in favour of protesters.

UGC refers to internet content (text, images, videos and sound clips) that is created and uploaded to the internet by users, usually for no explicit financial gain, but rather for enjoyment or passion. UGC is created usually by amateurs, rather than professionals. It includes blogs, video clips, audio clips (podcasts), as well as comments on internet forums or "status updates" on social networks like Facebook or micro-blogging platforms like Twitter. In MENA, UGC created on mobile phones enabled protesters or witnesses to report on events live and to communicate with others and spread their message. Social networks like Facebook and the micro-blogging platform Twitter were used to disseminate this content.

Twitter and Facebook revolutions?

Can the uprisings in Egypt and Tunisia, as well as others in the MENA region, be called Twitter or Facebook revolutions? Was social networking unique to these protests? Has similar usage been seen before elsewhere? Was UGC, created on mobile phones and distributed over platforms like Facebook or Twitter, among the causes of these uprisings?

The usage of mobile phones, social networking websites and UGC in protests in MENA is not unprecedented. Twitter was used in protests in Moldova and Iran in 2009 and both cases were referred to by some as Twitter revolutions.[1] The popular ousting of President Joseph Estrada in the Philippines in 2001 was referred to as an "SMS revolution" due to the use of text messages to mobilise protests. It was described as "arguably the world's first 'e-revolution' – a change of government brought about by new forms of ICTs."[2]

Many feel that the role of UGC and social networking should not be overstated,[3] that these were not the cause of protests and uprisings in any MENA country. The causes involve a combination of decades of repression, political and economic marginalisation, the long-term structural decay of effectiveness and legitimacy in some state institutions, and soaring food prices, along with a desire by citizens for political representation and participation and the recognition of their human rights. On the ground, popular sentiments, grassroots organising and allegiance of the state security forces are important factors.

1 The term was applied by Evgeny Morozov to the Moldovan protests in 2009. See Morozov, E. (2009) Moldova's Twitter Revolution, *Net Effect*, 7 April. neteffect.foreignpolicy.com/posts/2009/04/07/moldovas_twitter_revolution; see also his other posts, More analysis of Twitter's role in Moldova, *Net Effect*, 7 April. neteffect.foreignpolicy.com/posts/2009/04/07/more_analysis_of_twitters_role_in_moldova and Moldova's Twitter revolution is NOT a myth, *Net Effect*, 10 April. neteffect.foreignpolicy.com/posts/2009/04/10/moldovas_twitter_revolution_is_not_a_myth Morozov has since criticised the Western media's haste to apply the term to Iran and protests and uprisings in MENA, as well as admitting that he might have hastily applied the term to Moldova. He writes about it in his 2011 book, *The Net Delusion: The Dark Side of Internet Freedom*, Public Affairs, New York.

2 Cout, J. (2001) *People Power II in the Philippines: The First E-Revolution?*, Overseas Development Institute. www.odi.org.uk/resources/details.asp?id=3147&title=people-power-ii-philippines-first-e-revolution

3 The debate between techno-sceptics and techno-idealists with regards to the role of ICTs in Tunisia and Egypt is well outlined in Vargas, J. A. (2011) Egypt, the Age of Disruption and the "Me" in Media, *The Huffington Post*, 7 February. www.huffingtonpost.com/jose-antonio-vargas/egypt-age-of-disruption-me-in-media_b_819481.html; see also Kravets, D. (2011) What's fueling Mideast protests? It's more than Twitter, *Wired Magazine*, 28 January. www.wired.co.uk/news/archive/2011-01/28/middle-east-protests-twitter.

TABLE 1.

ICT access in MENA

Country	Mobile cellular subscriptions per 100 inhabitants	Fixed internet subscriptions per 100 inhabitants	Estimated internet users per 100 inhabitants	Fixed broadband subscriptions per 100 inhabitants	Facebook users	Facebook users per 100 inhabitants
Algeria	93.8	...	13.5	2.3	1,138,240	3.00
Azerbaijan	87.8	5.9	27.4	1.1	184,660	2.00
Bahrain	177.1	10.0	53.0	9.6	232,960	29.00
Egypt	66.7	2.8	24.3	1.3	5,651,080	7.00
Iran	70.8	...	11.1	0.5	no data	no data*
Iraq	64.1	...	1.1	0.1	254,840	less than 1
Israel	125.8	...	63.1	25.8	308,760	40.00
Jordan	95.2	3.9	26.0	3.2	954,580	15.00
Kuwait	129.9	...	36.9	1.5	525,000	17.00
Lebanon	56.6	...	23.7	5.3	969,240	23.00
Libya	148.5	12.0	5.5	1.0	191,120	3.00
Mali	34.2	0.2	1.9	0.0	44,360	less than 1
Mauritania	66.3	...	2.3	0.3	33,700	1.00
Morocco	79.1	1.5	41.3	1.5	2,158,680	7.00
Oman	139.5	2.8	51.5	1.4	156,200	5.00
Palestine	28.6	...	32.2	5.0	no data	no data
Qatar	175.4	10.4	40.0	10.4	405,100	24.00
Saudi Arabia	174.4	7.3	38.0	5.2	2,489,320	9.00
Sudan	36.3	...	...	0.4	no data	no data*
Syria	45.6	3.6	20.4	0.2	no data	no data*
Tunisia	95.4	4.0	34.1	3.6	1,708,700	16.00
UAE	232.1	30.5	75.0	15.0	1,689,300	36.00
Yemen	35.3	1.9	10.0	0.2	107,520	less than 1

* Denotes lack of data due to the US comprehensive economic embargo on Iran, Sudan and Syria. There is no official Facebook data for these countries due to the trade embargo – technically they are not supposed to be offered Facebook, which is a US product.

Sources: International Telecommunication Union 2009 (www.itu.int/ITU-D/ICTEYE/Indicators/Indicators.aspx) and Social Map (geographics.cz/socialMap, statistics are from May 2011)

ICT access in MENA

Calling the uprisings in Tunisia and Egypt Twitter or Facebook revolutions overlooks information and communications technology (ICT) access in these countries. In 2009 in Tunisia and Egypt there were only 34.1 and 24.3 internet users per 100 inhabitants respectively. In Egypt only 7% of inhabitants are Facebook users, while 16% are Facebook users in Tunisia. From the ICT access and usage figures listed in Table 1, there is little correlation between ICTs and the level of unrest.

Throughout MENA social networking users generally comprise a minority of the population. Claims that UGC speaks for the demonstrators must be taken critically. The usage of the internet in developing countries is often disproportionately urban. Media attention is generally drawn to urban protests, for example, Cairo, Alexandria, Tunis, Tripoli and Benghazi. Use of UGC and social media also often reflects income and literacy biases.

Nonetheless, many protesters used UGC to express popular demands. Linkages were demonstrated between the mobilisation of demonstrators by social media as well as offline (on-the-ground) mobilisation.[4]

UGC and social networking in MENA

The terms "Twitter revolution" or "Facebook revolution" may not be accurate. The assertions that "the revolution will be tweeted" and "the revolution will be streamed" have more credence in the cases of Egypt, Tunisia, Syria, Bahrain and Libya. Many used mobile phones to organise demonstrations and to spread their messages. UGC and social networking platforms play an important role in protests and political transitions, but not necessarily a decisive one.

4 Meier, P. (2011) Civil Resistance Tactics Used in Egypt's Revolution #Jan25, *iRevolution*, 27 February. irevolution.net/2011/02/27/tactics-egypt-revolution-jan25

Before investigating the usage of UGC, the context of its use in MENA will be examined by looking at internet freedom in the region.

Internet freedom in MENA

In November 2005, Reporters Without Borders (RSF) listed fifteen "enemies of the internet", four of which were in MENA: Libya, Saudi Arabia, Syria and Tunisia. In 2010, RSF listed twelve enemies of the internet, including Saudi Arabia, Egypt, Syria and Tunisia. In March 2011, only Saudi Arabia and Syria were "enemies of the internet", although Bahrain, Belarus, Egypt, Libya, Tunisia and the United Arab Emirates (UAE) were listed as "under surveillance". Saudi Arabia, Syria and Egypt had netizens in prison.[5]

Internet filtering is common in MENA. The OpenNet Initiative reports that Bahrain, UAE, Qatar, Oman, Saudi Arabia, Kuwait, Yemen, Sudan and Tunisia used Western technologies to block internet content, "such as websites that provide sceptical views of Islam, secular and atheist discourse, sex, GLBT [gay, lesbian, bisexual and transgender content], dating services, and proxy and anonymity tools."[6]

According to a 2007 study of Arab media, "the impact of censorship across the region is mixed." Despite persistent censorship, "governments have not been able to silence dissent on the internet."[7]

The use of UGC and social networking in protest in MENA

Mohammed Bouazizi was a poverty-stricken Tunisian vegetable trader from the small town of Sidi Bouzid who had been repeatedly harassed by the police, who often asked him for bribes and confiscated his wares. In the last encounter they beat him. After being denied an appointment with a local government official to discuss this harassment, he doused himself with fuel and set himself alight in a public square. He died in hospital weeks later.

News of Bouazizi inspired protests in Sidi Bouzid, elsewhere in Tunisia, and throughout MENA. Initially television and print media were slow to pick up on the story. Often state media in MENA avoided reporting on it. Some internet content (like YouTube) was blocked at the time by the Tunisian internet filter. Facebook, which was not blocked at the time, became an important platform for spreading news of Bouazizi and the Sidi Bouzid revolt. Twitter was also instrumental in covering the protests.

Around the globe, many used Twitter and Facebook as a first port of call for information about Tunisia. UGC about events in Tunisia served to inspire people throughout the region. Egyptian activist Gigi Ibrahim, upon witnessing the downfall of Tunisian President Zine al-Abidine Ben Ali, tweeted: "The Tunisian revolution is being twitterised...history is being written by the people #sidibouzid #Tunisia."[8]

In Egypt, Facebook and Twitter were used to announce and publicise the planned protests on 25 January 2011. Facebook groups such as We are all Khaled Said[9] and the 6th of April Youth Movement[10] called for demonstrations. The plans and message of the protest were also disseminated through conventional means like word of mouth, photocopies and emailing of a PDF file explaining the plans for the protests.[11]

Facebook was used to announce protests in other countries in the MENA region. Many protests in 2011 were supported by Facebook pages, events and groups. UGC communicated the messages of protesters nationally, regionally and globally, and provided live coverage, news and opinions. On Twitter, protests (both online and offline) had their own Twitter hashtags. The Twitter hashtags #SidiBouzid, #Jan25, #Jan30, #Feb14, #Feb17, #Mar11/#ksa/#tal3mrak,[12] #Yemen/#Yamen,

5 Reporters Without Borders (2005) The 15 enemies of the Internet and other countries to watch, *Reporters without Borders*, 17 November. en.rsf.org/the-15-enemies-of-the-internet-and-17-11-2005,15613.html; Reporters without Borders (2010) Web 2.0 vs Control 2.0, *Reporters Without Borders*, 12 March. en.rsf.org/IMG/pdf/Internet_enemies.pdf; Reporters Without Borders (2011) *Internet Enemies*, Reporters without Borders. march12.rsf.org/i/Internet_Enemies.pdf

6 Noman, H. and York, J. C. (2011) *West Censoring East: The Use of Western Technologies by Middle East Censors, 2010-2011*, OpenNet Initative. opennet.net/west-censoring-east-the-use-western-technologies-middle-east-censors-2010-2011

7 Hofheinz, A. (2007) Arab Internet Use: Popular Trends and Public Impact, in Sklar, N. (ed) *Arab Media and Political Renewal: Community, Legitimacy and Public Life*, IB Tauris, New York, p. 60.

8 Gigi Ibrahim (@Gsquare86) 17:28:11 Jan 14 2011 twitter.com/gsquare86. Tweet curated in Nunns, A. and Idle, N. (2011) *Tweets from Tahrir*, OR Books, New York.

9 See Anonymous, "اديعس دلاخ انلك - We are all Khaled Saeed", www.facebook.com/ElShaheeed as well as "We are all Khaled Said: Working against torture and inhuman treatment of Egyptians in their own country. Standing up against corruption in Egypt", www.elshaheeed.co.uk. The pages were created in response to the murder of Khaled Said. Said was beaten to death by police after being caught in an internet café attempting to upload footage of Egyptian police selling drugs.

10 See "6th of April Youth Movement - ةكرح بابش 6 ليربا.", www.facebook.com/shabab6april

11 See a copy in English and Arabic in Madrigal, A. (2011) Egyptian Activists' Action Plan: Translated, *The Atlantic*, 27 January. theatlantic.com/international/archive/2011/01/egyptian-activists-action-plan-translated/70388. Interestingly, the document stated not to use Twitter, Facebook or other websites for dissemination as "[t]hey are all monitored by the Ministry of the Interior."

12 Tal3mrak means literally "May God prolong your life" and is used to address the wealthy and powerful respectfully in the Gulf region. It is also used sarcastically to make fun of rich and powerful figures and has been used to make fun of the king of Saudi Arabia around the Arab world. See Shibab-Eldin, A. (2011) #Tal3mrak: A Hashtag Challenges Saudi Arabian King, *The Huffington Post*, 31 August. www.huffingtonpost.com/ahmed-shihabeldin/tal3mrak-a-hashtag-challe_b_941231.html

#Kuwait, and #Syria were used for protest in Tunisia, Egypt, Sudan, Bahrain, Libya, Saudi Arabia, Yemen, Kuwait and Syria respectively.

UGC acted as a conduit for news around unfolding events not covered by or outside the reach of the conventional media. Micro-blogging and picture and video sharing over mobile phones became avenues to disseminate and consume news about protests. The nexus of UGC and mobile phones is an important tool for protesters to inform the world of their demands, the events surrounding the actual protests, and the nature of police, military and civilian responses. UGC often offers views and perspectives that state-run and conventional media do not offer, as well as images that other media cannot record. In Syria, where access by international journalists has been almost completely restricted, mobile phone videos have become one of the few ways to report on protests.

State responses to UGC and social networking

Many have commented on the power of social media in the hands of protesters and activists. What of state responses to UGC and social networking during the protests? How have UGC and social networking websites been used by incumbent regimes in response to protests?

Goliath and the mouse? Twitter revolutions and cyber crackdowns

An online campaign by the International Society for Human Rights (ISHR) depicts challenged incumbent leaders gripped by fear of the revolutionary potential of ICTs. The presidents of Iran, Zimbabwe, Venezuela and Cuba, Colonel Muammar Gaddafi of Libya and North Korea's Kim Jong-il, are portrayed cowering in near paralytic fear of a computer mouse, jumping on furniture and hanging from chandeliers and curtains in an attempt to flee.[13] The real balance of power in the electronic terrain, however, is not necessarily in favour of the mouse. The campaign could have been balanced with other images: boots crushing mice, keyboards and mobile phones after being identified as threats for spreading content. Or perhaps the regime's technicians unplugging the mice, terminating lines of communication.

UGC and the infrastructures through which it flows are areas of contestation between protesters and pro-incumbent groups, not necessarily balanced in favour of those creating content for protest.

Some governments used internet filters to block content during the protests. In Tunisia, Egypt, Libya, Syria and allegedly Gaza there were state crackdowns on UGC and the internet in general through internet blackouts and slowdowns.[14]

The Mubarak regime virtually shut down all Egyptian access to the internet from midnight 27/28 January until 2 February 10:30 GMT.[15] In Libya, the internet was blocked to most Libyans from the beginnings of the protests in areas under Gaddafi control.[16] Hours after the internet had gone back up, Egyptian security forces arrested, detained and harassed bloggers and Facebook and Twitter users who had shared content or publicised and attended events.

In Tunisia, the Ben Ali regime stole usernames and passwords for Facebook, Twitter and online email accounts by injecting Java scripts into the content of these pages before they were sent to end-users.

Twitter and Facebook have been used by security and intelligence agencies to identify and locate activists and protesters. In North Sudan, where Facebook groups announced protests against the regime, the government actively monitored social networking websites. When protests did happen, many potential demonstrators found police waiting for them and were arrested.[17]

In Azerbaijan, influenced by events in Egypt, a number of Facebook pages and groups called for protests in early 2011. An opposition activist was arrested and charged with possession of narcotics. Many believe he was detained for comments he made on Facebook calling for Egypt-style protests.[18] Amnesty International called the charges a "pretext to punish Jabbar Savalan for his political activism and to discourage other youth activists from exercising the right to freedom of expression."[19]

13 The campaign cannot be found anymore on the ISHR website (www.ishr.org), but it can be found in many other places online, for example at Duncan (no surname given) (2010) ISHR Scared Dictators and The Mouse, *The Inspiration Room*, 24 September. theinspirationroom.com/daily/2010/ishr-scared-dictators-and-the-mouse

14 Global Voices (2011) Syria: Reports of Internet Blackout, *Global Voices*, 3 June. globalvoicesonline.org/2011/06/03/syria-reports-of-internet-blackout; Occupied Palestine (2011) Latest Updates on #Gaza | #GazaBlackOut", *Occupied Palestine*, 10 August. occupiedpalestine.wordpress.com/2011/08/10/latest-update-on-gaza-gazablackout. The Gaza case may have been an accident, or an attempt to stop a planned terror attack, but it still may represent a crackdown on the internet during protests and unrest.

15 Internet access during the Egyptian revolution can be graphed on Google Transparency (transparency.google.com); see is.gd/VwQM29. The web was not entirely blocked: the ISP Nour, which ran the stock exchange, was functional. The web more correctly slowed to a microscopic trickle into Egypt.

16 See Google Transparency for Libya from mid-February on at is.gd/XKhikC and is.gd/jTwlIS

17 Meier, P. (2011) Civil Resistance: Early Lessons Learned from Sudan's #Jan30, *iRevolution*, 31 January. irevolution.net/2011/01/31/civil-resistance-sudans-jan30; Babington, D. (2011) Sudan's cyber-defenders take on Facebook protesters, *Reuters*, 30 March. reuters.com/article/2011/03/30/us-sudan-internet-feature-idUSTRE72T54W20110330.

18 Krikorian, O. (2011) Azerbaijan: Blowing Up in Their Facebook, *Global Voices Advocacy*, 10 March. advocacy.globalvoicesonline.org/2011/03/10/azerbaijan-blowing-up-in-their-facebook/.

19 Cited in Ibid.

Crackdowns on internet communications during protests were not only witnessed in MENA in 2011, but also in the United States (US) and United Kingdom (UK). In response to protests in the UK, the government has asked for cooperation from Research in Motion (RIM) – the creators of the Blackberry smartphone – to provide it with encryption keys in order to be able to eavesdrop on the Blackberry Messenger service (BBM). The UK government has summoned Twitter, Facebook and RIM to a meeting discussing ways to restrict the use of social media during civil unrest.[20] The San Francisco Bay Area Rapid Transit (BART) authority (a state-owned transport corporation) shut down mobile phone access at subway stations as a response to planned protests against the killing of a homeless man by the BART Police.[21]

Problems presented by the use of UGC in struggles for democracy and human rights

Social media and surveillance

As WikiLeaks' Julian Assange recently noted, the internet is not only a force for openness and transparency, "it is also the greatest spying machine the world has ever seen."[22] Social networking platforms often link an online identity to a real name, home town, occupation, interests, pictures, and network of friends – providing many opportunities for surveillance.

Information on social networks may potentially be mined by third-party applications and advertisers. Facebook's API,[23] which is a language or set of commands for retrieving information from Facebook, is openly accessible by anyone turning their account into a developer account. The API makes it easy to obtain and analyse such information.[24]

20 Somaiya, R. (2011) In Britain, a Meeting on Limiting Social Media, *The New York Times*, 25 August. www.nytimes.com/2011/08/26/world/europe/26social.html?_r=1&src=tp

21 For an overview of the operation in protest against BART see: The War and Peace Report (news show), 16 August 2011, *Democracy Now!* www.democracynow.org/2011/8/16/stream and Vince in the Bay, Disorderly Conduct - Operation BART Recap (podcast), 17 August 2011, www.blogtalkradio.com/vinceinthebay/2011/08/17/disorderly-conduct--operation-bart-recap-1

22 The Hindu (2011) World's greatest spying machine, *The Hindu*, 6 April. www.thehindu.com/opinion/editorial/article1602746.ece.

23 API originally stood for Advanced Programming Interface, but is now more commonly known as Application Programming Interface. An API is "a particular set of rules and specifications that software programs can follow to communicate with each other. It serves as an interface between different software programs and facilitates their interaction, similar to the way the user interface facilitates interaction between humans and computers." en.wikipedia.org/wiki/Application_programming_interface

24 Moderated, of course, by the user's privacy settings.

Mobile phones and geolocation

Facebook and Twitter, as well as mobile phone applications, offer geolocation functionality, which may add location to a user's content. The position of a mobile phone can be tracked by mobile operators, and potentially by governments or third parties. Under certain circumstances the use of the mobile internet can actually enhance the surveillance capabilities of repressive regimes.

Removal of UGC from social networks

Facebook policies can often result in the Facebook pages of political activists being shut down. The "We are all Khaled Said" Facebook page, which was used (among others) to call for protests on the 25 January revolution in Egypt, was actually opened in June 2010 but was quickly shut down by Facebook. This was because the user who opened the account – "El Shaheed" – was not using a real name. Facebook's terms of service prohibit the use of fake names or monikers.

In the UK in April 2011 a group of students from University College London called UCL Occupation, protesting over fee increases and cuts to higher education funding, claimed that in twelve hours Facebook had deleted over 50 Facebook profiles of activists in the UK.[25]

Guy Aitchison, a student at UCL and blogger for openDemocracy.net, said:

> These groups are technically in violation of Facebook's terms of agreement (...). But the timing – on the royal wedding and May Day weekend – is deeply suspicious. (...) [T]his purge of online organising groups could be linked to the wider crackdown on protest by authorities in Britain. Either way, it is a scandalous abuse of power by Facebook to arbitrarily destroy online communities built up over many months and years [which] provide a vital means for activist groups to communicate with their supporters.[26]

Facebook officially responded to UCL Occupation with the following explanation and advice:

> Facebook profiles are intended to represent individual people only. It is a violation of Facebook's Statement of Rights and Responsibilities to use a profile to represent a brand,

25 UCL Occupation (2011) Over 50 political accounts deleted in Facebook purge, *UCL Occupation*, 29 April. blog.ucloccupation.com/2011/04/29/over-50-political-accounts-deleted-in-facebook-purge

26 Aitchison, G. (2011) Political purge of UK Facebook underway, *OurKingdom*, 29 April. www.opendemocracy.net/ourkingdom/guy-aitchison/political-purge-of-uk-facebook-underway

> business, group, or organization. (...) If you would like to continue representing your organization on Facebook, we can convert your profile to a Page.[27]

In Palestine a page calling for a "Third Palestinian Intifada" was shut down. It was seen by some as hate speech and reported to Facebook.[28] Many wondered why all other Arab countries were allowed to have pages dedicated to a "day of rage" against their governments, but one was not allowed for a protest against Israeli occupation.

These examples demonstrate that it is not users of the platforms, but the social networking or content platforms themselves, that have ultimate control of their content.

Reliability and veracity of UGC

UGC can be used for misinformation and propaganda. UGC presents problems with regards to the reliability and veracity of information. A famous example from MENA was that of the "lesbian Syrian blogger" who turned out to be a married US man.[29] This ended up being counterproductive for the protest movement and fuelled rumours of foreign intervention in protests, propagated by the Syrian government. Social networks can be mechanisms for spreading rumour and falsehood. As there is usually no moderation of this content, it is the responsibility of the user to critically examine the veracity of UGC.

Sockpuppetry and astroturfing

"Sockpuppets" are an important problem in UGC. Wikipedia defines a sockpuppet as "an online identity used for purposes of deception within an online community" and, in earlier usage, "a false identity through which a member of an Internet community speaks with or about himself or herself, pretending to be a different person."[30] "Astroturfing" is using sockpuppets on a larger and organised scale, designed to fake the appearance of grassroots or "netroots" movements (conventionally the word "astroturf" refers to synthetic grass). Astroturfing can disseminate views that appear to be legitimate and spontaneous, but are actually campaigns by political or commercial identities.[31]

Members of the hacktivist collective Anonymous claim to have discovered the existence of an advanced astroturfing software allegedly commissioned by the US Air Force.[32] This software can create online identities with corresponding social networking profiles on multiple platforms, which can create content with identities that appear contingent to previous posts, as well as according to culture, age or gender. This software is also a surveillance platform, as "fake friends" on social networks to monitor unsuspecting users.[33] The possible existence of this software raises important concerns about the nexus of UGC and astroturfing.

Conclusion

UGC, social networks and mobile phones are not unequivocally tools for the benefit of protesters, but rather a part of a contested terrain used by both governments and protest movements in societal conflicts and transitions. Social networking sites like Facebook and Twitter could be used to spy on protesters, find out their real-life identities and make arrests and detentions.

These dilemmas will remain relevant in Egypt and Tunisia now that political transitions have started. Egypt and Tunisia both remain under military rule. Democracy and freedom to create and distribute content will not necessarily prevail. Neither will the role of UGC and social networking sites cease to be of relevance.

UGC is still being used actively in Egypt and Tunisia to expose violations of the security forces. In Egypt, the military recognised the power of Facebook and made a Facebook page after the fall of Mubarak to try to garner support and make peace with the protesters.

The transition in Egypt and Tunisia is still unfolding – elections need to be planned, political parties organised, reorganised and new ones formed. These processes cannot be conducted today without the internet and ICTs.

Some issues the online activist needs to bear in mind include:

27 UCL Occupation (2011) Facebook forced to respond to our campaign for restoration of accounts, *UCL Occupation*, 29 April. blog.ucloccupation.com/2011/04/29/facebook-forced-to-respond-to-our-campaign-for-restoration-of-accounts

28 Neroulias, N. (2011) Jews Pressure Facebook over Palestinian Intifada Page, *The Huffington Post*, 31 March. www.huffingtonpost.com/2011/03/30/jews-pressure-facebook-ov_n_842741.html

29 Al Hussaini, A. (2011) Lesbian Blogger is Married American Man, *Global Voices*, 13 June. globalvoicesonline.org/2011/06/13/syria-lesbian-blogger-amina-is-a-married-american-man

30 en.wikipedia.org/wiki/Sockpuppet_(Internet)

31 en.wikipedia.org/wiki/Astroturfing; see also Monbiot, G. (2011) The need to protect the internet from 'astroturfing' grows ever more urgent, *The Guardian*, 23 February. www.guardian.co.uk/environment/georgemonbiot/2011/feb/23/need-to-protect-internet-from-astroturfing

32 Bright, P. (2011) Anonymous speaks: The inside story of the HBGary hack, *ars technica*, 15 February. arst.ch/o9q

33 Anonymous (n. d.) Operation Metal Gear, *AnonNews*. anonnews.org/?p=press&a=item&i=752

Anonymity and monikers

User-generated content can, if not used carefully, expose content creators to surveillance. Many UGC platforms do not allow for anonymity. In light of the concerns raised above about astroturfing and sockpuppetry, anonymity is not ideal for activism, especially if the source of the activism is not known. Nonetheless, in the context of repressive regimes, the protection afforded by anonymity does have its merits.

Anonymity cannot and should not, as Randi Zuckerberg, ex-marketing director of Facebook has suggested, "go away."[34] Despite calls by some authorities – the British Police for example – to end the use of anonymous monikers on platforms like Twitter,[35] many platforms will not do this. There are legitimate reasons (including personal security) for activists not to use their real names. Content creators should be informed about the possibilities of creating content anonymously and securely and decide whether to use real names or monikers. If anonymity is chosen, creators of content must be aware that small things like a network of real-life friends, one picture or an accidental use of geolocation could expose a user's identity.

Safe and informed use of social networking

UGC and social networking present the challenge of balancing activism with privacy and online safety. Different platforms offer different strengths and weaknesses regarding the often diverging goals of activism and privacy: Facebook does not allow for anonymity, and the use of monikers is not permitted, while Twitter does allow monikers.

Facebook users need to be aware of the range of possible privacy settings and their implications. Privacy settings can protect users, but minimal privacy settings in certain conditions may be useful for online activism to build and coordinate communities, and spread content virally.

Each platform for the creation and dissemination of UGC, as well as each social networking website, has terms and conditions which users should be aware of. Users should also be aware of the national legal and regulatory environments governing privacy and the internet in the countries in which these UGC platforms are hosted.

Backup and mirroring of content

At the end of the day, it is the social networking platform or content platform on which the content is hosted that has the ultimate control over their online content. Unless, of course, users have this content backed up or mirrored (duplicated on another website).

There are alternatives to Facebook

It would be beneficial if activists were afforded access to social networking tools that they could exercise more control over, especially with regards to the hosting of their content, and their privacy and anonymity.

There are alternatives to social networking platforms such as Twitter or Facebook. The social networking platform Diaspora is nodal and peer-to-peer. Users can host their own identities or "pods", and choose from a range of hosts to host their pod on.

Self-hosted or smaller social networking platforms have many advantages. However, they may not be able to invest as much in security as their larger counterparts. Even big "brand" social networks can experience problems securing private data.

UGC under surveillance

If the avoidance of state surveillance is required, certain practices should be followed wherever possible when disseminating UGC. Platforms offering end-to-end encryption should be defaulted to wherever possible. Facebook, Twitter and other social networking applications, web-based email and web-based applications should always be accessed through HTTPS encryption if it is available (by typing https:// instead of http:// before a web address).[36] HTTPS will help avoid the stealing of usernames and passwords as well as eavesdropping. Anonymising tools such as proxies, virtual private networks (VPNs) and Tor can also be used for protecting the identity of content creators, as well as for circumventing filtering and censorship. Tor has been particularly helpful in protecting activists and journalists in the MENA region.[37] ■

34 Bosker, B. (2011) Facebook's Randi Zuckerberg: Anonymity Online "Has to Go Away", *The Huffington Post*, 27 July. www.huffingtonpost.com/2011/07/27/randi-zuckerberg-anonymity-online_n_910892.html

35 Chen, A. (2011) Clueless British police suggest Twitter require real names, *Gawker*, 26 August. gawker.com/5834776

36 The Electronic Frontier Foundation has a plug-in for Firefox which can be downloaded from its website (www.eff.org/https-everywhere). The plug-in will instruct the browser to always connect to HTTPS (if available) when viewing a website.

37 Zahorsky, I. (2011) Tor, Anonymity and the Arab spring: An Interview with Jacob Appelbaum, *Peace and Conflict Monitor*, 1 August. www.monitor.upeace.org/innerpg.cfm?id_article=816

The internet and social movements in North Africa

Ramy Raoof
Egyptian Blog for Human Rights
ebfhr.blogspot.com

Creating free space

Many taboos and "red lines" are imposed on offline spaces like newspapers and TV channels in several states in North Africa, as well as many limits on freedom of expression and the right to assembly. It is not easy to establish a newspaper in Libya or a human rights organisation in Algeria or to call for a march in Bahrain.

Cyberspace is almost the only free space for many groups and individuals to practise not only their right to freedom of expression and speech but also to practise their right to assembly and to form associations and groups with common interests.

Since 2004, Egyptian netizens and bloggers have been able to utilise online platforms for different causes effectively. Many taboos were broken by online spaces, empowering offline media to address several topics that they considered "red line". These topics included torture in police stations, sexual harassment issues, religious minorities, violations committed by Mubarak supporters, etc.

Human rights NGOs, bloggers and journalists played complementary roles at that time – and still do – confronting violations and providing immediate help to victims and those in need. Journalists used to share information and pass multimedia recordings of torture to bloggers so that they could post them online when their editors refused to publish details of the cases in newspapers. This fear was due to local laws or the response from security authorities or even that a publication would lose advertisements.

During the revolution, the Egyptian cyberspace erupted in extremely rich content, which took different forms – text, videos and pictures. Two main things affected the content in cyberspace: the first was what happened on the ground and the second was the accessibility of communications platforms.

From 14 January to 24 January 2011, netizens kept sending invitations to demonstrate on 25 January – National Police Day in Egypt – against corruption, unemployment and torture. In order to motivate participation, netizens posted human rights reports and statements on the status of human rights in the country online, as well as video clips of different torture cases, and pictures and footage from previous peaceful assemblies. Practical information was also provided, such as legal and medical tips for participants taking part in peaceful assemblies, tactics for using online platforms and mobile phones to organise, the locations and timings of demonstrations on 25 January, and hotline numbers for immediate legal and medical help from human rights NGOs.

From 25 January to 6 February 2011 Egyptians experienced a series of crackdowns on communications platforms. Activists' mobile lines and hotline numbers were shut down and social media websites (including Twitter, Facebook and Bambuser) and newspaper websites were blocked, while landlines did not work in some areas in Cairo. Later, when communications were restored, netizens gradually posted what had happened when communications were shut down, including content showing violations and violence committed against peaceful demonstrators. The timeline of the communications shutdown by the Egyptian authorities is shown in Figure 1.[1]

Before the internet was totally blocked, some activists were able to post information, videos and pictures from demonstrations and to cover what was happening offline. This was very important: besides offering concrete evidence to the world of the clampdown, it proved the government was just spreading rumours and false information of the security situation. There had been, until now, a big gap between what individuals posted and circulated online and what the state-run media broadcasted and published. At times this gap was extreme. For example, when netizens and activists posted pictures online of hundreds of thousands of demonstrators in Tahrir Square, the state media was showing a picture of an almost empty square which it called "live" footage!

Although some downplay the role that the internet played in the revolution, during the uprising online platforms were the only space where Egyptians could share what they really faced and went through.

Of course, many taboos are broken in offline spaces, but still – even now – online platforms are in some cases the only space where Egyptians can address topics that offline platforms cannot. These include human rights violations committed by

1 Online version of the diagram: flic.kr/p/9RNhpz

FIGURE 1.

Timeline of the communications shutdown in Egypt during the revolution

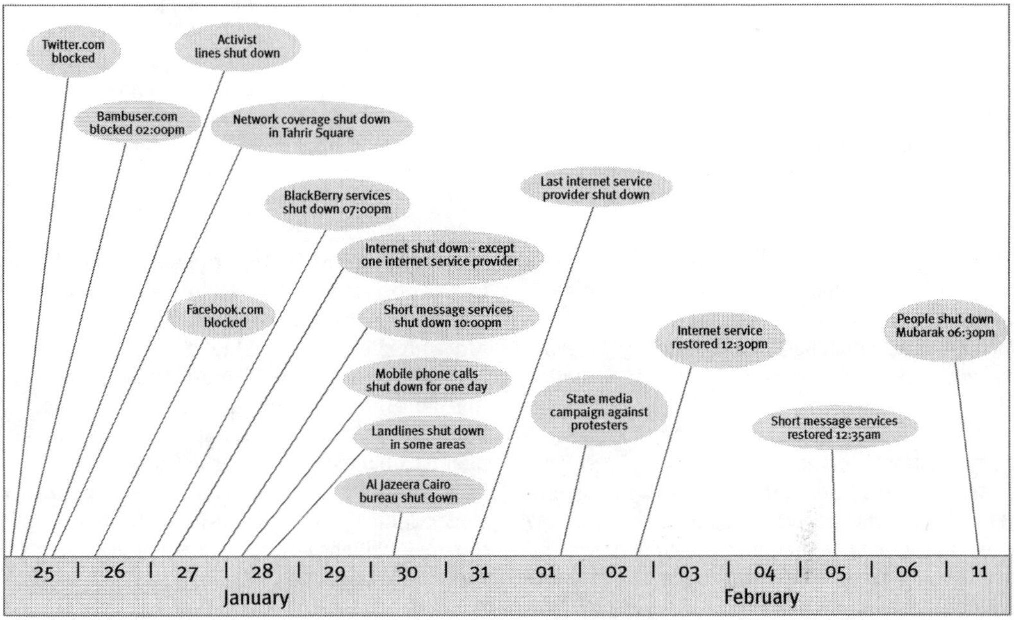

military officers and other topics related to the army. These online spaces continue to put pressure on the authorities to address issues in the offline world.

Nevertheless, it is important not to magnify the role of the internet during the revolutions and uprisings; the Egyptian revolution is not a "Facebook revolution" or "Web 2.0 revolution" or similar meaningless terms. But online platforms were the media arm for Egyptians during the revolution, a space for Egyptians to share their experiences and thoughts and to show the truth of what happened.

Circumventing repressive regimes

Online spaces are frequently utilised to expose human rights violations that governments try hard to keep unknown. Videos published online showing particular violations taking place create a strong wave of resistance over time in different online and offline platforms – like the videos exposing police corruption in Morocco[2] and torture in police stations and violence in Egypt.[3]

During the revolution in Tunisia, the Tunisian cyberspace in general – and blogosphere in particular – was almost the only source of information, pictures and videos of what was happening on the ground. Offline platforms did not pick up on what happened in Tunisia in the beginning and even when coverage took place it was limited.

In Libya, Tunisia and Syria, where there is excessive control on offline media platforms, the internet was the place where individuals could share what was happening.

Media tent in Tahrir Square

One of the first media tents set up in January in Tahrir Square was organised by a group of friends (including bloggers, human rights defenders, political activists) using their personal laptops, cameras, memory sticks, hard disks, cables and other devices that might be needed. We also put up a sign[4] that said "Point to upload pictures and videos". The main thing we did was gather all kinds of multimedia from demonstrators in Tahrir Square, then made the content available online.

For me, doing this was very important because I believed that making those pictures and videos public would help everyone to really understand what was happening on the ground. It would allow them to follow the situation and be able to assess it, as well as have an overview of what happened

2 Video from July 2007: youtu.be/K6FCsv8RhsM and October 2008: youtu.be/4XpMmyUVdLo

3 Video from November 2006: youtu.be/HMeXkZX9_E8 and youtu.be/YVxeyq__KD4

4 flic.kr/p/9eEabY

in different cities in Egypt, given that those people who had pictures or videos were not only from Cairo.

Providing the content[5] also helped to prove that the government at that time was just spreading lies and rumours and manufacturing fake images of the protests. The content that we uploaded proved that violations were taking place, whether a video showing police shooting at peaceful demonstrators, or a picture showing a sniper pointing his gun at someone.

Challenges facing online communities

There are several challenges facing online communities and activists. These frequently relate to the violation of an individual's privacy and legal threats that any netizen could face based on their online activity.

These threats have become more intense due to international companies providing technical surveillance and monitoring systems to governments around the world. These companies simply develop programmes that enable governments and security agencies in the ruling regimes to violate anyone's privacy, monitor anyone's activity and impose censorship. Consequently, they are helping governments to fabricate cases against political activists and human rights defenders on charges like "destabilising order", "defaming state leaders", "spreading rumours to overthrow the regime" and many other charges that regimes set to minimise the work of civil societies and activists towards securing human rights.

For example, in 2009 – and maybe even earlier – a European-based company with its headquarters in the United Kingdom called Gamma Group International offered the State Security Intelligence (SSI) in Egypt security software. SSI units describe this software in their internal communications in August 2009 as a "high-level security system that has capabilities not provided in other systems. Its most prominent capabilities include hacking into personal Skype accounts, hacking email accounts associated with Hotmail, Yahoo and Gmail, and allowing the complete control of targeted computers." In December 2010 the SSI reported that the software can "record audio and video chats, record activity taking place around hacked computers with cameras and make copies of their content."

This is just what we knew after Egyptians stormed SSI headquarters, discovering the documentation.

Even without the use of such programmes, netizens might face trial due to content posted online. This happened to human rights activist Nabeel Rajab, director of the Bahrain Center for Human Rights. Rajab was criminally charged in April 2011 for publishing images on his personal account on Twitter.[6]

Twitter and Facebook usage in North Africa

The Dubai School of Government issued a report in May 2011 on social media in the Arab region; the statistics on Twitter and Facebook usage in North Africa are presented in Table 1.[7]

From the numbers in the table, it is clear that the percentage of Twitter and Facebook users is not high compared to the population sizes. Consequently, online content does not have a high, direct impact on offline communities. Instead it can be said to influence offline activist platforms, which in turn may influence offline communities.

Conclusion

Each space used to share information and knowledge has its own key players, target groups, and positive and negative points. There are differences, not gaps, between the press and radio stations. There are also differences between online and offline tools and communities, and these differences are normal – the "gap" should not be the main concern.

Individuals and groups use online tools to complement their offline work in mobilising people for events, and online tools are used to provide coverage of and document what is happening offline. The relationship between both online and offline communities can be complementary.

"Crossposting" is the main way that online communities help spread information and create a wave or buzz on particular incidents. Bloggers from Syria, Bahrain, Morocco and other states played an important role by crossposting the content coming out of Tunisia and Egypt. This pushed offline media to use online content in their work, enabling more people to become aware of what was happening and helping the content reach more and more communities.

The internet is a free space that enables individuals and groups to practice their rights in a different way when they have no space offline. Online tools

5 Content available online through torrent links: is.gd/bAFmHg and is.gd/SaZJVZ and pictures available at: flic.kr/s/aHsjtogRvz

6 www.anhri.net/en/?p=2412

7 www.dsg.ae/NEWSANDEVENTS/UpcomingEvents/ASMROverview2.aspx

TABLE 1.

Twitter and Facebook users in North Africa

Country	Population	Twitter users (average between 1 Jan and 30 Mar)	Facebook users (4 May)
Algeria	35,953,989	13,235	1,947,900
Egypt	85,950,300	131,204	6,586,260
Libya	6,670,928	63,919	71,840
Morocco	32,770,852	17,384	3,203,440
Sudan	44,103,535	9,459	443,623
Tunisia	10,476,355	35,746	2,356,520

help social movements to better communicate, share their ideas and achieve impact and improvements. Building movements and improving human rights and political situations can only be done offline with the mobilisation of people, using all available tools, including the internet.

I joined the street demonstrations in Egypt on 28 January. Before that, together with my colleagues, I was providing legal and medical assistance as well as documenting violations. In the beginning, for me, the day was just another demonstration that might continue for several days and end up in a brutal clampdown by the police. On 2 February I realised it was a revolution, and people would not leave the streets until Mubarak was brought down.

During the revolutionary events, and on a daily basis, it was clear that we went through a wide range of feelings. You get angry, upset, aggressive, afraid, feel courage and fear and suddenly happiness and hope.

The most important thing that made me feel comfortable and believe that anything is possible was that I was not alone in the streets. Many people were around helping, showing support and solidarity. This would not be possible on the internet alone. ■

Workers' rights and the internet

Steve Zeltzer
LaborNet
www.labornet.org

Communication, solidarity and the internet: How the internet, information technology and new media are shaping the world working class

From textile factory workers at the Egyptian Mahalla textile plants, to Chinese workers in Honda factories, to Wisconsin public workers: social networks, the internet and new communications technologies are playing a critical role in linking up workers locally, nationally and internationally.

In each of these struggles the use of mobile texting, Twitter, YouTube and video streams is playing a vital role in helping to get the word out, defending against repression and linking up with workers throughout the world.

The global economy and the drive for greater profitability is the key driving force in the development of communications technology. International production lines are linked up through the internet, and the export and transfer of labour through the use of the internet is endemic.

Central to the power and information network of working people globally has been the rollout of mobile phone coverage. In 2010 there were 4.6 billion mobile phones in service and this is set to go to five billion by 2011. Even in parts of Africa where only 5% of the population has electricity, workers globally, and particularly migrant workers, are now linked up through their mobile phones.

One of the first uses of the internet and the web for education and solidarity was the Liverpool dockworkers strike in 1995. The 500 dockers who were members and local leaders of the Transport and General Workers' Union (TGWU) refused to cross a picket line. This solidarity action was labelled as illegal under the Thatcher anti-labour laws, and the dockers not only faced a fight with the government laws, but also the acceptance of these laws by their national union. The workers, in order to fight back, had to break the information blockade. LaborNet, in collaboration with the Association for Progressive Communications (APC) in the United States (US), working with APC member GreenNet in the United Kingdom (UK) and labour supporters Chris Bailey and Greg Dropkin, developed the first international web page to support a struggle globally.[1]

The web page allowed the Liverpool dockworkers to bring their struggle to Australian dockers as well as longshore workers throughout the world. It included messages of solidarity and helped solidify an international defence campaign that even included workers' action by dockers in the US, Canada and Japan against the ship the Neptune Jade.[2]

One of the lessons of this struggle for the working class was that the anti-labour laws and restrictions on solidarity, and the corporate effort to prevent knowledge of workers' struggles and solidarity efforts, could be overcome using the internet. In fact, during the West Coast boycott of the Neptune loaded by the union-busting company, video footage was provided to CNN for broadcast in the UK for the first time showing that the struggle had international support.

This multimedia use of computer networks, video and the media has been replicated many times worldwide, and the growth of social media and live streaming now make this a 24-hour-a-day occurrence.

Temporary workers and communication

Capitalists have also sought to use technology to control temporary workers. A document called The Beeper Revolution from Korea tells how workers were contracted by being beeped on their mobile phones, and had no contact with other workers. This also prevented workers from linking up with each other and beginning to organise. The atomisation of workers, who do not work together in the old way through a union hall, but only when beeped or called, is a major obstacle to organising workers.

This is especially the case with the use of temporary workers on a global level, such as in Spain and other parts of Europe, as well as in Korea, where 30% or more of the work force are temporary workers. In Japan where these mostly young workers are called *Freeta* workers, their marginalisation through their isolation is a conscious policy of the corporations and their governments. They have done this through deregulation and anti-labour laws, which inhibit unionisation and collective action.

1 eastbound.eu/site_media/pdf/060111bailey.pdf
2 www.youtube.com/watch?v=F3Wva4XbMVs

In one document called Workers Under Surveillance and Control: Background, presented by Korean professor Kang Soo-dol of Korea University at the Third Annual Seoul International Labor Media conference in 2001, it was pointed out that this means of controlling and using labour was critically connected to the use of digital and communication technologies.[3]

The great fear of capital is that through their collective power, labour will refuse management control and threaten their power to govern. This fear was confirmed in the 1997 general strike in South Korea, when the young Korean Confederation of Trade Unions (KCTU) led a general strike in part through the use of computer networks. At the 1999 Second Seoul International Labor Media conference, reports were presented about the Seoul Subway Workers Union's use of a computer users group (CUG) to help organise the general strike. Trade unionists reported that they had to go underground to conduct the strike, and did this through the use of computer networks to keep their communication open in the successful strike. This was also the first general strike in which workers used video to document the strike throughout the country with the development of a labour video network.

The growth of LaborFests[4] and international working class film and video festivals have also become a tool for the expansion of communication and knowledge about labour and the democratic struggles of workers throughout the world. The first LaborFest in San Francisco in 1994 has now expanded internationally with film festivals in Turkey, Korea, Japan, Argentina, South Africa and other countries around the world. These can also be streamed live, and the development of an international labour video channel on the internet and cable would be a powerful vehicle for building solidarity and increasing education.

The use of a variety of communication technologies in labour struggles is a vital lesson of the new age of telecommunications. This was also the case with the Egyptian Mahalla workers who used their mobile phones to organise workers' actions and overcome the government control of information. As suggested, the use of mobile phones has become a historic vehicle for workers' and peoples' struggles throughout the world. Today, the Mahalla workers not only use their mobile phones for mobilisation, but also use social media sites like YouTube to get their action plans out.[5]

Another report, by Hossam El-Homalawy, a journalist and labour activist, shows how the role of the mobile phone and computer networking was critical in the building of the workers movement in Egypt – and in fact led to the foundation of the mass movement that removed Mubarak.[6]

Mobile phones also have the potential to be used to spy on workers and to prevent their struggle to unionise for labour rights. The most shocking case is again in Korea, where the Korea Samsung workers were seeking to organise. They visited their labour lawyer to find out what their rights were and when they returned to the factory, their boss repeated word for word what they had questioned their lawyer about. Their phones had been used to track their locations and record their private meeting with their lawyer by the virulently anti-labour Samsung Corporation.

Again, the independent labour media movement was able to develop a video about how mobile phones are being used against the workers. Seoul-based Labor News Production made a documentary called *Big Brother is Watching: The Other Side of Samsung* (2006), which was also screened to workers around the world, including in Turkey, Argentina and the US.

Tracking workers on the internet

Another dangerous use of ICTs is the use of the internet in the tracking of union activists and organisers, as well as sick and injured workers, to allow employers to gather information that will help them terminate their contracts. Today, everything that is done on the internet stays in the internet world. Actions including labour rallies, strikes and other activities are now being recorded both by the mainstream media and independent journalists, and this material, once posted, is traceable on a global level.

Artificial intelligence developed by Google and other corporations is now being put to use to collect and examine, effectively amounting to spying on people to determine what they are interested in for future sale of products. This includes book publishers such as Amazon and other online consumer businesses. The information about the books you buy and look at are now being held by private corporations that have private interests. And some of this information is made public. To find out if a worker is looking up books about labour history, for example, you could do a search under US laws and most laws around the world.

3 lmedia.nodong.net/maybbs/view.php?db=nodong&code=lmedia_pds&n=165&page=14

4 www.laborfest.net

5 www.youtube.com/watch?v=Z6UC9Lme7PE

6 blip.tv/file/4699784 and blip.tv/file/4700355

Digitalisation of the health industry threatens privacy rights

In a world with private control of health care, this is especially the case with the digitalisation of medical records by private health care companies and capitalists, who seek to limit their liabilities.

A powerful example of this is the recent case of Adventist Health System. IT worker Patricia Moleski was ordered by the company to delete the electronic records of injured workers to negate workers compensation due to them. She was also ordered to delete records of deaths and other malpractices that had become corrupted due to a computer glitch. The failure to have backup records in an electronic medical system and the lack of any serious regulation potentially allow the massive manipulation of information, threatening basic human rights for workers and the public.[7]

The development of communications technology and the digitalisation of our society have generally left organised labour behind, despite the work that has been done. Most unions in the world do not do media training and do not educate their members in the use of technology and the dangers of it to their unions and the public. Issues of net neutrality and calls for a strong independent media that would support workers' causes are usually not addressed.

Tech workers organising on a global level grows

The potential for organising technology workers globally is growing. IBM workers, who are pro-union, have organised and some important struggles have developed over freedom of information.[8]

Ken Hamidi, an employee of Intel who installed systems, was injured on the job while driving. He continued working until he could not do the work and complained about growing health problems. Intel refused to take care of his injury and as a result Hamidi formed an organisation called FACE Intel (Former and Current Employees of Intel). He then was provided with the email addresses of over 30,000 workers by a supporter, and sent out messages to Intel workers throughout the world. For this action, Intel went to court and got an injunction that charged that Hamidi had entered the "chattel" of Intel by sending the messages. With support from the US trade union federation AFL-CIO and the Electronic Frontiers Foundation, as well as LaborNet, Hamidi was successful in defeating this effort to repress his free speech. The effort to prevent workers and unions from sending email to their fellow workers and getting information out through email was thwarted.[9]

The fight to defend the workers who make technology is critical. The brutal conditions faced by Foxconn workers in China, leading to many suicides, show the real story behind iPhones and the other new communications tools. Workers and human rights supporters have mobilised nationally and internationally to demand justice for these workers.[10]

Foxconn even sought to force the workers to sign documents pledging that they would not commit suicide, working through the government trade union federation ACFTU in 2006. But this meant very little when it came to conditions on the factory floor for workers, as their slave-like conditions continued under the new "union agreement".[11]

This is not to say the conditions of workers even at technology companies like Google are proper. At Google workers are separated by coloured badges and lower-level workers are discriminated against in the company on the grounds of the colour of the badge they wear. A former Google videographer declared:

> Speaking for myself, what worries me is that there is apparently a class of workers (yellows) who are denied privileges that are given to other workers of an equivalently non-skilled or impermanent nature (reds)... The only differences between these two classes of workers are the exact nature of their work (data entry versus, for example, janitors), and their overall racial mix. Neither of these reasons is a legitimate reason to withhold a privilege like free transportation from one group while granting it to the other, in my opinion. You, of course, may not agree.[12]

Labour using social media to organise: A double-edged sword

There is no question that social media have become vital tools in protecting democratic and labour rights. These tools have helped link up trade unionists and human rights organisers throughout the world. At the same time, however, workers are now being fired by their boss for putting material about their job on their Facebook page in their own time.

7 www.youtube.com/watch?v=F91hN9nR1KA

8 www.endicottalliance.org

9 www.faceintel.com/hamidismessage.htm

10 www.youtube.com/watch?v=V3YFGixp9Jw

11 www.boingboing.net/2011/05/05/foxconn-workers-forc.html and www.workerscapital.org/connected/news/in-focus-students-and-labour-activists-protest-foxconns-working-conditions/#In%20Focus

12 Andrew Norman Wilson recorded the segregation of Google workers in this video: vimeo.com/15852288

In a recent US Federal Labor Relations Board case, the board ruled that the actions of five workers who had been fired for using Facebook to publicise bad working conditions were not cause for firing.[13]

This effort by employers and corporations to silence their workers who use Facebook and the internet is growing. In a recent case in the UK, Uncut reported that UK Facebook had illegally removed material and sought to change workers' pages.[14]

Additionally, governments have sought to shut down labour and civil rights organisations' websites in many countries throughout the world, including the shutdown of the internet in Egypt during the recent uprising. This will likely take place again as mass movements seek to break the information blockade. The likelihood of this in most industrialised countries however is quite small, since the shutdown of the internet would result in the complete shutdown of the entire economy. In the US and Europe, the closure of the internet would virtually close the world economy from the airlines to all financial transactions. This would obviously be a doomsday scenario for those governments that have contemplated these tactics to silence critics using the internet.

This includes attacks on independent media, and, again in Korea, the suppression of independent media groups such as MediAct has brought international solidarity and protests.[15] APC took up an international campaign to defend this community media centre.[16]

The worldwide growth of independent labour media platforms has led to significant and powerful examples of using streaming media to defend workers struggles. Sendika.org, a project of LaborNet Turkey, supported the hunger strike by fired Tekna Tobacco workers in Istanbul by live streaming their strike and interviewing the workers about why they were taking the action.[17] The live video streaming reached an international audience and solidarity was expressed through SMS text messaging.

This was a concrete international expression of solidarity for their hunger strike and showed how workers can link up directly. Videos about these struggles were also streamed worldwide, including one called *The Wind Blows From The Workers*.[18]

Pizzas from Egypt in the Wisconsin struggle: Will the revolution be televised?

The most recent example of social media in the labour struggle was a major battle in Wisconsin to defend public workers against the attacks by Governor Scott Walker. While workers and students were occupying the capitol building, labour and community supporters were using tweets to organise food and other supplies. Tens of thousands of workers were mobilised to support a workers' picket line minute by minute also through the use of Twitter and other social media including live streaming on smartphones.[19] There was also an explosion of labour music videos, giving an important cultural expression to this struggle, including *Cheddar Revolution* and *Union Town*.[20]

When someone in Egypt helped buy a pizza for the workers occupying the capitol building, workers knew that their struggles were crossing all borders in a way that was impossible in the past.

The digitalisation of the world and the growing awareness of the world working class on how these communications and media tools can be used to build their unions and support their democratic workers' rights will only grow in the future. The development of a powerful world working class mass movement offers the potential to change the fundamental dynamics of who controls and runs the world, and these tools are critical to these developments. ■

13 www.sfgate.com/cgi-bin/article.cgi?file=/n/a/2011/05/18/national/w151508D64.DT

14 www.guardian.co.uk/technology/2011/apr/29/facebook-accused-removing-activists-pages and www.guardian.co.uk/uk/video/2011/feb/10/uk-uncut-protest-movement

15 labornetjp.blogspot.com/2010/02/movement-to-support-independent-media.html and www.facebook.com/group.php?gid=273091817582&ref=nf

16 www.apc.org/en/news/south-korean-govt-threatens-public-media-centre-me

17 Background about this struggle can be found at: www.sendika.org/english/yazi.php?yazi_no=29021

18 iscinet.org/index.php?option=com_content&view=article&catid=45%3Avideolar&id=168%3Atekel-direnii&Itemid=92

19 The use of the smartphone to stream labour struggles directly onto websites is already taking place through www.ustream.com and other servers.

20 www.youtube.com/watch?v=a5ZT71DxLuM&feature=player_embedded; www.youtube.com/watch?v=rCNaBe2Sl10; www.youtube.com/watch?v=9nGeWyV4Vec; www.youtube.com/watch?v=wTHo5CBeIRk; a report of this was made by J. Eric Cobb, executive director of the Building Trades of South Central Wisconsin, in a recent speech in San Francisco: www.youtube.com/watch?v=o4zzzFcjkJ

Sexuality and women's rights

Jac SM Kee and Jan Moolman
Association for Progressive Communications (APC)
www.apc.org

Rights and the internet: Sexuality and women's rights

The universality of human rights means that, sometimes, the specific needs of sections of society, due to the multiple forms of discrimination and inequality faced, can disappear from the understanding and translation of rights into reality. Women's rights movements have struggled for decades to gain the recognition that women's rights are human rights, culminating in the 1993 Vienna Declaration that states that "the human rights of women and of the girl-child are an inalienable, integral and indivisible part of universal human rights." With the increasing urgency to apply the human rights framework to understanding the impact of the internet on all facets of our lives, closer attention needs to be paid to how this might impact on women and people of diverse sexualities in different contexts, to ensure that the principle of universality is truly universal in the sense of being applicable to all people, equally. This report attempts to foreground some of the key insights from the work of the Association for Progressive Communications (APC) in the area of women's rights, violence against women and sexual rights in relation to the internet.

Role of the internet in realising rights

Public participation, right to assembly and citizenship

The findings from APC exploratory research into the area of sexuality and the internet (called EROTICS) as well as our work on information and communications technologies (ICTs) and violence against women in twelve countries clearly indicate that the internet is a critical space in the struggle for fundamental rights and freedoms. This is especially true in contexts where civil liberties are restricted or threatened. In contexts where people are discriminated against because of their gender or sexual identity, the restriction of and threats to their basic rights is a daily struggle and reality. For them, the internet is an especially vital space for democratic deliberation and political contestation where different actors, struggles and concerns are able to converge to inform or transform norms and public opinion and, in turn, policy that regulates their lives. It is a site where transitional or long-term alliances are forged in the form of informal social groupings, communities of shared interests or communication spaces for action. Here, the internet convenes an especially vital public sphere due to the multiple barriers to access found in more traditional forms of "publics", like the media or political representation, due to their marginalised position in society.

Feminist and sexual rights activists in the Democratic Republic of Congo turned to the internet as the only viable safe space to organise against a proposed homosexuality bill, in a climate of extreme intolerance and violence in the region. In Lebanon, the queer movement named the registration of www.gaylebanon.com as a historical marker of when the sexual rights movement began to formally organise in the country, and has since moved to greater visibility in physical spaces. Black lesbians in South Africa mobilised support for a pride march and organised mass solidarity for cases in court against "corrective rape" through online platforms for communication and information dissemination. These examples clearly show the democratising potential of the internet in enabling the public participation of people who face great risk to their personal safety in organising for change.

Self-representation, expression, writing history and countering discriminatory norms and culture

As noted by Frank La Rue in his report to the 17th session of the United Nations Human Rights Council in March 2011, the right to freedom of opinion and expression is critically facilitated by the internet, and is both a fundamental right on its own as well as an enabler of a broad range of human rights. In terms of the heavily regulated realm of sexual speech in all parts of the world and the barriers to accessing channels of communication like the mass media, the internet at present provides a relatively more open space for non-normative expressions, subaltern histories and less readily accessible information to proliferate and be obtainable. This can have an important impact of participating in the shaping of history and culture, and to dismantle discriminatory norms that contribute to inequality and discrimination.

In India, the EROTICS research uncovers the complex ways that young women experiment with the ideas of "sexy" through self-representation in dating, matrimonial and social networking sites. Through this, they are able to push the boundaries of cultural and social barriers that place intense scrutiny on the sexuality and mobility of women and girls. Mothers create popular blog sites that provide peer support and information and commentary on contemporary issues, challenging the traditional and patriarchal discourse in India that holds motherhood in a sacred and moral position. In Lebanon, an important strategy of the queer feminist movements is in writing, documenting and analysing personal and political accounts of their activism and sexuality, which acts to resist the colonisation of perspectives and knowledge by people outside of their community. Women's rights activists and women survivors of violence in Pakistan and the Philippines challenged the dominant construction of victimhood in situations of domestic violence by creating powerful digital stories. The digital stories enable them to take control of the narrative and to tell the complex realities of domestic violence through their own words and experiences, and present an important and often missing account of their strategies of survival as active subjects instead of passive victims of violence.

Autonomy, integrity of the body and right to security of the person

The ability to access relevant and meaningful information is critical to enable individuals to make informed decisions about their lives. It allows informed consent, the exercise of self-autonomy, and the realisation of a broad range of rights, such as the right to education, health and safety. Meaningful access to the internet and the engagement with online spaces and communities can greatly enable the capacity of individuals who face discrimination and inequality to exercise their right to self-determination and integrity of the body.

The EROTICS research showed that transgender people in South Africa are able to access online information on medical procedures of gender transitioning, including their risks, details of trustworthy medical practitioners and the experiences of others who have gone through the procedure. This helps them make an important decision about their own lives and bodies. In India, where arranged marriages by parents are commonly practised, young women are able to gain greater control over their choices of life partners through a range of online matrimonial sites. The internet in India has also become a significant, albeit controversial, site for sex education on a range of topics including HIV/AIDS, contraception, menopause and sexual pleasure. It meets an important information gap faced by young people in schools where sex education is regarded with alarm and in moralistic terms, with India banning sex education in twelve states and the United States (US) emphasising "abstinence only" sex education.

In the US, young people under the age of seventeen are unable to access unfiltered content in publicly funded libraries. Added to the lack of comprehensive sex education in schools, this has an impact of significantly limiting their right and evolving capacity to exercise agency and decision making about a critical component of their development.

In situations of violence against women, where many victims are socially isolated as a key tactic by abusers, the internet can be a critical space for getting information on how to safely exit the violent situation and to get support and help.

Challenges, barriers and limitations

Infrastructure and access

At the most basic level, there is a persistent gender divide in society. Despite rapidly increasing levels of internet penetration in all countries, particularly through the use of mobile phones, literacy levels in terms of language and technical skills, relevant content and costs are still significant determining factors in achieving access. Given the gendered dimension of technology, economic empowerment and control over resources, these act as barriers to equal access and engagement with internet technologies.

Shared or public internet access points, which can help address some of the cost issues, provide a limited solution to access for women and girls. As touched on earlier, the only law that mandates restriction to internet content in the US applies to publicly funded libraries, which affects approximately 77 million users, and can disproportionately impact on the poorer sections of the community. In India, cybercafés are dominated by men and a culture of masculinity, with increasing state regulation placed on their operation including taking photographs of users, collection of users' personal data, and restrictions on their physical location and arrangement, in part for reasons of controlling consumption of pornography. Submitting personal information without a corresponding data protection policy means that women and girls who use cybercafés can become subjects of harassment by predominantly male cybercafé managers, making them unviable and unsafe internet access points for women and girls.

Laws and policy

National policies on gender and ICTs are primarily viewed through the framework of economic development. This translates into initiatives and budgetary allocations that only aim to build the capacity of women to improve their income, and usually through a very limited lens. For example, in Malaysia, the recent national development plan sees ICTs as being beneficial for women because they enable them to work "flexi-hours" while still juggling their domestic responsibilities. However, such work, which is often considered low skilled and dispensable, does not provide an adequate social safety net with women being the first to lose their jobs during times of economic instability.

In many parts of the world, new legislation and policies are being developed to regulate the free flow of information on the internet. These are often accompanied by the mobilisation of anxieties around the dangers of sexual content and the risks of online interaction, the most familiar being the need to regulate or prohibit pornography, and increasingly, content or activities that are harmful to children. However, such measures often hide other agendas and interests. For example, a draft bill proposing a ban on sexual content on the internet and mobile phones submitted to the South African Department of Home Affairs in May 2010 claimed to have the best interests of women and children in mind. In fact, the bill was drafted by an organisation known to be anti-choice and homophobic, which raises serious questions about the actual intent of the proposed bill. Further, this runs counter to the constitutional guarantee of the right to freedom of expression and information in the country. In Brazil, the controversial cyber crime bill known as the "Azeredo Bill" that was fronted on the grounds of addressing paedophilia has its roots in the banking industry wanting to shift liability for internet fraud onto the shoulders of its customers instead of on banks.

Regulatory measures are also often introduced or passed at great speed with little public consultation, as shown by the EROTICS research. Legislation can include provisions with wide-ranging impact on expression, including censorship, mandated blocking and filtering of content, and invasions of privacy, such as increased surveillance and data retention. They can have a disproportionate and wide-ranging effect on the ability of marginalised sections of society to use the internet in the exercise of their rights. For example, in Indonesia, the anti-pornography bill was recently used to block a website that features information on the rights of lesbian, gay, bisexual and transsexual people.

Privacy, safety and violence against women

Privacy and anonymity are critical components of meaningful access to the internet, particularly by people who face great risk to their personal safety should they be "outed" through their internet activity. This can range from young women who are using the internet to challenge the boundaries of acceptable sexual expression, as we found in a case in India; to people of diverse sexualities who are exploring their identity and building communities, as in a case in Lebanon where homosexuality is criminalised; to women's rights defenders who are using the internet to provide support, document violations and organise for change, such as abortion rights activists in parts of Latin America.

There is a need to ensure greater protection of the right to privacy and security when it comes to the internet. Content regulation is almost always accompanied by surveillance measures, and in the face of missing privacy protections, this raises serious questions about the vitality of online spaces in advancing social justice.

It also bears reminding that even with the potential of the internet to realise freedoms, many women and girls still need to negotiate existing cultural and social barriers to fully and meaningfully engage with online spaces. The EROTICS research in India showed how young women have developed strategies to avoid surveillance of their activities by their family and boyfriends, and to manage the real risks and dangers that they can face online, including that of harassment, manipulation of photographs and violation of their right to privacy.

Technology-related violence also acts as a significant barrier to women's meaningful engagement with the internet. Cyber stalking, online sexual harassment, blackmail through the use of private and often sexualised information, photographs and videos, and the forwarding of content that depicts, promotes and normalises violence against women are becoming increasingly documented and faced by women and girls who use the internet. They create a hostile online environment and can cause women and girls to disengage from the internet due to fear for their safety. They also contribute to the creation of a communication culture that is discriminatory and tolerant of violence against women.

Conclusion

It is clear that when internet-related rights are examined through the lens of the diverse realities of women's lives and from the vantage of sexual rights, it provides a richer, nuanced and more comprehensive analysis of the different dimensions that need to be considered in the realisation of the internet's potential for fulfilment of human rights. Such an effort is necessary to ensure that our collective struggle to promote the transformative impact of the internet is one that is inclusive of diversity and affirming of equality. ■

Internet charters and principles

Internet charters and principles: Trends and insights

Dixie Hawtin
Global Partners and Associates
www.global-partners.co.uk

Introduction

A growing phenomenon in the internet governance arena is the emergence of charters and sets of principles which aim to guide policy making and to influence the behaviour of different stakeholders using the internet. The phenomenon is predominately driven by two separate but overlapping purposes: to articulate and promote a particular vision of the internet; and as an alternative to legislation and ex-ante regulation which is often considered ineffective, impractical and/or harmful.

This report provides an overview of the trend. It examines the different types of charters and sets of principles that are emerging and analyses the opportunities and challenges these present for freedom of expression and association on the internet.

Background

The internet developed in a "laissez-faire" environment – where regulation did exist it was mainly aimed at ensuring that the sector was open and competitive, for example, through unbundling and common carrier obligations. However, it has grown to be a foundational infrastructure for social, economic, political and cultural life. At the same time, a number of significant challenges have emerged, such as protecting privacy and combating the rise of cyber crime. The combination of these two factors has led to a growing consensus that the internet is too important to be left alone. The pressing debates now are about the content, form and processes by which governance is exercised.

Governing the internet is a challenging undertaking. It is a decentralised, global environment, so governance mechanisms must account for many varied legal jurisdictions and national contexts. It is an environment which is evolving rapidly – legislation cannot keep pace with technological advances, and risks undermining future innovation. And it is shaped by the actions of many different stakeholders including governments, the private sector and civil society.

These qualities mean that the internet is not well suited to traditional forms of governance such as national and international law. Some charters and declarations have emerged as an alternative, providing the basis for self-regulation or co-regulation and helping to guide the actions of different stakeholders in a more flexible, bottom-up manner. In this sense, charters and principles operate as a form of soft law: standards that are not legally binding but which carry normative and moral weight.

On the other hand, there is an increasing array of attacks on the open nature of the internet from governments (both authoritarian and democratic) who seek to control the environment and from businesses who seek to monetise it. Concerned that the capacity of the internet to support freedom of expression and association is being eroded, civil society groups are developing charters and sets of principles to push back against these threats by articulating and campaigning for a progressive approach towards the internet.

A summary of internet charters and principles

An enormous variety of charters and principles have been developed, each involving different models, stakeholders and issues. It is possible to divide these into a number of broad groups, although the examples outlined below are not exhaustive:

- **Civil society charters and declarations** John Perry Barlow's 1996 Declaration of Cyberspace Independence is one of the earliest and most famous examples. Barlow sought to articulate his vision of the internet as a space that is fundamentally different to the offline world, in which governments have no jurisdiction. Since then civil society has tended to focus on charters which apply human rights standards to the internet, and which define policy principles that are seen as essential to fulfilling human rights in the digital environment. Some take a holistic approach, such as the Association for Progressive Communications' Internet Rights Charter (2006) and the Internet Rights and Principles Coalition's (IRP) Charter of Human Rights and Principles for the Internet (2010). Others are aimed at distinct issues within the broader field, for instance, the Electronic Frontier Foundation's Bill of Privacy Rights for Social Networks (2010), the Charter for Innovation, Creativity and Access to Knowledge (2009), and the Madrid Privacy Declaration (2009).

- **Initiatives targeted at the private sector** The private sector has a central role in the internet environment through providing hardware, software, applications and services. However, businesses are not bound by the same confines as governments (including international law and electorates), and governments are limited in their abilities to regulate businesses due to the reasons outlined above. A growing number of principles seek to influence private sector activities. The primary example is the Global Network Initiative, a multi-stakeholder group of businesses, civil society and academia which has negotiated principles that member businesses have committed themselves to follow to protect and promote freedom of expression and privacy. Some initiatives are developed predominantly by the private sector (such as the Aspen Institute International Digital Economy Accords which are currently being negotiated); others are a result of co-regulatory efforts with governments and intergovernmental organisations. The Council of Europe, for instance, has developed guidelines in partnership with the online search and social networking sectors. This is part of a much wider trend of initiatives seeking to hold companies to account to human rights standards in response to the challenges of a globalised world where the power of the largest companies can eclipse that of national governments. Examples of the wider trend include the United Nations Global Compact, and the Special Rapporteur on human rights and transnational corporations' Protect, Respect and Remedy Framework.

- **Intergovernmental organisation principles** There are many examples of principles and declarations issued by intergovernmental organisations, but in the past year a particularly noticeable trend has been the emergence of overarching sets of principles. The Organisation for Economic Co-operation and Development (OECD) released a Communiqué on Principles for Internet Policy Making in June 2011. The principles seek to provide a reference point for all stakeholders involved in internet policy formation. The Council of Europe has created a set of Internet Governance Principles which are due to be passed in September 2011. The document contains ten principles (including human rights, multi-stakeholder governance, network neutrality and cultural and linguistic diversity) which member states should uphold when developing national and international internet policies.

- **National level principles** At the national level too, some governments have turned to policy principles as an internet governance tool. Brazil has taken the lead in this area through its multistakeholder Internet Steering Committee, which has developed the Principles for the Governance and Use of the Internet – a set of ten principles including freedom of expression, privacy and respect for human rights. Another example is Norway's Guidelines for Internet Neutrality (2009) which were developed by the Norwegian Post and Telecommunications Authority in collaboration with other actors such as internet service providers (ISPs) and consumer protection agencies.

Advocacy, campaigning, dialogue and networking

Civil society uses charters and principles to raise awareness about the importance of protecting freedom of expression and association online through policy and practice. The process of drafting these texts provides a valuable platform for dialogue and networking. For example, the IRP's Charter of Human Rights and Principles for the Internet has been authored collaboratively by a wide range of individuals and organisations from different fields of expertise and regions of the world. The Charter acts as an important space, fostering dialogue about how human rights apply to the internet and forging new connections between people.

Building consensus around demands and articulating these in inspirational charters provide civil society with common positions and tools with which to push for change. This is demonstrated by the number of widely supported civil society statements which refer to existing charters issued over the past year. The Civil Society Statement to the e-G8 and G8, which was signed by 36 different civil society groups from across the world, emphasises both the IRP's 10 Internet Rights and Principles (derived from its Charter of Human Rights and Principles for the Internet) and the Declaration of the Assembly on the Right to Communication. The Internet Rights are Human Rights statement submitted to the Human Rights Council was signed by more than 40 individuals and organisations and reiterates APC's Internet Rights Charter and the IRP's 10 Internet Rights and Principles.

As charters and principles are used and reiterated, so their standing as shared norms increases.

When charters and statements are open to endorsement by different organisations and individuals from around the world, this helps to give them legitimacy and demonstrate to policy makers that there is a wide community of people who are demanding change.

While the continuance of practices which are detrimental to internet freedom indicates that these initiatives have not, so far, been entirely successful, there are signs of improvements. Groups like APC and the IRP have successfully pushed human rights up the agenda in the Internet Governance Forum. Other groups are hoping to emulate these efforts to increase awareness about human rights in other forums. The At-Large Advisory Committee, for instance, is in the beginning stages of creating a charter of rights for use within the Internet Corporation for Assigned Names and Numbers (ICANN).

An alternative to hard law

An increasing number of governments around the world are introducing new laws and regulations designed specifically to govern internet communications. These can have adverse implications for freedom of expression and association. One illustration of this is the increasing trend of governments placing formal requirements on intermediary service providers to monitor the activities of their users. This effectively stifles innovation among service providers and reduces the range of platforms that people can use to express themselves and associate online. On a global level, there are increasing calls for a global treaty to govern the internet. Many human rights advocates are concerned that, given the present push back against human rights standards by powerful countries, the outcome of such a treaty may erode rather than advance freedom of expression and other rights. Policy principles offer a more flexible alternative, enabling coordinated policy making without running the risk of enshrining detrimental standards in international law, or stifling innovation. Freedom of expression and association are already enshrined in internationally legally binding conventions such as the International Covenant on Civil and Political Rights. Many argue therefore that we do not need new legal standards, but to find ways of enforcing those which already exist in the context of digital communications.

Furthermore, processes for defining policy principles tend to be more open than those establishing international conventions or national law, allowing civil society greater opportunity to influence and shape the approaches adopted. Over time, charters may help to forge international agreement around the normative dimensions of internet policy. The influence and input from civil society can be inferred from the fact that most sets of principles invoke similar language to that of civil society declarations – particularly with respect to freedom of expression.

Nonetheless, principles will not automatically promote human rights; for example, the OECD Communiqué, while widely praised for following a multi-stakeholder process and recognising principles including freedom of expression and access to infrastructure, also includes language that would push intermediaries to police and enforce laws on their networks. Because of this it is an ongoing challenge to ensure that the principles approach furthers rather than reduces respect for human rights.

Charter overload?

A growing concern is that there are now too many different charters and principles. This could fragment civil society efforts: when different groups congregate around different sets of principles they have less power than if all civil society groups were to promote the same set. However, those charters and principles which are high quality and perceived to be legitimate are likely to stand the test of time, being adopted by a critical mass of stakeholders. Those with less support will be neglected. Furthermore, different kinds of charters may be useful in different contexts. For example, the Brazilian principles are useful for advocacy in Brazil as they were formulated by local stakeholders for a national audience. However, charters with a more specific international orientation may be more useful in international advocacy work.

This viewpoint, however, neglects the fact that charters with support from economically and politically powerful groups are more likely to prevail. Civil society declarations usually do not have the same power as those developed by large companies, powerful governments or intergovernmental agencies. Because of this there is no guarantee that these will provide adequate protections for freedom of expression and other public interest dimensions of the internet. This is exacerbated by a lack of meaningful multi-stakeholder participation in the formulation of many charters and declarations.

The proliferation of charters and principles can also contain conflicting standards. This enables governments and companies to pick and choose those standards which are most in line with their own interests. Similarly, soft law and voluntary standards can lack effective enforcement and accountability mechanisms, allowing stakeholders leeway in how they interpret and implement the standards. Charters can be manipulated to support brand and image without actually resulting in a change in policy or practice.

Conclusion

The proliferation of charters and sets of principles in recent years has been, to date, a positive phenomenon, raising awareness about the importance of protecting and promoting freedom of expression and association; building consensus about what international human rights standards mean in the internet environment; and allowing diverse actors to feed into internet governance processes. As new charters and declarations continue to emerge, the challenge for human rights advocates is to push for policy coherence between different initiatives and to ensure that rigorous protection of human rights is upheld in them all. A further challenge is to ensure that governments and companies act in accordance with the charters and policy declarations that they sign up to, scrutinising their policies and behaviour to guarantee that they are in line with their commitments.

While charters and declarations are important tools in internet governance, recent years have seen growing calls for formal and binding international treaties on the world stage. Any standards that are codified in the future are likely to follow the course of emerging agreement around existing charters and declarations. Because of this it is critical that civil society engage with all ongoing processes to promote the highest protection for human rights in the emerging consensus on internet governance norms and principles. ■

Mapping rights

Mapping internet rights and freedom of expression

David Souter
ict Development Associates
david.souter@runbox.com

Introduction

The intersection between the internet and human rights, including freedoms of expression and association, is increasingly important as the internet becomes more universal, and increasingly complex as the internet affects more aspects of society, economy, politics and culture. This report suggests two ways to map this intersection, and raises a number of questions that need to be considered by those concerned with the internet, with rights, and with wider public policy.

The first of these mapping frameworks is based on the location of rights within current debates about internet public policy. The second is based on the relationship between the internet and the framework of rights set out in the Universal Declaration and the International Bill of Human Rights.

Internet public policy, rights and freedom of expression and association

A number of attempts have been made to map debates around internet governance (decision making that concerns the internet itself) and internet public policy (decision making that concerns the interface between the internet and other public policy domains). Many of these, like that of the Working Group on Internet Governance in 2004, locate issues along a spectrum from

- Highly internet-centric issues such as critical internet resources, through
- Issues which are internet-specific but have public policy implications such as spam and cyber crime, and
- Issues of wider public policy which are strongly impacted by the internet, such as intellectual property, to
- Broad public policy issues such as development and democratic participation.

While this is useful, the increasing complexity and reach of the internet into public policy make it insufficient for in-depth analysis. Research for the Association for Progressive Communications (APC) and other civil society organisations, presented in Italy in 2010, suggests that more complex mapping is required to place rights issues such as freedom of expression within the broad picture of debates around internet public policy. This more complex mapping focuses on two dimensions, concerned respectively with issues and with institutions and stakeholders.[1]

Mapping internet issues enables us to identify a number of core themes within current internet debates. Some of these are concerned with technical issues such as internet standards and coordination/administration; some with broad issues of public policy such as economic interchange, development and environmental impact; some more specifically with issues of rights, culture and governance. They can be illustrated conceptually as in Figure 1, each section of which can be broken down into more specific issues if required. The section that is concerned explicitly with rights is located at the bottom of the diagram.

The value of mapping issues in this way is twofold. Firstly, it helps to move beyond a broad discussion of the overall interface between the internet and rights towards a more nuanced discussion of the relationship between the internet and specific rights, such as freedom of expression and association. A lot of current debate is based around the idea that the internet necessarily enhances human rights, or that particular decisions regarding the internet necessarily threaten rights. Looking at individual rights issues and debates more specifically enables us to build a more sophisticated understanding of what is happening and why.

Secondly, it helps to identify links between rights issues and aspects of other public policy domains which have significant rights implications, but which appear in different areas of the map. Examples of these include affordability aspects of "access" and diversity aspects of "culture".

The rights issues identified in Figure 1 are wide ranging, including freedom of expression and consumer rights, privacy and defamation, intellectual property and child protection. This is not a comprehensive list, and individual rights agencies will have different priorities. They can also drill down in

1 A full report on this research can be found at: www.apc.org/en/pubs/books/mapping-internet-public-policy

FIGURE 1.

Mapping internet public policy issues

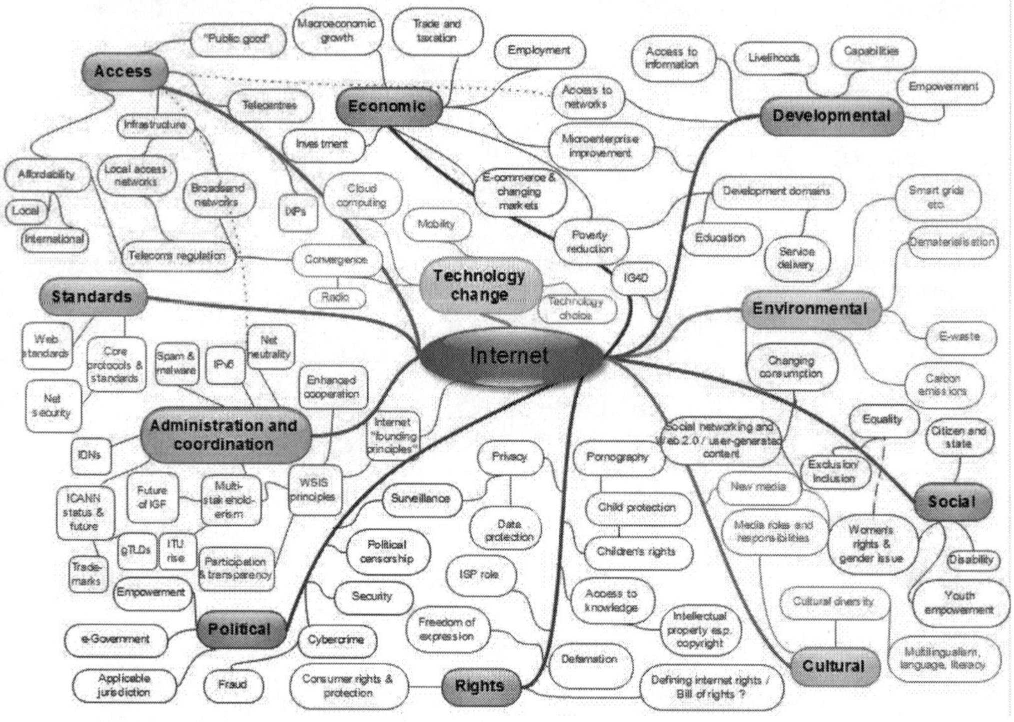

each of these to a deeper level of granularity, and to considering the implications in different national contexts in which rights are more or less guaranteed in law and practice and more or less established as public norms.

The second dimension of this mapping exercise is concerned with institutions and stakeholders. To understand how decisions concerning the internet and rights are taken, and where the pressure points at which rights agencies can exert influence lie, it is necessary to map the decision-making environment that overlays these issues of internet public policy. In practice, that environment includes diverse institutions from both mainstream public policy and internet governance contexts. Decisions or outcomes concerning the extent of freedom of expression, for example, emerge from the interaction between international rights frameworks, national governments, private businesses such as internet service providers which can open or close access to information or expression, citizens who use the internet as a means of expression (and often to bypass legal constraints), and civil society organisations, some of which seek to broaden freedom of expression and some to place boundaries around it.

This is a complex multi-stakeholder environment, but it is possible to overlay a map of the authority of different institutions on the kind of issues mapped in Figure 1 in order to gain clarity about which institutions exert decision-making power, whether globally or in national contexts. Figure 2, for illustrative purposes, suggests the principal areas in which the Internet Corporation for Assigned Names and Numbers (ICANN) influences internet public policy.[2]

The final aspect of this mapping exercise to consider here is the relationship between internet rights and rights in general. Two issues are important.

The first concerns the relationship between internet rights, human rights (as set out in the Universal Declaration) and other rights which individuals may hold (including, for example, consumer rights and employment rights, which result from legislation that is enacted at national level). There is often confusion between these, while there are also significant areas of overlap and interpretation, which have been changing over time. Article

2 Thanks to Dr. Konstantinos Komaitis for input on this diagram.

FIGURE 2.

Mapping internet public policy – the example of ICANN

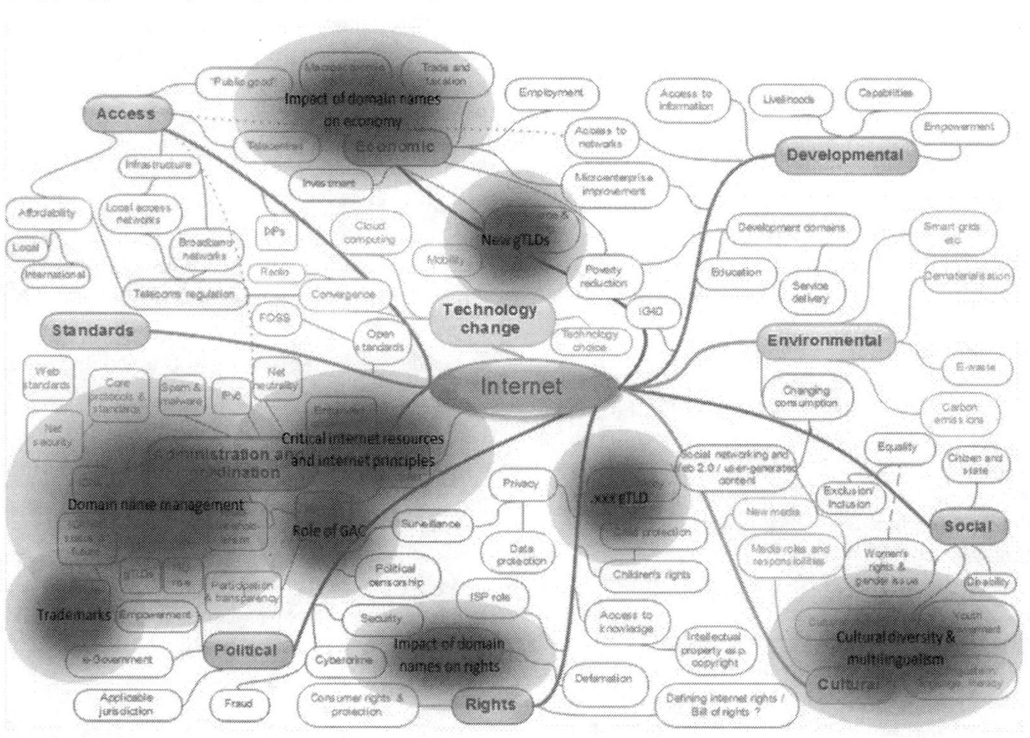

19 of the Universal Declaration, for example, grants everyone the right "to seek, receive and impart information and ideas through any media and regardless of frontiers." Does the reference to "any media" imply a right of access to media such as the internet, or merely a right to make use of such media as are available to the individual at the time and place in which s/he lives? Opinion on this is divided and has been changing over time as the internet has grown in reach and in importance.

The second concerns the relationship between internet rights and mainstream human rights advocates and networks. As in other interfaces between information and communications technology (ICT) specialists and those in other public policy fields, there can be a substantial difference of perspectives here:

- Mainstream human rights advocates tend to build their analysis of rights issues, threats and opportunities on the international Covenants, on interpretations by UN and other international agencies, and on international and national legal instruments to enable individuals to exercise their rights.
- Internet rights advocates, by contrast, often build their analysis of rights on the founding principles and ways of working of the internet, which enable people to extend the exercise of rights by bypassing constraints rather than through legal instruments.

These are significantly different paradigms, and they raise important questions about whether there is at present a consistent understanding of the relationship between internet rights and mainstream human rights amongst those who are concerned with the legal framework for rights and means for their expression. This is especially significant where the second mapping framework discussed in this article is concerned (see below).

It is also important to recognise that these debates are taking place within a multi-stakeholder context. Rights debates are not the preserve of rights activists, but are part of a broader discourse that involves governments, intergovernmental organisations, international non-governmental institutions, businesses, civil society organisations with varying perspectives, and individual citizens whose rights are under discussion and who have highly varied views about them. The significance which multi-stakeholder participation has achieved in internet governance adds to the complexity of this multi-stakeholder context, as does the exceptional prominence in the internet world of non-governmental international entities such as ICANN and the Internet Engineering Task Force (IETF).

Human rights, internet rights and freedom of expression

The second mapping exercise which is proposed here also concerns the relationship between internet rights, human rights and rights in general. Particular attention has been paid in discussion about the interface between the internet and rights to ways in which the internet has enhanced opportunities for people to exercise freedom of expression, obtain access to information (freedom of information) and organise collectively (freedom of association). How do these relate to the broader rights regime?

The international human rights framework as we know it was established by the Universal Declaration of Human Rights (UDHR) in 1948 and subsequently entered into international and national law in the 1960s/1970s through the International Covenants on Civil and Political Rights and on Economic, Social and Cultural Rights. It also includes other international instruments such as the UN Convention on the Rights of the Child.

Discussions of the UDHR often present it as a list of individual rights which have cumulative force, the most prominent of which tend to be those concerned with freedom of conscience (Article 18), freedom of expression (Article 19) and freedom of association (Article 20). Some of that discussion appears to give those articles primacy over other rights within the Declaration. In practice, however, the Declaration recognises that the exercise of rights can be conflictual – that there are occasions on which the exercise of two different rights, or of the same right by different people, can be incompatible – and therefore involves the need for balance. Article 29 addresses this in two ways, by asserting that the rights set out in the Declaration are "subject only to such limitations as are determined by law solely for the purpose of securing due recognition and respect for the rights and freedoms of others and of meeting the just requirements of morality, public order and the general welfare in a democratic society."

Article 29 is obviously open to interpretation, and the relationship between it and Article 19's guarantee of freedom of expression is central to many contests over censorship and other constraints on freedom of expression/publication. These arise generally, in relation to different interpretations of the imprecise terms "morality, public order and general welfare in a democratic society", but also specifically, in relation to constraints on the scope of freedom of expression or publication which are implied in other articles of the Declaration. These arise in:

- Article 3, which asserts the right to life, liberty and security (the root of constraints against incitement to violence against the person, hate speech, etc.)
- Article 7, which guarantees protection against incitement to discrimination
- Article 11, which guarantees legal protection against "arbitrary interference with ... privacy [and] correspondence" and against "attacks upon ... honour and reputation"
- Article 27, which asserts a right to intellectual property ("protection of the moral and material interests resulting from any scientific, literary or artistic production") and, arguably
- Article 10, which guarantees the presumption of innocence (often interpreted as imposing constraints on the reporting of criminal arrests and trials).

These articles represent limits to the scope of freedom of expression as declared in Article 19. In practice, all societies have imposed constraints on freedom of expression, for a variety of reasons ranging from political censorship and protection of social or religious norms to protection against incitement to racial hatred and protection of individual rights of privacy. Some restrictions on publication have high levels of public support, particularly where it is perceived to conflict with privacy (e.g. health records, credit card information and other personal details) or with children's rights. While no articles so clearly affect freedom of conscience or association, many governments have interpreted "morality, public order and general welfare" as enabling them to restrict the latter.

Debates concerning what, if any, boundaries should be placed around freedom of expression and association were current long before the Universal Declaration, let alone the internet, and this is not the place to rehearse them further. What is significant here, however, is that the internet has greatly extended the ability and means to exercise freedom of expression and association, changed the ways in which they are being exercised, and thereby altered the balance which prevailed in the pre-internet era between Articles 19, 20 and other rights. This is why the meaning of freedom of expression is now central to discussion of international and national rights regimes.

There are four main ways in which the internet has impacted here which are important from a public policy perspective. Internet specialists need to understand the dynamics of these from that perspective in order to address the implications of internet rights effectively.

Firstly, the internet – particularly the web and social networking – has changed the nature of publication. Rather than being largely restricted to a relatively small number of official agencies and businesses, the opportunity to publish has become effectively universal, making constraints on publication (in its widest sense) more difficult or impossible for governments to enforce. This is particularly important in the expression of opinion, where it is analogous to the early impact of the printing press 600 years ago.

Secondly, it has made it much easier for those who wish to publish or access material which is illegal in a specific jurisdiction to bypass legal constraints. The most prominent area of debate here has concerned pornography, particularly child pornography, but there are wider public policy issues around questions such as restrictions on religious content in some jurisdictions, the publication of incitement to racial hatred, the marketing of pharmaceuticals and weaponry, the sharing of identifying information and the publication of websites and online content which are designed to extort money.

Thirdly, it has made it much easier to publish material anonymously. On the one hand, this has encouraged transparency, freedom of expression and association, especially where these have been constrained. On the other hand, it has disrupted the balance between freedom of expression and the rights concerning privacy and defamation which are included in Article 11 of the UDHR.

Fourthly, it has made the protection of intellectual property rights much more difficult, disrupting the constraint of freedom of expression where these are concerned which was set out in Article 27 of the Universal Declaration, as well as the elaborations of that balance in international intellectual property law.

The internet's ability to change the relationship between different types of rights, generally in favour of freedom of expression and association, is substantial and significant. For most within the internet community, this has been a matter for celebration. Some activists and internet users have also seen it as an opportunity to ignore or overturn legal constraints which they oppose, particularly where intellectual property is concerned. Other rights organisations argue that a legal framework is the only way in which the exercise of rights can be effectively enforced. Governments and others have sought to find ways of adjusting legal frameworks to accommodate new internet realities, with varied success from their and from citizens' points of view.

The question of whether the internet changes the rights and freedoms set out in the Universal Declaration is not new but is important. The argument here is that it changes the ability to exercise those rights, and that this has changed the meaning of rights to stakeholders in ways that were not envisaged when the Declaration was agreed. That makes the relationship between the internet and the international rights regime a significant public policy issue, which governance institutions and other stakeholders must address. Those who are concerned about rights and internet rights need to understand and analyse what is happening, whether they see it as an opportunity to extend the exercise of rights, sustain the existing rights regime, or move towards a new understanding of rights and the exercise of rights for a post-internet era. Mapping the impact of the internet on rights and on their exercise is an important step in that direction. ■

Country reports

Introduction

Alan Finlay

The authors of these country reports were encouraged to select a story or event to write about that illustrates the role of the internet in defending human rights. The result is a rich collection of reports that approach the topic of the internet, human rights and social resistance from different angles – whether discussing the rights of prisoners to access the internet in Argentina, candlelight vigils against "mad cow" beef imports in South Korea, the UK Uncut demonstrations in London, or online poetry as protest in China.

The contexts in which these stories occur are diverse, with different implications for social mobilisation using the internet. In many, the potential of the internet to galvanise progressive social protest has proved critical. In the United Kingdom (Open Rights Group) events demonstrated how social media have become the "standard mobilisation toolkit" for civil protest. In Bosnia and Herzegovina (owpsee foundation), "Facebook, with all the criticism of its privacy and security, is today the space where grassroots initiatives and informal groups in Bosnia Herzegovina start their activities, connect with each other and *do* things."

These reports also show how the internet has an extraordinary power of making visible that which many would prefer to keep secret. Indonesia (EngageMedia Collective Inc.) demonstrates how difficult and delicate documenting the invisible can be – and the country report is worth reading for practical (and ethical) issues to take into consideration. "Making visible" is not only a way of documenting and speaking out, and of mobilising widespread support for a cause; it is also used to hold authorities accountable for their actions. Activists in Jordan (Alarab Alyawm) "always take into consideration the worst that the police could do. Because of this they assign some participants the task of documenting everything in the events, especially if police attack demonstrators."

While countries like Iran (Arseh Sevom School) look to create a "halaal" internet – "one that is pure from immoral websites" – Morocco (DiploFoundation) shows how the internet can disrupt entrenched ideas of citizenship:

> [T] he common citizen (...) took refuge in the social and citizen media channels to lead a radical change of the idea of the state-citizen relationship. This relationship was based on a top-down approach to decision making when it came to state policies – while the internet helped to make these decisions evolve around the citizens' needs.

In Tunisia (Arab World Internet Institute), the internet catalysed an essentially "leaderless" revolution, and in Costa Rica (Sulá Batsú), "the essential part [of the internet] is the spirit and the power of organising without organisations."

Reports show that it is not always civil society organisations with formal mandates that galvanise social resistance. Often protests are catalysed by self-organising individuals who meet online and instigate protests and campaigns for change, and who otherwise would have very little to do with civil society causes. Resistance to importing "mad cow" beef into South Korea (Korean Progressive Network Jinbonet) is sparked by spontaneous interactions amongst young people: "In the beginning, the most energetic participants were young people who had spent the entire day at school and used the internet and SMS to organise their friends and debate various issues."

The role of satire in social protest is seen in a number of reports collected here. In China (Danwei) this is felt in poems written in response to a hit-and-run incident involving the son of a deputy director at a public security bureau (known as the "My dad is Li Gang" online protests), made all the more striking in that they draw on classical Chinese poetry and philosophy:

The philosopher Mencius (*Mengzi* in Chinese, 372-289 BC) said:

> 君子穷则独善其身
> 达则兼善天下
> If a gentleman is poor, he does good works in solitude; if he is rich, his work is for the good of the whole world.

The Li Gang version:

> 穷则独善其身
> 富则开车撞人
> If a gentleman is poor, he does good works in solitude; if he is rich, he drives his car into people.

But what is equally striking is that many authors – often long-time activists for internet rights – show a growing ambivalence to the idea of the internet as simply a positive social phenomenon. The role of the internet activist, the reports suggest, is an increasingly complex one; and few unequivocal statements can be made about its social agency. Countries such as Bulgaria (BlueLink Foundation) show that as much as the internet can be a force for progressive political change, it offers a vehicle for reactionary politics too – a different kind of "social resistance". In that country reactionary groups are incisive in using the internet to push their agenda:

> [E]xtremist online groups are meeting more frequently offline than online social activists. While social researchers point out the growing number of Facebook groups and causes in support of neo-fascism, reminiscent of Hitler's treatment of minorities, and protest against social policies supporting the long-term unemployment of Roma, offline incidents show the neo-Nazis do act in accordance with their claims. In the summer of 2010 two cases of violence emphasised the fact that the problem of intolerance is not a dormant or discursive one any more.

The revolutions in North Africa have shown how social media can be an ally in the organisation and mobilisation of people, but also how authoritarian regimes use the internet to counter progressive social and political change. Similarly, in Thailand the internet has been used effectively to support the conservative politics of the monarchy, as Arthit Suriyawongkul (Thai Netizen Network) observes: "What can then be called a 'digital witch hunt' emerged, as users began hunting down those who were against the monarchy."

The tension between online activism and social mobilisation in public is felt throughout these reports – at times with a sense that it is difficult for authors embedded in internet practice and thinking to find words for "offline" protest and demonstration. Even though the idea that the revolutions in North Africa were "Twitter revolutions" or "Facebook revolutions" has been debunked by most, there is still a tendency to think of the internet not just as an alternate public sphere – a place of multiple counterpublics – but as something more literal: a vehicle for the creation of "cyber*countries*" populated by "netizens" that can, the South Korean report suggests, offer "cyber asylum".

While these are just ways of describing the phenomenon that the internet has become, some of the reports suggest a growing discomfort with the internet as a place of refuge, with its negative implications for active engagement in civil protest. Many reports mention the difficulty of translating support for a cause expressed through clicking on "Like" or "I'm attending" buttons on a Facebook page into public mobilisation. As Iran puts it: "The internet has also effectively turned the activist into a solitary, protesting computer user, fighting against multiple government computers."

This attention to the dangers of over-relying on the internet for social mobilisation is felt sharply in countries that either do not have access or adequate infrastructure (whether through censorship or underdevelopment). In Lebanon (Mireille Raad), for instance, activists felt excluded from the social protests taking place in the region:

> With the Arab Spring and revolutions being shared online, activists in Lebanon are feeling helpless not being able to broadcast their opinions and take on events that directly affect their own country. This showed the Lebanese that they are actually suffering from a subtle and worse form of censorship.

In Kazakhstan (Adil Nurmakov), even the most creative online interventions – a "remixed" and "redubbed" *Shrek* animation satirising a referendum – have little widespread impact because of the low levels of access in the country. In a different way, Japan shows that, in the wake of the recent tsunami, even highly developed countries face the danger of over-dependency on technology for civic mobilisation and communication.

The power of the internet to "make visible" also has the inverse effect of a kind of visibility that impacts negatively on other rights, particularly when it serves the state. In the Netherlands (Institute for Information Law), advocating for privacy rights is a key concern – it is a country that could be "sleepwalking into a surveillance society."[1] While the internet can "protect" against authoritarian regimes, it can also expose those who are already vulnerable. In Thailand:

> The personal data of victims, including their home addresses and phone numbers, were posted online. One person was even physically threatened, as the groups tracked down with reasonable accuracy – within a one-kilometre

1 Richard Thomas, the English Information Commissioner, quoted in Ford, R. (2004) Beware rise of Big Brother state, warns data watchdog, *The Times*, 16 August 2004.

radius – where she lived (probably using social media), and offered a cash bounty to anyone who would "surprise" her at home.

But it is precisely this ambivalence towards the internet that makes the focus on online social activism for human rights such an important area to explore – and these reports, from 55 countries across the globe, make an important contribution to the discussion. The stories captured here have implications for everyone engaged and concerned with the state of the world we live in. And, as you will see, there are many worrying trends, as much as there are moments of unexpected community, of spontaneous and shared struggle made possible by the internet.

Many of these reports also offer practical advice and solutions to harness the potential of the internet to galvanise progressive social resistance effectively – actions steps for civil society – and offer ways to avoid its pitfalls. But they are not just for ICT4D specialists or internet activists. They unpack in a concrete way the growing implications of the internet for the political sphere – and the widening possibilities for social activism and engagement that are opening up for the person in the street. ■

ARGENTINA

ACCESSING THE INTERNET AS A RIGHT IN PRISONS

Nodo TAU
Florencia Roveri
www.tau.org.ar

Introduction

In Argentina – as in many other countries across the world – the conditions of confinement in prisons do not guarantee life. People in jails are deprived of more rights than their freedom. Prisons do not ensure access to health, education, food, hygiene, dignified conditions in cells and decent treatment of prisoners. The main problems that affect the conditions in correctional facilities are overcrowding and institutionalised violence.

Meanwhile, public policies that address these issues are influenced by two factors. On the one hand, facing a sense of an increase in violent crime, middle and higher social income groups demand tougher penalties, with a reprehensible disregard for the conditions under which sentences are enforced. This claim is amplified by the media. On the other hand, the political power responds to this situation with a so-called "punitive demagogy",[1] deciding to construct more prisons and increasing police controls, detentions and imprisonment. These measures do not resolve the problem, falling more severely on impoverished classes and favouring the penal system as a tool for solving social conflicts.[2]

The precarious conditions of confinement and the absence of public policies based on civil rights are worsened because of the opacity and inaccessibility of the country's prisons. Any resource that enables voices to be heard on the plight of prisoners helps to illuminate the darkness of the prison system. In this context, access to the internet for prisoners, besides offering them a source of information, and a way to communicate with the outside world and to organise collectively, serves as a medium for free expression that is indispensible to their right to tell their own stories.

Prison policy

The Argentine Constitution specifies in Article 18:

> The prisons of the Nation shall be healthy and clean, and used for security and not for undue punishment of the prisoners confined therein. Any action taken under the pretext of a precautionary measure that leads to the degradation of prisoners beyond what the measure requires shall make the judge that authorises this action responsible for the decision.[3]

Argentina, as a federal republic, has a federal penitentiary service and several provincial services with their own regulations. Law 20.416 governs the performance of the federal service, defining as its main functions:

- Ensuring the safety of persons in custody, and that the prison regime contributes to preserving or improving their moral conditions, education and physical and mental health.
- Promoting the social rehabilitation of convicts.

The numbers appear to contradict these objectives. According to a 2008 report from the National System of Statistics on Enforcement of Sentences (SNEEP),[4] the prison population is 54,537 (increasing from 29,690 in 1997). This means 137.22 prisoners per 100,000 inhabitants. These figures place Argentina in sixteenth position in the world, based on official data from each country.[5] As for the status of the sentence, 47% are convicted and 52% are awaiting trial.[6]

SNEEP is meant to publish periodic reports to assess the implementation of prison policies, but it has not published reports since 2008, and when it does there are many inaccuracies. Its statistics do not count police station holding cells, for instance, which are also overcrowded, making it difficult to evaluate the number of prisoners in terms of prison

1 CELS (2011) *Derechos Humanos en Argentina. Informe 2011*, CELS and Ediciones Siglo XXI, Buenos Aires. www.cels.org.ar/common/documentos/CELS_FINAL_2011.pdf

2 CELS (2008) Capítulo III: La situación carcelaria: una deuda de nuestra democracia, in *Derechos Humanos en Argentina. Informe 2008*. www.cels.org.ar/common/documentos/carceles_ia2008.pdf

3 www.argentina.gov.ar/argentina/portal/documentos/constitucion_nacional.pdf

4 www.jus.gov.ar/media/108979/Informe%20SNEEP%20ARGENTINA%202008.pdf

5 International Centre for Prison Studies (2009) *World Prison Population List*, King's College, London. www.kcl.ac.uk/depsta/law/research/icps/news.php?id=203

6 www.jus.gov.ar/media/108979/Informe%20SNEEP%20ARGENTINA%202008.pdf

capacity, and to define measures to address the problem.

Other sources indicate that in the first half of 2010, 3,849 acts of violence were reported in the country's prisons, which gives an average of 10.5 cases per day.[7] Of the total, 929 were cases of prison staff violence against inmates, and 849 were fights between inmates. Another 348 cases were labelled as "self-harm" and 282 as "accidents", data that may be related to acts of violence that have been covered up. Another statistic from 2006[8] shows that only 3.44% of the cases are brought to trial and only 0.36% result in a sentence.

Most actors in the judicial system seem to have become accustomed to the conditions of the prisons and the institutional violence and do not report either.[9] Paradoxically, some groups of inmates consider these conditions necessary to learn to survive in violent prisons. These facts place the problem in the complex field of cultural attitudes.

Given the continuing violation of detainees' rights, in May 2005 the Supreme Court declared the United Nations (UN) Standard Minimum Rules for the Treatment of Prisoners[10] as the guideline for all detention institutions to follow. Furthermore, in June 2006, Argentina ratified the UN's Optional Protocol to the Convention against Torture and other Cruel, Inhuman or Degrading Treatment or Punishment through Law 25.932. The protocol establishes a mechanism of prevention through regular visits to facilities, but the issue is still pending, and the mechanism is not yet in place.[11]

Silenced facts behind the walls

Institutionalised violence is more difficult to attend to because of the opacity and inaccessibility of prisons. Although inmates have set ways that allow communication with the outside world, and have contact with state and social actors that work to improve their prison conditions and to institutionalise their demands, a shadow is cast over much of what goes on in prisons.

Among state actors, the Prison Ombudsman's Office[12] is in charge of protecting inmates and controlling penitentiaries. Amongst civil society, the work of the Centre for Legal and Social Studies (CELS), the Coordinator Against Police and Institutional Repression (CORREPI) and the Coordinator of Work in Prison (CTC) stand out. They work on the institutionalisation of inmate demands and they all refer to the difficulties in accessing prisons. They also participate in so-called "dialogue tables", which are meetings of "pavilion representatives",[13] prison authorities and external actors. These sorts of initiatives are valuable mechanisms but not always conducive to hearing complaints from prisoners.

Prisoners' rights to communication should not be affected except in those cases in which a sentence explicitly states that they may not communicate with the outside world. Law Enforcement 24.660, which regulates the implementation of sentences,[14] defines in its Article 158 that "inmates have the right to communicate regularly, orally or in writing, with their family, friends, lawyers, and representatives of government agencies and private institutions with legal status who are interested in their social reintegration" and in Article 164 it states that "they have the right to be informed of events of national and international life through social communication media." The law also refers to a document dealing with "Rules of Inmate Communication", which expands on the legal provisions above.[15]

From day-to-day descriptions of life in prison, detainees report that telephones are frequently inaccessible for long periods of time.[16] Mobile phones are forbidden, but many inmates manage to smuggle them in. However, if authorities allow prisoners to have phones, they would, for instance, be able to log them and track their use in crimes, and would avoid the difficulty of having to make sure that the phones are not smuggled into the prisons. Mobile phones have also been used for recording and reporting violence.[17]

Voices passing through walls...

> *We cannot break down the walls and gates but what we can do is allow the voices of those who are sentenced to silence and oblivion to pass through them.* – Rodolfo Walsh Agency

The headline shouts: "Model Rehabilitation Institute: 114 fatalities in less than 10 years". The article

7 www.comisionporlamemoria.org/comite/informes/informe_2010.pdf

8 Ministerio Público Fiscal (2006) *Informe Anual al Congreso de la Nación*. www.mpf.gov.ar

9 CELS (2011) Op. cit.

10 www.spf.gov.ar/pdf/ReglasMinimasparaelTratamientodeReclusos.pdf

11 www.cels.org.ar/common/documentos/mnpt_proyecto.pd

12 Procuraduría Penitenciaria de la Nación: www.ppn.gov.ar

13 The prisons are divided into so-called pavilions.

14 www.infoleg.gov.ar/infolegInternet/anexos/35000-39999/37872/texact.htm

15 www.spf.gov.ar/index.php?option=com_content&view=article&id=108&Itemid=35

16 Information obtained through email interviews with prisoners of Regional Unit 3 and the Coronda Penitentiary.

17 www.enfoque365.net/N19146-torturas-en-crcel-argentina-fueron-filmadas-y-difundidas-por-internet-y-telfonos-celulares.html

was published by "Ciudad Interna" (Inner City) – the blog of a group of inmates in a so-called model prison in Coronda – after the death of four detainees during a conflict. The article complains that the measures that authorities take in general after this kind of episode amount only to punishment and confinement. Because of this, most conflicts result in the death of inmates.

Coronda, the biggest prison in Santa Fe province, is called a "model" prison because it used to have a school, a sports field and housed the workshop of a garment and shoes manufacturer that offered the possibility of social reintegration after prisoners had served their sentence. Political prisoners were jailed there during the last military dictatorship (1976-1983) and – more recently – it was the scene of an uprising which ended with fourteen prisoners killed, in April 2005.

After the uprising, a group of inmates started meeting with the objective of publishing a magazine written entirely by them. They were assisted by two journalists who ran a workshop. The publication was called "Coronda: Ciudad Interna" and it was the first step towards a bridge that the group started to build, linking them to the outside world. Later they started a radio station for inmates,[18] and then began to negotiate for access to the internet.

There is no legislation in Argentina that prevents access to the internet in jails. In several prisons it is used in distance learning projects, generally in penitentiary libraries.[19] In Coronda internet access for distance learning was already in place through an agreement with the University of Litoral.[20] However, Ciudad Interna wanted to extend the time of this access. With the support of a group of lawyers they prepared a habeas corpus in which they argued that "digital exclusion means the deprivation of the human right to communicate," conceiving communication through the web "as an extension of human possibilities." They stated: "Nowadays the internet enables us to transcend the prison walls, to take our complaints to the outside, to train ourselves in a job, to keep in contact with the world in order to intervene in reality and thus to have the possibility, perhaps, to transform our present condition of exclusion and marginalisation."

The group finally obtained access to the internet. The technology and the connection they got was unstable – and only a few computers were available. They shared these with all of the prisoners, which made communication difficult and slow. In turn they complained that this was an "excuse used by penitentiaries to leave us cut off [from the outside world]."

Generally, access is restricted in terms of time. The prisoners who do get access send email and search for information; also, "some prisoners have met girls with whom they begin a relationship, others have found jobs they can go to when they get out." Others use instant messaging (IM) to "chat" – during a recent conflict an inmate used IM to contact a CTC staff member who called the prison authorities. Instantaneous communication by chat or mobile phones (when they are smuggled in) facilitates rapid intervention to avoid increasing tension.

Computer rooms are frequently the birthplace of training and communication projects. "Once we had the connection, we did not know anything about internet and there was no one to teach us. People from outside helped us to create email accounts and later the blog," Ciudad Interna said. The magazine and the blog are mainly dedicated to complaints about violations of human rights. When an article deserves more attention, they also use email to circulate it. "The group called this procedure 'la gatilladita' [little trigger] because we reach our contacts directly and they do not need to consult the blog."

In a recent post, the prisoners published a historical analysis of penitentiary service in Argentina.[21] They wrote:

> Navigating in this expansive virtual field, we learn about how what was used as a military structure became a prison. But because not everything is on the internet, we will provide reliable information – not disseminated by the mass media – with the intention that an ill-informed society gets to know about prison conditions in increasingly crowded jails. ... As it stands, bad men continue to control [prisoners]... torturing and killing... without anyone doing anything to stop it.

After publishing the article on the blog, they also sent it out by email. Nine websites republished the post – including some recognised independent media.

This example shows the potential of the internet as a medium to publish to the outside world, and as a source of information and means of contact and socialising. Today Ciudad Interna is a self-managed

18 www.ciudadinterna.blogspot.com

19 Román, A. (2008) *Pensar Internet como elemento de reinserción en los penales argentinos*. www.biblioteca.jus.gov.ar/roman_bteca_pen.pdf

20 www.unl.edu.ar/noticias/leer/7351/Acuerdo_entre_la_UNL_y_la_provincia_por_la_Educacion_en_Prisiones.html and www.uba.ar/extension/trabajos/uba.htm

21 ciudadinterna.blogspot.com/2011/04/pareciera-que-del-titulo-de-esta-nota.html

media site produced by detainees, with the help of former detainees, and even relatives and working professionals.

Similar experiences are found elsewhere: La Cantora[22] from Unit 4 in Bahía Blanca; the blog Caracoles en Red (Snails on the Web)[23] from the Federal Psychiatric Hospital in Buenos Aires; Rompiendo el Silencio (Breaking the Silence), [24] a blog by Unit 3 and the blog Mujeres tras las rejas (Women Behind Bars) by Unit 5, both in Rosario.[25] These publications form a network, so that if one is silenced, the others sound the alarm.

Conclusions

- The prison system in Argentina is not able to guarantee human rights due to structural and cultural limitations. In addition, it is also difficult to know what goes on inside prisons. Any means to shed light on prison conditions could help in making the public aware, and reporting on the situation. Self-managed projects and spaces promoted by civil society organisations contribute to this possibility.
- Although there is no legislation that prevents inmates from accessing the internet, it is not guaranteed for all detainees – only for those who organise and complain to the authorities.
- Internet access would allow inmates to maintain contact with their families, to keep informed about their communities, their country and the world, to build capacities for social reintegration, and to remain emotionally healthy.
- The web, specially the blogosphere, is very useful when it comes to awareness of what happens inside prisons, and for reporting on the violation of rights.

Action steps

- Contribute to the debate about the importance of guaranteeing widespread access to the internet in prisons.
- Promote the creation of internet access points, so that all prisoners have the possibility to send email or find information. Access can offer various forms of assistance and help, as well as training.
- Discuss the ban on mobile phones in prisons, and promote the use of wireless connectivity.
- Demand that data collection tools be developed so that quantitative and qualitative information on various issues in prisons can be collated to inform policy. This could also be used to collect stories on the use of the internet in prisons to analyse the potential of the internet to rehabilitate prisoners. ■

22 www.lacantora.org.ar/inicio.php
23 caracoles-en-red.blogspot.com
24 rompiendoelsilenciou3.blogspot.com
25 mujerestraslasrejas.blogspot.com

AUSTRALIA

BLOCKING CONTENT, BLOCKING RIGHTS

EngageMedia Collective Inc.
Andrew Garton
www.engagemedia.org

Introduction

The Australian government's response to WikiLeaks' publication of leaked United States (US) State Department diplomatic cables in November 2010 sought to criminalise both the organisation and its founder and editor-in-chief, Australian citizen Julian Assange.

In spite of significant public and media industry support for WikiLeaks, both Australia's Prime Minister Julia Gillard and Attorney-General Robert McClelland placed their support squarely behind the US[1] and its persecution of Assange, WikiLeaks and its staff.[2]

Parallels emerged with the Howard government's[3] dispassionate response to David Hicks and Mamdouh Habib,[4] two Australians held without charge and in violation of their basic democratic rights in the US military prison in Guantanamo Bay.

The call from Australia's political leadership to seek legal grounds for Assange's arrest and to criminalise the work of WikiLeaks, when no legal grounds existed for either,[5] also reignited debate about the Labor Party's single-minded efforts to introduce a controversial mandatory internet content filter.

The writer and commentator called Stilgherrian asks, "Why aren't our politicians considering us citizens and our rights?" It is these rights, the democratic rights of all Australians who are finding their voice and the will to question and act through the internet, that are at odds with the so-called clean feed internet filter. The clean feed drew so much public condemnation, and with a minority government comprised of independents and Greens with no stomach for an internet service provider (ISP)-level content filtering system, that it was shelved until at least 2013 – though the impetus for its creation is far from idle.[6]

Policy and political background

The ease by which Australia complies with international conventions, from cyber crime to intelligence gathering, draft or otherwise, describes an increasing gulf between Australian politicians and the citizens they are meant to represent. Through the 1990s Australia continued to display the tolerance, empathy and cultural diversity that grew from the 1970s with the abolition of the White Australia Policy (1973),[7] its intake of Vietnamese and Cambodian refugees (1976) and, a decade later, the creation of the Office of Multicultural Affairs and the Australian Council of Multicultural Affairs (1986), both of which were to create a National Agenda for a Multicultural Australia. Another decade on and the political climate in Australia was about to change.

In 1996, only four months after the Howard government took office, they came good with an election pledge and closed down the Office of Multicultural Affairs. Multiculturalism was to be "zeroed", instructed the new treasurer, Peter Costello. The remaining Department of Immigration and Citizenship would have the majority of its funds withdrawn.

The breakdown of an increasingly educated, knowledge-focused and pluralist society was on its way. With massive cuts to higher education and a gradual decimation of humanities, language and religious studies to follow, it would be another four years before the curtain would seek to be drawn on Australians' right to privacy and free speech online.

1 Nicholson, B. (2010) WikiLeaks acts 'illegal': Gillard government, *The Australian*, 10 December. www.theaustralian.com.au/in-depth/wikileaks/wikileaks-acts-illegal-gillard-government/story-fn775xjq-1225968584365

2 AAP (2011) Australia 'helps US target WikiLeaks staff', *The Australian*, 13 February. www.theaustralian.com.au/news/breaking-news/australia-helps-us-target-wikileaks-staff/story-fn3dxity-1226005158805

3 John Howard was the 25th prime minister of Australia, representing the Australian Liberal-National coalition, which led the federal parliament from 11 March 1996 to 3 December 2007.

4 Lander, K. (2004) Government sceptical over Hicks torture claims, *Lateline*, 20 May. www.abc.net.au/lateline/content/2004/s1112658.htm

5 Hayward, A. (2010) Law not broken but WikiLeaks illegal: PM, *Nine News*, 17 December. news.ninemsn.com.au/article.aspx?id=8185173

6 Moses, A. (2010) Conroy's net filter still alive and kicking, *Sydney Morning Herald*, 10 September. www.smh.com.au/technology/technology-news/conroys-net-filter-still-alive-and-kicking-20100910-1540s.html

7 Fact Sheet 8 – Abolition of the 'White Australia' Policy. www.immi.gov.au/media/fact-sheets/08abolition.htm

On 11 September 2001, John Howard, visiting the US, invoked the ANZUS Treaty and strengthened military ties with the US, unquestioningly entering both Iraq and Afghanistan. This stirred the flame of hate for minorities, particularly asylum seekers in Australia. The freedom to seek refuge and asylum from abuse on Australia's shores would be severely tested.

It was in this climate of fear, suspicion and increasing contempt for informed public discussion and transparency that the subsequent Australian Labor Party which came to power proposed the much maligned mandatory clean feed filter, and the measures that would follow as it simmered on the policy back burner.

Blocking content versus blocking rights

Much like the rest of the developed world, Australians, who once hailed theirs as "the lucky country", live in an environment governed by economic concerns, fluctuations in currency markets, increasing interest rates and threatening statistics. Traditional media are struggling to define themselves through headlines that continue to opine economic peril. Many leading politicians are turning their back on our experts. Given a minority government, held together by three independents and the Greens, the only wedge of common sense and courage in a political environment that is by and large conservative, is driven by short-term goals and ambitions.

> *The definition of insanity is doing the same thing over and over again and expecting different results.* Albert Einstein

When the clean feed was introduced it met with unparalleled backlash from the public, civil society and ISPs. The clean feed's architect, Senator Stephen Conroy, Minister for Broadband, Communications and the Digital Economy, continued to back it time and time again. Tests proved the technology would slow internet usage, but Conroy persisted. Industry leaders suggested it would hamper internet usage and stifle innovation. Conroy ignored their concerns and pressed harder. Campaign after campaign ridiculed the proposal and sought to test the minister's expertise, which appeared limited.

Conroy continued to condemn those who were against the policy as supporters of the kind of information he was wanting to protect Australians from. It was not until a leaked blacklist of sites appeared on WikiLeaks that the proposal started to come undone. It took an election to see the policy put on the proverbial back burner. But what is driving the clean feed? We are not quite done with it yet.

> *It is not the government's role to be a net nanny. It is the role of every single household.* Rob Oakeshott, independent member of the House of Representatives, Australia

Since 1 July, leading Australian ISPs, including Telstra, Optus and Primus, have voluntarily undertaken, with the support of their industry association, the Internet Industry Association (IIA), to implement the blocking of sites on an Interpol list of child abuse websites.[8] At the same time, the Australian Communications and Media Authority (ACMA) is compiling a list of its own, and it is seeking to have sites on its blacklist reviewed by the Classification Board. ACMA's list is said to include "material that meets the criteria for Refused Classification under the National Classification Code for containing offensive depictions or descriptions of children." It is under this basis that the Classification Board will formally classify sites for the filtering scheme.

Nevertheless, while the ACMA administers a co-regulatory scheme for online content,[9] at the time of writing the Classification Board has not yet set out guidelines for the classification of online content as it has done, for example, for films and more recently computer games.[10] It is also not yet clear which of Australia's ISPs will agree to implement it.

The IIA is less than enthusiastic about the ACMA blacklist. The government sees the implementation of the Interpol blacklist as an "interim step", fuelling speculation by the IIA that the government's mandatory filter could be taken up by ISPs through a "backdoor" mechanism. However, the IIA's scheme, according to Electronic Frontiers Australia (EFA), provides "no clear governance and oversight from the people affected by it."

The EFA is concerned that being an international list that no Australian agency can contribute to without international cooperation, the Interpol list will not satisfy the government. David Cake, EFA's chair, suggests that this position will not only "make legislation perhaps easier to sell, but it opens the way for further (perhaps non-legislative) additions to the filter – and the decision to add this filtering scheme, as a voluntary industry scheme, is one with virtually no consumer or civil society input."

8 Moses, A. (2011) Internet censorship machine quietly revs up, *Sydney Morning Herald*, 20 July. www.smh.com.au/technology/technology-news/internet-censorship-machine-quietly-revs-up-20110720-1hooy.html#ixzz1V4sQXzkP

9 Australian Communications and Media Authority, Online regulation. www.acma.gov.au/WEB/STANDARD/pc=PC_90169#coreg

10 Classification Board, Guidelines for the Classification of Films and Computer Games. www.comlaw.gov.au/comlaw/management.nsf/lookupindexpagesbyid/IP200508205?OpenDocument

But it is not all about protecting Australians from content governments do not wish them to see. There is an increasing desire to know what people are saying to each other, both online and through the myriad of communications devices in use.

> *In Australia the quality of debate has largely been deplorable: soporific on one side and hysterical on the other, ugly, dumb and bullying, marked by a "Gotcha!" approach in sections of the media, with relentless emphasis on fear, the short term, vested interests and a mindless populism.* Barry Jones, Honorary (Professorial Fellow), Melbourne Graduate School of Education at University of Melbourne

As the appetite for a more informed conversation in the national media increases, one may not be wrong in thinking that Australians are turning to the internet to stay informed. Here independent media and public debate are flourishing. This has, in turn, inspired a new form of media within national institutions such as the Australian Broadcasting Corporation's popular *Q and A*[11] and the Special Broadcasting Service's *Go Back to Where You Came From*.[12] We may well be seeing an increase in the number of informed, politically literate and active citizens in Australia. If this is the case, why then seek to criminalise the tools we use to both inform and protect ourselves?

The story is the same the world over. Activists have been using computer networks since their appearance in the mid- to late-1980s. With every technological advance, activists migrated from one platform to another exploiting their use to give voice to the unheard, to document the perils of the unseen, from the forests of Borneo to the streets of Egypt. When once their communications were secure, or relatively unknown, new technologies have made activists vulnerable, but they have also made them inventive. So long as an open internet can be maintained, that inventiveness will serve the cause of free speech and open democracies – but it can also harbour and protect the practices of really bad people.

> *Governments will always try to monitor citizens' "secure" communications – and corporations will always help them.* Dan Gillmore, director, Knight Center for Digital Media Entrepreneurship, Arizona State University

Governments across the planet seek to profoundly change the way activists and the general public at large communicate with each other. Western governments will, on the one hand, speak out against the restrictions imposed on internet access during the uprisings in Egypt, but will call for similar impositions when the hard issues need to be addressed and citizens demand that they are. Australia is no exception.

A proposal on data retention, inspired by the European Union's Data Retention Directive,[13] is being driven by the Australian Federal Police and could see all web browsing history of Australian internet users logged for law enforcement to access.[14] A representative from the Attorney General's Department stated that the Department is "considering the merits of comparative data retention proposals to enable security and law enforcement agencies to maintain access to telecommunications information to assist with investigations."[15]

The Environment and Communications References Committee of the Australian Senate produced a report in April 2011 analysing whether Australia should implement such a plan. A report[16] considering the adequacy of protections for the privacy of Australians online made five key suggestions that government should consider prior to proceeding with data retention legislation,[17] asking the Australian government to:

- Produce an extensive report analysing the costs, benefits and major risks of data retention legislation
- Demonstrate that retaining data is necessary for law enforcement purposes
- Quantify and justify the costs to ISPs of implementing a data retention law
- Assure citizens that data retained will be stored securely and subject to appropriate accountability mechanisms
- Consult with a wide range of stakeholders, including NGOs which the government has yet to consult.

11 www.abc.net.au/tv/qanda

12 www.sbs.com.au/shows/goback

13 eur-lex.europa.eu/LexUriServ/LexUriServ.do?uri=OJ:L:2006:105:0054:0063:EN:PDF

14 Jacobs, C. (2010) AFP pushing for invasive data retention, *Electronic Frontiers Australia*, 7 September. www.efa.org.au/2010/09/07/afp-pushing-for-invasive-data-retention

15 Parenell, S. (2011) Canberra rethinks retention regime on ISP subscriber records, *The Australian*, 26 July. www.theaustralian.com.au/news/investigations/canberra-rethinks-retention-regime-on-isp-subscriber-records/story-fn8roe18-1226101609674

16 Senate Environment and Communications References Committee (2011) *The adequacy of protections for the privacy of Australians online*. www.aph.gov.au/senate/committee/ec_ctte/online_privacy/report/index.htm

17 Electronic Frontiers Foundation (n.d.) Mandatory Data Retention. www.eff.org/issues/mandatory-data-retention

So far the recommendations remain as such: recommendations with no clear indication as to whether they will be taken up in any form.

Conclusions

What is the problem these measures are designed to address? Filters can be circumvented. Data can be encrypted. Voices that wish to be heard will find a way to reach communities that wish to listen and really bad people will pay to conceal their activities.

The internet has given Australians a means to not only express their democratic rights, but also to exercise innovation in the use of those rights for public debate. This report has described a vigorous, determined, all-embracing attack on those rights through political posturing targeting a fearful population and conservative values. It is wrong to not stand up against child abuse, for instance; but when this is used as an argument to stymie all manner of online content, one can only wonder why the same approach is not taken to shut down the operations of those who would pollute the Artesian Water Basin through the controversial practice of coal seam mining.

There are millions of websites that host questionable content. It would seem far easier to put an end to the practices that harm the health of all people both now and into the future than to attempt to narrow the means by which we can inform ourselves of such folly. Perhaps therein lies the answer.

> *Call it draconian or whatever they like, but any society needs supervision and regulation.* DD, online comment to *The Age* article, "Censoring mobiles and the net: How the West is clamping down"[18]

Perhaps Australians prefer to be protected, to be supervised and regulated. Perhaps Australians do not wish to be reminded that they are, no matter where they came from, part of the rest of the world.

There is need for "protection", but by whom and for what end or gain? Responsible parenting, for instance, is simply that. But the nanny state appears to want to parent all Australians, at the expense, it seems, of the liberties expressed online. Self-regulation is an option that the IIA is exploring. It has worked in the past, in other information communication sectors, the motion picture industry for instance.

In 1966 the Motion Picture Association of America, in response to what were already considered antiquated censorship restrictions of their industry, came up with a rating system of their own. A form of industry self-regulation created avenues for an independent scene that saw no reason to rate itself whatsoever. The independent filmmakers of the past decade have sought to make films on their own terms and employ alternative forms of distribution. Theirs is a world that seeks not to stifle, but to open debate on all issues; not to criminalise taboos or critique, but to encourage a more open and honest society where the majority take responsibility for their actions, where their elected leaders protect, but do not parent, and seek to educate and nurture their constituencies. Censorship limits life, but life knows no limits. Australians would do well to not think only of themselves as living in the "lucky country", but as responsible, creative and nurturing citizens on a lucky planet!

Action steps

- Support initiatives that promote an open internet. Become a member of EFA.
- Join GetUp.org.au and advocate for the maintenance of civil liberties when they are challenged.
- Engage in public debate on the issues raised in this report. Publish your own views or support the views of those whom you respect and raise the calibre of discussion from passive acceptance to being informed and active in shaping the future of your community, your nation and its contribution to the planet at large.
- Find the means to use social media sites for local, community initiatives. Just as Australians gathered on social media sites during unprecedented natural disasters in early 2011, from Cyclone Yasi to flooding across the state of Queensland, local use of these tools will strengthen their everyday use and further prevent intrusion into their use by governments and civil authorities. ■

18 Moses, A. (2011) Censoring mobiles and the net: how the West is clamping down, *The Age*, 15 August. www.theage.com.au/technology/technology-news/censoring-mobiles-and-the-net--how-the-west-is-clamping-down-20110815-1itsx.html#ixzz1V5lJBiiv

BANGLADESH

CAMPAIGNING AGAINST WAR CRIMINALS ONLINE

VOICE
Ahmed Swapan Mahmud and Farjana Akter
www.voicebd.org

Introduction

Bangladesh attained independence after a nine-month war against Pakistan in 1971, during which local collaborators set up by fundamentalist political parties engaged in genocide. The United Nations Human Rights Commission (UNHRC), in its 1981 report on the occasion of the 33rd anniversary of the Universal Declaration of Human Rights, stated that the genocide committed in Bangladesh in 1971 was the worst in history. It is widely accepted, both inside and outside of Bangladesh, that a total of three million Bengalis were killed by Pakistani troops and their local allies. The UNHRC report said that even if a lower figure of 1.5 million deaths were accepted, the killings took place at a rate of between 6,000 to 12,000 per day, lasting for 267 days of carnage. This made it the most intense genocide in history.

We achieved our independence through a sacrifice of human lives. We had to undergo tragedies of unprecedented proportions. What finally helped us to drive the occupation forces out of our sacred land were our indomitable spirit, sheer grit and determination more than anything else. At the same time one should also recall with gratitude the support provided by our neighbour India, both militarily and by the Indian people.[1]

The genocide in 1971 was helped by many local fundamentalists, including members of the religious Jamaat-e-Islami party. They formed a militia which allegedly helped identify victims and also took part in the killings. Their leaders were absolved after the war and are now prominent opposition political figures.[2] The government wants to put them on trial, but they claim they are innocent and that this is a political move.

On 25 March 2010, after 39 years of independence, the current government of the Awami League party formed the International Crimes Tribunal, dedicated to the prosecution of war crimes committed during the 1971 war of independence. The people of Bangladesh have been united since independence to bring all war criminals to justice and punish them for war crimes and crimes against humanity. They are waiting to hear the verdicts against the hated war criminals.

While the peoples' movement against war criminals started at independence, it is now stronger than ever before, largely because of new media. By using the internet, young people have promoted the movement. They have successfully spread its message, not only in Bangladesh but all over the world, by blogging, using social networking sites, and online web forums.

Policy and political background

Bangladesh has a comprehensive information and communications technology (ICT) policy, which was passed in 2002, and a National Telecom Policy, which was passed in 1998. The present government has placed considerable importance on ICT issues and on the digital rights of people. Around 10 million people now use the internet, while in 2008 the number of users was around 4.8 million.

A National ICT Task Force has been formed and a programme called the Support to ICT Task Force (SICT) has been initiated by the government to help with implementation and monitoring. The government has also started a multi-stakeholder e-government forum. This includes several important ministries, academics, NGOs and the private sector.

In 2007, during a military caretaker regime, the country lacked freedom of expression both in print and electronic media. One of the most highly circulated newspapers, *Prothom Alo*, had to suspend the publication of its weekly satire supplement called *Alpin*. Cases were filed against the editor, publisher and cartoonist of the Bangla daily *Prothom Alo*. *Saptahik2000*, a popular magazine supplement, was stopped because of a story where the writer compared Kaaba Shareef (a holy place in Mecca where the prophet Muhammad was buried and where the holy pilgrimage takes place) to a brothel.[3]

1 www.thedailystar.net/suppliments/2011/26_march/pg2.htm

2 www.secularvoiceofbangladesh.org/Fotoes/Report%20on%20the%20war%20criminals..%A8%A8/Report%20on%20the%20war%20criminals.htm

3 www.e-bangladesh.org/2007/09/20/attack-against-freedom-of-speech-bangladesh-cartoon-controversy-update

The military government also set guidelines for TV talk shows and other programmes.

Before coming to power, the present government always spoke in favour of freedom of the press and freedom of expression – but now that it is in power, the situation has not improved. The electronic and print media are simultaneously being pressurised by the ruling party. Private TV channels have shut down and one channel did not get permission to broadcast, while others have received licences and will be on the air soon. In 2010 Facebook was banned for days because it published a cartoon of the prime minister in a commentary on a religious matter.

Newspapers in Bangladesh are already compelled to self-censor to avoid any form of harassment by the state. Bangladesh has a Right to Information (RTI) Act and a commission has been formed under the Act. The RTI Act is expected to create a more open and democratic society. But this does not seem to have happened yet. Under the established exceptions and for security reasons the government has blocked people's right to know.

The role of ICTs in citizen mobilisation

ICTs have had a great impact on numerous peoples' movements in the world because of their ability to allow the general public to participate. The role of online social resistance is very important. The internet allows people to communicate, exchange ideas and organise themselves. It also facilitates a kind of political process that is different to the conventional political system. A group of people sharing a common interest and vision collectively have greater capacity and resources to campaign when using the internet.

It has been said that online media allow easy access to information. The internet is a place of free-flowing information where people can express anything anytime. It is a unique place to build people's mobilisation and give them a voice against an unjust and unfair society.

In the case of Bangladesh, the internet can be used to publish photos, videos and documentaries which offer solid evidence of the genocide in 1971. The war left three million people dead, and 200,000 women were assaulted. All these hated activities were perpetrated by local collaborators such as the Rajakar (also spelled Razakar), Al Badar and Al Sham militias.

The online campaign against war criminals is intensifying. Different groups have been created for the cause on social networking sites like Facebook and Twitter. These groups are very active in distributing messages to their lists. YouTube also helps to distribute videos. A Facebook group named "50,000 BANGLADESHIS UNITED AGAINST WAR CRIMINALS AND RAJAKARS OF 1971 BANGLADESH" has published an official list of Razakars. Groups called "Trial For War Criminals In Bangladesh" and "Stand Against RAJAKAR" are vigorously pushing policy makers for justice.

Independent writers, bloggers and journalists have formed a pressure group to push for the prosecution of war crimes. For example, War Criminals in Bangladesh[4] is a very strong blog which publishes photos and stories of atrocities committed by Razakars in 1971. Sachalayatan[5] is another very prominent blog in Bangladesh. It focuses on all kinds of injustices in society. It publishes articles and critical perspectives on war criminals in Bangladesh. Sachalayatan is playing a very decisive role in the campaign.

Amar[6] is another blog run by enthusiastic online activists. Recently they established an online research foundation. The main objective of the foundation was to include young people in research on struggles for freedom, and to make this research available online. As part of its campaign, Amar also organises meetings and seminars on online campaigns against war criminals.

The International Crime Strategy Forum (ICSF)[7] is an active and strong online coalition against war criminals in Bangladesh. The ICSF had been formed to promote the cause of justice and at the same time to facilitate the fair trial of the perpetrators of the 1971 war crimes, irrespective of where they now live, their political connections or their status in the society. Through this campaign the ICSF wants to strengthen the movement against war criminals by instilling a sense of justice, independence and freedom in the hearts of future generations. The ICSF has been providing reference resources to the public using the internet. For instance, it has set up the e-Library 71[8] which includes reference materials on the 1971 genocide.

To make the campaign more effective, the ICSF has been running an online media archive.[9] This archive contains recent media reports and blog coverage related to war crime prosecution in Bangladesh. It also has a group blog platform to discuss and analyse current developments related to war crimes and criminals of 1971 generally and prosecution initiatives specifically.

---

4 warcriminalsinbangladesh.blogspot.com

5 www.sachalayatan.com

6 www.amarblog.com

7 icsforum.org

8 icsforum.org/blog/category/archives/e-library-71

9 icsforum.org/mediarchive

New media are being used to organise protests on the ground. These include demonstrations and the collection of signatures for campaigns. These activities push the government to take action.

Conclusion

Online campaigns and resistance are stronger than movements on the ground, and have grabbed attention nationally and internationally. The end result is that the government has considered it its moral and political duty to bring war criminals before tribunals. It has started to try war criminals – a move which has been encouraged by people's activism.

Action steps

- Lobby government for access to the internet.
- Mainstream ICT policy development.
- Online campaigners should include key policy actors when dealing with important national issues.
- Content should be in both local and international languages so that everybody can access it.
- Visual media should be emphasised when seeking to influence public opinion.
- There could be more coordination among online groups and blogs. ■

BENIN

ICTS IN EDUCATION IN BENIN: ELUSION AND THE LIGHT OF HOPE

CréACTION BENIN
Barnabé Affougnon
www.ogouman.blogspot.com

Introduction

The era of people sitting around a tree for endless discussions is now past. Now is the time of screens, paper and multimedia, with the internet as a cornerstone. This is a fast world, full of images, texts and sounds, moving as fast as light. However, to keep pace with that light, the true light, is not an easy task. We mean the light which can help get rid of ignorance; the light that brings in changes in businesses, moving them to develop.

To ignore new technology is to be a misfit in today's world. It is to lag behind a story that humankind has made up. We spoke to Cedric, a student in sociology. A writer and poet, Cedric got a scholarship for Brussels as a writer-in-residence. One of the requirements was that he had to use a computer with an internet connection while in residence. Too bad, he knew nothing about computers, even though he attended computer classes when he was in high school. Basically, the courses were theoretical and insubstantial.

Meanwhile, his colleagues, African or European residents, were making good use of the machine, proudly showing documents they had produced in a relatively short time.

Ironically, Cedric is from Benin, a country where computer and internet classes in a number of schools are compulsory, and the use of technology is encouraged and advertised by the media. However, learners continue to be introduced to technology "in theory", rather than practically. The government exercises no control over information and communications technology (ICT) training programmes. The education system continues to be run with flaws, and there is almost no curriculum guidance.

The French political document, the Declaration of the Rights of Man and Citizen of 1793, states in Article 3: "All men are equal by nature and before the law." This right is inalienable. But culturally, this right is problematic. People in all continents have not received the same education, do not have the same history; therefore, they do not have the same opportunities. In this context, even Cedric was lucky.

The challenge of ICTs in education in Benin

The national strategy for ICTs in Benin is well defined. By 2025, Benin must become "the digital district of Africa". This strategy has two essential components. The first component relates to the development of e-business. The second component takes into account e-government and e-education. The aim is to connect all government and educational institutions in order to boost development at the national level.

Unfortunately, in practice, this is more difficult. The ICT learning programme is not yet widespread in schools. Therefore, the digital gap is getting wider. The rate of internet use is still very low in Benin. Among over 200 students surveyed, only 3% have a computer and 15% use the internet for their studies. The reasons given are threefold. The first is economic. The students do not have the money to buy computers. The purchasing power of these learners does not allow them to acquire these materials. The second reason relates to the teaching system. There are few teachers and lecturers who can teach computer classes. Mostly they are individuals who have attended introductory courses in computers and the internet, and have only partial knowledge of the discipline.

The last reason relates to the difficulties in learning how to use technology well – which comes from using technology regularly.

Because of these factors, we can say that access to knowledge is unevenly shared.

Sad fate, sad situation for Cedric, a young student of eighteen, registered for his first year in sociology and anthropology at the University of Abomey-Calavi in Benin, truly immersed in this reality. Lured by the attractive and misleading advertisements of ICTs in education in one of the computer schools in the city, Cedric realised he had been duped. What motivated Cedric to register at that school was the computer classes it claimed it taught there. To have a good command of typing, being able to use the internet, chat, find information, was a dream for the young learner, a step towards reality.

But by the end of the year, the only things he knew were the definitions of the different parts of a computer: screen, keyboard, mouse, monitor, hard disk, computer. Generally, the computers he used were first-generation computers (Pentium 1) or second-generation (Pentium 2), largely because they were less expensive to buy. But these computers are subject to untimely breakdowns and malfunctions during training programmes. The Pentium 3s that are found in some schools are considered luxury items, sophisticated objects placed on desks and covered up for protection.

Another serious problem is the instability of electricity supply. There are frequent power cuts. When they occur, classes automatically stop, given the absence of generators. Classrooms are also not air-conditioned. And up to eight students cluster around a single computer to work. The time spent at the keyboard was considered short. "The class was a boiler and everyone was fighting to breathe easily," Cedric told us in our interview with him.

Given the lack of laws and regulations, educational institutions lure young pupils and students to their classes through what amounts to false advertising. The practical arrangements put in place in these schools are outdated and do not facilitate access to quality training. Unfortunately, this sorry and even illegal situation continues, and is legitimised by a number of school authorities who have the protection of a few political leaders.

As a result, despite attending the school, Cedric has not yet discovered the advantages and benefits of using a computer and the internet. The students know nothing about discussion groups or social networking. Cedric has just a poor idea of these tools, which many students of his age in other parts of the world manipulate skilfully.

The right to access the internet

My mother often says, "The five fingers are not equal, yet they are all together." The realities of Benin are not those of Togo, neither those of the Ivory Coast nor of France. The needs expressed in these countries reflect the existing emergencies there. In Benin, education is an "emergency" and the state is well positioned to help Cedric recover his right to access the internet, one that allows him to access information.

The educational system in Benin, despite the noticeable progress made since the *Conférence Nationale des Forces Vives de la Nation* (National Conference of Active Forces of the Nation) in 1990 has faltered. Several ongoing reforms do not appear to be working, especially those related to new teaching programmes. One is the teaching of ICTs. Unfortunately, many schools in Benin have no electricity, no telephone lines. The cost of hardware is still too high given the budget allocated to each school for operating expenses. This all contributes to the failure of ICT projects in the educational arena such as the GLOBE Project in 1996, NTIC-EDUC in 2000 and the Project for Introducing Computers in Schools (PIIES), based in the Ministry of Primary and Secondary Education.

A reluctance is also observed in the school system where teachers who are computer illiterate do not want to admit it, because they are afraid of losing their jobs. Following our investigations, it turned out that many educators do not want to be taught about computers in their schools at risk of being treated as if they belong in the backwaters of this changing century. Some argue that they are no longer able to learn anything. Why?

They refuse to face the new difficulties a computer introduces into their lives. This narrow-minded attitude reduces the chances of introducing these tools into school programmes.

Cedric lives this policy failure.

Conclusions

The growing development of ICTs has profoundly changed people's ways of thinking and acting in the community. ICTs contribute to the strengthening of social ties. Basic computer literacy and a good command of IT applications are essential to getting to know the realities of the changing world.

Unfortunately, Western countries have a clear lead over the Southern ones. The result is a digital divide which is a key factor of underdevelopment. ICT development initiatives and forums are set up by multinational corporations, political leaders and members of civil society in an effort to bridge the divide – regional and international summits such as the World Summit on the Information Society being one such effort.

In Benin, efforts to promote an enabling environment for the use of ICTs continue. The state's regulatory framework, including tax exemptions for hardware, and the numerous ICT projects, including an increase in the number of cybercafés in major cities, help to some degree. Schools and universities have been gradually introducing computer and internet training programmes in their classes.

However, real difficulties remain: the availability of computer hardware, the training and capacity of teachers who are responsible for teaching the discipline, financial difficulties relating to the management of computer rooms. As a result, like the computers they use, the training of students is still not reliable. The courses are unregulated and inconsistent. There is a mismatch between the training promised and the course content in the programmes. Teachers are not evaluated by the state. The student performance officially recorded is not credible.

Yet the need for training remains high. It is only by meeting this demand properly that we can build an "Emerging Benin" where socioeconomic and intellectual development is supported by ICTs.

Action steps

- The state should back up its ICT policies and visions by supporting ICT education programmes in schools and universities.
- State strategies should involve both national and international NGOs.
- Computer education should be integrated into all public schools and universities.
- Computer classes should be part of free education at primary school.
- Computer courses should be a separate subject in official exams – it should no longer be an optional subject.
- Courses should be run enabling teachers to build their ICT capacity.
- The state should gradually build rooms specifically designed for computer classes.
- All schools and universities with computers should be connected to the internet.

Action steps for directors and heads of schools

- The heads of schools should develop objective criteria in the selection of teachers to ensure quality training for learners.
- The internet should be used for knowledge sharing among teachers, including courses and curricula.
- New computer hardware should be installed to facilitate effective learning. ■

BOLIVIA

THE NEW INSTITUTIONAL ADVOCACY:*
A HUMAN RIGHTS MODEL FOR THE INFORMATION SOCIETY

REDES Foundation
J. Eduardo Rojas
www.fundacionredes.org

Introduction

The Bolivian Constitution promulgated on 9 February 2009 restores a new historical process of structural reconstruction that proposes to change the neoliberal corporate state model into a community-orientated one. But since then, the country has experienced social, political and economic restructuring characterised by excessive state centralism, which has gradually affected all spheres of daily life, including internet development.

In November 2009 the federal police closed down the Cyber Crime Division, arguing that there were not enough cases to justify it. Since then, the situation has not changed. Between 2009 and 2011, the mass media reported on an increase in violations of human rights on the internet and using mobile phones, principally against young people, women and families.

In response to this situation, since April 2010 the REDES Foundation has implemented a programme called ENREDOMINO: Developing Active Citizenship in the Information Society. This involves several initiatives led by volunteers, including highly qualified professionals, unleashing new kinds of support for legislative reforms and for processes of creating awareness and sharing information about human rights in the information society.

A national culture of human rights in the information society

Bolivia has a short history of developing the information society. Between 2004 and 2005, a National Strategy for Information and Communications Technologies for Development (ETIC) was passed. This was the result of a multisectoral process that mobilised different sectors of the population. Nevertheless, due to the political instability and change of leadership that took place until 2006, this strategy was not adopted by the government, even though it has been inserted in the current National Plan for Development. In August 2010, believing that the ETIC was still in a stage of "formulation", the Agency for the Development of the Information Society in Bolivia (ADSIB), part of the Vice-Presidency of the State, decided to create a brand new Digital Agenda, restarting the entire planning process from scratch.

Over the last five years the state has invested in several infrastructure projects led by governmental entities. Some of the projects include: the installation of the Túpac Katari satellite; a project called Bolivia: Territory with Total Coverage (TCT) by the state-run telecommunications company ENTEL; One Computer Per Teacher, a programme by the Ministry of Education; and the academic network called CLEAR, run by the vice ministry. Though Bolivia has several initiatives aimed at reducing the digital gap, it does not have many initiatives aimed at eliminating the information and knowledge gap.

Institutional advocacy in the ENREDOMINO programme

Between 2009 and 2011 the situation of human rights in the Bolivian information society can be summarised as follows:

- The new Bolivian Constitution assumes a human rights approach to societal affairs, and this facilitates a human rights approach to the internet.
- However, no state policies dealing with access to information on the internet integrate a human rights approach.
- No state actor has promoted human rights on the internet.
- At the same time, there is evidence of the population's overexposure to online crimes (e.g. cyber bullying, trafficking and child pornography).
- There are no approaches, methods or educational strategies that promote the responsible use of the internet or mobile phones.
- There are no experiences on human rights approaches documented in the domain of information and knowledge.
- Internet governance does not exist in Bolivia.
- No actor assumes leadership for directing the development of the digital culture with a multisectoral or transdisciplinary approach.

* Refers to the defence and promotion of human rights in the information society, working with professionals and volunteers from the REDES Foundation.

- Old ways of violating human rights are reproduced online and are not addressed, due to the lack of institutional capacity.

In April, 2010, the REDES Foundation presented the results of research – conducted using its own resources – on access to and social use of the internet in Bolivia. The results found that no initiatives existed promoting the responsible use of the internet, specifically those incorporating a human rights approach. This demonstrated the extreme vulnerability of children, teenagers and women in the online world. Despite the impossibility of raising financing, we decided to create the programme ENREDOMINO (a combination of the three words EN-RED-DOMINO, which can be translated as "In the network – or on the internet – I dominate"). The agenda of the programme rests on the assumption that volunteer professionals might take advantage of their institutional experience and initiate activities based on their networks and commitment to human rights.

In May 2010, a contest for producing mobile videos called filMóvil was held. With the support of more than ten institutional allies and 30 young volunteers, students gathered in the cities of La Paz, Cochabamba and Santa Cruz for the competition. The mass media was informed about the initiative, and Facebook was used intensively to promote it.[1] Nevertheless, the experience did not have good results because the daily use of the mobile phone was centred on the consumption of telecommunications services and not on the creative use of the video camera. The lack of technical support for the production and editing of mobile videos was also a problem. The volunteer professionals identified the importance of creating videos and educational animations to be distributed using manuals for audiovisual production; "how to" manuals for uploading information to the web; and primers on cyber crimes. On two occasions they ran courses on producing digital and interactive mobile content for students from rural areas. This material is available freely on the ENREDOMINO educational portal.[2]

Towards the end of 2010, the portal received the institutional support of the Vice Ministry of Science and Technology, linked to the Ministry of Education, the Office of the Ombudsman and ADSIB. This promoted the portal across the whole country and unleashed a variety of activities that influenced the development of the internet with a human rights approach. Amongst the actions that stand out:

- Conferences were held on legislative reforms and the right to information at the Bolivian Catholic University, UDABOL University, San Andrés University (UMSA) and the Department of Education.[3]
- The issue of digital violence was inserted into a law on school violence presented to the Commission on Human Rights in the Legislative Assembly.[4] The TV programme *Renew You* on the state television channel also devoted a special programme to digital rights.
- Articles were published on the internet about human rights in the journal *DiálogosTransdisciplinarios en la Sociedad de la Información* (Transdisciplinary Dialogue on the Information Society). In December 2010 an issue of this journal was dedicated to the subject Identities in the Information Society.[5] In addition, a publication was released with the help of the Office of the Ombudsman in October 2011 exploring the subject of human rights in the information society.
- The National Centre for the Democratisation of Digital Culture[6] was created in the city of Cochabamba to prepare teenagers and women for the responsible use of social networks. This is co-managed by the CREPUM foundation.[7]
- The Vice-Presidency invited the REDES Foundation to draw up a new model of regulation for information and communications technologies (ICTs) in Bolivia.[8] This directly influences ICT and telecommunications law in the country. It emphasises human rights, and focuses on important aspects of the internet such as electronic signatures, e-commerce and e-governance, democratisation of frequencies, telecommunication price control, and universal services projects.
- A national citizen group was created called Bolivians for the Right to Communication and Information.[9]

1 www.facebook.com/pages/ENREDOMINO/104743696237782

2 www.enredomino.fundacionredes.org

3 www.conaric.org.bo/site/php/level.php?lang=es&component=36&item=1

4 noviolenciabolivia.blogspot.com/2010/11/presentacion-del-anteproyecto-de-ley.html

5 fundacionredes.org/index.php?option=com_content&view=section&layout=blog&id=4&Itemid=11

6 www.fundacioncrepum.org/index.php?/2011040557/Ultimas-noticias/crepum-inaugura-en-cochabamba-el-centro-nacional-de-democratizacion-de-la-cultura-digital.html

7 Institution specialising in traditional family development.

8 comunicacionconderechos.org/index.php?option=com_content&view=article&id=93:comunicacion-con-derechos&catid=44:noticias&Itemid=131

9 www.facebook.com/pages/Bolivians-por-el-derecho-a-la-Comunicaci%C3%B3n-e-informaci%C3%B3n/188422331209779

- A seminar called Perspectives and Challenges of the Information Society in Bolivia[10] was organised to commemorate Internet Day on 17 May 2011. It addressed a human rights agenda for the internet and was broadcast on television with the support of national and international partnerships.
- We ran a digital journalism workshop[11] with a human rights approach to train 22 journalists from the city of La Paz.
- A proposal for national research into interactive digital content generation was designed in September 2011.
- An agreement with the Communications Ministry was reached to provide technical advice on the right to communication and information to 300 teenagers using filMóvil educational units set up in La Paz (September-November 2011).

These activities marked a turning point in the recent history of participatory construction of the information society in Bolivia. The programme continues to be run by ENREDOMINO, attracting the support of new professionals, young people and institutions interested in collaborating on initiatives that have a structural impact, low operating costs and the potential to create employment options for Latin American professionals.

Most of the interventions were reported on television channels with national coverage, in print, on the websites of institutional partners, and on social networks.

The new model for institutional advocacy in the information society in Bolivia

This relates to how an institution that has no economic resources may influence several issues related to human rights in the information society in Bolivia. The analysis can build a new "model of institutional advocacy" capable of being replicated by the global community.

Five elements determine the effectiveness of new institutional advocacy: a) a clear vision of the work proposed, b) activism based on professional experience, c) transdisciplinary research/action, d) management of information and knowledge for social innovation, and e) self-sustainability that combines volunteering with professional services.

Clear vision of the work proposed A view that proposed the use of ICT for development has been replaced with a programmatic approach that promotes collective structural construction of the information society, allowing anyone in any context to be part of the re-shaping of his or her own local-global environment.

This vision is summarised as follows: 1) to build and promote a human rights approach through the strategic use of the internet and mobile telephones, 2) to influence cultural patterns that violate human rights that are reproduced in the information society, 3) to create real and virtual scenarios of global and local promotion and exercise of human rights and prevention of human rights abuses, 4) to demand that we act on and denounce all practices that violate the human rights of future generations through the internet and mobile telephony, 5) to promote the development of technological skills for the exercise of citizenship, 6) To educate people about the functioning of the internet so that they can surf without risk, and 7) to undertake structural reforms based on a human rights agenda in the information society.

Recognition of technical and professional experience We are all part of building the society we live in, so it is necessary to assume social responsibility for our environment. REDES suggests that we realise present opportunities by projecting their implications for the future, but considering the lessons of the past. Under this logic, all activities and all employment opportunities result in activism as a way of life. This recognises the potential of all people to imagine and create new forms of social life. It calls for sensitivity and social solidarity, and an awareness of the opportunities opened up by institutional experience and vocational placement for proactive proposals that contribute to living well.

Transdisciplinary research/action All activities should be informed by transdisciplinary research with particular emphasis on disciplines such as sociology, communications, anthropology, psychology, law, public management, information technology, telecommunications and interactive digital content production. This allows the intersection between human rights and the internet to be recognised in the everyday experience of the general population. Everyday communication is the best example of a transdisciplinary approach, and easily articulates various areas and approaches to knowledge and information.

Management of information, knowledge and capacities for social innovation REDES developed a set of activities that allow using, sharing, creating and disseminating information and knowledge to promote human rights and the internet, involving individuals and organisations interested in these issues. In all cases, information management is directed to realise "actions and events" that are innovative, whether as a focus (e.g. the information society), as a method (e.g. filMóvil) or as knowledge (e.g. transdisciplinary research).

10 www.gobernabilidad.org.bo/noticias/13-web-20/824-organizan-simposio-nacional-por-el-dia-del-internet-en-bolivia

11 www.fundacionperiodismo.org/moodle

TABLE 1.

Economic-technological vs. social innovation

Type of innovation	Economic-technological innovation	Social innovation
Capital	Capital intensive	Intensive human intellectual capital, relationships and networks
Basic orientation	To create monopoly situations (single product) that generate high returns	To cover the extensive needs of social groups at low cost with high impact
Rights protection	Added to ensure the investment effort and sustain the monopoly	Very low: knowledge is free for public access
Complexity	Increasing level of technology	Growing at the interpersonal level; nominal risk of failure to use technology due to a lack of know-how.

Given this, information management and knowledge for social innovation can be compared to a traditional model of economic-technological innovation, as shown in Table 1.[12]

Self-management model that combines volunteering with professional services The volunteer work of highly trained professionals in some cases turned into job opportunities for consulting services. In these cases, professionals voluntarily devoted various percentages of their salaries to support the project activities in ENREDOMINO. These operating expenses subsidised income, electricity, rent and materials production. The system is open, free and contributions are made voluntarily, building trust among the team of professionals involved.

Conclusions

Bolivia has a weak digital culture because of low internet penetration levels. In 2011 a penetration rate of 1.2% was reported, which is equivalent to twelve people in 1,000 having an internet connection at home. A country with such low levels of digital inclusion must promote causes and advocate with the support of traditional media (TV, radio and newspapers), interpersonal communication (conferences, courses, workshops) and strategic alliances with institutions and individuals involved in the field of ICTs. In this context, it also reduces the possibilities of social organisation and resistance in cyberspace.

According to the National Institute of Statistics, in 2008 it was estimated that about 26% of the population accessed the internet via public access points (telecenters and cybercafés) and household connections. In April 2010, ENREDOMINO research on internet use among teenagers in the city of La Paz showed that all teenagers interviewed know how to search for information on the internet; seven out of ten are distracted in their search navigation by pop-ups or hyperlinks; and that all are only aware of the search engines Google, Yahoo or Windows Live. Seven out of ten accepted unknown contacts on social networks, and three out of ten follow up casual online encounters in real life. In no cases were there explicit references about searching for information geared to the practice of their own human rights. It was found that the internet also reproduces old patterns of human rights violations, which affect three main population groups: young people, women and families.

There are two events which have highlighted the quiet work of ENREDOMINO activists: a) the WikiLeaks case and b) the design of a new regulatory model for ICTs in Bolivia. Both of these events were widely reported in the media and sensitised the Bolivian population to the importance of the internet and human rights.

Action steps

- Replace digital literacy with education in a human rights approach to technology and knowledge. Encourage the production of interactive digital content, strengthening gender rights in the region using the filMóvil methodology licensed under Creative Commons.
- Coordinate interventions that offer short-term, high-impact structural support, and which involve actions for strengthening social innovation.
- Broaden the base of actors who interact through converging media, such as internet activists, bloggers, TV presenters, students, opinion leaders and print journalists. All of these actors need to share in urban interventions and social innovation.
- Develop strategies that synchronise governmental policy with public strategy.
- Explore the potential of mobile telephony to promote human rights in the information society. ■

12 Based on Morales, A. (2009) Social Innovation: An area of interest for social services, *Ekain*, June.

BOSNIA AND HERZEGOVINA

IS ONLINE MEDIA AN ALLY FOR SOCIAL JUSTICE? TRAPPED BETWEEN HATE AND INFLAMMATORY SPEECH

oneworld - platform for southeast europe (owpsee)
Valentina Pellizzer
www.oneworldsee.org

Introduction

Bosnia and Herzegovina is a small country in southeast Europe.[1] There are a number of well-known words and phrases that locate it in the geopolitical landscape: "Former Yugoslavia", "Balkans wars" (1992-1995), "Dayton Peace Agreement", "Srebrenica", "genocide", "war", "rapes", "ethnic division", "Serbs", "Bosnians/Muslims", "Croats", "reconciliation", "mass graves"... The list goes on.

If we consider the information and communications technology (ICT) context, there are interesting phenomena that can be observed which are a reflection of the highly fragmented and still conflict-ridden macro-political situation. Bosnia and Herzegovina still does not have a National Agency for the Information Society. However, it has three academic research networks (BiHARNET, FARNET and SARNET),[2], in line with the three ethnic groups in the country, and the top-level domain .ba is not the default for public institutions in the country. The use of the three telecom operators (BH Telecom, M:tel and Eronet) also corresponds roughly to the three ethnic communities. Nationalism is strong and *otherness* is the main draw card used by political parties to divide people.

Policy and political background

If we look at freedom of expression and association, access to information, and media freedoms generally, Bosnia and Herzegovina has an advanced legal framework.[3] But if we scratch the surface, what emerges is a divided country. According to a recent analysis: "Most divisions are along ethnic lines. Public broadcasters and privately owned media reflect this situation. (...) Incitement of ethnic intolerance is present in much of the media, including public broadcasting. Internet fora disseminate discriminatory rhetoric and hate speech."[4] Only half of the existing 12,000 NGOs are active, and, according to another analysis, "The early concentration on service delivery militated against the development of NGOs with a social vision and the capacity to campaign and advocate."[5] Political participation is low. Apathy and disillusionment are common denominators among people.

Bosnia and Herzegovina is still an international protectorate with an ethnic constitution. Due to ethnic vetoes, it is still without a national government after the October 2010 general elections.

The country has a high level of corruption, and is ranked 78 out of 178 on the Corruption Perceptions Index (CPI).[6] The unemployment rate is 27%, and there is no strategy to remedy this.[7]

Self-regulation safeguards online media content under the auspices of the Press Council's Code of Conduct, which focuses on professional media. The Communications Regulatory Agency (RAK) is in charge of TV and radio, as well as, more recently, mobile short messaging service (SMS) content.[8]

The role of the internet in public demonstrations in Bosnia and Herzegovina

It is always problematic to say that a specific event can come to define social resistance in a particular context. In my experience, as a feminist and human

1 See the Bosnia and Herzegovina country report in GISWatch 2007: www.giswatch.org/en/2007

2 See the Bosnia and Herzegovina country report in GISWatch 2008 and 2009: www.giswatch.org/en/2008 and www.giswatch.org/en/2009

3 "BH is the most advanced in the legal environment and the least advanced in the quality of journalism." ARTICLE 19, the Global Campaign for Free Expression, International Federation of Journalists (2005) *Case Studies of Media Self-Regulation in Five Countries of South East Europe: Bosnia Herzegovina.*

4 South and East Europe Media Organisation (SEEMO) (2011) *Press freedom in the western Balkans and Turkey*. www.seemo.org; Marko, D. et al. (2010) *Izbori 2010. u BiH Kako su mediji pratili izbornu kampanju*, Media Plan Institute, Sarajevo.

5 Sterland, B. and Rizova, G. (2010) *Civil society organisations' capacities in the western Balkans and Turkey*, TACSO.

6 The Corruption Perceptions Index (CPI), compiled by Transparency International, ranks countries according to perception of corruption in the public sector. The CPI is an aggregate indicator that combines different sources of information about corruption, making it possible to compare countries. www.transparency.org/policy_research/surveys_indices/cpi

7 "By Southern Tier Central and East European (CEE) averages, Bosnia and Herzegovina (BH) continues to lag considerably in economic and democratic reform progress and remains ranked near the bottom, second only to Kosovo. (...) Democratic reforms have stagnated at best in BH since the mid-2000s. (...) Overall, BH's peace and security score is sub-average compared to its neighbours; only Albania and Kosovo are ranked lower." USAID Strategic Planning and Analysis Division, Europe and Eurasia Bureau (2011) *Bosnia and Herzegovina Gap Analysis*.

8 Press Council and Code of Conduct: www.vzs.ba and www.vzs.ba/index.php?option=com_content&view=article&id=218&Itemid=9; the Communications Regulatory Agency (RAK) issued a fine for inappropriate SMS content displayed during a TV broadcast. rak.ba/eng

rights activist, I have witnessed a series of small and very often unrelated events that contribute to what we may consider the "story" of social resistance in a country, sometimes culminating in a "big event" that is the start of the realisation of a long-nurtured common social cause.

So, my story would have its prelude in February 2008 and its "happening" during the 2010 political elections and their immediate aftermath. Without the prelude, I would not be able to show how the internet can bypass ethnic divisions and the gatekeeper logic which is rife in Bosnia and Herzegovina society.

In 2008 internet penetration in Bosnia and Herzegovina was approximately 20%, and broadband access was expanding in towns. The use of new media was gaining momentum, with users eager for direct participation. However, websites were not yet seen as relevant to the formation of public opinion[9] by politicians and NGOs.

In February, a seventeen-year-old boy, Denis Mrnjavac, was stabbed to death on a public tram by three boys without any apparent reason.[10] Real-time information provided by internet sites resulted in widespread public compassion and rage. Demands that politicians attend to public safety and develop a youth strategy were met with arrogance and insensitivity. On 6 February, a public demonstration with more than 10,000 people took place. Over the following three months, public demonstrations were coordinated using the net. During the next administrative elections, those politicians who had been scornful of public demands lost their seats in towns and cantons.

In 2008, when the administrative elections took place, the internet can be said to have been *the* tool that led to democratisation and direct participation by the public. Ordinary citizens fought for a cause they felt was worthy enough to stand for. A 360° rebellion against politicians took place; but also against NGOs perceived as being donor dependent (and therefore driving their agendas), or as extensions of political parties – a class that lives off citizens' accounts but are not accountable to them. I would say that the internet opened up a new, free space for civic discussion and activism. Participation in discussion forums broke the feeling of being alone; people had the opportunity not only to safely express their own visions and ideas, but also to discover similar thinkers. Forums were flexible enough to allow a range of people to participate, from professional activists to ordinary citizens, who used the opportunity to define the agenda for discussion.

The anonymity that the internet provided made people feel safe. This is very important in a hierarchical society which very easily stigmatises diversity. At the same time, violent reactions were "only verbal" and controlled by moderators and by the active participation of other users.

In 2010 the political situation had become critical: corruption was worse, and state as well as other institutions had become bankrupt. An increase in tension could be felt throughout the year, as well as a rise in nationalist rhetoric and threats of secession and a vicious cycle of accusing different ethnic communities for the crises.[11] Meanwhile, access to the internet grew and expanded, and in 2010 internet penetration reached 50%. 3G services started to be provided by the three telecom operators.

General elections were scheduled for 3 October that year. With the increase in access, and popularisation of the media (more people began to have access to the media), incendiary comments became a way to increase readers. On the internet, comments showed the face of a polarised society where aggressive, inflammatory, sexist and elitist expressions are the norm.[12] Fights even erupted online amongst the activist community, mainly due to inexperience with online communications, but also because of the rigid mindset that is used to hierarchy rather than horizontal decision-making processes.

The enthusiasm and the connection felt between activists and the online professional media were already a thing of the past. The media became more interested in propaganda than in information. Both online and traditional media,[13] either public or private, had shown their loyalties to political parties and had become an integral part of the electoral machine.

9 The internet is the second most-followed medium in Bosnia and Herzegovina after TV. Media Plan Institute (2010) *Internet – Sloboda bez granica.*

10 See the Bosnia and Herzegovina country report in GISWatch 2008 for more information on the expansion of online media and the online community. www.giswatch.org/en/2008

11 "Bosnia and Herzegovina is politically and ethnically divided. Most divisions are along ethnic lines. Public broadcasters and privately owned media reflect this situation. There are three public TV channels: one covers the Bosnian Federation, the second addresses Republika Srpska and the third encompasses the whole territory. The Bosnian-Herzegovina public RTV is under constant political pressure from all ethnic groups. Incitement of ethnic intolerance is present in most media, including public broadcasting. Internet fora disseminate discriminatory rhetoric and hate speech." SEEMO (2011) op. cit.

12 "...destructive, mutually exclusive, ethnic politics." Commission of the European Communities (2010) *Bosnia and Herzegovina Progress Report.*

13 "In addition to the three state- and entity-wide public broadcasting systems, there are a total of 183 electronic media outlets in BiH – 42 television and 141 radio stations. This remains far more than the country's limited advertising market can support. Most radio stations are local and either limit their broadcasts to entertainment or focus on local political and ethnic interests. Most of the 128 registered print media are characterized by strong divisions along ethnic and ideological lines. Total circulation of the seven daily newspapers does not exceed 90,000 copies." Freedom House (2010) *Freedom of the Press 2010 - Bosnia-Herzegovina.* www.freedomhouse.org/template.cfm?page=251&year=2010&country=7786

Once more, but more structured and technically wise than in the past, websites and blogs managed by civil society organisations and activist groups started to appear. They developed online applications to help visualise the political situation, including the corruption and lies of the political elites.

The issue was how to reach people who had lost trust in politics and who preferred entertainment to engagement. How could we provide information to counteract demagogy; how could we bypass the poison of *otherness* and make people feel that diversity was a positive factor, that they could become messengers of possible change? The fact that the majority of this kind of information produced was coming from civil society activists, and was free to reuse, had a multiplier effect on our efforts. Tools such as "Truth-Meter", "razglasaj.ba" and "Clean Up Parliament"; Abrashmedia's online radio and video production; the blog called *Gdjelova* ("where is the money"); the online and offline guerrilla activism done by Pritisak ("Pressure"); the Glavuse ("Bigheads")[14] from Akcija Gradjana ("Citizens Action"):[15] all of these initiatives confirmed the emergence of a network of net activists who collaborated across the main cities of Banja Luka, Sarajevo, Tuzla, Zenica, Mostar and beyond to bring about change.

Civil activists used their own websites and tools not only to produce information and bypass mainstream indifference, but to open a direct dialogue with users/voters. They provided searchable and verifiable information that anyone could access when deciding if and why to vote. Without this strategic online engagement of civil society, clearly supported by foreign donors, voter participation would have been lower. Participation rose to 55% of eligible voters and resulted in a change of government in the entity of the Federation of Bosnia and Herzegovina and a troubled victory for the Dodik presidency in the entity of Republika Srpska.[16] It was strategic to gain the trust of Bosnia and Herzegovina's growing community of netizens which, even if still not ready to engage in the street, was hungry to read, search and listen to evidence-based news. Access to the internet, the continuous production of information and citizen journalism had proven successful and made people feel their vote was necessary.

Social networking and building civil society

Facebook is, without any doubt, the key tool used to pass on information and attract readers in Bosnia and Herzegovina. Grassroots and activist groups such as Dosta, Akcija Gradjana, Zenica, Abrashmedia, Protest.ba, Ostra Nula and many others constantly use it to promote their causes, share information and generate debate. In this context the lesbian, gay, bisexual, transsexual and queer (LGBTQ) community is the only community which remains careful to avoid the use of open groups or pages. The patriarchal and sexist Bosnia and Herzegovina society is aggressively hetero-normative and actively dislikes and stigmatises alternative sexual orientations.[17]

Facebook, with all the criticism of its privacy and security, is today the space where grassroots initiatives and informal groups in Bosnia and Herzegovina start their activities, connect with each other and *do* things. It represents the main communication infrastructure for activists, followed by Google Groups, which is considered as the best tool for setting up mailing lists and spaces for private conversation. Both applications answer activists' needs to have access to tools that are free of charge and user friendly. Facebook, and recently Twitter and Google+, are considered a public sphere where the majority of people connect and where activists can promote their causes and reach the support of critical masses. Whenever there is an action to be taken, the first step is setting up a Facebook group and sending out "friend requests". More and more debates are moving from forums to Facebook pages and groups.

Netizens understood that the mainstream media will, most of the time, ignore their calls, or will reformat the information disseminated to suit their needs. Because of this, the trend is moving from social network spaces to the creation of websites where information can be published more formally. Another trend is to publish information on a friend's blog as well as on activist websites. And it is the "share" and "like" features of social networks that bridge the gap between all these disparate groups and initiatives. The "share" and "like" functions that are linked to blog posts have become an index of social consent or dissent on certain issues.

14 Caricatures of politicians' heads were made out of papier mâché.

15 www.dosta.ba, www.akcijagradjana.org, www.istinomjer.org, www.rasglasaj.ba, www.pritisak.org, www.izaberi.ba, www.cistparlament.org, www.abrashmedia.info, www.ostranula.com, www.protest.ba, www.pulsdemokratije.net

16 Bosnia and Herzegovina encompasses two entities with their own governments and parliaments: the Federation of Bosnia and Herzegovina and the Republika Srpska (also known as the Republic of Srpska).

17 "In a study from Bosnia and Herzegovina 77% of respondents believed that accepting homosexuality would be detrimental for the country." Council of Europe (2011) *Discrimination on grounds of sexual orientation and gender identity in Europe*. See also the report from the first Queer Sarajevo Festival (2008) at www.oneworldsee.org/node/17219 and owpsee (2008) CoE Resolution Condemns Discrimination and Violence against LGBT Community, 3 October. www.oneworldsee.org/node/17247

Considering the active online links between social networks, it is important to raise awareness on the content and privacy policies implemented by these global providers.

The current scenario shows a slow but constant migration from anonymity/nicknames used in public forums, to people writing under their real names.

At the same time, public discourse remains polarised and trapped in a cycle of hate speech and discrimination. The internet has liberated activist groups from a dependence on editors and journalists,[18] but not from reproducing stereotypes.

Conclusions

Members of the new activist scene were disappointed during 2011 by the fact that Bosnia and Herzegovina, despite corruption, poverty and politicians' arrogance, did not follow the examples seen in the Arab world revolution. Activists started accusing what they considered overly easy "one-click activism" and criticised the minimal commitment required from "like" and "I'm attending" functions on Facebook pages when calling for participation in public demonstrations. Too often these amounted to little more than small groups of people.

Netizens seemed to forget the essence of our fragmented and divided society, where people are locked in exclusive collective identities and do not see themselves as citizens. The internet and social networks have created a breakthrough, a space where people can act and communicate more fluidly. At the same time, after an initial period of openness, many comments on websites and on Facebook groups and pages started to reflect a growing presence of extremist and intolerant groups – often from people in the diaspora, who share the language but not the territory. At times this amounted to a rude duel involving religion, ethnicity and identity, which began to monopolise public discourse and divide, threaten and pressurise people.

Nevertheless, the online space remains one of the spaces where identities can be shared, merged, and changed. That is why it is important to learn how to mediate and control online violations, without allowing censorship or control using internet service providers (ISPs).

Disillusionment is good when it generates awareness. Social resistance now involves building up nodes of trust, connected offline and online. Activists have started producing and collecting alternative stories in alternative languages. Social networks can be the gear but never the engine of social change. Technology needs to be understood and learnt, activists need to own and control their communication infrastructure and, in this way, to connect better and in a safer way. Without guaranteeing private conversation, emerging local groups will remain sporadic and fragile. The final stage of Bosnia and Herzegovina's social resistance is the public acceptance of humanist and secular positions, and the authentic protection of freedom of expression of the LGBTQ community.[19] So, to be continued...

Action steps

- There is no technology that can work for social activism if people are not ready to take risks and stand for their opinions, and to defend human rights and freedom.
- Socially engaged ICT geeks should be strategically placed when there is a need for a quick response in setting up online tools and services.
- It is important to always use tools which people already know, share and understand.
- It is important to be aware of existing technology and to adapt it. Updates in local languages on "how to" use the tools and "tips and tricks" for online activists are necessary.
- Privacy and security information sheets are necessary to prevent misuse or damage to activists' reputations and causes.
- The creation of a common, shared communication infrastructure and networks database that can be used on demand is needed.
- Encourage informal meetings of ICT geek and grassroots and social activists, as well as informal meetings on online content, including the use of stereotypes and inflammatory language. ■

18 Media Plan Institute (2010) Op. cit.

19 See the ILGA Rainbow Europe Map and Index (May 2011) at www.ilga-europe.org/home/publications/reports_and_other_materials/rainbow_map_and_index_2011 and www.pulsdemokratije.ba/index.php?l=bs&id=1170

BRAZIL

FROM A CYBER CRIME LAW TO AN INTERNET CIVIL RIGHTS FRAMEWORK

GPoPAI-USP
Pablo Ortellado
www.gpopai.usp.br

Introduction

In 2007 a law establishing penalties for cyber crimes was on the verge of being approved in the Brazilian Senate. The bill had been discussed in Congress for eight years, but it was significantly altered at the last stages of the legislative process in order to include provisions of the European Convention on Cybercrime. With such changes – activists argued – the government would criminalise everyday practices of consumers and would open the way for criminalising file sharing.

Civil society activists and academics started pressurising senators to change the proposed law. As the campaign gathered momentum it turned into a massive campaign against criminal law being applied in the context of the internet and a positive push for a civil rights framework for the internet. After activists managed to persuade Brazilian President Luiz Inácio Lula da Silva of the importance of a rights framework for the internet, the Brazilian government set up a model participatory process for drafting the legislation, which is now ready to be debated in Congress.

Early legislative process

On 24 February 1999 Deputy Luiz Piauhylino submitted the proposed law on cyber crime (PL 84/1999)[1] to the Chamber of Deputies (the lower house of the Brazilian Congress). The bill established criminal penalties for damage to computer data, unauthorised access to a computer or computer network, unauthorised use of data, the introduction of malware and publishing of pornography without warning. On 5 November 2003, after four years of legislative processes, the bill, with minor alterations,[2] was approved by the Chamber of Deputies and subsequently submitted for further approval by the Senate. Nearly three years of additional legislative processes ensued in the Senate. In June 2006, an opposition Social Democrat senator, Eduardo Azeredo, proposed an amendment[3] incorporating provisions in accordance with the European Convention on Cybercrime[4] – a convention to which Brazil was not a signatory. The amendments created broad definitions for the crimes, which could result in criminalising trivial things like unlocking mobile phones or making backup copies of DVDs. It could also oblige internet service providers (ISPs) to identify users and log all internet connections in Brazil, opening the way for the criminalisation of file sharing.

The change to the legislation was backed by a coalition of strong corporate and state interests, including the Brazilian Federation of Banks (FEBRABAN), which wanted stronger criminal sanctions to fight bank fraud; police organisations and public prosecutors who wanted identification and logs to help investigative work; and the copyright industry which wanted a way to identify users, as well as criminal penalties, to combat "piracy".

After the amendments were included in the bill, civil society groups and academic experts grew concerned with the potentially negative outcomes of the proposed legislation and became involved in the process by opening up discussions with senators from the ruling Workers' Party. In 2007, Senator Aluizio Mercadante of the Workers' Party began negotiations with Senator Azeredo to incorporate minor changes that civil society was demanding. In June-July 2008, a new version of the legislation was agreed on by Social Democrat and Workers' Party senators.[5] But because the bill had been further amended it had to be once again approved in the Chamber of Deputies.

Civil society campaign against the cyber crime bill

Four days before the amended bill was to be voted on again in the Senate, university professors André Lemos and Sergio Amadeu and internet activist João Caribé

1 www.camara.gov.br/proposicoesWeb/prop_mostrarintegra?codteor=284461&filename=Tramitacao-PL+84/1999

2 www.camara.gov.br/proposicoesWeb/prop_mostrarintegra?codteor=284469&filename=Tramitacao-PL+84/1999

3 www.safernet.org.br/site/sites/default/files/PLS_Azeredo-CCJ-versao-protolocada-em-20-06-2006-1.pdf

4 conventions.coe.int/Treaty/en/Treaties/Html/185.htm

5 www6.senado.gov.br/diarios/BuscaDiario?tipDiario=1&datDiario=26/06/2008&paginaDireta=23637

launched a petition asking for senators to veto the proposed legislation.[6] One week after it was launched, the petition gathered nearly 30,000 signatures, with this number growing as the campaign evolved (it had gathered some 160,000 signatures by July 2011).

The debate became so polarised that the Brazilian Ministry of Justice intervened in order to work on a compromise between supporters of stronger criminal penalties and advocates for more freedom on the internet. NGOs and academic groups, such as the Getúlio Vargas Foundation's Centre for Technology and Society[7] and the University of São Paulo's Research Group on Public Policies for Access to Information (GPoPAI),[8] produced technical studies that were sent both to the Ministry of Justice and the Congress highlighting the negative effects of the bill and asking for it to be stopped. Mainstream media gave broad coverage to the controversy – turning what was on the face of it a sectoral concern into a major political topic polarising Brazil's two largest political parties. In 2008 and 2009, industry, civil society and police institutions organised seminars all over the country, and Congress called for several public hearings. The topic was so controversial that even though it had been discussed in Congress for ten years, it had not been settled (and remains unresolved at the time of writing this article – August 2011).

From a criminal law to a civil rights framework

A significant twist in the debate occurred when Professor Ronaldo Lemos from the Getúlio Vargas Foundation published an article[9] arguing that a civil regulatory framework had to precede a criminal framework for the internet. Slowly, the idea that civil law must precede criminal law gained support and became part of the demands of activists opposing the cyber crime bill. Lemos' idea was that we needed a regulatory framework – that is, regulation of the internet services provided to customers which is especially clear on civil liability. However, activists expanded the idea to include a civil *rights* framework – a change probably inspired by discussions at the Internet Governance Forum on a Charter of Human Rights and Principles for the Internet.[10] The demand became an integral part of the campaign and found its decisive moment at the 10th International Free Software Forum (FISL) that took place in Porto Alegre in July 2009.[11] FISL is an annual free software forum, similar to Linux World, although significantly more political. At the tenth forum, organisers decided to place the threats to a free internet at the core of the proceedings. Both President Lula and Chief of Staff Dilma Rousseff (now the president of Brazil) spoke at the closing conference of the event. In his speech, Lula criticised the cyber crime bill as a threat to freedom of information and said that his government would be willing to do whatever was necessary to correct the situation, including changing civil regulation.[12] The Ministry of Justice promptly reacted to the remark by starting a process to build a civil rights framework for the internet in October 2009.

The public consultation for the civil rights framework

The Ministry of Justice decided that the public consultation process should follow the open and participatory nature of the internet, and so opted for a three-step process. First, it commissioned a comparative study of civil regulations of the internet and, based on experiences in other countries, it came out with a systematic list of topics that the civil rights framework should encompass. This list[13] was then put out for public consultation for a period of 45 days, and posted to a website which allowed free comment and input, including suggestions for the removal or addition of clauses. Comment was unmoderated and did not require logging in. More than 800 contributions were received during this phase of the consultation.

The contributions were then consolidated and a draft revised text was published[14] for further public discussion and comment. An additional 1,168 contributions were received by May 2010. Public debate spilled over onto blogs, into public seminars and the press – which itself followed the debate closely. The process, given its openness and participatory nature, was so successful that it quickly became an international benchmark for participatory and transparent law making.[15]

6 Lemos, A., Amadeu, S. and Caribé, J. (2008) Pelo veto ao projeto de cibercrimes: em defesa da liberdade e do progresso do conhecimento na Internet brasileira. www.petitiononline.com/veto2008/petition.html

7 Centro de Tecnologia e Sociedade (2008) Comentários e Sugestões sobre o Projeto de Lei de Crimes Eletrônicos. www.culturalivre.org.br/artigos/estudo_CTS_FGV_PL_crimes_eletronicos.pdf

8 Grupo de Pesquisa em Políticas Públicas para o Acesso à Informação (2008) Carta ao Ministro da Justiça. www.gpopai.usp.br/wiki/images/f/ff/Contribuicao_pl.pdf

9 Lemos, R. (2007) Internet brasileira precisa de marco regulatório civil, *UOL*, 25 May. tecnologia.uol.com.br/ultnot/2007/05/22/ult4213u98.jhtm

10 For more information, see the website of the Internet Rights and Principles Coalition at: internetrightsandprinciples.org

11 fisl.softwarelivre.org/10/www

12 The full speech is available on YouTube: www.youtube.com/watch?v=JqULQ5Yv3vw&feature=related

13 culturadigital.br/marcocivil/consulta

14 culturadigital.br/marcocivil/debate

15 It has since then been adapted to other law-making processes such as the reform of copyright law.

Current state of affairs and the new legislative agenda

As of August 2011, both the cyber crime bill and the civil rights framework proposal have re-emerged as public topics for debate and discussion. A wave of hacker attacks on government websites in July 2011 and the fact that the civil rights framework is about to be sent to Congress reignited the controversy. Because the cyber crime bill was still considered excessive, Deputy Paulo Teixeira called for public consultation on an alternative cyber crime law.[16] The draft consisted of a cyber crime law which was much more limited in its reach, and much more practical. Civil society campaigners and government officials are now rebuilding their legislative agenda in order to defend the joint approval of the civil rights framework and the new cyber crime bill. If both proposals are approved, the experience would stand out as a model of democratic process in which strong civil society mobilisation succeeded in defeating powerful corporate and state interests, and securing a public-interest legal framework.

Action steps

Given the context of the above discussion, the advocacy focus areas for civil society appear clear:

- Work towards the approval of the civil rights framework for the internet.
- Work towards rejecting Senator Eduardo Azeredo's cyber crime bill.
- Work towards the approval of Deputy Paulo Teixeira's alternative cyber crime bill.

16 edemocracia.camara.gov.br/web/seguranca-da-internet/wikilegis/-/wiki/Projeto_de_Lei_Alternativo/In%C3%ADcio

BULGARIA

IS FREEDOM OF EXPRESSION AND ASSOCIATION ON THE NET WORKING ON THE STREET?

BlueLink Foundation
Vera Staevska
www.bluelink.net

Introduction

With global and national analysts emphasising a growing number of human rights violations in Bulgaria in 2010, it is no surprise that online activists are sounding the alarm that human rights are similarly not well protected online. Ethnic discrimination, police violence, the detention of asylum seekers, repression on freedom of speech and surveillance, pressure over media and personal communication, political pressure on the judiciary system, child abuse and anti-gay and lesbian aggression are the key human rights violations according to several institutions. Amnesty International,[1] the European Union (EU) Fundamental Rights Agency,[2] the United States (US) Department of State[3] and the Bulgarian Helsinki Committee have identified negative developments in all major spheres of human rights protection compared to previous years.

With regard to human rights on the internet in Bulgaria, this report will focus on two aspects of freedom of expression and association online:

- Discursive dominance of hate speech in online activism that raises several questions: Is this freedom not used to violate the rights of vulnerable groups? Is civil society too weak to prevent undemocratic forces from exploiting online freedom? And if this is so, do we need this right to be checked and regulated?
- The Bulgarian perspective of the internet as a basic human right (the right to access vs. the right to privacy).

Policy and political background

In recent years Bulgaria's continuous transition to a "normal" country in the Western mould has been accompanied by the growing resentment of its citizens over the failed promise of democracy. The dominant model is one of paralegal, post-communist "elites" in power with little cultural capital, but exerting an economic power that is the result of shady deals during the privatisation of state property. The "normalisation" of the state regime is currently going through what can be called a "feudal" stage with crime bosses having political impact. This stage has shown the general public that the Bulgarian transformation has been manifestly undemocratic and has failed the promise of liberal development and civic rights. The ideas connected to Western-type democracies have consequently been losing their appeal, and "human rights" and "civil society" are widely perceived as ideologemes that veil corrupt practices of stealing EU and international funds with no effect on the average Bulgarian's life. Online discourses of hate and virtual communities based on intolerance are now striking, given that many used to assume that the internet was a tool to fight oppression.

At the same time, authentic movements for social change come up against this paradigm of state control, which is being reinforced by capitalist monopolies. The pressure for elites on free speech that is a result of the political economy is evident in digital rights violations – both through illegal surveillance and official attempts at introducing legislation to grant the state control of internet communication. This paradigm of state control is specific to Bulgaria due to economic monopolies being closely intertwined with political power and the shady privatisation of prior communist-state properties. However, its discourse benefits from the Western European model of capitalism, which also imposes state control over internet consumption due to producer concerns over the free use of their products – a concern which the Western democracies explain as protecting copyright and stemming from the need for protection against piracy and cyber crime. Though broadband access has been a basic right in Finland since 2009,[4] EU policies stress child protection and commercial rights rather than free access to online communication, as the debates[5] around the

1 www.amnesty.org/en/region/bulgaria/report-2010
2 fra.europa.eu/fraWebsite/attachments/AR_2010-conf-edition_en.pdf
3 www.state.gov/documents/organization/160182.pdf
4 articles.cnn.com/2009-10-15/tech/finland.internet.rights_1_internet-access-fast-internet-megabit?_s=PM:TECH
5 www.edri.org/files/EDRi_ecommerceresponse_101105.pdf; www.edri.org/files/shadow_drd_report_110417.pdf

E-Commerce Directive (2000/31/EC) and the Data Retention Directive (2006/24/EC) show.

And even as the EU secures measures aimed at online privacy and anonymity of retained data, national legislation can easily bypass this to secure legal state surveillance, as has been the case in Bulgaria.[6]

Freedom of expression and association online used to violate the rights of vulnerable groups and to promote hate speech

A wave of racism and homophobia can be observed online in Bulgaria, as tolerance becomes associated with state and international support for Roma and homosexuals. This support is felt as "positive discrimination" – discrimination that grants Roma specific goods that are not accessible to others and thus neglects the needs of the majority. And – ridiculously – spontaneously formed online civic groups are very often formed in reaction to the overly political correctness and thus, for intrinsically non-civic goals – for example, the extermination of minorities in different forms.

On the other hand, traditional civic rights movements have gone online too. Though online activism seems to be the fashion and a lot of online "profiles" are adorned with affiliations to internet causes in defence of human rights, fewer participants are seen at offline meetings and protests that have the actual weight when attempting to change official policies.

In fact, extremist online groups are meeting more frequently offline than online social activists. While social researchers point out the growing number of Facebook groups and causes in support of neo-fascism, reminiscent of Hitler's treatment of minorities, and protest against social policies supporting the long-term unemployment of Roma,[7] offline incidents show the neo-Nazis do act in accordance with their claims. In the summer of 2010 two cases of violence emphasised the fact that the problem of intolerance is not a dormant or discursive one any more.

On 4 June 2010 a meeting was organised in support of human rights of Asian immigrants in Bulgaria. A group of several young people headed for the meeting were stalked in a public transport tram and publicly beaten up with metal posts by fifteen neo-Nazis. The human rights meeting itself was attended by only 100 participants. Another case in line with growing racism is the group beating of Roma by neo-Nazis in close proximity to the Presidency building in central Sofia on 11 June 2010. A murder case of a boy, beaten to death in a park, happened in 2008 – and was only solved in June 2010 when the police arrested a group of youngsters who said they beat the boy because he "looked like a gay".

Of course, civic reaction to these stories and a growing number of online protests against xenophobic aggression marked the end of 2010 – including responses from new human rights protection groups,[8] statements by the Bulgarian Helsinki Committee[9] and the Bulgarian Greens,[10] and a well-attended flash mob in the centre of Sofia, protesting human rights violations and aggression.[11]

However, the tendency towards intolerance and aggression is not checked and is the most popular cause in Bulgarian Facebook life. Opposition to the attempt to legalise state control of online content, including from bloggers and online activists, has amounted to some 5,700 signatures online,[12] while people who have declared online that they refuse to pay taxes for non-paying Roma citizens total some 20,841. Extreme groups declaring that "Roma should be turned into soap", or making similar statements, are created and deleted daily.

In 2011 hate speech flourished in reaction to a street murder by the driver of a crime boss who had been linked for years to political corruption and cited as a "Roma king". Online and offline protests against "Roma crime" began, and calls for the "protection of Bulgarians against Roma" have flourished.[13] Attempts to review the crime as part of political-criminal monopolies in Bulgaria have been ignored in favour of an ethnic perspective on the case. Several big cities have witnessed street rallies against "tsiganisation"[14] and Roma crime.

6 store.aip-bg.org//publications/ann_rep_eng/08.pdf

7 balkans.blog.lemonde.fr/2011/02/21/sur-facebook-aussi-on-naime-pas-les-roms; www.julianpopov.com/main_page.html?fb_1383111_anch=9636455; www.dnevnik.bg/analizi/2010/01/26/848230_ekaterina_i_iskreno_sujaliava_za_hitler; www.capital.bg/politika_i_ikonomika/bulgaria/2010/10/12/974755_edna_po-razlichna_kauza

8 stopnazi-bg.blogspot.com/2011/02/25022011.html

9 e-vestnik.bg/9284

10 www.zelenite.bg/3059

11 nookofselene.wordpress.com/2010/06/11/anti-nazi-protest

12 www.facebook.com/group.php?gid=357395585520

13 english.aljazeera.net/news/europe/2011/09/201192653812872853.html; www.turkishweekly.net/news/124179/170-arrested-in-bulgaria-after-second-39-roma-protests-39-night.html

14 This term is becoming very popular in Bulgaria. It comes from "tsigane" the polite everyday word for "Roma" ("tsigane" = "gypsy"). "Tsiganisation" is used to indicate that the society is changing from a "Bulgarian" to a "tsigane" society.

At the same time, social networks are becoming the playground of users "deleting" friendships on the basis of support for or opposition to hate speech groups and causes.[15] Attempts to clarify that the crime had no ethnic character and to bring the issue back to a crime of politically protected classes and corruption of police practice[16] are almost unheard, and largely regarded as yet another dismissal of the citizens' rights of ethnic Bulgarians.

However, the case has provoked official reaction against hate speech, with an emphasis on hate speech on the internet. This official response is needed, since a lot of the street aggression against Roma was initiated on Facebook and online forums. Bulgarian Chief Prosecutor Boris Velchev has ordered that the prosecution of hate crimes be intensified, which should have been current police practice if Bulgarian law was abided by anyway.[17] According to Articles 162 and 163 of the Criminal Code, hate speech and provocation of aggression in written or oral form, including online communication, is a criminal offence, subject to a fine of BGN 5,000 to 10,000 (approx. EUR 2,500 to 5,000) and incarceration of two to four years.

Online media and forums should cooperate with police to enforce the illegality of online hate speech. However, prosecution against hate speech is often opposed on the grounds of the right of freedom of expression when specific cases are investigated, and priorities between these different human rights are never clearly set. According to the Bulgarian Constitutional Court, freedom of speech should be granted to all kinds of ideas, including shocking and offensive ones. Because of this Bulgaria still needs public debate and regulation of freedom of speech and its limitations in cases when other basic human rights are concerned.

The Bulgarian perspective on the internet as a basic human right: The right to access vs. the right to privacy

Since 2010 the world has been celebrating the power of the internet as a tool for mass protest movements (in Egypt, Libya, etc.) and has subsequently pleaded the guarantee of access to internet action as a basic right. However, Bulgaria still suffers from self-censorship in online communication and passive activism of internet users – mainly due to internet privacy issues and legal and illegal state surveillance. In a broader perspective, the EU context of the right to access is fighting a powerful counterforce that argues the necessity of state intervention for internet security. This paradigm presumes the internet is intrinsically a tool for cyber crime and violating others' rights (e.g. piracy and child abuse).

As pointed out in the Bulgaria country reports in GISWatch 2009 and 2010,[18] Bulgaria has been witnessing a state strategy to legalise the traditional practice of surveillance over private communication, including online communication. Since 2010 this has been continued. As an NGO called Access to Information Programme pointed out in its annual report,[19] we are again witnessing attempts to pass the draft bill to the Electronic Communications Act (ECA), which

> (...) aimed to provide the Ministry of Interior with unauthorized direct electronic access to the communication data retained by providers of electronic services (...) i.e. information on who, where, when and with whom one has written or spoken by electronic means (through mobile phones or the internet). (...) [Since May 2010] the ECA provides for two categories of access to traffic data. One is the data used by the security services for the purposes of their operational activities, and another is the access of the prosecutors and investigative services for the purpose of specific criminal proceeding. The two types of access are treated differently – the first one requires a court warrant and the second not. Thus, the standard for securing the rights of individuals is lower than before the 2010 amendments to the ECA.[20]

Given this background, Bulgaria's concern with internet rights is quite different from the surging global cry for securing internet access as a tool for human rights movements. Whatever the country-specific debates and consequences, social uprisings in North Africa and the Middle East since 2010 have been fought online as much as in the streets. Oppression has been seen to fight back by stopping internet access. In reaction, in June 2011, the UN declared internet access a basic human right.[21] However, in Bulgaria the struggle is not to secure access to internet communication but rather to secure the right for this communication to be

15 globalvoicesonline.org/2011/09/25/bulgaria-clashes-between-roma-people-and-ethnic-bulgarians-in-katunitsa

16 stopnazi-bg.org/declarations/73-konfliktat-v-katunica-ne-e-etnicheski

17 www.dnevnik.bg/bulgaria/2011/09/27/1164246_koga_ezikut_na_omrazata_e_prestuplenie

18 www.giswatch.org/en/2009 and www.giswatch.org/en/2010

19 store.aip-bg.org /publications/ann_rep_eng/2010.pdf

20 Ibid., p. 19.

21 www2.ohchr.org/english/bodies/hrcouncil/docs/17session/A.HRC.17.27_en.pdf

free. Since surveillance results in censorship and more commonly in self-censorship, the efforts of Bulgarian activists have been focused on ensuring legislation that enforces online privacy. This digital activism is not fighting for offline change, but for the tools that might some day help bring it about. Ironically, nobody would think of denying anyone internet access in Bulgaria, largely because it is far from the active online causes and communities that result in offline protests and change as seen elsewhere.

The official Bulgarian discourses – and for that matter EU discourses – stress security and consumption on the internet rather than freedom and social bonding. The national one due to political oppression, the EU one due to the commercialisation of policies. The result in Bulgaria is a relatively high technological society where information and communications technologies (ICTs) are only passively used.

The passivity of virtual activism has often been lamented. The fact that online campaigning and free expression and association on the net have no or insufficient offline impact is well known. However, an analysis is needed on why some societies (arguably Egypt) do and some (e.g. Bulgaria) do not achieve offline social change by means of online campaigning and the free expression and association that the internet provides.

In this context Bulgaria continues to be marked by fighting for the right to allow online activism but not practising it yet, and, as mentioned, the right to access to the internet has never been denied. One reason is perhaps that this is the characteristic of consumption-oriented societies where social goals are not priorities for the individual – that is, the characteristics of societies where social bonds are weaker.

One interpretation for the Bulgarian case could also be that, similar to other post-socialist societies, Bulgaria is experiencing a rise of individualistic, hedonistic attitudes to technology. This is a result of an erroneous vision of post-totalitarian transition focused on capitalism and consumption, rather than democracy, civil liberties, or public participation in governance and decision making. On the one hand, the internet has proven to be a powerful tool for civic activism and collective work – the civil sector of the 21st century cannot do without online collaboration. But on the other hand, within an individualistic culture, there is a "dark side" to the world wide web that facilitates a post-modern hedonism and undermines collective social links. And that is why public pressure for legislation that secures online activism is very weak and limited to the very few activists who were the first to take up the cause of digital rights in Bulgaria.

Conclusions

The growing tiredness of democracy is threatening to bring extremist aggression to the centre of Bulgarian public norms. Online communication stays virtual when defending human rights, but spills over onto the street when violating them. In this context, digital activists need more support from human rights NGOs and workers, in order to secure privacy rights online and to join forces in using ICTs to reinforce weak community links and democratic values.

Action steps

- Besides protests against state surveillance of online communication there is a need for formal regulations to limit violations of human rights online, in whatever form that violation occurs (writing, images, video, etc.).
- Digital rights advocacy should be combined with the concrete development of ICT tools that practising human rights activists can use to popularise "active" online activism – that is, tools that help to create a political effect offline. Good practices that are inspired by activist platforms used locally and abroad and slowly encourage supporters to go beyond the "like" function include spasigorata.net (online civic alerts on forest crime), sofia.urbanotopia.eu (online civic alerts on urban problems), fairelections.eu (online civic alerts on election fraud), and vote.bluelink.net (an online election mechanism for internal selection of NGO representatives for governmental committees).
- NGOs need to push state institutions into providing spaces for online consultation and services that help citizens exercise their rights. Some of the platforms cited above are examples of how civil society groups can start a service that should be provided through e-government, and then push the government to follow up and support the piloted e-tool.

CAMEROON

THE INTERNET AND MOBILE TECHNOLOGY IN SOCIAL RESISTANCE AND PUBLIC DEMONSTRATIONS

PROTEGE QV
Sylvie Siyam, Serge Daho and Emmanuel Bikobo
www.protegeqv.org

Introduction

Cameroon is a central African country with a population estimated at just over 19 million in 2009.[1] According to International Telecommunication Union (ITU) figures, the country had 750,000 internet users as of June 2010; this means 3.9% of the population and a penetration rate of 4%.[2] Since 6 November 1982, Cameroon has been under the leadership of President Paul Biya.

After the troubled period of 1990-1992, during which the opposition staged huge civil unrest rallies to force the head of state out of power – called "Opérations Villes Mortes" (Operation Dead Cities or Ghost Towns) – the country enjoyed a decade of relative stability. However, this came to an end in February 2008, when riots over food prices (later called "hunger riots") erupted in several cities, with infrastructures ransacked, cars and vehicles smashed, shops burnt down and many deaths reported.

Since the hunger riots, 23 February has been the day in the year when discontent Cameroonians take to the streets to demonstrate or to commemorate the February 2008 martyrs.

Echoing what happened in Tunisia and in Egypt, this year's demonstrations were to be different, according to the hopes and aspirations of protest organisers. During the weeks before the February demonstrations, they announced that this year was the start of Cameroon's "Egypt-style" revolt: "After Egypt, Cameroon next" was a message that spread throughout the internet and on flyers. There were calls for a popular peaceful revolution and for President Paul Biya to step down.

Cameroonian authorities reacted by suspending MTN mobile Twitter service[3] for security reasons. In fact, the government had grown increasingly wary of the role Twitter and other social networks could play in sparking an Egypt- or Tunisia-style uprising.

Policy and political context

Since Cameroon achieved independence and asserted its sovereignty at the international level, its successive constitutions have proclaimed its people's commitment to human rights as set out in the charter of the United Nations, the Universal Declaration of Human Rights, and the African Charter on Human and People's Rights.

It is therefore fitting that the current Constitution of 18 January 1996, amended in April 2008, grants constitutional status to all international legal instruments duly ratified by Cameroon, giving them precedence over domestic legislation.

At the national level, the preamble to the Constitution declares the Cameroonian people's commitment to the following values and principles which are guaranteed to all citizens, without distinction based on sex or race, amongst others:

- The freedom of communication, expression and the press
- The freedom of assembly and of association.

Numerous institutions and laws deal with the freedom of expression and communication in our country. These include, to name just a few:

- The National Commission on Human Rights and Freedoms created by Biya in February 1992. This governmental commission has conducted a number of investigations into human rights abuses and has been involved in training officials in matters of human rights.[4]
- Telecommunication Law No 98/014 of 14 July 1998, which regulates telecommunications, but does not deal with internet access.
- Law No 90/052 of 19 December 1999 on social communication.
- Law No 2010/012 of 21 December 2010 on cyber security and cyber crime.

These guarantees, while important, are deficient because there appear to be no provisions which limit how and when these freedoms can be restricted.

1 en.wikipedia.org/wiki/Cameroon
2 www.internetworldstats.com
3 MTN, a mobile telephony company, is the only service provider offering access to Twitter in Cameroon.
4 United States Department of State (1999) *Country Reports on Human Rights Practices for 1998*, Washington.

The suspension of MTN's Twitter service from 8 to 18 March 2011 came as a violation of both Article 19 of the Universal Declaration of Human Rights and the freedom of communication guaranteed in national legislation. It also prompted fears of an attempt by the Cameroonian authorities to suppress the use of social networks, which had played a crucial role in the political unrest in the Arab world. Speaking on behalf of the government, Tchiroma Bakary, the minister of communication and government spokesman, told the Agence France Presse that it was the government's job to protect the nation.

How significant is the internet in social protest in Cameroon?

Some opposition political parties, associated with certain figures of civil society in the diaspora, launched a series of messages commemorating the February 2008 events using printed leaflets and a campaign blog called the Collective of Democratic and Patriotic Organisations of Cameroonians in the Diaspora (CODE).[5] The Facebook page of writer Alain Patrice Nganang[6] and SMS text messages were also used. An event was planned during what had become known as "martyrs' week". This started modestly on the due date, 23 February 2011. Protesters in Douala and in Yaoundé were quickly outnumbered by police. Cameroonian authorities were on a high alert over possible riots and flooded the two major cities with armed police and gendarmes controlling major access roads, central squares and government buildings. Vehicles entering the cities were stopped and checked. The troops monitored any unforeseen gathering of people that could form the nucleus of a protest, asking them to disperse.

Protesters found a difficult environment partly due to the massive police presence, and also because most of the calls for Cameroonians to stage an "Egypt-like" revolution indeed had come from the diaspora, with even independent media in Cameroon giving protests calls little attention and main opposition figures remaining silent. Many Cameroonians therefore felt the initiative was not from within the country and disconnected from local realities. Outside the cities of Douala and Yaoundé, there were no reports of protests.

Besides this massive deployment of troops on the streets, the government blocked MTN's Twitter service for almost ten days. This raised a fundamental question: Was the internet power enough to threaten our government? As a communication medium unique in its kind, and unlike any other medium before, the internet allows individuals to express their ideas and opinions directly to a world audience and easily to each other. This power to give and receive information, so central to any conception of democracy, provides a vital connection between the internet and human rights and could be considered a threat to repressive regimes.[7]

Because of this, the blocking of MTN's Twitter service can be seen as a human rights violation by Cameroonian authorities. Reporters Without Borders condemned the lack of transparency surrounding the block and feared its implications for online freedom of expression in Cameroon. It said: "We hope the blocking of Twitter via SMS is not a prelude to other kinds of censorship of mobile phone services or tighter controls on the internet. Everything suggests that the authorities are trying to stop microblogging. We deplore the apparent readiness to impose censorship for the least reason, especially when the target is the peaceful expression of opinions."[8]

Yet social networks do not have many users in Cameroon. Facebook, for example, is used by only 1.5% of the population (176,666 Facebook users on 31 December 2010; a 4% penetration rate in the country according to ITU figures).[9] Only around 50 people were affected by the suspension of MTN's Twitter service – so was it worth blocking it?

According to John Clarke,[10] in order to make a case for disobeying the law as a significant element of social mobilisation, it is necessary to establish three things. First, you have to demonstrate that the society you propose to challenge is very seriously unequal and unjust. If the grievance does not rise to this standard, there is little basis for taking defiant action. Second, you have to show that the state structure and laws of this same society serve, in a fundamental fashion, to perpetuate the injustices you are opposing. Third, beyond demonstrating a deep degree of unfairness, you have to show that the historical record and the present situation would suggest that defying the rules of society offers the distinct possibility of success.

5 lecode.canalblog.com

6 www.cause.com/causes/387444

7 Centre for Democracy and Technology (2000) *The Internet and Human Rights: An Overview*. www.cdt.org/international/000105humanrights.shtml

8 www.ifex.org/cameroon/2011/03/25/twitter_blocked

9 www.internetworldstats.com

10 Clarke, J. (2003) *Social Resistance and the Disturbing of the Peace*. www.ohlj.ca/archive/articles/41_23_clarke.pdf

Were these issues combined in Cameroon's case? Yet Bakary attacked the protest organisers saying they wanted to "destroy the nation".

Conclusion

Article 19 of the Universal Declaration of Human Rights states: "Everyone has the right to freedom of opinion and expression; this right includes freedom to hold opinions without interference and to seek, receive, and impart information and ideas through any media, and regardless of frontiers." Therefore, no matter what the means, government restrictions on speech or access to the speech of others violate basic freedom of expression protections.

Though we have to acknowledge that few things could be more threatening to some regimes than access to and use of a medium that knows no boundaries and is very hard to control, protecting freedom of expression on the internet is crucial because free expression is the foundation of democracy, essential to the individual's pursuit of happiness and a tool that provides protection for other fundamental human rights.

It may have been that the government's response to the protests was an anxiety about foreign influence in local affairs – including the influence of Cameroonians abroad. The internet is yet to be used as the most effective means for communicating human rights or to expose human rights violations. Online campaigns inside Cameroon were accompanied by print campaigns, as a matter of necessity. And activists used a website run by exiled Cameroonians to urge their fellow countrymen to learn from the revolutions in Tunisia and Egypt.

Action steps

A number of steps should be taken to address the concerns described above:

- Policies that limit censorship of online communication should be formulated.
- Law No. 90/052 of 19 December 1999 on social communication should be amended to take into account the internet.
- The legislation setting up the National Commission on Human Rights and Freedoms should be reformed to conform to the UN principles relating to the status of national institutions to guarantee its independence.[11]
- Citizens are not mere consumers of content, but also creators of content on the internet. Taken as an analogy, activists should not only use the internet to call for protest, but also to formulate ideas that can contribute constructively to the development of a country.

11 UN General Assembly resolution 48/134 of December 1993, annex.

CHINA

THE INTERNET: CHINA'S FOURTH ESTATE

Danwei
Jeremy Goldkorn
www.danwei.org

Introduction

China's investigative journalists and a small group of news publications have become increasingly bold over the last decade. But the internet is now the most powerful force in China's emerging rights movements, the exposure of abuses of power, freedom of expression and the development of a real civil society. Emboldened by several high-profile cases of injustices brought to light by online activism, concerned citizens and reporters are taking to social media to air their grievances and attract publicity to their cases.

The official response usually includes repression of information. The Chinese government continues to operate the world's most extensive censorship apparatus, affecting both traditional media and the internet. Because of this and other factors, not all citizen grievances or activist and journalist campaigns are successfully exposed on the internet.

Nonetheless, the huge numbers of Chinese citizens online – more than 450 million people at the time of writing – and the blazing speed with which social media spread certain kinds of information mean that news about breaking events can no longer be hidden by the authorities.

To understand how the internet is changing challenges to the abuse of power and social resistance in China, it is useful to look at two events that took place in late 2010 and July 2011:

- "My dad is Li Gang" – a fatal hit-and-run accident by a well-connected young man who was exposed online in October 2010
- The Wenzhou high-speed railway disaster on 23 July 2011.

Precedent: The brick factory slave children

Precedents were set many years before the "My dad is Li Gang" scandal broke on the Chinese internet. The watershed moment was perhaps the 2007 exposure of a brick kiln run using slave labour.

In June 2007, an internet user posted a letter to a Chinese internet forum appealing for help. The authors of the letter were some of the parents of more than 400 children who had been kidnapped and forced to work as slaves in a brick factory in Shanxi province. After finding out where their children were imprisoned, the group of parents attempted to rescue their children, but were prevented by security guards and local police working in cahoots with the brick factory's owners.

Within a week of publishing their appeal for help online, the affair became a cause célèbre, and the Shanxi provincial government shut down the factory and liberated the children. The nationwide scandal erupted online first, driven by citizen anger, while the traditional news media had to play catch-up. The first traditional media to report on the case were the more commercial and independent local news organisations, but within a week of the scandal breaking online, even the highly controlled central government news organisations such as Xinhua News Agency were forced to publish stories about it.

This pattern has been repeated many times since 2007: an outrage of some kind occurs; citizens post text, photos or videos about it on the internet; the postings are forwarded virally; and only then do the traditional media catch up and report, usually followed by government action. Once the public outcry has been appeased, censorship usually steps up again, and many of the internet postings about it disappear.

Case 1: My dad is Li Gang

The "My dad is Li Gang" case followed the same pattern. Baoding is a city of more than 1.5 million people in north China's Hebei province. On 16 October 2010, a 22-year-old man named Li Qiming was drunk and driving his Volkswagen Magotan down a street inside the campus of Hebei University in Baoding to take his girlfriend back to her dormitory.

Li drove into two rollerblading university students, Chen Xiaofeng (20) and Zhang Jingjing (19). Chen died soon afterwards and Zhang was seriously injured. Li ignored the injured students and drove away. Before he left the university grounds, some campus security guards tried to stop him, but he screamed out of his car window, "Sue me if you dare! My dad is Li Gang!" and drove off.

Li Gang was the deputy director of the Baoding public security bureau (i.e. police authority) in Beishi district, where Hebei University is located.

Li Qiming was not pursued or arrested after the incident, even when Chen died of her injuries the next day. Some bystanders had seen the accident and Li's escape and complained of it to local news media and on the internet. But nothing happened to Li, and there was evidence to suggest a cover-up was orchestrated to keep the news out of the media. The police did not investigate.

Some students who had witnessed the accident continued to post about it online. In particular, they focused on Li's words, "My dad is Li Gang." Four days after the accident, a blogger organised an online competition which required entrants to use the phrase "My dad is Li Gang" in a poem written in classical Chinese style. There were hundreds of submissions and thousands of users voted for their favourite poem.

The phrase became an internet meme: photoshopped images and spoof videos of George W. Bush and other famous figures appeared using "My dad is Li Gang" to signify arrogance, corruption and a lack of decency.

By 20 October, the "My dad is Li Gang" case was famous and newspapers started reporting on the case. On 22 October, Li Qiming appeared on the country's most highly censored and conservative media platform: the state-owned broadcaster CCTV's news channel. He wept and apologised for his deeds, but if anything the apology further enraged his online critics.

There were two important factors behind the strong online reaction to the Li Gang case. Firstly, the catch phrase "My dad is Li Gang", which rolls off the tongue in Chinese (*wo ba shi Li Gang*), made the case memorable and inspired all kinds of darkly humorous creativity.

Secondly, there is a growing resentment felt by ordinary young Chinese people about the conspicuous wealth gap that now exists in China between a tiny privileged elite and the rest of the country. This is clearly expressed in the Chinese online slang for the children of the rich and powerful: *fu er dai* (literally second-generation rich) and *guan er dai* (second generation of government officials). By contrast, many internet users identify themselves as *pimin* – rabble (or literally "buttocks people").[1] Li Qiming's expensive car and his confidence that he could escape even being questioned after a fatal accident that he caused made him a perfect symbol of the *fu er dai* and *guan er dai*, and the *pimin* rose up in rebellion online.

As the anger seemed to be directed against the system, not just Li Qiming, government censorship efforts stepped up. The story was scrubbed from some news websites. In the last few days of October, directives from government propaganda organisations, leaked onto the internet, ordered the media to stop "hyping" the Li Gang case. Li Qiming remained at liberty.

But the stink over Hebei University and Li Qiming would not go away, partly because people continued to circulate fresh information about the victims and Li Qiming, and viciously funny "My dad is Li Gang" jokes.

Despite restricted media coverage and a perception that the authorities were reluctant to investigate the case properly, Li Qiming was arrested in January 2011, and sentenced to six years in jail and a large fine at his trial at the end of that month.

Li remains in jail, and "My dad is Li Gang" remains a popular catch phrase on the Chinese internet.

Case 2: The 23 July Wenzhou high-speed rail crash

Just after 8 p.m. on a Saturday night, 23 July 2011, a bullet train on one of China's new high-speed railway lines smashed into the back of another train that had stalled on the tracks.

At 8:47 p.m., a passenger on the stalled train with the pseudonym Yangjuan Quanyang tweeted from her Sina Weibo microblog: "Help, the train D301 is derailed just ahead of South Wenzhou Station, passengers are crying and we cannot find any train crew, please help us!"

Since its launch in summer 2009, the Twitter-like Weibo, operated by established news portal Sina.com, has become one of China's most popular web services and a powerful tool for the exposure and viral spread of information. Weibo played a large role in the aftermath of the Wenzhou crash.

Late into Saturday night when most journalists and government information minders were sleeping, news of the crash circulated on Weibo. Yangjuan Quanyang's tweet was widely cited by media as the tweet that broke news of the crash.

By Sunday, the official death toll was above 30 and officials were blaming the accident on a lightning strike, an explanation that did not satisfy an outraged citizenry on the internet.

Claims emerged in news reports and on the internet that the rescue effort had stopped after only five hours of work. As much as ten hours after that, the final survivor was rescued, a two-and-a-half-year-old girl.

1 "Pi" literally means buttocks or "arse"; "min" means people. Rabble is probably the best translation to convey the sense of the word, but does not have the connotations of rudeness and slang. The phrase could also be translated as "ordinary bums".

Even worse, on Monday, eye witnesses posted photos and video to the internet that appeared to show some of the wrecked train carriages being buried, less than 48 hours after the accident.

One video showed a carriage being pulled from the railway viaduct. What looks like a dead body appears to fall out of a window to the ground. It looked like evidence was being covered up and nobody believed that a thorough investigation could be made in such a short amount of time. A Ministry of Railways spokesperson told the media that the carriages were being buried because of marshy ground underneath the viaduct, saying that they needed a solid platform for rescue equipment. He concluded his statement with the words, "Whether you believe it or not, I believe it," which quickly became an internet meme and, again, the source of darkly critical jokes.

The initial official explanation of the cause of the accident – that the first train was struck by lighting – was widely criticised on the internet and it fed into an already toxic public opinion of China's railway authorities. In the first half of the year, as the high-speed rail project was being hyped by foreign media and hailed as a glorious achievement of the Chinese Communist Party, doubts started to emerge. In February, Minister of Railways Liu Zhijun lost his job and an investigation began into charges of corruption. Some media organisations and bloggers reported tales of massive corruption: huge bribes and kickbacks, and stories that Liu used some of his ill-gotten gains to keep eighteen mistresses in a life of luxury. There were suggestions that quality was sacrificed for speed and that some of the corruption in the Ministry of Railways meant that inferior construction materials were used to allow officials to embezzle the money they saved.

The combination of public suspicions about the railway authorities and the poor handling of the rescue emboldened journalists and editors. In the week after the accident, small news magazines, websites, newspapers, and even the normally conservative CCTV News produced investigative reports and highly critical commentary. Even the Communist Party mouthpiece newspaper *The People's Daily* said in an editorial that China should not pursue "blood-stained GDP" – that growth should not take precedence over people's lives.

The period of openness did not last long: eight days after the accident, news of the accident and its investigation disappeared from newspaper front pages. Propaganda organisations began warning news media of consequences for failing to toe the new line, which amounted to "keep quiet, don't investigate and use only authorised reports."

Two poems from the "My dad is Li Gang" online protests, with their implied classical poetry references

The final couplet from the Tang Dynasty poem "Seeing [my friend] Xinjian Off at Lotus Tower", a sad poem about two friends parting:

洛阳亲友如相问
一片冰心在玉壶

If my friend at Luoyang asks of me, you may answer: "He's keeping his pure heart and affection in a jade vase, forever."

Li Gang version:

洛阳亲友如相问
就说我爸是李刚

If my friend at Luoyang asks of me, you may answer: "My dad is Li Gang."

The philosopher Mencius (*Mengzi* in Chinese, 372-289 B.C.) said:

君子穷则独善其身
达则兼善天下

If a gentleman is poor, he does good works in solitude; if he is rich, his work is for the good of the whole world.

Li Gang version:

穷则独善其身
富则开车撞人

If a gentleman is poor, he does good works in solitude; if he is rich, he drives his car into people.

There is no doubt that the blitz of media and internet reporting on the accident will result in a more thorough investigation. But it remains to be seen how transparent the authorities will be about the results.

Conclusions

The Li Gang and Wenzhou train crash cases illustrate how the internet is allowing Chinese citizens and activists to expose abuses of power – but not all such cases will captivate the public, and the results are mixed, depending on official sensitivity to the case.

A key factor in most successful cases is that the wrongdoing has some resonance with China's internet demographic, which is largely made up of under-40s with middle-class aspirations. In the two cases discussed here, resentment about the behaviour of the privileged elite and frustration with a train system that has been held up as a national achievement were key in inspiring a strong online response.

The two cases above can be contrasted with attempts by online activists to organise a "Jasmine Revolution" along the lines of the Egyptian and Tunisian uprisings, which failed to elicit a response from the Chinese public and only resulted in a crackdown on activists, lawyers and journalists.

The key difference is that the Jasmine Revolution calls had no concrete goals, nor did they attempt to redress a specific wrong, but rather to start a movement challenging the political system. Not only do such movements cause much harsher repression and censorship from the authorities, they do not generate a sympathetic response from ordinary people on the internet.

Action steps

The following key points are useful learning experiences for any civil society action planned for the internet:

- Publicising a grievance or a cause in China is complex. However, the internet has become the key tool for this type of communication, and the Weibo service is currently the most active and useful method.
- Calls to investigate a specific case of wrongdoing, especially when it involves common resentments, are more likely to be heard. Abstract targets and calls to change the political system do not go anywhere.
- Eye-witness accounts, photographic and video evidence, particularly of violent or fatal events, are the most likely materials to attract citizen interest. ■

COLOMBIA

SOCIAL MOBILISATION FOR THE DEFENCE OF DIGITAL RIGHTS AND AGAINST THE "LLERAS ACT"

Colnodo
Lilian Chamorro Rojas
www.colnodo.apc.org

Introduction

The governmental interest to control the use of the internet has become a reality in some countries through the introduction of controversial laws such as the Sinde and Hadopi Laws in Spain and France,[1] respectively, or laws introduced – albeit with public consensus – in Chile and Canada. International organisations have warned about the danger of restricting access to the internet without careful consideration of the implications, given the relevance the internet has for democracy and people's rights.[2]

The Colombian government has submitted a bill as part of the preconditions to sign the Free Trade Agreement (FTA) with the United States (US), known as the Lleras Bill. It has been widely criticised by many sectors of society because it goes against basic rights such as the freedom of expression and civil and political rights. The response from these sectors has been to organise a campaign against the bill using the internet and the media.

Policy and political background

The protection of intellectual property rights (IPR) has been an ongoing issue related to trade, at the national and international level. In Colombia this issue has been discussed in the National Council for Social and Economic Policy (CONPES)[3] plans and documents on intellectual property for 2008-2010.[4] According to many sectors these ignore the new uses and trends of digital media, such as free software and free licences among others, and only address traditional entertainment and cultural media.[5]

Likewise, in the present government's National Development Plan, intellectual property is defined as strategically necessary to promote innovation in the country and essential to negotiate and establish international trade agreements – therefore the need to make the required adjustments to the law.[6]

In the FTA with the US there is a chapter on IPR with an annexed letter on the responsibility of internet service providers (ISPs) to fulfil the function of protecting IPR.[7]

As a response to this requirement included in the FTA, on 4 April 2011, the Colombian government submitted Bill No. 241 of 2011, better known as the Lleras Bill. This bill aims to regulate the responsibility for infractions of the law regarding copyright and related rights on internet. Many sectors have opposed the bill, especially those that have been working for the promotion of Creative Commons licensing and GPL (General Public License), among others.

At the same time, a joint declaration on freedom of expression and opinion on the internet issued by representatives of the United Nations (UN), the Organization for Security and Co-operation in Europe (OSCE), the Organization of American States (OAS) and the African Commission on Human and People's Rights (ACHPR) has contributed with strong arguments for the defence of citizens' digital rights.[8]

Challenging the control of the internet

On 4 April 2011, Minister of the Interior and Justice German Vargas Lleras tweeted the following on his Twitter account @German_Vargas: "Let me tell you that today we have submitted the bill on copyrights. No more piracy on the internet. Authors, singers, composers are supporting us."[9]

Soon his message was retweeted and people reacted either with alarm[10] or jubilation.[11] The bill

1 alt1040.com/2011/01/ley-francesa-antidescargas-ley-sinde
2 Joint Declaration on Freedom of Expression and the Internet. www.cidh.oas.org/relatoria/showarticle.asp?artID=849&lID=1
3 CONPES is the body responsible for formulating economic policy in Colombia. For more information see: www.eltiempo.com/archivo/documento/MAM-221821
4 www.derechodeautor.gov.co/htm/Planeacion/Audiencias%20Publicas/2008cp3533.pdf
5 equinoxio.org/destacado/carta-abierta-conpes-plan-accion-sistema-propiedad-intelectual-2647
6 National Development Plan 2010-2014: "Prosperity for All", Executive Summary. www.dnp.gov.co/PORTALWEB/LinkClick.aspx?fileticket=4-J9V-FE2pl%3d&tabid=1238
7 www.tlc.gov.co/eContent/newsDetail.asp?id=5023&IDCompany=37&Profile=
8 http://www.cidh.oas.org/relatoria/showarticle.asp?artID=849&lID=2
9 twitter.com/#!/German_Vargas/status/54966217961779201
10 twitter.com/#!/ppco/status/54967808211173377
11 twitter.com/#!/Juliana_M_L/status/55086053769490434

was soon shared on the net.[12] In less than 24 hours net surfers had started the hashtag #leylleras[13] to exchange information on the subject. Despite the efforts of Vargas Lleras and Senator Roy Barreras (who had submitted the bill) to popularise the tag #leyderechosdeautor (#copyrightlaw), the hashtag #leylleras became widely popular and the bill became known as the Lleras Bill by the media and other social networks.[14]

Bill 241 is defined as the bill "[b]y which responsibility for infractions against copyright and related rights is regulated". Vargas Lleras warned in his blog: "Those who continue to support piracy, now beware! From now on, the law will punish them with prison – and severely – if Congress passes the bill."[15] The bill will punish ISPs and internet users by blocking or banning content or by cancelling internet accounts. Likewise there will be changes to the penal code, among other controversial issues.[16]

It is not surprising that people and groups working on issues such as free culture, free software and freedom of speech on the internet – who knew about similar processes in Spain and France[17] – became worried and began to meet virtually and face to face to discuss the bill and organise campaigns.

One of these meetings took place in Bogota. Carolina Botero, one of the supporters of Creative Commons in Colombia, got together with free software activists for the first time to discuss the bill. Given her involvement in promoting "copyleft"[18] in the country, Botero was up to date on laws concerning copyright, was in contact with the Colombian Copyright Office (DNDA) and knew about the government initiative to legislate on the issue.[19] However, she had been expecting wide consultation on the bill and the involvement of citizens in this consultation. When Carolina and others realised the bill was submitted without any consultation[20] they started a review of the bill and invited other people and groups to join in. Ultimately, the group RedPaTo2 (Net for All) was created, and according to Freddy Pulido from RedPaTo2,[21] it is open to all members of the public – artists, academics, scholars, technicians and lawyers, among others. RedPaTo2 aims for the drafting of a consensual bill with the participation of all citizens. To do so, they are working on the internet and meeting face to face,[22] campaigning in social networks and the media, informing the public, and making alternative proposals to the Lleras Bill.

Likewise, there is also a group called ReCrea,[23] formed by professionals – mainly artists and content creators – whose goal is the promotion of culture and education in Colombia. Its main objective is to make remixing of content legal by proposing the inclusion of an article in the bill.[24] This would enable reproduction without payment and/or require the user to obtain the permission of authors to use their cultural, scientific and medical work, as well as fragments of protected materials, mentioning the source, title and author and making sure that the final product is used for non-profit purposes.

Other movements with more political purposes, such as the recently created Partido Pirata de Colombia[25] (Pirate Party of Colombia), have also expressed their views on the bill and are generating content regarding the bill on blogs and social networks.[26]

The group Anonymous, known in several countries of the world for their protests and distributed denial of services (DDoS) attacks, has also taken action against the Colombian government and senators involved in passing the bill. They have attacked Colombian President Juan Manuel Santos' Facebook profile and the Twitter account of former president Alvaro Uribe.[27] In an interview given to the magazine *Enter*, specialising in technology in Colombia, Anonymous declared they want to spread information about the Lleras Bill in the media and to the general public.[28] Likewise, in an interview given to the newspaper *El Tiempo*, they explained in detail their reasons for rejecting the bill.[29]

12 twitter.com/#!/Legal_TIC/status/55012429775642624

13 twitter.com/#!/carobotero/status/55359278982242305

14 equinoxio.org/estancias/reacciones-contra-la-ley-lleras-11065 and www.delicious.com/knowledgefactory/leylleras?page=20, cited in www.enter.co/otros/la-transformacion-de-la-industria-cultural-primer-debate-sobre-leylleras

15 germanvargasllerasmij.blogspot.com/2011/04/se-regulan-los-derechos-de-autor-en.html

16 Colombian Congress Bill No. 241 "By which responsibility for infractions against copyright and related rights is regulated".

17 The Sinde Law in Spain and Hadopi Law in France.

18 en.wikipedia.org/wiki/Copyleft

19 Audio available at: aumana.typepad.com/el_complejo_de_prometeo/2011/01/director-nacional-de-derechos-de-autor-cuenta-lo-que-nos-espera-en-el-2011-en-pi-en-colombia.html

20 www.openbusinesslatinamerica.org/wp/2011/06/18/leylleras-cronica-de-una-polemica-social-anunciada

21 Interview on 4 July 2011.

22 Blog: redpatodos.co/blog; wiki: redpatodos.co/wiki; email list: lists.redpatodos.co/listinfo.cgi/general-redpatodos.co; Twitter: @RedPaTo2; identi.ca: identi.ca/tag/leyllera

23 www.recrea.co/sobre-recrea

24 www.recrea.co/comunicado/propuesta-recrea

25 www.soypirata.org

26 On Twitter @ppco and on Facebook at es-es.facebook.com/pirataco?sk=wall

27 alt1040.com/2011/08/anonymous-inicia-ataque-contra-el-gobierno-de-colombia

28 www.enter.co/internet/anonymous-habla-sobre-detenciones-en-espana-ley-lleras-y-onda-larga

29 www.infografiando.com/2011/04/entrevista-de-anonymous-colombia-el.html

There are other groups that have contributed to the discussion on blogs, networks and audio and video platforms.[30] The media have also contributed to the discussion by presenting different points of view.[31]

It is necessary to pause a moment to understand in more detail what has prompted this movement, given that the discussion is not limited to the articles of the law, but that the movement's foundation was laid before the tweet of Minister Vargas Lleras. Whereas the government's goal through the CONPES documents, the National Development Plan and the FTA has been to strengthen intellectual property and copyright, surfers have been using and promoting virtual tools to freely exchange, copy and co-create intellectual creation. "Here we are all co-creators," said Alejandra Bonnet, a member of ReCrea, in one of the talks organised in the Senate.[32] The bill served as a catalyst for these persons to gather around a theme. While not all groups use the same strategies, and there are points of disagreement among them, in the comments made on articles of the bill there are common elements.

One of the points of contention for critics of the bill is that judges will be excluded from the act of censoring, and an ISP can simply block content that is identified by an author or creator as infringing the law. This, as Carolina Botero explains, "changes the presumption of innocence, and puts at risk the due process of law and rights such as the freedom of expression and opinion, with disproportionate sentences for the alleged offenders, not only in the process but also in the suggested contractual provisions for the ISPs."[33] According to Juan Carlos Monroy of DNDA, the legal possibility of blocking content is already in place in the law, and the bill aims for the "detection and blocking of content" without a judge's sentence given that the justice system does not have the infrastructure required to implement the law.[34]

Another point of contention is the violation of the right to privacy, given that the bill allows passing on information about the alleged offender without due process.[35] Likewise, the possibility of preventing people who break the law more than once from accessing the internet is considered a violation of laws already in place. Here, according to UN Special Rapporteur Frank de la Rue, the bill violates Article 19 of the International Covenant on Political and Civil Rights, which stipulates the right of all individuals to seek, receive and impart information and ideas.[36]

Both defenders and critics of the bill are in agreement that it is a copy of the Digital Millenium Copyright Act (DMCA), which was adopted in 1998 in the US,[37] and that it does not take into account the deficiencies of the law in Colombia regarding modern technologies or the fact that Colombia belongs to the Inter-American Commission on Human Rights where "all dispositions on civil rights must be submitted to a judicial process."[38]

These groups have carried out several actions aimed at modifying the bill.[39] Social mobilisation has led Congress to organise discussion forums on the bill. The social movements have also organised meetings and invited people to discuss the issues. A session in Congress that was seen by more than 2,000 people on the internet all over the country was unprecedented – with viewers tweeting their comments.[40]

Some senators have listened to the objections. One of the senators opposing the bill organised several meetings aimed at sharing information.[41] The government's proposed dialogues on the bill[42] have not been accepted by the social movements, given that they have no impact at the level of Congress where the bill has been discussed.[43]

RedPaTo2 has submitted alternative models to the bill based on Chilean and Canadian laws, and expressed well-founded objections to some of the articles, such as the need to include exceptions for disabled people, among others. Likewise, it petitioned Congress to make the process more transparent and to work on consensus building in drafting the bill.[44]

In order to be approved, the bill has to pass four stages. The first one – in the First Commission of the

30 www.netvibes.com/hiperterminal#LeyLleras

31 www.enter.co/search/leylleras?t=c

32 www.enter.co/internet/internautas-hablaron-con-los-ponentes-de-la-leylleras

33 www.openbusinesslatinamerica.org/wp/2011/06/18/leylleras-cronica-de-una-polemica-social-anunciada

34 Conversatorio de Ley Lleras realizado en el Campus Party, Bogota, 2011.

35 www.openbusinesslatinamerica.org/wp/2011/06/18/leylleras-cronica-de-una-polemica-social-anunciada

36 www.enter.co/internet/onu-da-otro-golpe-a-leyes-antidescargas

37 www.enter.co/internet/%C2%BFpara-quien-legislamos-segundo-debate-inspirado-por-leylleras

38 Contribution made by Lorenzo Villegas, solicitor for Google Colombia, during the debate on the Lleras Bill in Congress. www.ustream.tv/recorded/14950504#utm_campaign=unknown&utm_source=14950504&utm_medium=social

39 RedPaTo2 submitted an open letter with 2,300 digital signatures before the debate of the bill. See: redpatodos.co/blog/ley-lleras-a-primer-debate

40 www.elespectador.com/opinion/columna-277957-librecultura-el-proceso-legislativo-leylleras

41 redpatodos.co/blog/y-ahora-que

42 Like the blog derechodeautor.wordpress.com launched on 6 April after the debate on social networks had begun.

43 www.karisma.org.co/carobotero/index.php/2011/04/12/participar-en-leylleras-una-cuestion-de-fondo-y-de-forma

44 redpatodos.co/blog/comentarios-juridicos-ponencia-primer-debate-ley-lleras

Senate – was already passed with seven votes in favour and three against, with some modifications to the articles but not the substantial ones expected by the activists.[45] This proves the urgency the government has in passing the bill instead of reaching a consensus.

The debate is not over yet. There are still three stages left before the bill is passed, and social movements have not given up the hope of securing a law that protects authors' copyrights and also the rights of internet users.

Conclusions

The mobilisation that the Lleras Bill has generated has shown the social changes brought about by the internet, not only regarding copyrights and intellectual property, but also regarding digital rights and citizens' participation in democracies.

On the one hand there are the industries and people that support and defend the traditional use of artistic and intellectual creations, and advocate for tools and content created to be protected by copyright. On the other hand, there are those who have found ways to access information that was previously inaccessible and, as they point out, they have transformed themselves from mere consumers to creative producers, generating new ways of creating and distributing their work. Therefore, it is important to consider both the needs of copyright holders and the need to have access to knowledge and information, which is a basic element in the promotion of culture and education. It is also important to highlight that what we are looking for is not the suppression of any of the alternatives of cultural creation, such as Creative Commons, but the *simultaneous* recognition of alternative models of cultural creation that have arisen in the digital era.

It is obvious that there is no consensus regarding digital rights and their impact on human rights. While governments are trying to control the internet, users are trying to defend freedom of expression and the information it provides. In this regard, the UN and other international organisations, in their declarations on human rights and the internet, have taken a big step forward by providing guidance to lead the discussion on key themes such as the freedom of expression, censorship and internet neutrality, among others.

Finally, this situation shows the changes that are beginning to take place in our democracies. The internet is a space that has allowed people to share, discuss and make proposals, something that has taken many governments by surprise. However, as Pulido points out, there is a lack of real participation beyond discussing or sharing information – therefore the need to get people involved in legislative matters.

Action steps

Considering the mobilisation that has taken place around the Lleras Bill, and the shared experiences of some of the actors involved, it is possible to identify the following actions:

- Share and disseminate information.
- Convene stakeholders to analyse and tackle the issue. Find people who can translate the jargon into something understandable for the general public.
- Get together in an organised manner. Define common objectives and the strategies that follow, with clear and agreed rules.
- Assemble a group of trusted people to carry out the activities – again, with clear and agreed rules.
- Search for appropriate technological tools to share information in a team, appointing people for administrative matters. For example, RedPaTo2 has chosen several ways for communicating, such as a blog to publish press releases and documents, using micro-blogging tools such as Twitter and identi.ca, and using EtherPad[46] for creating documents in a group, among others.
- Establish contact with the media and, if needed, with legislators supporting the mobilisation of people.
- Keep the topic in the spotlight by publishing information and organising virtual and non-virtual forums and debates.
- Participate in all the spaces in which the issue is debated or solved.
- Submit proposals to actors responsible for the decision making, as well as the general public.
- Support the process by broadcasting the sessions and debates of legislators and by publishing all related documents. ■

45 www.lasillavacia.com/historia/la-leylleras-un-proyecto-que-pone-en-jaque-al-congreso-25255

46 ietherpad.com

CONGO, REPUBLIC OF

VIOLATING PRIVACY ONLINE IN THE CONGO

AZUR Développement
Romeo Mbengou
www.azurdev.org

Introduction

The internet is revolutionising social, economic, cultural and political life across the world. It has brought an avalanche of opportunities to its millions of users, and has become a tool that we cannot do without; almost all services, administrative or otherwise, depend upon it either directly or indirectly. It also contributes positively to human rights in countries like our own, especially with regard to freedom of opinion and expression as set out in Article 19 of the Universal Declaration of Human Rights and Article 19 of the Constitution of Congo.

However, measures to prevent the abuse of the internet are lacking, and the absence of these measures impacts negatively on human rights.

There are many reasons for this, including the public's ignorance regarding its rights and how to demand them. There is also an absence of specific laws defining and punishing certain online violations of rights.

In this report we present some cases of human rights infringements, in particular those that relate to invasion of privacy on the internet.

Political and legislative context

The internet is governed by various laws that regulate information and communications technologies (ICTs) in the Congo. These include a 2001 law on freedom of information and communication; a 2009 law regulating the electronic communications sector; another law from 2009 which sets up a regulatory agency for the sector; and Decree No. 2010-554 (adopted in July 2010) which requires subscribers to landline and mobile telephone services to register with their identity documents, and deals with the storing of electronic communication data by service providers.

It is important to emphasise that this legal framework establishes and guarantees freedom of access to sources of information through the internet (Article 174 of the 2001 law, Article 3 of the 2009 law on electronic communications) and, by extension, freedom of expression. However, its limitations regarding the protection of privacy and of personal data should be noted. In this environment, besides criminal activity, the invasion of privacy is common practice.

This situation is exacerbated by the fact that many in the Congo are new to the internet – and it is becoming more popular. There is a widespread lack of awareness of online rights and security, and little legal knowledge amongst the general population.

In such a context, it is no surprise to note serious violations of human rights.

The violation of privacy on the internet

The following two cases were widely reported.

Case 1

This involves the director of a well-known company in Brazzaville, the capital, and one of his secretaries, who were away on work together in an African country. They were both married and were having an affair.

During their trip they photographed their sexual encounters and uploaded them onto the director's laptop. When the director returned to Brazzaville, his laptop encountered a problem and he handed it in to be repaired. In the course of his work, the maintenance technician discovered the file containing the images of the director and his secretary. The technician, under the pretext that he would not have been paid by the director, circulated the images by email. These very intimate and somewhat pornographic images, which showed the faces of the two, were circulated to hundreds of email addresses.

Case 2

In a similar vein, the second case involves a young woman who was raped in the Mansimou district close to the Djoue River in a suburb of Brazzaville. She was photographed while unconscious. The image of the young woman stripped almost naked was sent to hundreds of people via email. The woman herself may never have known that her picture was circulated online and the perpetrator never cared.

Situations like this arise regularly but are not reported; and the victims are not even aware that they have rights which they can demand. These two stories highlight the weakness in the regulation: public awareness.

The respect of the right to privacy amongst individuals

Nowadays technology puts powerful surveillance tools in the hands of individuals – for example, a mobile telephone equipped with a camera and internet connection, or digital cameras, which can be used to invade the privacy of others.

On the other hand, the November 2009 law on electronic communications and the 2010 decree on identification of subscribers show that the state has seemingly unlimited power to invade the privacy of its citizens in the interest of security.

There are no precise descriptions of situations which justify intrusions of privacy by the state in the decree. It seems that the state can access personal data under any pretext without the consent of the individual concerned, who can do nothing to stop it from happening.

The general public's poor understanding of ICT issues

Many people do not know that the publication of images in contexts such as those described above constitutes a serious infringement of their right to privacy, and that no one has the right to publish these images without the consent of the people involved. For various cultural reasons, it seems that people are not concerned about the protection of privacy on the internet.

There are lawsuits about defamation involving traditional forms of libel (particularly involving print and broadcasting media), but there are almost no cases of legal action for people whose privacy is invaded on the internet.

Roger Bouka, executive director of the Congolese human rights watchdog OCDH, says that:

> We believe that the dignity of all human beings should be respected, and it is not right for people to violate the privacy of another person. At the very least we believe that measures aimed at the protection of the individual, their privacy and their physical and moral integrity on the internet are necessary.

What happens is this: due to the fact these technologies are new and therefore not yet fully understood by the general public, people are still only interested in the advantages of the internet and are not concerned about the damage the internet can do in society.

Many of the people interviewed for this report recognised that the protection of personal privacy on the internet is still a worrying issue in the Congo, which in part is explained by the lack of stringent regulations.

The violation of people's privacy on the internet is also to an extent synonymous with violence, as Sylvie Niombo, executive director of AZUR Développement, points out:

> There is an intersection between the violence perpetrated against women and young girls and the manipulation of the use of information and communication technologies. A person forwarding emails which explicitly talk of or allude to violence incites violence in exactly the same way as publishing private images of a young girl or woman. This is the case when it comes to the circulation of images showing women committing adultery – this is like being lynched naked in public on the internet.

There have been cases reported of violence against women and young girls after their partners, husbands or fathers have read private email messages. Cases of this sort are discussed in the issue paper on the use of ICTs and perpetration of violence against women and young girls in the Congo, written by Niombo in 2009 and published online by the Women's Networking Support Programme of the Association for Progressive Communications (APC WNSP).[1]

A large majority of the people interviewed in this study think that the general public is very unaware of these sorts of privacy issues. The general public has a poor understanding of the risks and their rights in relation to the handling of their personal information. "There are currently no laws relating to the protection of private information that explicitly guarantee respect and sensitivity in the handling of personal data. However, such legal protection and rights are only useful to people who are aware of their existence and know how to use them to their advantage," says Davy Silou, an IT consultant.

The lack of awareness also explains the lack of stringent regulations relating to the protection of private information. Alain Ndalla, director of new technologies at the Ministry of Post and Telecommunications, admits that a large part of the telecommunications sector is not regulated. He states that a series of measures are in the process of being introduced in order to guarantee better protection of individuals on the internet. He highlighted that "texts on cyber security and cyber

1 www.genderit.org/content/violence-against-women-and-information-communication-technologies-congo-country-report

crime will be made available to users of ICTs and will therefore protect the consumers and users. Punitive measures will also be put in place to punish those who commit acts of internet crime."

Internet regulations do not sufficiently protect human rights

One must recognise that in the Congo the applicable law on privacy generally falls under Article 9 of the French Civil Code, which is not the result of a Congolese legislative process and does not take into account the reality of the local situation, in particular the general public's illiteracy and lack of access to ICTs.

Although the law that was brought into effect in 2009 makes provisions for the protection of the privacy of internet users, it does not provide precise descriptions of what we mean by privacy on the internet and the measures guaranteeing its protection. Article 124 of the law stipulates that "online communication between members of the public is free. The exercise of this freedom can only be limited if it violates respect for human dignity, freedom and other people's property."

With such legislative and regulatory imprecision, victims of privacy violations are to an extent disarmed. In both cases highlighted earlier in this report, the victims have not sought reparations.

In addition to this legislative and regulatory imprecision, the judicial authorities and police forces have a poor record of investigating and prosecuting acts that infringe people's dignity on the internet. Very few in the police force or even judiciary are well informed on the types of internet crime that affect Congolese citizens: this is in part because these crimes are not reported. However, there is also a need to reinforce the capacities of the judiciary and police.

It is also important to note that the general slowness of legal proceedings make the public reluctant to pursue legal action against infringements of their dignity, as they have little confidence that their case will be pursued..

The problem of ICT governance in the Congo cannot be ignored.

The government, the private sector and civil society must commit to increased investment in the field of the protection of personal privacy on the internet. This is all the more important given the high number of people – the majority of them young adolescents – with mobile phones in the Congo, and with increased numbers accessing the internet at internet cafés.

Conclusion

This report has highlighted several problems linked to the internet and human rights. If the government is in the process of enabling the development of a true information society, it is clear that in the Congo the balance between the individual's freedom of expression and the protection of human rights still has not been found.

This is explained by the absence of adequate regulation of the issue of privacy as well as a lack of public awareness of the risks linked to ICTs.

It is therefore imperative that all the parties involved (NGOs on ICTs and human rights, the government and international organisations) further commit themselves to actions that will lead to the protection of privacy and human rights in general.

Action steps

In order to improve the protection of privacy and personal information on the internet, it is necessary that certain measures be taken by different stakeholders.

Civil society

- It is necessary that NGOs working on ICTs launch publicity campaigns on the various kinds of privacy and personal information violations and the legal measures that can be taken to redress them.
- A collaborative effort between various NGOs working on ICTs and human rights is necessary in order to encourage the authorities to adopt more proactive measures that protect human rights on the internet.
- Increased cooperation between the judiciary and police force and organisations working on ICTs and human rights is necessary.

Government

- It is necessary that the authorities adopt laws that adequately protect human rights on the internet.
- Members of the judiciary and police administration need to be educated on the issues relating to the protection of human rights on the internet.

International organisations

- International organisations should make more financial contributions to public awareness campaigns on the use of ICTs and individual privacy rights. ■

COSTA RICA

ICTS AND ENVIRONMENTAL ACTIVISM IN COSTA RICA

Sulá Batsú
Kemly Camacho
www.sulabatsu.com

Introduction

The Costa Rica report for GISWatch 2011 is based on a global problem: the exploitation of natural resources by international companies in the poorest countries in the world. At the moment, natural resources are scarce and very valuable. At the same time, they are often located in remote regions where the most excluded social groups are situated. Natural resources have been part of the culture and daily life of the communities living in these geographical locations.

Excluded populations have fewer opportunities for education, health, employment and other social rights. As a consequence, these social groups have fewer opportunities to access information and to voice their feelings and visions. They suffer an important information gap, which is partly the result of the digital divide.

In addition, there is a disconnect between rural areas and urban areas. Decisions as to the exploitation of natural resources by international companies are made in the urban areas and are implemented in the rural areas after no consultation with communities, and no information to support their implementation or regarding their social and economic consequences.

Social movements against mining

Cutris in San Carlos is situated on the northern Costa Rican border. This is a protected rainforest area and is the habitat of endangered species such as yellow almond trees, green macaws and manatees. Despite this restriction, in 2008 the former government, led by Oscar Arias, gave the Canadian Infinito Gold Company the concession for mining gold in over 300 hectares of this region in order to extract one million tons over ten years. The opencast mining operation – known as the Crucitas gold mining project – would have created an 85-metre pit and provoked serious environmental impacts.

Amongst other things, the mining operations were to involve the use of cyanide, a highly toxic substance which would be transported by land and by sea, creating dangers not only for Costa Rica but for the entire region along the transport route. The health of families and workers was expected to be seriously impacted by the mine, while technical studies demonstrated the inevitable danger for aquifers.

Different expert studies from institutions like the University of Costa Rica and national and international environmental organisations like AIDA[1] also showed the environmental, economic and social dangers posed by the Crucitas mining project. The Arias government, despite having promoted its "Peace With Nature" programme, declared the project to be in the public interest and of national importance.

The Infinito Gold Company has always disputed arguments related to the environmental consequences of the mining operation. They counter-argued that the project would generate employment in a region where people do not have any other opportunities and promised to reforest the devastated area. They never accepted the danger of the opencast mining.

This case is relevant because despite the declaration of public interest, the government's support and the important investment made by the Canadian Infinito Gold Company to promote the project, a social resistance movement at the national level has halted the Crucitas gold mining operation. An Administrative Court has not only annulled the concession granted to the Infinito Gold Company, but has also ordered it to pay for environmental damage already caused. Furthermore, it recommended putting now ex-president Arias on trial for declaring the project in the public interest despite the fact that it would have a negative impact on the environment and people. Subsequently, the Costa Rican government has declared a moratorium on all proposed opencast mining. This was an important success for popular movements in the country.

The role of ICTs in environmental struggles

Information and communications technologies (ICTs) – in particular social networks, email and mobile phones – have played a very important role in

1 www.aidambiental.org

this social resistance movement. They facilitate the dissemination of citizen information, popular mobilisation and communication between multiple and diverse social groups.

The Cutris-San Carlos story shows four key elements that characterised the role of ICTs in the environmental social resistance movement:

New media versus traditional media

The Infinito Gold Company made a substantial investment in a campaign to promote the benefits of gold exploitation in Crucitas. It used television, radio and newspapers in this campaign. It also set up an Infinito website[2] connected to social networks – but could not generate active participation on the site.

In contrast, social groups working against mining in Crucitas did not have enough resources to use the mass media. Instead they used social networks, email lists and mobile phones to express their disagreement and mobilise public opposition. There is 43.7%[3] internet penetration in Costa Rica, while 34.28%[4] of the population are social network users, as compared to 95% television and 99% radio penetration.[5] Despite this, the social mobilisation using comparatively low-cost ICTs was successful. By July 2010, 70% of Costa Ricans were well informed about the potential hazards of opencast mining in Crucitas and were against the project.

The information shared on these networks was developed and updated constantly by citizens, without control or restriction. Very often it was more significant and effective than the information produced by traditional media. It became so influential that traditional large-scale media tried to "infiltrate" social networks, looking for up-to-date information provided by social movements and circulated amongst their networks.

Online-offline links

There is a reciprocal relationship between online and offline activities. Social resistance is based on a permanent cycle where digital activities influence local actions and citizen action is followed up online. Innovative strategies and solutions, collective decisions and collaborative analysis in digital spaces used in local actions constitute the power of social resistance.

One good example is "La Marcha por la Vida" (The March for Life),[6] a walk from Crucitas to San José in July and San José to Crucitas in August (some 200 kilometres each way). The objective was to inform and protest. The march was conceived and popularised using Facebook, YouTube and email. It began with only 45 people but participation grew during the march itself and through using the internet. In the end it achieved national media coverage and was followed daily on Facebook, creating a "virtual march" with many expressions of support both online and offline.

Graphics, videos, photos and relevant documents were uploaded to digital spaces, some later printed on t-shirts and stickers, and used to inform live discussions and video forums, amongst other actions. Community activities were also popularised using videos, photos and audio uploaded to the internet, creating an online-offline dynamic which is crucial in creating a popular movement.

Bridging the urban-rural gap

One importance of ICTs is their ability to connect rural and urban populations, specifically when it comes to environmental protests. In general there is a significant social gap between rural and urban areas including a wide digital divide. Despite this divide, the protection of environmental resources connects rural and urban interests, and ICTs strengthen the communication of information between organisations and people in both locations.

Bloque Verde (Green Bloc),[7] an environmental organisation, uploaded examples of urban culture, such as dance, music and graffiti, expressing concerns about natural resource exploitation and the threats to rural life. At the same time, rural communities voiced their visions using digital audio and images on platforms such as Fuera de Crucitas (Get Out of Crucitas),[8] an active digital space created by the community in San Carlos. The result was a continuous exchange of knowledge and information between people with a common cause in rural and urban areas.

Mix of voices for information transparency

Another key role of ICTs during the Crucitas social resistance was to provide the Costa Rican people with varying and different information from diverse actors with multiple opinions: studies from academia, manifestos from civil society, political discussions from the Legislative Assembly, international agreements signed by the country, the position of the Infinito Company, as well as the rural community's opinion.

2 www.infinito.co.cr
3 www.internetworldstats.com/am/cr.htm
4 www.socialbakers.com/facebook-statistics/costa-rica
5 www.conicit.go.cr/documentos/costaricadigital.pdf
6 www.fueradecrucitas.blogspot.com
7 www.bloqueverde.blogspot.com
8 www.fueradecrucitas.blogspot.com

This included blogs such as "Ni una sola mina" (Not A Single Mine),[9] which guaranteed information transparency and diversity for citizen decision making. Environmental organisations and the cultural sector also played an "infomediation" role, translating into different languages and choosing appropriate media to better communicate between social actors and regions.

The viral effect of ICTs also favours disclosure at the international level. The process was, as a result, followed by various international media (albatv.org, laprensa.com, elnuevodiario.com), observatory institutes (conflictosmineros.net) and environmental organisations (humboldt.org.ni), mostly in Latin America.

This role was crucial in demonstrating the importance of information sharing in allowing citizens to make informed decisions.

Conclusion

- The use of social networks by itself does not define a social movement as inclusive and democratic, nor does it guarantee successful results.
- Traditional media are losing their power to connect with the public.
- ICTs promote new communication and information processes and through these can encourage new forms of organisation and ways to produce knowledge. The essential part is the spirit and the power of organising without organisations.[10]
- Mixed voices, multiple sources of knowledge and diverse information are basic conditions for an informed public, a new interest in political participation and solid community decision making. ICTs are playing a key role in facilitating these conditions.
- Social resistance is based on a combination of online and offline spaces, interaction between different geographical areas and exchange through different social actors with different languages. Infomediation and infomediators are key to facilitate communication in communities of diversity.

Action steps

- Create open spaces with appropriate ICTs to connect with popular movements in a meaningful way.
- Prioritise infomediary roles to connect multiple sources of knowledge.
- Remember offline spaces – not everything happens in the digital space.
- Develop citizen capacities to use ICTs.
- Prioritise digital audio, video and images for meaningful public impact.
- Follow your collective feelings and do not centralise processes – be open to any opinion and information. ■

9 www.niunasolamina.blogspot.com

10 Shirky, C. (2008) *Here Comes Everybody*, The Penguin Press.

CÔTE D'IVOIRE

INTERNET-ENABLED CITIZEN ENGAGEMENT DURING THE 2010 ELECTIONS

nnenna.org
Nnenna Nwakanma
www.nnenna.org

Introduction

At the start if its independence in 1960, Côte d'Ivoire was ruled by Félix Houphouët-Boigny, in a manner described as "authoritarian and paternal". In the 33 years of his rule, Côte d'Ivoire enjoyed relative economic and social stability as well as growth, with its economic capital, Abidjan, becoming what is known as the "Paris of Africa". On his death in 1993, Houphouët-Boigny was succeeded by Aimé Henri Konan Bédié, who was ousted from power by a military coup on Christmas Eve in 1999. General Robert Guei, the head of the military junta, managed to organise a presidential election, albeit amid civil crisis, which saw Laurent Gbagbo come into power in 2000. However, it would be another decade before elections would be held again, sparking civil unrest.

2010, the long-awaited elections and the "ivoire-info-techpreneurs"

The 2010 presidential elections were five years overdue. Several postponements had ended up galvanising ordinary citizens into civil action. In Côte d'Ivoire, presidential elections are the first in a series of elections. They are followed by legislative, regional and finally, municipal elections. The presidential elections are carried by a simple majority – by a candidate winning 50% of all valid votes plus one. In the case of no clear winner, a second round is organised as a run-off for the two candidates with the highest number of votes.

The government had coupled voter registration with a national identification process. This meant that a maximum number of voters were expected. At the end of the initial phase of registration, 5,784,490 voters were cleared for the process. Another feature of the elections was the number of presidential hopefuls. There were fourteen in all, including a woman, a comedian, a human rights activist and a farmer. The state-run national broadcaster indicated that each of the candidates was going to "face the nation" for 90 minutes and answer questions. A face-to-face live debate was also scheduled for the two run-off candidates.

Voter mobilisation moved from the streets online. Gbagbo launched a much-hyped website. His major challenger, Allasane Dramane Ouattara, launched his too, which was radio and TV enabled. Then followed the YouTube channels, the Facebook groups and the Twitter accounts, with politicians maximising the potential of online media interventions.

Wonzomai, the Ivorian version of Ushahidi

Wonzomai – meaning "witness" in Beté, the major language in the western part of the country – was the first internet-enabled citizen engagement initiative dealing with election issues.[1] It allowed individuals to report diverse incidents, from traffic conditions, fraud and security, to voting conditions, as well as to share official government information. Citizens could call, text, send email or use the Twitter hashtag to report incidents, which were then mapped.

#CIV2010 – Côte d' Ivoire online

In the middle of October 2010, immediately after the launch of Wonzomai, the Twitter hash tag #CIV2010 was launched. Its aim was to engage citizens on Twitter on all election issues. #CIV2010 allowed voters to track candidates, post pictures, analyse TV debates, campaign for votes, report issues and much more. #CIV2010 users chose not to obey the government injunction to not publish the first round of election results, since the injunction specifically focused on national and foreign media in Côte d'Ivoire. As a result, many of the #CIV2010 users felt they were not obliged to respect this.

The first leg of the presidential elections went relatively well and was declared peaceful across the world. This gave more impetus to the "ivoire-info-techpreneurs". They started meeting regularly on Friday evenings for drinks, forging friendships and comradeship. Then came the famous presidential face-to-face debate between Gbagbo and Ouattara. Once the debate was officially set for Thursday 25 November, the web went into a frenzy. It was going to be the first debate of its kind – the very first – in the recent history of the nation. The capacity of the live web stream of the national broadcaster was

1 www.wonzomai.com

increased to cater for more viewers. Those three hours were going to see the most viewers in the history of Ivorian TV.

Shocker!

About ten hours before the debate, the online platform was shut down. Viewers were required to pay a monthly or quarterly subscription for access. #CIV2010 took up the issue. Citizens pay for public TV already and, by law, access to the state broadcaster could not be restricted online. Especially not on such a day! The TV officials said they were not aware of the changes and that the board of the broadcaster had not been informed. In three hours, the ivoire-info-techpreneurs were able to track down the fraudster responsible for the shutdown. He was an employee of the broadcaster's web solutions provider. They reported his acts, informing the national broadcasting authority and the office of the prime minister. The national TV channel came back online for free after four hours of intense internet-enabled activism!

The debate lasted three hours and nine minutes. Every word was live-tweeted. Every question, every gesture. #CIV2010 users were doing direct translation of the presidential candidates' comments straight into English – in the same way the official results of the first round of presidential elections were live-tweeted. Beginning from the Thursday of the live debate to the time of this report, #CIV2010 has been in the Top 10 Trending Twitter Topics in the French language.

When crises set in

After waiting for run-off results for three sleepless nights, ivoire-info-techpreneurs knew danger was ahead. And the crises certainly came. The Independent Electoral Commission announced Allasane Dramane Ouattara winner of the polls. The Constitutional Council overrode the results of the Commission and gave victory to incumbent president Gbagbo. Each "president" held to his victory, formed a cabinet, and was intent on exercising power. The international community aligned itself with the Electoral Commission and held the challenger as victorious.

By this time #CIV2010 had established itself as the "other country" – a cyber country that offered a parallel expression of people's rights and needs. All stakeholders were using the hashtag. The two presidential camps were there, their propaganda too. Violence erupted. As clashes raged on the streets of Abidjan, details could be read on Twitter minutes after events unfolded. Photos, numbers, reports, eye-witness accounts! The international media was shut down, and Twitter became the "official" media platform for Côte d'Ivoire.

Managing the humanitarian crises

With the outbreak of post-electoral violence, citizen mobilisation took a different turn. While information battles were raging on #CIV2010, the need for humanitarian aid and support loomed large. Private vehicles had been snatched by armed combatants, banks had closed their doors, cash flow was meagre and medication for the sick was dwindling. Then came the curfew, which started at midnight and only ended at six in the morning. There was an unprecedented breakdown of the social system. As if all of that was not enough, mobile phone text messaging (SMS) services went down too. Movement was limited, phone calls down to the minimum, hunger was everywhere and the number of people hospitalised increased. At this time, gas stations had closed, shops too. Some hospitals ran out of medication, public transport was non-existent and heavy gunfire could be heard even before the curfew started!

The ivoire-info-techpreneurs decided to use the Wonzomai solidarity platform and weave in a kind of internet-enabled emergency centre. Médecins Sans Frontières (Doctors Without Borders), the Red Cross, and the United Nations were the only international organisations offering help in the country at the time. The solution to this was the CIVSOCIAL project.[2] The project consisted of six different hubs:

- A call centre in Accra, staffed by volunteers
- #CIVSOCIAL and #CIVAUTO hashtags on Twitter
- A website with a fundraising component[3]
- A Facebook group
- A Blackberry group
- A Skype group

All of the above functioned 24/7. Emergency messages poured in. In the first days, cases were mainly from wounded people who needed care, sick people who needed medication, pregnant women who needed attention, and families who needed food. Since many people did not have airtime to make calls and SMS services were down, they would "flash call" the centre, which would call the number back. #CIVSOCIAL would then forward the message to all of the six gateways listed above. Once a solution was found, it was relayed to the person in need.

A quick list of resources was drawn up: pharmacies, available medication, clinics that could receive patients, UN vehicles that could transport people, medical personnel willing to do consultations, points where food could be bought, etc. Patients and doctors met via remote conferencing using the call centre

2 civsocial.akendewa.org

3 www.gofundme.com/civsocial

in Accra. A husband helped his pregnant wife deliver her baby relying on a doctor's instructions via a conference call! At the height of the crises, the mobile telecommunication companies joined #CIVSOCIAL, donating airtime to allow for basic calls. Internet service providers also joined the effort, offering two weeks of free internet access to allow #CIVSOCIAL to continue its work. International media helped, publishing interviews and calling for donations. In less than 72 hours, the project raised well over USD 4,000.

The war on PayPal

At a time when #CIVSOCIAL had peaked, another drama reared its head. PayPal France would not release the donated money. One of the ivoire-info-techpreneurs, whose PayPal France account was used as an emergency measure, was told that in France you cannot use a personal account to receive a public donation. The information was shared with the Skype "situation room" and, in one sitting, the #CIVSOCIAL group decided to take the war to PayPal. A formal online petition was launched and in less than 24 hours over 1,000 signatures were received in support, each signature triggering a tweet! Bloggers followed, and the international media were happy to report on the crisis. PayPal reacted swiftly and the funds were cleared. The ivoire-info-techpreneur actually received a hand-written note and a digital photo frame from PayPal as a peace offering!

At the time of this report, the daily sound of gunfire has died down considerably: one camp has apparently won the war and the country is now picking up the pieces. Nonetheless, stolen cars have yet to be returned and #CIVAUTO is still functional, and being used to track the stolen cars and to deal with other vehicle-related issues, such as those that were abandoned. The call centre has been discontinued, and the ivoire-info-techpreneurs are now using #CIVNEXT to track and monitor the next steps after the crises, while #CIV2010 still remains as an information and political propaganda platform.

Moving forward: Lessons, trends and conclusions

Citizen mobilisation on Twitter has earned respect

Undoubtedly, the huge mobilisation of citizens on Facebook and Twitter has earned respect for the citizens themselves. At one point in time, even the G8 countries had officials posted to follow #CIV2010. Official communications from France, China, the European Union and the United States on Côte d'Ivoire were all posted on Twitter using the #CIV2010 hash tag. Recently, Prime Minister Soro Guillaume, after asking his advisor Alain Logbognon to engage citizens on Twitter and on #CIV2010, signed up himself as @Boghota and has held serious discussions with citizens on Twitter.

Online humanitarian actions are translating to concrete offline activities

The number of offline cases solved by internet-enabled mobilisation before, during and after the Côte d'Ivoire crises is significant. Lives were saved. People in France donated clothing and medication through #CIVSOCIAL which was then flown down to Abidjan. Recently, a blood donation drive was also organised in support of the wounded in the war.

Concerted coordinated action to (re)claim rights

It was of particular interest to note that citizen internet-enabled mobilisation is a realisation of the coordinated power of the people. The case of PayPal was one in which the ivoire-info-techpreneurs felt that "this is a war we can win, so we must fight it," with striking success.

Increase in web activism and greater use of social media

Before #CIV2010, web activism and social media were more or less a domain for the ivoire-info-techpreneurs. But the crises have given rise to increased web engagement with greater use of social media, particularly Twitter. With the realisation of the power of social media and networks, the country has learned that these platforms can become real citizen hubs and are critical for policy makers, businesses and governance.

As Côte d'Ivoire rises from the destruction brought on by war, its citizens are looking forward to a new and a better country. The internet will enable them to monitor governance, keep engaged and mobilise for or against causes in the future. Twitter and Facebook have proved powerful, and ordinary citizens have shown capacity.

Action steps

- Use informal face-to-face meetings to strategise, and to plan a tech hub for the country.
- Use Twitter and Facebook as platforms for citizens to keep watch over policies and promises made by the government.
- Promote increased citizen reporting on the legislative and municipal elections in 2011.
- Generate interest in social media amongst the new political leaders. At the moment, Alain Logbognon is the new minister of youth, employment and civic service. He sets time aside to interact on Twitter. The aim is to have more ministers do the same. ■

CROATIA

FIGHTING FOR A FREE MEDIA

ZaMirNET
Danijela Babic
www.zamirnet.hr

Introduction

The reorganisation of the Croatian media landscape began in the early 1990s, with the transition from the socialist system to a democratic political system and liberal market economy. Yet building a legal environment that enables a free media given an authoritarian past is a considerable undertaking. The criminalisation of journalistic work, including defamation and libel laws, is generally considered to be a direct threat to media freedom. In 2011 the government proposed changes to the Criminal Code that included severe penalties for libel – even jail. At the same time, gaps in the current legal system could be seen as attempts to silence civil society. For example, the newly established Electronic Media Agency,[1] a regulatory body in the field of electronic media, finances the Fund for Promotion of Pluralism and Diversity of Electronic Media with 0.5% of the total annual gross income earned in the previous year by all media service providers offering and engaging in radio and TV media services. However, websites – which are the main publication platforms for civil society organisations – cannot apply for money from this fund.

Policy and political background

The Constitution[2] of the Republic of Croatia guarantees freedom of expression and freedom of the press. It bans censorship, and journalists are entitled to report and to access information. The Constitution also guarantees the right of correction if legal rights are violated by published news.

The Croatian media are governed by the Law on Media,[3] the Law on Electronic Media,[4] the Law on Croatian Radio-Television[5] and the Law on the Right to Access Information.[6] The Law on Media as well as the Law on Electronic Media reaffirm that freedom of expression and freedom of the media are guaranteed. The Law on Media also stipulates the obligation of the government to stimulate and protect the pluralism and diversity of media by financing programmes and interventions from the state budget. Concerning the rules for civic journalism, the Law on Electronic Media regulates electronic publications and forbids hate speech as well as content that offends human dignity and contains immoral and pornographic content or might seriously impair the physical, mental or moral development of minors.

The media are indirectly governed by the Criminal Code and Civil Code through provisions regarding defamation and libel.

Challenges to free media in Croatia

The existence of a free and independent media is generally considered vital to democratic governance. In its recent history Croatia has experienced most of the problems that post-socialist states have faced regarding the media: self-censorship, pressure by advertisers and political groups, threats against journalists, especially investigative reporters, the crisis of the public broadcaster, the use of hate and nationalist speech, etc. In the latest Freedom House report on press freedom, published in 2011, Croatia is tied with Burkina Faso in 85th place on the global press freedom rankings (out of 196 states).[7] It gives the country a "partly free" status considering the legal, political and economic environment.

Even though the legal framework ensures freedom of expression, political and corporate pressures can still be felt. For example, in February 2009, Interior Minister Tomislav Karamarko brought a criminal case against journalist and blogger Zeljko Peratovic for "disseminating information likely to upset the population," after Peratovic accused him of obstructing an investigation into the death of a witness in a war crimes case. According to Freedom House, legal harassment against Peratovic continued in 2010.[8]

1 The Agency was established in 2009 based on the Law on Electronic Media (OG 153/09).
2 OG 56/90, 135/97, 113/00, 28/01, 55/01
3 OG 163/03, 59/04
4 OG 153/09
5 OG 137/10
6 OG 172/03, 144/10, 37/11, 77/11

7 www.freedomhouse.org/template.cfm?page=251&year=2011
8 www.freedomhouse.org/inc/content/pubs/pfs/inc_country_detail.cfm?country=8021&year=2011&pf

In April 2010, Zagreb police searched the home of famous blogger Marko Rakar and interrogated him after Rakar published a leaked list of registered war veterans on his blog. According to Human Rights Watch, "the government had resisted efforts to release the list, which civil society activists believe contains [the names of] people fraudulently receiving pensions as war veterans."[9]

Moreover, the changes to the Criminal Code proposed in 2011 provide that a journalist found guilty of libel could face imprisonment of up to a year, and a fine equalling half of the journalist's annual wage.

The example of blogger Damir Fintic, who has been sentenced to prison for a comment published on his blog[10] back in 2005, underscores the potential impact of defamation and criminal libel laws on new media – especially when they are misused by a government that feels threatened. The critical comment on his blog was related to a post about Vukovar's mayor Vladimir Stengl and his wife, and the person commenting on his blog had written critically about circumstances in relation to a real estate purchase by the Strengl family.[11]

Prison sentences for libel were abolished in 2006, but reappeared in the new proposal for legislative change, causing strong reactions from journalists and international free press watchdog organisations who argued that the government should rely on civil rather than criminal remedies. Zdenko Duka, president of the Croatian Journalists Association, warned that truth was not a defence for libel charges under the proposal, and that journalists could be subject to penalties for reporting items judged not to be in the public interest.

Eventually, the justice minister announced that the threat of jail will be removed from its draft law on defamation and libel.

In addition to the legal provisions explicitly targeting certain media content, there is indirect influence that can be exercised by way of both substantive rules and their application. There are certain shortcomings in current media regulations, particularly in relation to the status of the not-for-profit electronic publications of civil society organisations. The Electronic Media Agency keeps the records of the providers of audio and audiovisual media services and services of electronic publications. According to the Law on Electronic Media, the Agency is financed with 0.5% of the total annual gross income earned in the previous year by all media service providers offering and engaging in audio and audiovisual media services.

In 2011 the Agency notified civil society organisations running non-profit online newspapers that they are subject to that tax as well. As it came as a surprise, organisations could not have planned for such a cost within their budgets. Most of the non-profit media are funded through grants under strict financial rules from donors, and with no income from advertising mainly due to the lack of interest of the advertising industry. This means that every extra tax that is not budgeted for affects the sustainability of civil society media.

The Electronic Media Agency regulates TV and radio broadcasting but also manages the Fund for Promotion of Pluralism and Diversity of Electronic Media. The resources of the Fund are aimed at stimulating the production of programme content published by electronic media (television and radio) at the local and regional level, which is of public interest and is of particular importance. However, online newspapers run by civil society organisations are not eligible for these funds. Considering the fact that a concession is not available for online newspapers run by civil society, the reason why not-for-profit organisations should pay the operating fee to the Agency is not clear.

In an interview with Liderpress,[12] Damir Hajduk, a member of the Electronic Media Council, admitted the mistake and announced a public discussion on the criteria to register the electronic media. He also said that non-profit portals and blogs with several contributors will not be required to pay the fee – unless they publish media information aimed at a wider audience than they currently do(!). This explanation caused additional confusion since according to the Law on Electronic Media, electronic publications include edited websites and/or portals republishing electronic versions of printed articles in the press and/or media information available to the general public anyway. The public discussion on the criteria for the registry was held in March 2011 and the deadline for paying the dues to the Agency was May 2011. At the time of writing this report,[13] the new version of the criteria for the registry was not available on the Agency's website.

At the same time some other legal norms are not implemented properly in the country, as the MEDIADEM report on Croatia shows.[14] For example, Croatia

9 www.hrw.org/world-report-2011/croatia

10 www.vukovarac.net

11 www.croatiablognews.com/croatian-first-european-blogger-to-go-to-prison

12 www.liderpress.hr/Default.aspx?sid=122193

13 2 September 2011

14 Popović, H., Bilić, P., Jelić, T. and Švob-Đokić, N. (2010) *Media policies and regulatory practices in a selected set of European countries, the EU and the Council of Europe: The case of Croatia*, MEDIADEM. www.mediadem.eliamep.gr/wp-content/uploads/2010/05/Croatia.pdf

has a legal obligation to stimulate and protect pluralism and diversity of the media with support from the state budget. Since 2005 it was due to stimulate the programmes of local and regional media, as well as media intended to inform persons with special needs. It should have established new printed media, especially local and non-profit media, and supported the media published by non-governmental organisations. Unfortunately the state failed to carry out this obligation, according to the MEDIADEM report, due to a lack of money, as well as due to the rather marginal public interest in this media.

Although civil society online news portals cannot compete with corporate news portals in terms of resources available for content production and the number of visitors, they promote public interests often marginalised by the state or private sector. Civil society online newspapers will not be frequently visited if they do not have the resources to provide a quality product on a daily basis. Even the leading Croatian commercial online newspapers contain scarce news compared to advertisements, entertainment and lifestyle stories, as the publishers try to survive the recession. The MEDIADEM report noted that the political and economic crisis also incites the political elites to strengthen their interests in the media, and the media to rely more on public sources and funds. In this context independent, alternative and critical discourses are hard to maintain, the report concludes.

Conclusions

Democracy requires a media system that provides people with a wide range of opinion and analysis, facilitates debate and promotes the public accountability of the power holders.

In the process of democratisation, the concept of a legal enabling environment that supports a free and independent media is central. It is not only about the particular laws, but the institutional structure which administers those laws, including the courts and regulatory agencies. During the negotiations on Croatia's accession to the European Union, the Croatian media legislation was assessed as fully harmonised with European media standards and the *acquis communautaire*.[15] However, the inconsistencies of current legislation and practices clearly show that legislative changes are not rooted in coherent media policy aimed at supporting a free and independent media, but reflect a fast-changing interplay of different influences and interests. For instance, media run by civil society organisations seem to be neglected by the government when it comes to the measures that encourage their productivity. On the other hand, they were not ignored when legal instruments that repressed free speech were applied.

Action steps

Although the number of internet users is growing in Croatia and the media are being easily accessed online, the involvement of citizens in online content production is low. In the context of a transitional society where the level of consciousness about the value and functioning of free speech and its practice is low among the citizenry, this should not be surprising. It should also not be forgotten that in the 1990s, civil society activities were viewed as dangerous when not in accordance with state politics.

Such circumstances require that civil society organisations, as well as professional journalists associations, educate the citizenry about the role that the independent media play in society. It is also important to strengthen collaboration between professional journalists and civil society activists to influence the drafting of media legislation, so as to ensure the freedom of public expression. ■

15 Wikipedia defines this as the "accumulated legislation, legal acts, court decisions which constitute the body of European Union law." en.wikipedia.org/wiki/Community_acquis

ECUADOR

THE RESCUE OF A PRESIDENT: THE ROLE OF SOCIAL MEDIA IN INFORMING AND MOBILISING CITIZENS IN NATIONAL CRISES

IMAGINAR
Rossana Flores and Hugo Carrión
www.imaginar.org

Introduction

Since October 2008, when the new Ecuadorian Constitution was passed, the country has been undergoing significant changes in its legislative framework. In May 2009, the National Assembly (formerly the Congress) filed 293 new laws or legal amendments; and 24 months later, 68 of these new laws or amendments had been passed.

The new legislation has made changes in different areas, such as education, justice, citizens' participation, and public administration. One of the laws passed on 29 September 2010 was the Organic Law on Government Services which homologated the administration of the national police and army with that of the civil public administration.

The inadequate and insufficient dissemination of the contents of the law, in addition to the poor interpretation of the new laws by one sector of the police and army, led to police protests that initially seemed to be focused on the issue of wages, but that ended with the Ecuadorian president's kidnapping and an attempted coup. The results of the police protests that took place on Thursday 30 September, now called "30S" by the media, were unfortunate: eight casualties including policemen, soldiers and civilians. The national police's image was completely shattered and democracy staggered at a time when it seemed the phantom of presidential downfalls and moves to overthrow the government had finally been banished from Ecuador.

During the protests, information and communications technologies (ICTs) played a key role as alternative communication channels by transmitting the course of events live and encouraging citizen mobilisation.

Regulatory context

One of the main achievements in the new Constitution is the incorporation of the right for all Ecuadorians have to access to ICTs, as enshrined in Article 16. A debate on communication, freedom of expression, and the ownership of the media was held by the National Constituent Assembly, after which the Communications Law was declared a priority law that was to be issued immediately. Two years later, however, the debate is stagnant due to completely different positions on key matters.

On one hand, the national government claims the citizens' right to be informed. This administration is known for its extensive use of quite efficient government communication strategies, including a radio programme that is broadcast each Saturday where the president talks about his activities. The presidency also uses Facebook efficiently and a Twitter account with around 70,000 followers, making it the fourth most popular account in Ecuador, sharing honours with showbiz stars, singers and sportscasters. Furthermore, for the first time in our country, so-called public media has been created – one public television channel, one public radio station, and one public news agency.

On the other hand, the opposition and groups that object to the government's communication work, amongst other things, oppose government advertising, believing it is disproportionate compared to other advertising on media channels. They also object to the government's control of both public media and private media channels that were seized due to unpaid debts they held with several state banks. According to the opposition, the private media outlets now in the hands of pro-government administrators, which they call "confiscated media", have unbalanced the communications equilibrium in the country.

Police protests erupt...

On 30 September 2010 Ecuador lived an unprecedented episode in favour of democracy. Thousands of citizens filled the streets to protect the constitutional order by ensuring the will of the electorate who had voted for President Rafael Correa.

Since its return to democracy in 1978, Ecuador has lived through several incidents of political instability that have ended in overthrowing constitutionally elected presidents. From 1997 to 2006 Ecuador had seven presidents, excluding a fleeting triumvirate in 2000. These periods of instability have taken place after massive demonstrations by citizens who sought fundamental change in the country's political management. Back in 2003, a citizen movement called "Los Forajidos" (The

Outlaws), protesting with the cry of "All leave!", not only demanded that ex-President Lucio Gutiérrez step down, but that all appointed politicians vacate their positions, showing the little credibility the political class enjoyed.

Since 2006, after the election of Correa, Ecuador has experienced stability. This in spite of the changes made by the establishment of the Constituent Assembly with full powers to issue a new Constitution, as well as the passing of a significant number of laws, many of which affect private interests in many sectors. After almost four years in office, Correa still enjoys a historic general admiration of the people.

The police protests erupted after the passing of the new Organic Law on Government Services. This law eliminated all bonuses and additional benefits for all government employees, including the police and the military. On the morning of 30 September 2010 the media reported on a police strike that was taking place in Regimiento Quito, the National Police headquarters in the capital of Ecuador, where the strikers refused to work until the law passed the night before was revoked.

Immediately after learning about the strike, Correa went to the police headquarters to talk to the demonstrators and, in his words, share the advantages of the law. When he arrived, however, they greeted him with insults which led to a heated speech by Correa, after which he decided to leave, since no dialogue was possible. The demonstrators blocked his exit and the situation turned violent: live images transmitted scenes of aggression against the president, who started asphyxiating when tear gas was used, before he was taken to the police hospital which is next to the police headquarters.

Confusion reigned in the country while the news reported on thefts, looting and chaos throughout the country after almost the entire public forces decided to join the strike. The police who guarded the National Assembly had taken over the building and stopped members from entering. The runway of Mariscal Sucre Airport in Quito had also been blocked by some members of the air force. The people's attention, however, was focused on the news on the president's situation.

Around noon, Correa made a phone call to the public radio station and reported a coup against his government, and that he had been kidnapped and was unable to leave the hospital. "Policemen are trying to get into my room; if something happens to me, [I send] my endless love to my country and my family, wherever they are," he said. After these words, thousands of citizens gathered around the hospital and the Presidential Palace where the ministers and other public officials were organising the president's rescue, as declared by Minister of Foreign Affairs Ricardo Patiño. The people, however, were violently and disproportionately attacked by the police when they tried to reach Regimiento Quito.

Early in the afternoon, Correa electronically signed Executive Decree No. 488, which declared a state of exception,[1] and issued a world press release explaining the situation in the country. This resulted in international support. After the decree was issued, the government started an indefinite and uninterrupted national TV and radio transmission, and interrupted private radio and TV broadcasting to unify all the media around the official reports of the situation. The decree also authorised the armed forces' mobilisation to protect citizen security.

Police demands and violence rose while the president refused to revoke the approved amendments. The Chief of the Armed Forces Joint Command, General Ernesto González, as well as the high military command, reiterated their support to the president, promised to restore the country's stability, and requested the approved law's revision. However, official information sources disregarded the armed forces' demands for the law to be revised.

Throughout the day, politicians opposing the government disseminated statements supporting the insurgents. The opposing members of the Assembly met in a hotel and demanded amnesty for the rebels. Counter-government demonstrators, gathered around the public media building, demanded that their points of view be published.

The national broadcasting of official news was interrupted at approximately 8:00 p.m. and the private media started transmitting the impressive military assault executed in the environs of the police hospital, during which the police and the army clashed. Correa was rescued by an elite army group, the Special Operations Group (GEO), and an elite police group, the Intervention and Rescue Group (GIR). Live TV broadcasts showed the president's convoy being fired upon.

Some minutes later, from the Carondelet Presidential Palace, Correa addressed the citizens who had gathered in Plaza de la Independencia with a speech describing that date as "one of the saddest" in his life and "without a doubt the saddest in his almost four years in office."

1 The state of exception restricts some civil rights, such as the free movement of persons, etc.

FIGURE 1.

Daily reach of leading online publications (percentages)

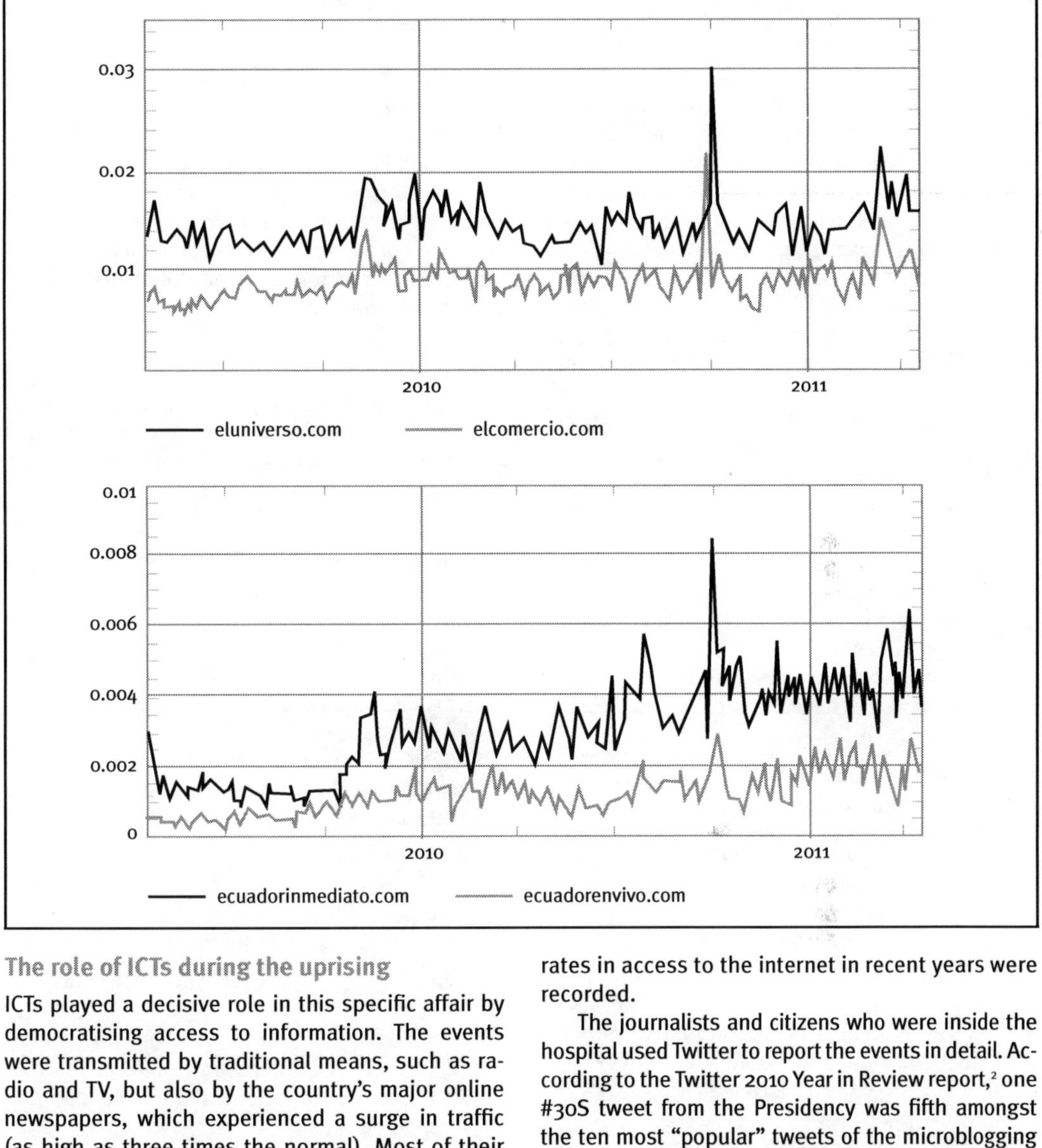

The role of ICTs during the uprising

ICTs played a decisive role in this specific affair by democratising access to information. The events were transmitted by traditional means, such as radio and TV, but also by the country's major online newspapers, which experienced a surge in traffic (as high as three times the normal). Most of their websites crashed and were inaccessible during the entire day. The online newspaper *ecuadorinmediato.com* turned out to be a special case – it quickly modified its format and was able to keep transmitting information. Other newspapers, such as *Hoy* and *El Comercio,* could only publish through Twitter because their conventional sites were no longer operating.

The graphs in Figure 1 illustrate the online traffic for the main digital publications. The peak corresponds to 30 September, when the highest rates in access to the internet in recent years were recorded.

The journalists and citizens who were inside the hospital used Twitter to report the events in detail. According to the Twitter 2010 Year in Review report,[2] one #30S tweet from the Presidency was fifth amongst the ten most "popular" tweets of the microblogging network worldwide. The Presidency's official Twitter account[3] reported on the "30S" events, while hashtag #30S described the police crisis, becoming a hot topic and trend on Twitter that Thursday.[4] It is worth noting that the Presidency's Twitter account is fourth among the country's most viewed accounts, with 70,000 followers (as of April 2011).

2 yearinreview.Twitter.com/powerful-tweets

3 Twitter.com/Presidencia_Ec

4 Trending topics are the most popular keywords used in Twitter at a given moment.

The debate shifted to other social networks, including Facebook. According to statistics, around 3.5 million Ecuadorians were Facebook members in August 2011 (i.e. around 25% of the population) – for every one internet user, one is a Facebook member.[5]

Mobile telephony kept relatives and friends informed and up to date concerning incidents that were taking place in different areas of the country. As would be expected, journalists also transmitted information to their respective media outlets using mobile phones – many of these journalists and camera people were assaulted by the police.

The electronically signed presidential decree authorised the armed forces' mobilisation and the control of information broadcast within the country, while private channels transmitted the news overseas via the internet, and this situation influenced the national chain's interruption.

The government's use of ICTs enabled it to neutralise a potential coup and to secure international support and solidarity. By means of social networks, the citizens mobilised to defend democracy. The information sought through the internet and the government's national chain fractured the monopoly that the traditional media had held in similar situations internationally in the past.

Conclusions

Society is unquestionably influenced by the people's access to new technologies. Although internet penetration in Ecuador is still low, it is significantly higher than it was five years ago – in 2006 it was below 5%, and by March 2011 this percentage had increased to four times that number.

The combined use of ICTs enabled the presence of more than one information channel. Through mobile technology, access to internet and social networks the citizens became information and news producers, which gave rise to a new type of journalism that some sectors have called citizen, social or participative journalism.

On the other hand, state regulations on the traditional media do not always include the new technologies where coverage and dissemination potential exceeds the national scope and opens the possibility of accessing plural and diverse information. Real-time updating of information generated by citizens and independent journalists is an invaluable source that secures the citizens' right to such access.

An innovative element was the government's use of ICTs in times of crisis which facilitated its decision making in the most decisive moments. The executive decree's electronic signature, mobile communication during the president's kidnapping, and the Presidency's communication through Twitter were fundamental in keeping the country informed and reaching a solution to the conflict.

Something that seems less innovative, but which was clear on 30 September, is that social networks and SMS are used to organise even more than to share media-related information. Once again, these technologies facilitated the citizens' immediate mobilisation.

Action steps

- Recommend that the government strive to increase broadband internet penetration as a way to access the means of communication and information.
- Implement ways of direct communication through the existing platforms between the leaders and the public and – along with this – recommend that the access of public officials and authorities to social networks not be restricted by means of technological tricks or administrative provisions. A proper understanding of the benefits of social technology and adequate training could lead to the creative use of this technology in favour of democracy and participation.
- Keep internet, social networks and other web applications away from the regulations that govern traditional media; and, in turn, promote neutrality in the network and its contents as an essential principle of the rights to communication.
- Establish social control mechanisms for the management and accountability of the information generated by the media and the government.
- Recommend that the media develop contingency plans for high information demand and increased traffic in particular crisis situations to insure the provision of continuous services.
- Promote the development of ethical codes and principles for the exercise of citizen journalism as a way to insure information quality, accuracy and veracity. ■

5 According to Ministry of Telecommunications statistics, internet penetration in Ecuador is 20%.

EGYPT

EGYPT'S 25 JANUARY REVOLUTION: THE ROLE OF THE INTERNET AND MOBILE TECHNOLOGY IN SOCIAL RESISTANCE AND PUBLIC DEMONSTRATIONS

ArabDev
Leila Hassanin
www.arabdev.org

Introduction

Were the internet and mobile technology the tipping point for Egypt's 25 January Revolution? Internet and mobile-based social networks like Facebook, Twitter, blogs and YouTube have been common tools for activism in Egypt for some time, as discussed in a previous GISWatch country report.[1] Though as much as they are tools for activists, they are also excellent tools for tracking and surveillance – an equally common practice by governments, the former Egyptian regime no exception.

So what was the difference between this revolution and previous attempts that used information and communications technologies (ICTs) to rally people to protest, especially attempts by youth groups such as the 6th of April Movement, independent activists and bloggers, and working professionals, be they journalists, lawyers or labour unionists? How did the revolution succeed despite nearly a week of internet, mobile, and in some areas, landline blackout?

This report maintains that as much as the internet and mobile technologies are important tools, without their broader amplification through more widespread traditional media like TV and newspapers and without a strong trigger changing the perception of the masses, these ICT tools are only minimally effective. Despite connectivity blackouts, social resistance and public demonstrations continued in Egypt; and as we are seeing, also in other countries of the region.

Policy and political context

The Mubarak regime had strongly promoted the spread of ICTs in Egypt. Connectivity and the development of IT skills were a cornerstone of Egyptian economic development – even though this approach proved to be a two-edged sword with the rapid development of Web 2.0 applications that spread the use of social networks, collaborative software, user-generated content, video sharing, and the like.

By 2005, the internet and mobile phones had become common tools for political activism. By 2008, the 6th of April Youth Movement Facebook page became a rallying point for activists. YouTube aired controversial footage. Twitter and mobile text messaging (SMS) were the chosen tools to organise demonstrations among core activists. The government responded by tightening control: the notorious emergency law, imposed for 30 years since President Anwar Sadat's murder in 1981, was extended to online content and mobile use. In a context of increasingly oppressive censorship targeting online activists, it was common for them to be harassed, arrested, and in cases, tortured.

Mobile ownership became traceable. The state established the National Agency for the Regulation of Audio and Visual Broadcasting (NARAVB), an enforcement body that engaged in the surveillance of radio, satellite and website content. As much as "venting" was allowed as part of a gesture towards freedom of political expression, laws and their enforcement were used to squash any content (or public demonstrations) that were remotely perceived as dangerous to the regime.[2] Resistance remained, but it never translated into widespread, lasting mass demonstrations.

A brave new change....

With the uprisings in Tunisia in mid-December 2009, culminating in President Zine al-Abidine Ben Ali fleeing from the country on 14 January, the unthinkable became reality: masses can uproot entrenched, authoritarian regimes, even in the Arab states. Traditionally the wider public did not get involved in protests; it was the domain of journalists, lawyers, human rights activists, and, in recent years, new clusters like "Kifaya"[3] and an increasingly secular youth. Tunisia was the long-awaited trigger that unleashed the flood of anger that had been building up for decades in all strata of Egyptian society.

In Tunisia, Facebook and Twitter were used to organise revolts. The same had been happening in

1 www.giswatch.org/country-report/20/egypt

2 Ibid.

3 Kifaya is an opposition movement that began in 2004. In Arabic it means "Enough". Kifaya operates in urban areas, especially Cairo and Alexandria, embraces a multitude of political views, from socialist to Islamist, and pushes for regime change. It has been built on grassroots protests.

Egypt. The Egyptian government had been anticipating protests – normally they did not last more than a couple of days, but this time it proved to be different. After several days of small demonstrations, mass rallies throughout Egypt were organised for Tuesday 25 January, the national holiday dedicated to the police force. The brutal police force was the most hated symbol of the regime. The government disrupted Twitter nationwide on the 25th in an attempt to dampen the protests. On the streets tear gas and rubber bullets were used. Facebook, intermittent SMS and emails continued to function, but some internet-based tools and sites needed proxies.

The national pride was ignited: with the success of the Tunisians' revolt, Egyptians could only blame themselves if they endured the Mubarak regime, especially as Ben Ali's and Mubarak's rule had many parallels. The Twitter hashtags #Egypt and #Jan25 were created and helped to consolidate tweets, updating the media worldwide as events unfolded. When protests continued into 27 January, the government shut down the internet completely shortly after midnight on the same day. The 28th was a Friday and mass riots were planned. The regime was reaching measures it had never used before to block communications: mobiles did not work anymore and landlines were dead in several of Cairo's districts.

To circumvent the silence, the hashtag #Jan-25voices was created by Scott-Railton in Michigan to relay the messages he would get through phone conversations with people in Egypt.[4] For the more tech-savvy, Telecomix[5] provided a dial-up connection.

By shutting down the internet and mobile communication for the public,[6] the Egyptian government set a precedent that had been inconceivable. The blackout remained for five full days: from 12:30 a.m. early on 28 January to 2 February, when connectivity was partially restored. This blackout reflected the regime's belief that it was still dealing with a limited number of activists, and not a national uprising. Egyptians who were not on the streets – and they were many – remained glued to their TV screens, following news minute by minute.

Protests widened and got bloodier, especially in the Suez canal cities, Northern Sinai and Alexandria. Military troops were deployed on the streets on 28 January. This was the same day Mubarak announced the sacking of his cabinet. The internet and mobile blocking had no obvious effect on calming the demonstrations. A deep feeling of dissatisfaction reigned.

Friday 28 January was a major rally day, the "Friday of Rage". Fridays after prayers at noon had become the spearhead of protests. More people joined the demonstrations, among them leading public figures. Police stations were set on fire. Mubarak "supporters" infiltrated Tahrir Square, stabbing people with knives, attacking them with sticks and rocks. The military let this happen, patrolling the peripheries of the rally without intervening on either side. On the evening of the same day prisoners were freed in an attempt to create havoc, increase crime and frighten people. General Mohammed El Batran, the head of prisons in Egypt, was fatally shot when he refused to obey the order to let the criminals out on the streets. Chaos was everywhere, protesters and the public were tense: there seemed to be no real protection from the military. The police forces had vanished from the streets.

From that Friday onwards neighbourhood groups had been formed by civilians. Each night men gathered under apartment buildings with weapons and sticks to protect their families and the streets. People barely slept and started stocking up on essentials.

On 1 February Mubarak declared that he was not going to run for re-election in September, a move many had anticipated anyway due to his age and health status. The message was taken as a stalling tactic, especially as Mubarak's son Gamal had been preparing to take over from his father. Mubarak's speech led to major protests around the country. Tahrir Square had its bloodiest day on 2 February, when thugs entered it on camels and horses attacking protesters with sticks, petrol bombs and stones. Protesters, who had generally been peaceful until then, grabbed whatever they could get their hands on to fight back. Three died and 1,500 were injured.

During the early morning hours of 3 February, grenades and Molotov cocktails were thrown from the 6th October bridge surrounding Tahrir Square. Shots were fired from different parts around Tahrir, killing and injuring protesters staying overnight in the square. The violence was intended to deter a mass protest planned for Friday 4 February. Since the internet was up again, video clips began appearing on YouTube, and tweets were constantly picked up by news agencies. Al Jazeera was one of the most active and influential news agencies in Egypt, making it the target of forceful government

4 Faris, S. (2011) Meet the Man Tweeting Egypt's Voice to the World, *Time*, 1 Feb. www.time.com/time/world/article/0,8599,2045489,00.html

5 www.telecomix.org

6 Online accessibility was maintained for specific security units and the military.

intimidation – especially as it was seen as the main information channel for the public.

During all this time military tanks were circling Tahrir Square and were present in other major cities in Egypt. The demonstrators had made it clear that they considered the military neutral, if not on their side. To keep the military separate from the regime was crucial for the continuation of the demonstrations. Yet the military's position remained opaque. Protesters feared that they might be turning against them.

It was clear that many protesters were willing to face death. On 4 February, Tahrir Square was packed and people demanded that Mubarak step down unconditionally. The government responded by changing the National Democratic Party's leader.

In Egypt the weekend is Friday and Saturday; Sunday is the first working day of the week. On Sunday 6 February, businesses, banks and working life resumed in Cairo. An eerie chasm was felt between the anti-government protesters and other sectors of society who were willing to accept that the regime was not going to give up, and wanted life to return to normal. This trend abruptly changed when activist Wael Ghonim was interviewed live by the Egyptian channel Dream TV on 7 February. This was shortly after he was released from ten days of solitary detention, during which he had been blindfolded the whole time. His release and the sincerity of his interview infused the country with renewed vigour to fight.

On 5 February WikiLeaks posted that Mubarak's wealth was estimated at around USD 70 billion. This news was picked up by most media and aired on satellite TV, incensing the masses.[7] From 9 February work stopped at government and public institutions, and hundreds of thousands of union workers went on strike across Egypt. The rallies were intense and the army said that there would be changes coming soon that the protesters would like. It was said that Mubarak was going to give his resignation speech on 10 February. He appeared on TV very late at night on the 10th, but repeated that he was not going to run for president in September. He also stated that he would remain president until then, although delegating his responsibilities to Vice President Omar Suleiman. The crowds went wild. There was an incredible sense of frustration, disbelief and of having been mocked. The Mubarak speech was so disconnected from reality it hardly seemed true. What worried the people were the conflicting messages that were emerging from the government. What was going on? Who was playing what game, and with whom? Was the military co-opting the regime?

The following day, Friday 11 February, masses of people took to the streets. For the first time demonstrations reached the presidential palace. Protests were all over Egypt, drawing numbers not seen before. That evening Suleiman declared on TV that the High Council of the Armed Forces was taking over the responsibility of temporarily governing the country, and that Mubarak was stepping down. The Egyptian revolution took eighteen days: events were organised and documented online, using mobile communication, and followed closely by the media.

Conclusions

That the internet and mobile technology had a strong role in Egypt's political change is indisputable. But in a country where around 20% of the population is connected to the internet, and with a 67% adult literacy rate, there are limits to the outreach and influence of online content and activism. The use of Twitter is even more restricted as it needs a smartphone, a pricey piece of technology and service for a gross national income (GNI) per capita of USD 2,070.[8] The events show that the intertwining of online, mobile and traditional media, especially TV, were crucial in sustaining mass revolts. Without TV picking up the online and mobile messages, most Egyptians would not have known what content was being shared by a relative minority.

Al Jazeera[9] was pivotal in relaying information during the Egyptian internet and mobile blackout, as were other satellite channels – Egyptians from all strata of society use TV satellites widely. Citizen journalism was extensively used and picked up by the media, and often the visuals on YouTube were more powerful than words. The ability to relay events nearly instantaneously from all areas of the country through online and mobile technology gave the professional media incredibly rich, up-to-date material, from the perspective of people on the street.

Still, the capacity of governments to completely block internet and mobile access remains a problem that needs to be addressed. In Egypt the government had always maintained a close grip on ICTs, despite telecom liberalisation efforts. Liberalisation was geared towards the financial benefits of an open market, rather than the reality of centralised

7 Though I found the strong reaction to the news a bit strange, as rumours about the Mubaraks' and their cronies' wealth were a staple in Egypt since the 1990s. It seems that seeing a clear figure of the alleged wealth at this junction in time was the last straw for the masses.

8 www.unicef.org/infobycountry/egypt_statistics.html

9 english.aljazeera.net

control.[10] This control was facilitated by a limited number of internet service providers (ISPs)[11] that offered the country online and mobile access. When the revolution came, the government simply declared martial rule, ordering the companies to cut off their services to the public. Vodafone has been a much cited example. Because it has a broad clientele and is headquartered in Paris, the assumption was that it should have maintained connectivity for longer and not succumbed so readily to regime orders.

It seems from recent events that even traditional media are not necessarily needed to keep social mobilisation going once it is in full swing, as is being seen in Libya, Syria and Yemen. The momentum is, instead, driven by the feeling in the bone marrow when the masses realise their power, when a retreat is impossible due to ingrained conviction, when the sense of right is fully awakened and when national pride is aroused.

Action steps

- Technical alternatives and solutions are needed to enable people to circumvent communications services when they are blocked.
- The ability to share online content through more traditional media so that a wider audience is reached is necessary. In democracy mass ignorance could be fatal to the revolution's aspirations.
- Visuals are often better than a thousand words. What is needed is a platform that can *show* events in the way that YouTube does, but for millions without computers or mobiles, such as billboards.
- There is a need to educate children and youth on how to use the online and mobile platforms responsibly, and how to follow reporting ethics.
- There is a need to continue to make certain platforms more user friendly and intuitive to grow the user base. The average user is not up to the technical skills and tinkering needed today to use many of the crucial online applications.
- Internet and mobile use for emergency situations should be part of public training, in the way that first aid is.
- There is a need to continue to push for conditions that provide internet access to the poor. Social networking sites rely on the use of expensive technology such as the smartphone that is currently marketed to higher income and higher skills customers only. ■

10 www.giswatch.org/en/country-report/civil-society-participation/egypt

11 The main ISPs are Telecom Egypt, Vodafone, Etisalat Misr, Link Egypt and Internet Egypt.

ETHIOPIA

BUILDING ACCESS AS A HUMAN RIGHT

Ethiopian Free and Open Source Software Network (EFOSSNET)
Abebe Chekol
abechekol@yahoo.com

Introduction

Ethiopia, the second fastest growing economy in sub-Saharan Africa,[1] is expanding access to information and communications technologies (ICTs), which are regarded as one of the engines of its ambitious economic growth plan, the Growth and Transformation Plan 2011-2015. Like many countries in Africa, the explosion of access to telecommunications services has been most prominent in the mobile market. The mobile penetration rate increased from less than 0.55% in 2005 to 4.89% in 2009. The expansion of the telecom sector has made record growth in the last two years or so since telecom provider ETC was renamed Ethio Telecom following the takeover of its management by the French telecom provider Orange. In July 2011, Ethio Telecom announced that it had exceeded 10 million mobile subscribers. The incumbent announced that the total number of clients, including fixed-line and internet subscribers, had reached 11.3 million clients.[2]

However, other telecom segments have not developed as quickly as the mobile business. The penetration rate of fixed-line subscribers, for example, increased from 0.82% in 2005 to 1.1% in 2009.[3] Internet access across Ethiopia is also very low. The penetration rate in the country is one of the lowest in Africa, standing on the same footing as Liberia at 0.5% in 2011.[4] But this penetration rate is slowly increasing as wireless broadband technology becomes more established and prices fall.

This report considers the progress achieved in the telecom sector in Ethiopia and its impact on the socioeconomic and political development of the country, with particular reference to the role of the internet and mobile in the socio-political landscape.

Policy and political background

The role played by ICTs in the socioeconomic and political development of the nation is well recognised in the emphasis given to the sector in recent years. Its significant contribution to GDP has been growing (for example, 1.38% in 2008). However, the sector remains a monopoly of the government with no clear sign of liberalisation in the near future. As a result, the sector has not been exploited to its full potential in the last few years through diversified and value-added services.

While the Constitution of the Federal Democratic Republic of Ethiopia guarantees freedom of expression and of the mass media, a number of people argue that some of the recently enacted legislation could potentially restrict such freedoms.

The recently enacted legislation regarding access to and dissemination of information is the Freedom of the Mass Media and Access to Information Proclamation (Proclamation No. 590/2008). This proclamation, in its Article 4 on Freedom of Mass Media, stipulates that "freedom of the mass media is constitutionally guaranteed. Censorship in any form is prohibited." Article 12 of this proclamation on the Right of Access to Information states that "all persons have the right to seek, obtain and communicate any information held by public bodies, except as expressly provided for by this Proclamation." As stated in this article, this right includes access to information from any public body by means of "diskettes, floppies or any other electronic mode or through print-outs where such information is stored in a computer or in any other device."

Furthermore, the Anti-Terrorism Proclamation No. 620/2009 provides the executive organs – for instance, the National Intelligence and Security Service – the power under court warrant to gather or collect information, intercept or conduct surveillance of telephones, faxes, radio, the internet, electronic, postal and similar communications, and to enter into any premise in secret to enforce that interception, or install or remove instruments enabling the interception.

Key issues

Over the past five years, mobile and internet services have made significant contributions to the socioeconomic and political participation of the

1 World Bank (2011) *Global Economic Prospects 2011*, The World Bank, Washington, D.C.
2 www.ethionet.et
3 www.itu.int/ITU-D/ict/statistics
4 www.internetworldstats.com

citizenry. In this regard, a couple of events can be cited that can demonstrate such developments in the country.

One example in the context of social contributions, particularly by mobile service, is the use of RapidSMS in UNICEF's work in supporting the drought-affected areas in Ethiopia in 2008. The impact of this service was dramatic in that UNICEF Ethiopia launched a massive food distribution programme to supply the high-protein food Plumpy'nut to under-nourished children at more than 1,800 feeding centres in the country.[5]

Previously, UNICEF monitored the distribution of food by sending a group of individuals who travelled to each feeding centre. The monitoring group wrote down the amount of food that was received and distributed, and if more food was needed. But there had been a two-week to two-month delay between the collection of that data and analysis, which in turn delayed action. In a famine situation, each day can mean the difference between recovery and starvation, or even death.

With the use of RapidSMS, the delay was completely eliminated. After a short period of training, monitors were able to enter information directly into their mobile phones as SMS messages. This data would instantaneously appear on the server and immediately be visualised as graphs showing potential distribution problems and displayed on a map clearly showing where the problems were. The data, therefore, could be seen not only by the field office, but by the regional office, supply division and even the headquarters, greatly improving response coordination. The process of entering the data into phones was also easier and more cost effective for the monitors themselves, leading to quick adoption of the technology. In this context, it is highly important to have accurate and timely data to make decisions, so that where there are problems, response can be quick, and resources effectively allocated to ultimately save lives. This is a highly dramatic result of the use of mobile technology in social services.

Mobile technology has also been instrumental for the active participation of citizens in the recent political history of the country. The denial of public access to SMS by states is not new in the mobile arena. The SMS ban was enforced during the political unrest that followed the highly contentious May 2005 elections. At that time, the Ethiopian government banned SMS because, it claimed, the main opposition party was exploiting it to organise activities during the elections – just as happens elsewhere. The opposition was particularly effective at using text messaging to mobilise its supporters and get them to the polling stations.

When the election result was announced and subsequently contested, the government moved quickly to shut down the SMS service to ensure the opposition party could not use it again.[6] The service, which was interrupted in June 2005, was restored only after two years in September 2007. The restoration of the service improved the political space and allowed for its use by different actors for socioeconomic development activities, as seen in the case of the RapidSMS service for humanitarian aid.

However, mobile services have not developed far beyond basic voice and limited data services. With the expansion of the currently limited 3G network as well as integrated IP networks as a result of Ethio Telecom's NGN (next generation network) project being finalised and implemented, Ethio Telecom is able to provide data services (simple text/email messaging as well as internet and value-added services) in addition to basic mobile telephony. As a result we see a number of initiatives that have contributed to the socioeconomic development of the country.

The Ethiopian Commodity Exchange (ECX) is one recent success story. It provides IVR (interactive voice response) and SMS-based mobile market information delivery to farmers and traders, avoiding the information gap between the ends of the chain.

Nevertheless, despite this potential for socioeconomic and political participation, the adoption and use of the technologies has been slow. A number of factors could be contributing, including the illiteracy rate, the relative affordability of the telecom services compared to the average income, and insufficient transfer of technology among professionals and technology firms.

The impact of the internet is lower compared to the increasing penetration of mobile. Ethiopia, with the second largest population in Africa, had only 445,500 internet users in early 2011 with a penetration rate of 0.5%. Given that broadband internet is underpinning the fundamental rights of citizens in a number of countries like Finland, providing access to basic connectivity is of paramount importance if countries are to benefit from the global economy, and to participate in increasingly global political spaces.

To bring isolated communities into the global socioeconomic landscape, a number of technology solution providers have developed new technologies

5 www.mobileactive.org/preventing-famine-mobile

6 www.balancingact-africa.com/news/en/issue-no-374/telecoms/sms-ban-lifted-in-et/en

to facilitate communication and access to information. Nokia, for instance, recognises the impact of illiteracy in this regard, and the launch of mobile handsets with local language support in a number of models by the company is a commendable start. And as much as technology providers make every effort to provide mobile operating systems as well as software applications in local languages, it is also in the interest of governments to open up their telecom networks to ensure the full participation of citizens in the information society – and in return utilise the network's full potential for their development goals.

Conclusions

It is widely acknowledged that the internet is still in its infancy in Ethiopia. Access is limited and slow. Where broadband is available, it is typically very expensive – far beyond the financial means of the majority of Ethiopians. This is evident from the low number of fixed broadband internet subscribers, which stood at around 3,500 subscribers in 2009. The challenge for policy makers is to ensure that networks are capable of delivering broadband internet access at affordable prices.

To this end, the government has pledged to dedicate 10% of its annual budget to the development and maintenance of telecom networks.[7] This effort will hopefully improve the expansion of the network and access to information and ICT services.

As seen in the examples above, the role of the internet and mobile in promoting the socioeconomic and political participation of the citizenry is of paramount importance.

Currently, satellite internet is available to some large corporations, but individuals are not permitted to have private satellite connections. Ethio Telecom also bans call back or use of modern technology such as voice over internet protocol (VoIP).[8]

Furthermore, like many countries in Africa, the new ICTs are unequally distributed in Ethiopia, so that to speak of a new communication revolution is still something that must be interpreted within specific social perspectives. Seen in a broad perspective there can be little doubt that the media and the rise of new communication systems have contributed to democratisation in many African countries – including Ethiopia, where at least it has given some people access to information and alternative viewpoints and to channels in which to express their opinions and dissatisfaction.

Action steps

Given the low penetration of ICTs across the country, the role of multimedia community centres is important. These would serve to draw wide and new popular sectors into a media environment.

Low literacy levels and the dominance of international (especially English) rather than local languages on the internet serve to limit the use of computers. These challenges are part of wider issues of underdevelopment central to the role and future of communication policies. This includes connectivity and capacity problems, content development, questions of costs, and unequal social and political access.

Today, access to high-tech communications is accepted as integral to modern life. Communication systems are essential for commerce, culture and politics. More and more they are becoming a basis for multifaceted development strategies. Given the role of media and communication for social change and the full participation of citizens in the socioeconomic and political development of the country, all-inclusive and gender-sensitive ICT policy implementation is essential to build the information society and benefit from the emerging information and knowledge economies. ■

7 en.wikipedia.org/wiki/Internet_in_Ethiopia

8 Adam, L. (2010) *Ethiopia ICT Sector Performance Review 2009/2010: Towards Evidence-based ICT Policy and Regulation.* www.researchICTafrica.net

FRANCE

CONSTITUTIONAL CHALLENGES TO A FREE INTERNET

VECAM
Frédéric Sultan (with La Quadrature du net)*
vecam.org

Introduction

The French Constitutional Council released its decision[1] regarding the controversial LOPPSI bill on 10 March 2011. Judges held that Article 4 of the bill, which allows the executive branch to censor the internet under the pretext of fighting child pornography, is not contrary to the Constitution. In doing so, the constitutional court has failed to protect fundamental freedoms on the internet, and in particular freedom of expression. Hope now lies with European institutions, which are the only ones with the power to prohibit or at least supervise administrative website blocking and its inherent risks of abuse.

The LOPSSI law collated many repressive measures on vastly unrelated subjects. The Constitutional Council found itself caught out in this strategy. While it did strike down some of the most shocking provisions, it left untouched those that seemed less harmful or were proposed in the name of noble goals, in spite of having a highly detrimental impact on civil liberties – such as the ones related to the internet.

According to Jérémie Zimmermann, co-founder and spokesperson for La Quadrature du Net:

> This decision on Article 4 is a great disappointment. It is obvious that internet censorship will not help solve the child pornography problem in any way, as experiments in other countries have shown.[2] After HADOPI's[3] internet access suspension measures, calls to ban WikiLeaks hosting and recent talks against net neutrality, France is siding with the group of countries hostile to a free internet by adopting administrative filtering of the internet."

The following analysis is based on a legal study on the screening measures published in 2009 by a team of European lawyers.[4] It attempts to identify – given the European Convention on Human Rights (ECHR) and related case law – a number of safeguards that must govern any action involving the freedom of communication on the internet. The review of arrangements for supervision of restrictions on fundamental freedoms in play shows that the administration of internet filtering violates some basic principles of the rule of law.

International law and the protection of freedom of expression and communication

Respect for fundamental freedoms is the legal basis of democratic societies and the rule of law. The highest legal protections are granted to fundamental freedoms. These protections are enshrined in law but also in national constitutions and international instruments, and it is traditional for judges to protect each of these levels. The foundation of this protection is the idea that people who enjoy these freedoms must be protected, especially from any interference by the executive and the parliament.[5]

Measures to regulate online communications may, depending on the various cases, violate one or more fundamental freedoms protected by constitutions and conventions:

* This report is based on two articles by La Quadrature du net: Le filtrage d'Internet viole l'État de droit, published 16 November 2010 (minilien.fr/aokwuy) and French Constitutional Council Validates Internet Censorship, published 11 March 2011 (minilien.fr/aokwuz). These are licensed CC-BY-SA, and were reworked with the approval of the original authors. Rewriting and translation by Frédéric Sultan, VECAM.

1 www.conseil-constitutionnel.fr/conseil-constitutionnel/francais/les-decisions/acces-par-date/decisions-depuis-1959/2011/2011-625-dc/decision-n-2011-625-dc-du-10-mars-2011.94924.html

2 See the letter sent by ISPs and the Dutch Task Force on Blocking Child Pornography: www.bof.nl/2011/03/07/dutch-providers-abandon-ineffective-web-bl...; similarly, Germany gave up on filtering as its efficiency could not be proven: www.laquadrature.net/fr/loppsi-comment-lallemagne-a-renonce-a-la-...

3 The French HADOPI law or Creation and Internet law (N°2009-669 of 12 June 2009), also referred to as the "law promoting the distribution of creative works and the protection of rights on the internet", was introduced during 2009 as a means to control and regulate internet access and encourage compliance with copyright laws. HADOPI is the acronym of the government agency created to administer it, the *Haute Autorité pour la Diffusion des Œuvres et la Protection des Droits sur Internet*.

4 Callanan, C., Gercke, M., De Marco, E. and Dries-Ziekenheiner, H. (2009) *Internet Blocking: Balancing Cybercrime Responses in Democratic Societies*, Aconite Internet Solutions. www.aconite.com/blocking/study

5 Terré, F. (2005) Sur la notion de libertés et droits fondamentaux, in Cabrillac, R. et al. (eds) *Libertés et droits fondamentaux*, Dalloz, Paris, p. 195.

- The first of these is, of course, freedom of expression and communication, as these measures prevent the transmission of information and access to this information by the public.
- The second is the right to respect for one's private life and correspondence. Whatever the techniques employed to intercept and block the offending content, private communications will be intercepted as well as criminal communications.

In the ECHR, freedom of communication is protected by Article 10, the second paragraph identifying cases in which this freedom may be restricted if it were to jeopardise "national security, territorial integrity or public safety." Measures are also necessary "for the prevention of disorder or crime, for the protection of health or morals, for the protection of the reputation or rights of others, for preventing the disclosure of information received in confidence, or for maintaining the authority and impartiality of the judiciary." Article 8 of the ECHR, which asserts the right to respect for one's private and family life, also provides a framework if this freedom comes under question.

Conditions on challenges to freedom of communication in European law

As evidenced by the second paragraph of Article 10, any questioning of fundamental freedoms protected by the ECHR must meet a number of conditions to be acceptable. With regard to freedom of communication and the right to respect for one's private life, such interference must, in addition to being required by law, pursue a goal called "legitimate" under the Convention,[6] and be "necessary in a democratic society". This last condition, which looks rather vague, seems to be the most important in terms of interference with freedom of communication, including blocking communications or removing content.

As judges of the European Court of Human Rights (ECtHR)[7] had the opportunity to point out in their jurisprudence, in a "society that wants to remain democratic", the notion of "necessity" of the interference implies that interference refers to "a pressing social need"[8] and is proportionate to the legitimate aim pursued.[9]

Let us examine these two aspects:

- One of the requirements attached to the pressing social need – for which the states have some discretion while remaining dependent on the decisions of the Court – implies that the restriction of liberty ordered must meet this need. So, the measure must be effective.
- Second, the measure must be proportionate to the aim pursued. The Court has distinguished several criteria to assess the proportionality of a restriction. With regard to the screening procedures or removal of content, the Court will check in particular if the purpose of the interference can be satisfactorily achieved by other means less restrictive to rights.

Are screening measures "a necessity in a democratic society"?

Do screening measures meet the criteria of efficiency and proportionality? Are they needed in a democratic society? To answer, we must obviously take into account the purpose (child protection or copyright, for example) as well as technical solutions to prevent access to litigious content. In the case where we seek to prevent access to child abuse content, which is undoubtedly the most pressing need that has been argued to date to justify screening measures, these measures have very different "legitimate aims" that are included in paragraph 2 of Article 10 of the ECHR. These are the protection of morals and protection of the rights of others – especially children and sensitive people who may find such images extremely traumatic – and the prevention of crime and punishment.

6 Article 10 refers in particular to the protection of morals, the protection of the reputation and the rights of others, the guarantee of the authority and impartiality of the judiciary, and the prevention of disorder and crime.

7 The European Court of Human Rights is a supra-national court, established by the European Convention on Human Rights, which provides legal recourse of last resort for individuals who feel that their human rights have been violated by a contracting party to the Convention.

8 See for example ECtHR, 21 January 1999, Fressoz and Roire v. France, Grand Chamber. In this case, the satirical newspaper *Canard enchaîné* had published the tax forms of the head of a big company. The Court concluded that the culpability of the newspaper for revealing secret information violated freedom of expression and the freedom of the newspaper to disseminate information by publishing a document as proof. It particularly criticised the lack of social need: "The need for any restriction on the exercise of freedom of expression must be convincingly established." cmiskp.echr.coe.int/tkp197/view.asp?item=1&portal=hbkm&action=htm ...

9 See for example ECtHR, 26 April 1979, Sunday Times v. UK. "Article 10-2 does not give the states an unlimited power of appreciation. In charge with the Commission to ensure compliance with their commitments (Article 19), the Court has jurisdiction to rule on whether a 'restriction' or 'penalty' is reconcilable with freedom of expression as enshrined in Article 10." The national margin of appreciation goes hand in hand with European supervision. It will be noted that the Constitutional Council employs similar words. See Decision No. 2009-580 DC of 10 June 2009, paragraph 15: "Freedom of expression and communication is all the more precious since its exercise is a prerequisite for democracy and a guarantee of respect for other rights and freedoms, and damage to the exercise of this freedom must be necessary, appropriate and proportionate to the aim pursued."

However, in each of these cases, technical problems with the screening procedures suggest that they are neither effective nor proportionate.

The availability of technical means to bypass screening curtails the effectiveness of these measures. A well-known method, often used by political dissidents in authoritarian regimes, is, for example, to set up a proxy (or encrypted "tunnel") to another computer or server connected to the internet. The criminal networks engaged in the business of child abuse content have long developed distribution channels impermeable to filtering techniques. Whether for prevention or suppression, filtering is totally ineffective in this regard.

Proportionality of filtering measures is also strongly questioned because of their lack of accuracy in implementation. There is broad consensus among experts who emphasise that no methods to block access to content can eliminate the risk of over-blocking perfectly legal sites. Several cases of over-blocking have been identified. In the United Kingdom, Wikipedia, which is one of the busiest sites in the world, was blocked for almost three days in late 2008[10] and blacklisted (secretly) by the Internet Watch Foundation (IWF), due to the publication of the original album cover of *Virgin Killer* by the rock band Scorpions, released in 1976. The cover shows a prepubescent girl posing naked. Because of these inevitable collateral effects, filtering is too dangerous compared to its objectives.

Finally, when the ECtHR assesses the necessary action, it seeks to determine whether alternative measures that are less restrictive of the fundamental freedoms at stake can meet the pressing social need. From this point of view, other measures are more satisfying than the screening procedures. The first one is that the removal of content from servers should be accompanied by international cooperation.[11] (A negative to this is that a study by two United States researchers shows that filtering has the effect of discouraging the activation of international cooperation policies already in existence.)[12] The second one is the possibility for users (parents) to install monitoring systems on their computers to block access. These filtering systems, on the edge of the network and much less intrusive, seem more proportionate to the objective.

10 Wikinews (2008) British ISPs restrict access to Wikipedia amid child pornography allegations, *Wikinews*, 7 December. en.wikinews.org/wiki/British_ISPs_restrict_access_to_Wikipedia_am...

11 Before ordering the blocking of the AAARGH site, hosted in the United States, the French judge had asked the US court to remove the offending content servers, but it refused, citing the protection of the First Amendment to the US Constitution .

12 Moore, T. and Clayton, R. (2008) *The Impact of Incentives on Notice and Take-down*, Computer Laboratory, University of Cambridge. www.cl.cam.ac.uk/~rnc1/takedown.pdf

The procedural framework of attacks on freedom of communication on the internet: The role of ordinary courts

Despite these factors, the French national legislature decided to address a pressing social need (the fight against child pornography) by restricting the freedom of online communication through content filtering. Article 4 of LOPPSI gives the executive power to delete information circulating on the internet. Contrary to its decision on HADOPI, the Constitutional Council has approved the legislation authorising the administrative authority to order measures that conflict with the freedom of online communication. The position of the Constitutional Council seems to be to find, for each case, a balance between protecting freedom of communication and other fundamental rights.

However, the traditional role assigned to the judicial authorities in European law should disqualify the competence of non-judicial entities to impose restrictions of freedom of communication on the internet, and this *a fortiori* when these measures conflict with other fundamental rights, such as the right to respect for one's private life.

Three principles justify the exclusion of non-judicial authorities when it comes to deciding on cases concerning the restriction of freedom of expression:

- **The declaration of illegality** The jurisdiction of ordinary courts is primarily because the judge alone can declare a situation the illegal abuse of freedom. In all liberal democracies, only the judge has jurisdiction to establish the illegality of content, situation or action.
- **The guarantees attached to any criminal charge** Restrictions on freedom of online communication should be accompanied by the guarantee of a fair trial (Article 6 of the ECHR).[13] Indeed, an administrative or judicial injunction of filtering, removing or blocking access to content, if it relates to offences of a criminal nature, seems to be a charge leading to the respect of guarantees attached to fair trial, including the right to be tried by an independent and impartial court.[14]

13 "[E]veryone is entitled to a fair and public hearing within a reasonable time by an independent and impartial tribunal established by law." Article 6-1 of the ECHR.

14 It could be an administrative authority, but the guarantees of Article 6 will apply. The European Court of Human Rights has accepted the validity of the method of administrative penalty under the European Convention of Human Rights and Fundamental Freedoms, but recalled the need to comply with the requirements of Article 6 (ECtHR, 21 February 1984, Oztürk v. FRG). Article 6 applies because the Court will consider administrative sanctions such as criminal charges (ECtHR, 24 September 1997, Garyfallou AEBE v. Greece), or because they feel they relate to rights and obligations of a civil nature (ECtHR, 8 December 1999, Pellegrin v. France).

- **Control of proportionality** The control of proportionality of measures intended to respond to an abuse of freedom of communication is a function traditionally the responsibility of the ordinary courts in democracies.

The role of prior judicial authority in monitoring violations of freedom of communication on the internet

Given these different observations (declaration of illegality, the right to due process and control of proportionality), the judge's role in monitoring violations of freedom of online communication seems essential.

Because of their ineffectiveness and their disproportionate nature, the screening procedures proposed in LOPSSI do not seem able to meet European standards and should be discarded.

Regarding the withdrawal of content, it seems more conceivable that the administrative authority may, for very serious offences, order a hosting provider to take down content. However, at this stage, concerned content will only be "potentially" illegal and the alleged offence needs to be prosecuted.[15]

Beyond these considerations, signatories to the ECHR have discretion regarding the definition of serious offences that can be subject to restrictions of freedom on the part of the administrative authority as a precaution. In reality, this is a choice of a political nature. In 2009, during the review of the Telecoms Package,[16] an amendment was made to this law twice ("Amendment 138") stating that only the judiciary should be able to impose restrictions on freedom of communication on the internet:[17]

> No restrictions may be imposed on fundamental rights and freedoms of end users without a prior ruling by the judicial authorities, notably under Article 11 of the Charter of Fundamental Rights of the European Union on freedom of expression and information, except when public safety is threatened.

It is regrettable that this principle has not been enshrined in European Community law. It would have allowed a rigorous defence of freedom of expression and communication in France.

Action steps

The freedom offered by the internet, such as free communication and other fundamental rights, must be strictly protected by law. The main issues to assert in the context of LOPSSI should include:

- A guarantee of the presumption of legality for any online publication
- We must oppose the requirement for filtering online content because it is disproportionate.
- Citizens must be sufficiently informed of orders to remove content, so that they can legally oppose it.
- Citizens must be sufficiently informed if their access to the internet is blocked, so that they can legally oppose it.
- The right to a fair trial must be guaranteed.
- The government should not be able to impose sanctions that have the effect of restricting freedom without trial.
- The opportunity to speak anonymously online must be guaranteed.

15 See on this issue the proposal of La Quadrature du net as part of the consultancy on the European e-Commerce Directive.

16 Package of five European Directives on the regulation of communications networks and services.

17 www.europarl.europa.eu/sides/getDoc.do?pubRef=-//EP//TEXT+IM-PRES...

INDIA

THE INTERNET AND THE RIGHT TO INFORMATION IN INDIA

Digital Empowerment Foundation
Ritu Srivastava and Osama Manzar
defindia.net

Introduction

The right to information is a basic human right for every citizen, and the internet is an effective medium to access information. The internet is considered one of the most democratic forums, where the expression of one's views knows few barriers and borders. But this does not mean that the freedom of speech and expression on the internet is absolute and unrestricted.

Transparency International's 2010 Index rates Denmark, New Zealand and Singapore the highest when it comes to granting their citizens the right to information.[1] Finland became the first country in the world to make access to the internet a legal right for all citizens in 2010,[2] and now the Netherlands has followed suit.[3] Although it is one of the world's largest democracies, India is also one of the few countries where most state information lies with governing bodies rather than being available publicly.

In India, 70% of the population lives in 638,365 villages,[4] represented by 245,525 panchayat offices, mostly located in the remotest regions of the country. However, rural India is not able to access information due to a lack of infrastructure and means to do so. At the same time, many do not know that they have a right to access information. According to the 2011 census, the literacy rate in India is just 64.32% – with illiteracy most prevalent in rural areas. This is the case even though the government introduced the Right to Education Act in 2004, which promised free elementary and basic education to all children. Yet 35% of the population is still illiterate, and only 15% of Indian students reach high school. Because of this it becomes more important to provide them a medium to access information in a way that they can understand.

Advocating the need for a citizen's basic right to demand information that affects their societal well-being and existence is a mandatory requirement of any democratic society. And it is a citizen's basic right in a democratic society to demand information which is held by governing bodies who are elected by the people to serve the people.

Because of this, movements like the National Campaign for People's Right to Information, Save the Right to Information and India Together have been advocating for the internet to be used to secure the right to information as a basic human right.

Birth of the "right to information" in India

It has been more than 60 years since India's independence – but it is only since 1996 that the government's stranglehold on freedom of information has been lessened. Prior to 1996, India was still burdened by the legacy of the Official Secrets Act 1923, put in place by the British government. This prohibited people from getting any information from government officials. The first step toward recognising the right to information as a basic human right came in 1996 through the establishment of the National Campaign for People's Right to Information (NCPRI),[5] but it took almost a decade to conceptualise the Right to Information (RTI) Act and to bring it into effect.

The "right to information" campaign started as the Mazdoor Kisan Shakti Sangathan (MKSS) movement in the early 1990s, which campaigned against rampant corruption in the system. It was pushing for transparency in the implementation of minimum wages in the remotest part of Rajasthan, one of the largest states in India. The spirit of this movement inspired the citizens and administration in the country. The advocacy work done by MKSS gave rise to the NCPRI, which set out to advocate for the right to information at the national level in 1996. Eventually, in 1999, then Union Minister for Urban Development Ram Jethmalani[6] issued an administrative order that enabled citizens to inspect and receive photocopies

1 www.transparency.org/policy_research/surveys_indices/cpi/2010/results

2 www.nytimes.com/2011/04/28/technology/28internet.html?_r=2&partner=rss&emc=rss

3 www.rijksoverheid.nl/nieuws/2011/05/24/verhagen-gaat-telecomwet-wijzigen-om-vrij-internet-te-garanderen.html

4 censusindia.gov.in/Data_Products/Library/Post_Enumeration_link/No_of_Villages_link/no_villages.html

5 righttoinformation.info

6 For more information on Ram Jethmalani see: en.wikipedia.org/wiki/Ram_Jethmalani

of files from his ministry. Disappointingly, the cabinet secretary at the time did not approve this order, which led to the campaign gaining momentum. The first national Freedom of Information Bill (2000) was introduced in Parliament in 2002. After a long struggle by the MKSS and NCPRI campaigns, the Right to Information Act formally came into force on 12 October 2005.

Through this Act, the Constitution of India has provided both the right to privacy and freedom of speech and expression as fundamental rights, but one right cannot override the other.

Regarding the use of information and communications technologies (ICTs), the government states in the RTI Act:

> Every public authority should provide as much information to the public through various means of communications so that the public has minimum need to use the Act to obtain information. The internet being one of the most effective means of communications, the information may be posted on a website.

Since independence, the RTI Act is probably one of the most influential laws that has been passed making access to information a basic human right. This Act enables citizens to demand information not only from the government and public authorities, but also gives power to citizens to access information from anywhere in the world using the internet as a tool to access the information.

Despite the fact that the spirit of freedom of expression is strong in India, it is still slow in making government information readily available, and government decisions transparent. It is also not easy for citizens to access information due to a lack of infrastructure or technological tools.

Because of this some have advocated for the internet to be used to ensure the right to information as a human right in India.

Using the internet to ensure the right to information in India

With more than 100 million internet users as of December 2010 (of whom 40 million use the internet via mobile phones), India boasts the third highest number of internet users in the world.[7] The internet's presence is reaching into every aspect of people's lives in India: in education, learning, health and, in this case, in helping citizens exercise their right to information.

The internet revolution first made a substantial difference in the lives of citizens when peasants, farmers and landholders of Rajasthan raised their voices demanding the ability to access land records directly through the internet. They were campaigning against rampant corruption and the manipulation of records that goes unabated in rural areas marked by stark poverty and feudalism. In response, an initiative was launched by the Rajasthan state government aiming to bring more accountability and transparency into the system of land records. The initiative enabled farmers to access their land and revenue records online by selecting their tehsil[8] name, account and serial numbers, and paying a fixed amount to the manager of the internet access point (such as a kiosk). Through this project, the state government helped 209 tehsils in the 32 districts of the state, and digitised the jamabandis (land records) of 37,980 villages – as many as 95,490 have been released. This initiative also released the revenue records of the period before April 1996, resulting in around 62,000 pending cases being settled.

The spirit of this movement inspired the Karnataka state government to launch a project called Bhoomi in mid-1999, which aimed to digitise land and revenue records. The Bhoomi project digitised 20 million rural land records of 6.7 million landowners through 177 government-owned and internet-enabled kiosks in the state. Now, farmers and landowners are able to receive their records by providing data such as ownership, tenancy, loans, nature of title, irrigation details, crops grown, etc. This small initiative helped farmers in many ways, from documenting crop loans and legal actions, to securing scholarships for school children.

This project impacted on the whole country, leading the central government to initiate a national-level Digitisation of Land Records project. The state governments involved include Madhya Pradesh, Andhra Pradesh, Gujarat and Maharashtra. Under this initiative, landowners are able to access digitised copies of records of rights, along with property boundaries.

This initiative formed the foundation of a nationwide project aimed at allowing citizens to access information. The Common Services Centres (CSC) programme was launched in 2006 with the goal of setting up 100,000 centres in rural areas across the

7 www.trai.gov.in/WriteReadData/trai/upload/PressReleases/823/Press_Release_Mar-11.pdf

8 A tehsil consists of a city or town that serves as its headquarters, possibly additional towns, and a number of villages. As an entity of local government, it exercises certain fiscal and administrative power over the villages and municipalities within its jurisdiction. It is the ultimate executive agency for land records and related administrative matters. en.wikipedia.org/wiki/Tehsil

country. The project enabled rural citizens to access real-time information as well as various e-government services.

The right to information is included in the National e-Governance Plan (NeGP), which calls for the internet to be used so that "all information covering non-strategic areas [is placed] in the public domain to enable citizens to challenge the data and engage directly in governance reform." The Plan also strengthens the right to information by providing for disclosure by governments in all non-strategic areas. All information should be digitally available as it is not possible to fulfil this requirement through traditional paper-based processes.

Another good example aimed at building transparency between government and citizens is the NREGA (Mahatma Gandhi National Rural Employment Guarantee Act) programme in the state of Andhra Pradesh. This enables hundreds of labourers to receive real-time information, including transactional information such as work done, wages paid, and assets acquired. All this information is publicly shared through the programme's website. They are able to receive this information through the internet or with the help of community-based organisations that provide the information over telephones.

There is now widespread awareness that accessing information is a basic human right and that the internet can help in securing this right. Many activists have taken the cause to the next level and use the power of social networking websites like Facebook and Twitter to spread awareness about the right to information.

One example was highlighted recently when veteran social activist Anna Hazare began a hunger strike, demanding the enactment of the Jan Lokpal Bill[9] that gives wider powers to the Ombudsman to keep corruption in check. The protest began on 5 April 2011. For four days Hazare's fight against corruption spread like wildfire across the internet and he became the most "searched" person on the Google India page. This was largely because of social media websites like Facebook, Twitter and YouTube that played an important part in stitching a nation of concerned citizens together. The 72-year-old activist became a worldwide celebrity on Twitter with tweets that were pouring in every minute and with more than 70,000 "likes" on Facebook. Thousands of youth joined the campaign and supported it in a non-violent way on Facebook and Twitter. Facebook pages such as "Mahatma Gandhi 2.0" and "India Against Corruption" reached over 145,000 "likes" within a day. Within four days, Hazare's non-violent social movement impacted on the central government, which accepted all the demands of the movement.

Another example is the CIC Online project, a key initiative of the Central Information Commission (CIC) and National Informatics Centre (NIC), under the aegis of the NeGP. Now we are also able to file complaints online,[10] and check the status of appeals when the right to information is denied. Effectively, CIC Online has institutionalised the convergence of ICTs with the Right to Information Act 2005.

Although these particular examples have shown the impact of the internet in realising the right to information as a basic human right in India, India has also failed in many ways due to a lack of infrastructure, or when citizens have been unable to utilise or access CSCs. The right to information could be successfully implemented if it could be directly correlated with a level of commitment within the state and central governments of both the political and administrative bureaucrats. It is essential that immediate and wide-scale dissemination of the content of the RTI Act as well as assistance in implementing the Act is provided to all concerned. The Act has also set down obligations on the state and central governments for its implementation and for setting up monitoring mechanisms.

There is a requirement to implement the Act uniformly across the country. No doubt, uniform implementation of the Act will bring transparency to governing bodies and authorities, which will be vital for the functioning of a vibrant democracy. It will create an environment of minimal corruption where governments are accountable to the people. This can be possible only when governing bodies and authorities allow citizens to access their information from anywhere and anytime. Because of this, it becomes necessary to make internet access a basic human right.

Action steps

In developing societies like India, ICTs play an important role in bringing disparate activist groups together. Some of the actions that could be taken include:

- In order to remove the constraints on accessing information, it is important to push for universal access to ICT infrastructure and the availability of information on the internet.

9 www.indiaagainstcorruption.org

10 rti.india.gov.in/index.php

- In an era of Web 2.0, it is important to have free and open models of knowledge creation that ensure protection against undue commercial influence over the free flow of information and knowledge.
- Panchayat Offices can be used as RTI filing centres or can be internet-enabled and converted to Public Citizen Offices (PCOs) where citizens can file RTI applications. The RTI fee could either be based on the rate of a call or decided by a PCO officer.
- In a country where the literacy rate is just 64%, and most are not able to use the internet, there should also be a way to utilise the power of mobile technology for the filing of RTI applications (for instance, using SMS).
- There is a need to properly catalogue, index, and digitise government policies, applications, schemes, papers, announcements, etc. so that these records can be easily accessed.
- Given globalisation, there is a trend towards developing worldwide restrictive intellectual property laws and practices and the coercive implementation of laws, often through technical restrictions. These need to be opposed.
- Civil society needs to identify political contours in the struggle for rights, democracy, equity and social justice, and in a way that enables them to campaign effectively for people's rights. ■

INDONESIA

DOCUMENTING TORTURE: THE RESPONSIBILITIES OF ACTIVISTS

EngageMedia Collective Inc.
Alexandra Crosby
www.engagemedia.org

The ways that human rights activists have employed new technologies have shaped the political upheavals that have punctuated Indonesia's recent history. Probably the best-known example is the footage of human rights abuses in East Timor during the late 1990s, which was televised globally and became one of the key factors in garnering international support for Timor-Leste's independence.[1]

The experience of the 1998 political uprising that overthrew the Suharto regime also showed the power of digital video in generating extensive socio-political changes by mobilising people in support of a new government. In the build-up to the end of the regime, footage of the shootings of Trisakti University students in Jakarta, much of which was "amateur" footage, was broadcast on television inside and outside Indonesia. These images sparked sentiments of national solidarity, leading to mass student protests in several cities across Indonesia, denouncing the New Order regime.

However, today, without the same momentum of mass direct action on the streets that characterised the end of the 20th century in Indonesia, the ways that video can be used to affect change are more ambiguous. Realising that they cannot rely on the foreign press to expose humiliating human rights violation cases, campaigners push their videos through other avenues – such as EngageMedia, YouTube and Facebook – where, instead of relying on news corporation producers, activists can become the producers and distributors themselves. But in becoming more independent, their responsibilities also shift, particularly when it comes to contextualising video information.

This report is concerned with what activists can do with video to improve the situation in West Papua and Indonesia more broadly: to stop human rights abuses, to bring perpetrators to justice, to prevent torture, and to end violence. Our approach is to compare the production and distribution of videos documenting incidents of abuse in order to deepen activist understanding of the mechanics of online distribution of video that has the purpose of social change. This focuses on the work of EngageMedia as one organisation investing in making this distribution not only more effective, but more mindful and secure.

Human rights abuses in West Papua and elsewhere

Indonesia ratified the UN Convention Against Torture in 1998, the same year the brutality of the New Order regime was meant to end. However, the Asian Human Rights Commission says, today "torture is in fact encouraged as a mean[s] of interrogation and intimidation by the police and the military."[2] Because military personnel enjoy special immunity from being tried in civilian courts, acts of torture continue to go unpunished.

Amnesty International reports that in recent years there have been a number of cases of intimidation and attacks against human rights defenders and journalists in Indonesia. Many of these cases have occurred in the province of West Papua, given "special" autonomy by the Megawati government in 2001. West Papua is one of the least accessible places in Indonesia and one of the richest in natural resources.

This report does not have the scope to cover the struggle for self-determination in West Papua. Suffice to say that allegations of torture in the region are hardly new. Since it became part of Indonesia in the 1960s, there has been both a resilient separatist movement and a strong military presence.[3] Amnesty International has documented how victims and witnesses in Papua have few available legal remedies

1 KUNCI Cultural Studies Center and EngageMedia (2009) Video Activism and Video Distribution in Indonesia. www.engagemedia.org/videochronic

2 Asian Human Rights Commission (2010) Indonesia: Video of the military torturing indigenous Papuans surfaced, press release, 17 October. www.humanrights.asia/news/press-releases/AHRC-PRL-021-2010

3 For background on the issues in West Papua, see Drooglever, P. (2009) *An Act of Free Choice: Decolonisation and the Right to Self-Determination in West Papua*, Oneworld Publications, Oxford.

to make complaints.[4] Perhaps more than anywhere else in Indonesia, human rights violations in West Papua have gone unchecked for decades.

As recently as July 2010, Tama Satrya Langkun, a Jakarta-based anti-corruption activist, was severely beaten by unknown persons in an apparent move to silence him. That same month, Ardiansyah Matra, a journalist covering corruption and illegal logging in Papua, was found dead in the province. Despite police investigations, no one has yet been held accountable for these attacks.

Documenting torture

On 30 May 2010, Indonesian military personnel tortured Tunaliwor Kiwo, a Papuan farmer, and his neighbour, using a number of methods, including clamping their genitals, burning them with an iron rod, trying to suffocate them with plastic bags and pulling out their fingernails with pliers. The incident was recorded on a soldier's mobile phone. The ten-minute torture video was released to the public on 18 October 2010, after being leaked to activists. The video was distributed on several websites including the Asian Human Rights Commission (AHRC) site from October and received international attention. Since then, the AHRC has reported attacks on their website along with the sites of several other groups who featured the torture video, including Survival International, West Papua Media Alerts, the Free West Papua Campaign, Friends of People Close To Nature and West Papua Unite. The video also appeared on YouTube.

Many questions arise from this incident, including whether or not this is part of a military culture in which such actions are not considered criminal. Why would a perpetrator want to take pictures of their crime? It is hard to believe that with the ease of upload/download technologies, a soldier would not understand how quickly a video such as this could be disseminated and circulated. Wondering the same about the documentations of abuses at Abu Ghraib, the great United States (US) philosopher Susan Sontag wrote that, rather than being trophies, these images are "inspired by the vast repertory of pornographic imagery available on the internet" and are evidence of the "increasing acceptance of brutality in American life."[5] Perhaps the same could be said of the mainstreaming of violence in Indonesian life – perhaps this acceptance is, sadly, universal. The mutilation of genitals in the cases of both Abu Ghraib and Kiwo's torture represents a violence that seems intertwined with the sexualisation of victims' bodies.[6] Clearly, video evidence of torture presents ethical dilemmas, not only around how it is made and released, but how it is watched and how those who watch are implicated in the processes of social change.

Responding to the public attention around the torture video, video testimony was produced by human rights activists in Jayawijaya. The video testimony was an effort to provide more direct evidence for the case and also to respond to some of the dilemmas mentioned above by contextualising the event. It was passed along to the Papuan Customary Council – Dewan Adat Papua – and handed to Human Rights Watch. The interview was conducted in Lani (the language of the Jayawijaya region – Papua has over 200 languages), which was later translated into Indonesian by a Lani activist, and subtitled in both Indonesian and English. In November, EngageMedia released both videos of the testimony, one with English subtitles,[7] one with Indonesian subtitles.[8]

Video testimony, as opposed to documentary, allows the victim to create his or her own narrative. But in order to be effective, to be able to circulate in the wider world, these narratives require a great deal of context. Translation and subtitling take on renewed importance because they are part of the process of getting as close as possible to the victim's expression of events and making that expression the core of social change campaigns. For such cases, EngageMedia is currently teaming up with Universal Subtitles, an open source, online system that enables collaborative translation and subtitling of video. The system can be accessed on the Universal Subtitles website itself, and can also be used in concert with other video sites such as EngageMedia.org, tapping into already existing networks and communities.[9]

4 See the following reports: Amnesty International Papua Digest, January 2011. www.amnesty.org.uk/uploads/documents/doc_21212.pdf; Open letter on unchecked police abuse in Nabire district, Papua (Index ASA 21/024/2009), 30 November 2009. www.amnesty.org/en/library/info/ASA21/024/2009/en; Unfinished business: Police accountability in Indonesia (Index ASA 21/013/2009), 24 June 2009. www.amnesty.org/en/library/info/ASA21/013/2009/en; Amnesty International's briefing to the UN Committee Against Torture (Index ASA 21/003/2008), 15 April 2008. www.amnesty.org/en/library/info/ASA21/003/2008/en

5 Sontag, S. (2004) Regarding The Torture Of Others, *New York Times Magazine*, 23 May.

6 Carby, H. (2004) A strange and bitter crop: the spectacle of torture, *openDemocracy*, 10 October. www.opendemocracy.net/media-abu_ghraib/article_2149.jsp

7 www.engagemedia.org/Members/dewanadatpapua/videos/kiwotestimony_rev_en.mp4/view

8 www.engagemedia.org/Members/dewanadatpapua/videos/kiwitestimony_id/view

9 The aims for this collaboration are to broaden access to critical human rights and environmental stories from within Southeast Asia, increasing regional and international exposure; develop a Southeast Asia network of volunteer translators and subtitlers of citizen media, human rights and environmental video content; enhance the communication between video advocates, campaigners and citizens in the region to develop shared understandings of the common issues they face; and provide easy access to television stations and other websites to pick up and run non-native language content.

Being sensitive to local languages is just one of the practical challenges of using video in torture cases. "Given the previous cyber attacks," says Enrico Aditjondro, EngageMedia's Indonesia editor, "the decision to publish the testimony was a calculated risk that required careful preparation to ensure the safety of all organisations and individuals involved." As well as Universal Subtitles, EngageMedia teamed up with Human Rights Watch and others to urge the Indonesian government to mount a thorough, impartial and transparent investigation into the episode. This collaboration is important in tracing the way video can be used in concert with human rights campaigns in raising public awareness and bringing about social change.

The Indonesian government responded with a rapid trial of the soldiers involved. The AHRC says the trial only came about after heavy national and international pressure, and the result does not provide an adequate remedy for the gravity of the human rights violations. The perpetrators have not been charged with their actual crime and AHRC rejects this trial as a conclusion of the case. This is not surprising, considering the track record of the Indonesian government in coming to terms with human rights abuses, evident in other cases such as the poisoning of human rights activist Munir Said bin Thalib in September 2004, and the failure to convict any of the generals accused of war crimes in East Timor or Aceh.

Aditjondro says EngageMedia learns from each of these experiences, and continues to face similar dilemmas, most recently concerning the publication of what is known as the "Ahmadiyyah Video". In February 2011, hundreds of villagers in Banten province, west of Jakarta, were filmed marching to a house where twenty Ahmadis[10] had met. The video shows three bloody bodies of Ahmadi men who had been stripped, beaten and dragged from the house to the ground outside. Police officers appear in the video, making no attempt to stop the killing, and scores of young men looked on, recording it with their mobile phones.[11]

EngageMedia and other independent media channels were immediately sent the footage by some of those who recorded the incident. While EngageMedia decided against posting the video on its site, journalist and human rights campaigner Andreas Harsono from Human Rights Watch used his own YouTube account to publish the video. Within minutes, he received numerous death threats. After receiving over 100,000 hits, the video was flagged and blocked. An anonymous uploader then re-posted the complete video on YouTube where it was still available at the time of writing, but viewers need to sign in to see it, due to the graphic nature.[12] Aditjondro says:

> For credibility and integrity, taking responsibility for videos like this is important when they go out in public. But such actions can also endanger advocacy work and made people associated to him [Harsono] vulnerable as well. The story of Andreas Harsono helped activists realise the security implications of doing digital campaigning, particularly those activists working in more repressive environments such as West Papua.

Aditjondro also says that EngageMedia, knowing that the videos would be on YouTube, was more concerned with contextualising the event, and posted a news story with links to the footage.[13] "Watching violence for the sake of it doesn't achieve anything," he says.

This incident, and the extrapolation of the torture video into Kiwo's testimony, also point out some of the responsibilities video makers and distributors have to their subjects and how people watch and interpret disturbing footage. While all activists have the same aim of exposing violations of human rights, not all campaigns take the same measures to make sure victims and their supporters have a voice and still remain secure.

In the case of the video of the torture itself, we cannot know how this video got into activist hands, whether it was intentionally or accidentally leaked. But, having the infrastructure in place for distribution, what we do with these opportunities in a way that is responsible and clear is a great challenge. This requires partnerships between technologists and human rights agencies. More than ever before, these networks must operate with an unprecedented level of security, speed and collaboration.

10 Ahmadis, who practice the Ahmadiyya form of Islam, have been subject to various forms of persecution since the movement's inception in 1889. Ahmadiyya is a controversial religious minority in Indonesia that rose sharply in the 2000s with a rise of Islamic fundamentalism. As of 2011, the sect faces widespread calls for a total "ban" in Indonesia.

11 Dewan, A. (2011) Why We Should Support Indonesian Schools, *New Matilda*, 16 February. newmatilda.com/2011/02/16/why-we-should-support-indonesian-schools

12 www.youtube.com/verify_age?next_url=http%3A//www.youtube.com/watch%3Fv%3DDWHzc8ZxRuQ%26feature%3Dplayer_embedded

13 EngageMedia (2011) Ahmadiyah bloodied video leads to calls for revoke of decree against religious minority, 14 February. www.engagemedia.org/Members/cikeusik/news/ahmadiyah-bloodied-video-leads-to-calls-for-revoke-of-decree-against-religious-minority

Concluding notes

Kiwo's story and the ways video has been generated from it tell us a great deal about the potential of information and communications technologies (ICTs) for human rights and social resistance. But they also relay the limitations of online video activism. Without an approach that also supports victims of human rights abuses in their day-to-day lives, in their own languages, what good is such evidence?

This report has focused on particular incidents because of the repercussions on activist security and because of the clear pressure they put on authorities. But this report concerned the impact of video in specific incidents. The story of human rights in Papua and other places is far more complex. Infant mortality, sexual health, land rights, access to basic human needs all indicate a grim situation for many indigenous people all over the world. Yet these stories are unlikely to receive many hits on YouTube. How can these issues also be integrated into a different type of activism, one that can move beyond the shock of violence shaming us into a real world response?

Perhaps more than any other medium, video has the power to reframe stories. Kiwo's story is much more than a file viewed in browsers and copied over servers. Taking responsibility for how videos effect change is about making them more than nameless images of violence.

Action steps

The immediate action to be taken around this incident is demanding the retrial of the soldiers who perpetrated the torture of Kiwo and his neighbour. This requires ongoing support for local activists in West Papua from regional and global networks.

More broadly, activists need to:

- Be informed. Listen, watch and read stories from West Papua at www.engagemedia.org/taxonomy/countries/WP
- Follow the AHRC campaign to end violence in West Papua at www.humanrights.asia/countries/indonesia/end-violence-in-west-papua
- Sign the petition opposing US cooperation with Kopassus (the Indonesian Special Forces Command) at www.gopetition.com/petitions/dont-train-indonesias-deadly-kopassus.html
- Consider security implications to filmmakers and witnesses when conducting video documentation of human rights violations
- Download *Video for Change: A How-To Guide on Using Video in Advocacy and Activism* from www.witness.org
- Visit Tactical Tech Security-in-a-Box at www.tacticaltech.org/securityinabox ▪

IRAN

THE INTERNET AND CIVIL RESISTANCE: FREEDOMS AND STATE REPRESSION

Arseh Sevom School
Sohrab Razzaghi
www.3rdsphereschool.org

Introduction

In recent years, the Iranian political-civil rights movement has used the internet as an important tool for free access to and exchange of information. This has broken the government monopoly on news media, expanded social networks, built capacity and empowered both citizens and activists. However, the government is alert to this potential, and has launched its own cyber war on activists. This report highlights the important but ambivalent role the internet plays in social resistance in Iran.

The internet, human rights, and civil resistance in Iran

Blogs have played an important role in the social struggle and civic resistance of the Iranian people. Civil rights activists in Iran have depended on blogs more than any other tool for expanding social networks, and engaging in civil resistance. Blogs offer a vibrant field for challenging dominant ideological and theoretical assumptions, and for news reporting on Iranian victims of human rights abuses. Writing blogs has given many Iranian men and women the ability to express their beliefs, demands and interests without censorship. They can create their own "cyber identity" without fear of being discovered (with the concomitant consequences), and can make their "hidden self" public.

Blogs are one of the most important political advantages progressive Iranians have in the internet world. In the Iranian calendar year 1383 (March 2004-March 2005), Iran ranked highest in the number of blogs produced in the world – and although that ranking decreased slightly last year (2010), Iran is still one of the top ten blog-producing countries in the world.

The women's movement in Iran was one of the first social movements to recognise the importance and influence of the internet. Women activists used the internet as their most important tool in information media for the purposes of advancing their social struggle. Iranian women have always been amongst the most marginalised groups in society, and because of this they have always been looking for opportunities to create alternative civic spaces, and exploiting those spaces for advancing Iranian women's collective struggle. For them the internet quickly transformed into an alternative civic space for social resistance, in place of the many political and social spaces in which women did not have and do not have much influence.

The women's movement was able to use the internet as a communications tool for spreading news about the conditions of Iranian women, breaking taboos, and mobilising and organising women in protests against anti-women legislation. The internet also allowed the Iranian women's movement the opportunity to connect with international women's movements and coalitions and raise awareness about the plight of Iranian women within international circles.

One of the successful strategies for using the internet in the social struggle has been the One Million Signatures Campaign for Changing the Discriminatory Laws against Women in Iran. In a short time, this campaign allowed Iranian women to shine light on some of the limitations of Iranian society, while demonstrating their qualitatively different experience in the world.

In recent years, civic activists have created campaigns in cyberspace for human rights issues, victims of human rights abuses, and focusing on single-issue civic demands. The campaign against stoning is one such campaign. Here a group of human rights activists wrote a letter addressed to the Chief of the Judiciary demanding the nullification of the Stoning Law and circulated it online to gather signatures. This letter presented brief reports of people who were awaiting stoning sentences and expressed the activists' criticisms about stoning being in conflict with Shariah (Islamic law), Iranian common law, and international human rights laws.

Other campaigns include: Opposition to the Imprisonment of Students Involved in the 1999 Tehran University Dormitory Attacks; Demanding Freedom for all Political Prisoners (presently 800 political-civic activists are imprisoned); the Campaign Against Sakineh Ashtiani's Stoning Sentence; the Campaign Against Execution; the Green Protest Campaign; and the Campaign for Freedom of Assembly and Association in Iran.

Censorship and the shutting down of websites and blogs represent some of the major difficulties that civil resistance in cyberspace faces. Just as the government censors and limits access to and the exchange of information between Iranian citizens, it continually employs new methods for filtering internet use. In response, civic activists have invented numerous methods for bypassing filtering. These include using filter "breaking" sites, proxies, exploiting alternative software, and Google caches, amongst others.

Another act of resistance against the regime's policies, especially the Iranian "Cyber Army" attacks – essentially online "troops" sent to stifle civil resistance – is the hacking of government sites and government-supported sites. In the last two years, civil activists have attacked government sites such as the Islamic Republic of Iran Presidency site, the Islamic Republic News Agency (IRNA) site, Fars News, Raja News, and many others – multiple times. Through this method, they have expressed their protest against government policies and programmes.

The Green Movement represented a qualitatively new experience in using the internet to further social militancy and expand civil resistance in Iran. This movement emerged from the womb of a wider-based social movement, which we can label the movement for political-civil rights. Its most visible moment of civic resistance was on 12 June 2009, the day of elections, when it took to the streets, demanding: "Where is my vote?" This movement constituted a reaction to the governing methods of Iran's rulers, the imposition of a particular kind of existence, the widespread violation of human and civil rights, and corruption and disorganisation within Iranian society. It called for a government based on the rule of law, the expansion of democratic relationships, and a commitment to standards and criteria of human rights and peace within Iranian society.

By using the internet, this movement was able to communicate the voices of Iranians to the outside word. By using new forms of internet media as a political weapon, Green Movement activists successfully brought the government's legitimacy into question, and dispelled the regime's myths.

Facebook, news websites and video exchanges on YouTube have been some of the main tools of civic activists in the political-social struggle against government deception and the widespread violation of human rights. For example, the video of the murder of "Neda Agha-Soltan" was first published on Facebook and shortly sent shockwaves across the entire world.

Another useful experience in using the internet for civil resistance in Iran comes from the actions of a group of youths who used it for resisting government policies and breaking cultural taboos. A group of young boys and girls used Facebook to organise a public water gun fight at the Water and Fire Park in Tehran. On the morning of Friday 29 July 2011, a considerably large group of people gathered at the park, and some families came out with their children as well, to play with water guns and relish the joy of being outside. However, the security forces reacted forcefully and swiftly, stopping the event and arresting a number of participants.

Meanwhile, alongside the expansion of the political-civil rights movement in Iran by using new communications tools to help democratise Iran, the false government has also attempted to use these tools to solidify its rule and silence the Iranian people's civil resistance.

Policy and regulation

In 2009, a new political class was able to come to power by widely manipulating the tenth presidential elections, with the full support of the military. These actions resulted in the formation of a garrison state, the expansion of populism in the societal and political spheres, the renewed rise of ideological discourses, and the suppression of the middle class and cultural classes. During the past few years, this new political class in Iran has attempted to make itself the sole power and independent actor in the fields of politics, society, economy and culture within Iranian society. It has also attempted to have a determinant role in all fields of Iranian life, and to govern Iranian society based only upon its ideological and theoretical assumptions. Effectively, it wanted to occupy all civic spaces, preventing alternative discourses from politicising society, and destroy all associations engaging in political resistance. The ultimate consequence of all of this was the obstruction and constriction of civil and political society, the limitation of political-civil freedoms, and the widespread violation of human rights in Iranian society.

This new political class, in advancing its project to homogenise Iranian society and social thought, has likewise attempted to promote and make dominant a culture of inertia and silence in Iran. It aims to disrupt, obstruct and control access to and the free exchange of information.

The most important programmes that the Iranian government has used to limit the people's right to access the internet, shut down communications and break up civil resistance in cyberspace include the following:

- Preventing the development of and investment in internet infrastructure, despite the fact that the Fourth and Fifth Five-Year Social-Economic Development Plans (2005-2009 and 2010-2014) emphasise the need to develop and invest in internet infrastructure.

  According to statistics presented by Iran's National Internet Development Management Centre, by March 2011, 32.66% of Iran's total population used the internet through various methods. In addition to dial-up internet, ADSL has been introduced in the country, and now wireless internet on the WiMAX platform is available. Based on a report by MATMA (National Internet Development Agency of the Islamic Republic of Iran), most internet users in the country are GPRS subscribers, and use their mobile phones to connect to the internet – constituting more than 41% of all internet users in Iran.

  However, by the end of the Iranian year 1389 (March 2011), 29% of all internet users in the country used dial-up telephone services to connect to the internet. Because of legal limitations for residential users, who constitute a large portion of internet users, high-speed internet bandwidth is only 128 kilobits per second in Iran (equal to 8.12 bytes per second), and high-speed bandwidth is generally limited. In addition to limited speeds, the high cost of high-speed internet and power instability can be added to the difficulties that Iranians face.[1]

- Shutting down access to and the free exchange of information and the obstruction of communication networks. The government has frequently resorted to disrupting or reducing Iranian internet speeds in the last two years – especially from 15-21 June 2009, and in the months following the 2009 elections. It is necessary to note that the Iranian government is the main provider of internet services in Iran through the Iran Telecommunications Company, and it can disrupt or obstruct internet access and the free flow of information at any time. In the year 1388 (March 2010-March 2011), a majority stake in the ownership of the government-owned telecommunications company was given to the Iranian Revolutionary Guard Corps.

- Widespread filtering of sites and blogs is one of the other actions the government has taken to stifle civil resistance and prevent access to and free exchange of information during recent years. Identifying "forbidden" pages and filtering them occurs via multiple methods. The common methods used are filtering based on IP addresses, domain names, page addresses, keywords and page content.

  For expanding the reach of filtering, Iranian officials use full-featured blocking software, which has been purchased from China and Russia. The criteria for identifying and blocking websites are determined and announced by the "Committee for Determining Examples of Criminal Web Content" comprised of representatives from the security institutions. Censorship and filtering in Iran happen through the main gateways, combined with the blocking of certain URLs. Iran is one of the ten countries named as "Enemies of the Internet" by Reporters Without Borders in 2011.[2]

- Online attacks by the government's Cyber Army is another strategy used to foil civil resistance. The identity of the Cyber Army was at first unclear, until Ebrahim Jabbari, Commander of the Iranian Revolutionary Guard Committee (IRGC) Ali Ibn Abi Taleb Ground Forces Regiment, announced on 20 May 2010, "Today, we witness that the IRGC has been successful in founding a cyber army that is only the second cyber army to exist in the entire world."[3] In May 2009, the public relations office of the Revolutionary and Public Court of Tehran announced that, following a series of complex intelligence operations, 30 people suspected of participating in the group called "cyber wars" were arrested. This action followed a wave of attacks against anti-government websites and blogs by the Iranian Cyber Army.

  Although the IRGC had clearly begun combating what it viewed as "immoral sites" through the creation of GERDAB (the Centre for Combating Organised Cyber Crimes), the IRGC did not begin confronting social-political media until a directive issued following the events of 12 June 2009, and the emergence of the Iranian people's political-civil rights movement. It appears that the IRGC, in addition to dominating all communications infrastructures and information networks in Iran, has direct responsibility for the guidance and management of "cyber wars" within the Iranian government. In addition to the Cyber Army, other institutions such as the IRGC

1 www.mehrnews.com/fa/newsdetail.aspx?NewsID=131042

2 march12.rsf.org/en

3 english.farsnews.com/farsnews.php

Department of Cyber Defence and the Security Police for the Exchange of Information (FATA) were also created in 2010. Alongside these institutions, "observational teams" and activity monitoring centres that track internet users are working hard, and the IRGC is making efforts to recruit hackers and computer security experts with very high salaries and benefits.

- Another of the government's actions to fight the "soft war" against cyber civil society was the allocation of a budget of 500 billion tomans (about USD 500 million) in the calendar year 1389 (March 2010-2011) to the Basij, paramilitary forces affiliated to the IRGC. The Basij have attempted to conquer Iranian cyberspace by producing pro-government content, using psychological warfare, and creating insecurity amongst Iranian social networks. In order to achieve their goal, namely, a "pure internet", the government has recruited 8,000 Basijis for this work. The Communications and Information Technology minister first brought up the idea of a "pure internet" in 2010. The minister claimed that within internet networks, "rogue elements" exist that have become a serious problem in real-world communities, and, on that basis, the government must protect the Iranian people from such harm. On 16 April 2011, the Deputy for Supervision and Coordination in Economic Policies for the First Vice President announced, "The first halaal internet network, one that is pure from immoral websites, has been launched inside Iran."[4]

Conclusion

The experience of Iran shows that just as much as the internet can be a productive tool for advancing democracy, human rights, and the political-civil rights movement, it can also be used in the service of authoritarian regimes, who use it to repress and identify civil activists and consolidate their rule over society.

Civil activists in Iran have used multiple methods to protest in the last two years, ranging from street demonstrations to online campaigns, blogging, producing and publishing video files using mobile phones, writing graffiti on paper currency, and even hunger strikes in prison. The use of social networks and the internet has played a very important role in publishing pictures, videos and news stories about protests, and helping individuals express personal opinions, reflecting the reality of events both inside Iran and in the broader world. In this respect, internet use has been an important political act.

Nonetheless, the internet can also deplete the energy of the opposition, and create artificial feelings of satisfaction, the consequence of which is inaction in the real world of activism. The internet has also effectively turned the activist into a solitary, protesting computer user, fighting against multiple government computers. Meanwhile, as everyone knows, "The revolution will never happen without revolutionary people."

Action steps

Despite all of their inherent limitations and challenges, the internet and cyberspace remain the most important tool for civil activists and the political-civil rights movement for access to and exchange of information, organising, mobilising society, and democratising the nation.

In response to the widespread governmental programmes to limit and restrict access to the internet, including its cyber war programme, an important step is the development of software and educating users in Iran in order to secure communication among social and political activists at home and internationally. ■

4 www.tabnak.ir/fa/news/158720

ITALY

BLOCKING ITALY'S "GAG LAW"

With the support of Centro Nexa
Arturo Di Corinto and Giacomo Mazzone
nexa.polito.it and
www.dicorinto.it/?s= internet+governance

Introduction

After many attempts to restrict freedom of expression on the internet, the Italian government has proposed a new anti-internet law, the so-called "gag law". The proposed law will create a very special situation in the country, compared to the other G7 economies.

In Italy, 96.1% of households have a television, but only 47.3% are connected to the internet,[1] suggesting how far Italy lags behind other G7 countries. The digital divide impacts negatively on the concrete possibilities of using the internet for human rights. For instance, according to the Organisation for Economic Co-operation and Development (OECD), Italy shows the lowest broadband penetration among G7 countries (20.5% in December 2009). The development of internet infrastructure suffers from a lack of investment in technological improvement: according to employers' association Confindustria,[2] information and communications technology (ICT) investment represents less than 2% of Italy's GDP; recently an important public investment to overcome the digital divide (800 million euro) was first announced and then stopped.

By the end of 2008, broadband access was available in almost 95.7% of Italy, but the statistics do not consider that most of this coverage comes from ADSL technology which presents technical difficulties in interfacing with traditional copper phone lines. Fibre-to-the-home (FTTH) and fibre-to-the-business (FTTB) connections remain limited, while the majority of internet users currently use household connections with an average download speed of 3-4 Mbit/s.[3]

On top of the scarce internet infrastructure, information and media literacy in Italy is limited. In 2009, according to Confindustria, 38% of Italian households had no computer literacy, and more than half of the IT users were not able to perform basic operations such as using spreadsheets or zipping files.

However, the recent success of mobile internet is opening new scenarios for the online world: if most 3G devices are still purchased by those who are already IT literate, the booming industry of smartphones in a country where 90% are mobile phone users is introducing a new wave of users to the internet.

Political context

Italy's president of the Council of Ministers, Silvio Berlusconi, is also a media tycoon, controlling directly or indirectly five out of seven of the major TV channels in the country. Because of this he is not interested in helping to democratise mass communication. On the contrary, he fears that he may lose control over the production of information and audiovisual content.

Since his first nomination at the head of the government in 1994, the main priority of Berlusconi has been to consolidate and increase his control over traditional media: television, press and publishing companies. In order to do so he had to violate or ignore (or even repeal) a certain number of safeguards that had existed in Italian laws and regulation, including the Constitution.

In fact, the Italian Constitution – written just after twenty years of fascist regime – recognises freedom of expression in its Article 21:

> (1) Everyone has the right to freely express thoughts in speech, writing, and through other means of communication.
>
> (2) The press may not be controlled by the authorities or be censored.
>
> (3) Seizing media assets is permitted only by judicial order stating the reason for the action, and only for offences expressly determined by the press law or for violation of the obligation to identify the persons responsible for such offences.
>
> (4) In cases of absolute urgency where immediate judicial intervention is impossible, periodicals may be seized by the judicial police,

1 www.istat.it
2 www.confindustria.it
3 www.sostariffe.it

who must immediately and in no case later than 24 hours report the matter to the judiciary. If the measure is not validated by the judiciary within another 24 hours, it is considered revoked and has no effect.

(5) The law may, through a general provision, order the disclosure of financial sources of publications.

(6) Publications, performances, and other exhibits offensive to public morality are prohibited. Measures of prevention and punishment against violations are provided by law.

The "gag law"...

Italy represents an interesting case study for online freedom of expression. It is a European democracy that has lived with the anomaly of a media tycoon in power for ten out of the last seventeen years. In fact, Berlusconi's massive conflict of interest impacts on the online world and is arguably at the heart of Italy's lack of internet infrastructure development.

The Italian establishment's hostility towards the internet is translated into two main behaviours by Berlusconi's power/political/media chain: either not developing any proactive policy to foster the online word and build internet infrastructure with public resources, or proactively trying to "regulate" the e-content sector and to undermine the public's perception of the internet.

Mainstream media and political leaders portray the internet most often as a threat to avoid than as an opportunity to grasp. Its negative aspects are constantly stressed, while the positive impact on freedom of speech is generally underestimated. This is particularly striking when dealing with libel and privacy concerns. The internet is often accused of spreading anxiety together with defamatory content, which in turn need to be blocked in some way in order to respect human dignity and the right to privacy.

However, Berlusconi and the Italian establishment have (so far) not succeeded in having any real influence on freedom of expression online, and the web is now enjoying a comparatively broader sense of pluralism and freedom. The indirect and "soft" strategies attempting to undermine online freedom of expression have so far been bypassed or ignored by users and e-content producers.

However, in 2010 newer, more aggressive strategies were put forward by the anti-internet establishment, and denounced by observers such as the Organization for Security and Co-operation in Europe (OSCE) Representative on Freedom of the Media and Reporters Without Borders.

After many attempts to restrict freedom of expression on the internet agora – the crusades against peer-to-peer file sharing (P2P), anonymity, the right to oblivion – the Italian government introduced a new anti-internet law. Called the "gag law" and also known as the Alfano Bill, it has resulted in widespread opposition in Italy. Article 29 of the proposed law for the first time imposes responsibilities on online sites – including amateur ones – that are equivalent to restrictions on the press. In the case of defamatory comments, the proposal requires a right to reply within 48 hours, obliging the blogger to correct news content as required by the Italian Press Law of 1948, which provides for harsh penalties when this is not done.

While the proposal lists internet sites as part of the media obliged to provide this guarantee, critics say that such a provision seems inappropriate for bloggers, amongst others who have no professional or legal support and risk a huge fine if they do not comply within the strict time limit. If implemented, such a measure will push most bloggers towards self-censorship.

This is probably the real aim of such a proposal, especially if we consider that all the cases that have been raised as justifications for such a measure have concerned Berlusconi and his sexual affairs, his party's scandals, or cases of organised crime suspected of being connected to political parties.

Unlike formal media companies, bloggers and most informal websites are not in fact able to assess the merits of a request for correcting information. Typically this involves a complex chain of professionals backed by a legal department. The law, in short, is intimidating: politicians do not care about correcting the blog of a sixteen-year-old written on her bed and read only by a few friends. They are interested in what you write about them on Wikipedia.it.

For all these reasons bloggers took to the streets on 1 July 2010 in Rome, teaming up with the Italian Journalists Union and many civil rights associations in an attempt to block the law.

The protests and widespread commentary on the law would not have been possible without an information campaign using, ironically, the internet. Some 240,000 signatures protesting the proposed law were collected on the site nobavaglio.it and another 90,000 via Facebook. The protests received further exposure through the mainstream media that could not ignore the news.

This attack is not isolated, but part of a general trend...

In the last five years, the internet in Italy has been subject to different legislative measures (or attempted measures) aimed to introduce new sets of regulations restricting users' rights to online information.

For instance, the "Pisanu Decree", justified as a temporary anti-terrorism measure after the attacks in the London underground in 2005, introduced the obligation for connectivity providers to secure administrative authorisation and to force those who access the internet at Wi-Fi hotspots and in internet cafés to register with an ID document. The measure has subsequently been extended by decree, with the end result of curtailing the development of free Wi-Fi in Italy, an anomaly considering that countries with a high risk of terrorist attacks such as Israel and the United States have no such laws, and Wi-Fi hotspots are widespread.

The "Gentiloni Decree", adopted in 2006, identified two main ways to block access to child pornography through domain name system (DNS) and internet protocol (IP) blocking. However, this does not pay due attention to the common practice of IP address sharing, which results in a potential risk of blackout for websites which share the same IP address with illicit ones.

In the few months preceding the announcement of the proposed "gag law", two other legislative initiatives raised concerns among online freedom observers. Firstly, the draft of a decree implementing the European AVMS Directive 2007/65/CE (the so-called "Romani Decree") extended part of television broadcasting regulation to audiovisual content on the internet, imposing unusual rules such as the obligation to obtain administrative authorisation for audiovisual streaming and a stricter copyright regime. Audiovisual producers and platforms, together with internet service providers (ISPs), expressed concerns about the repercussions of such a measure, given the possibility of being held liable for e-content hosted.

Secondly, a similar concern was expressed in the aftermath of a case known as "Google vs. Vivi Down",[4] in which the Milan Court found three Google executives criminally liable for data protection violations under the Italian Privacy Code because of a video temporarily hosted on Google Video. This case followed a large number of proposals from MPs that sought to introduce specific punishments for crimes committed on the internet.

4 www.reuters.com/article/2010/02/24/us-italy-google-conviction-idUSTRE61N2G520100224

These concerns were met with government assurances that it would intervene soon with specific proposals – assurance which amounted to little when the sentence on Google's executives was overturned by the courts and defined as a judiciary mistake.

Conclusions

The internet allows new voices to enter debates by reducing the influence of gatekeepers and by allowing citizen journalism to flourish. This is why those who seek to control traditional media organisations are "enemies of the net". It is also why the Italian internet community has opposed the new "gag law".

Now that the grip of Berlusconi's majority party over the electorate seems to be becoming weaker, it is very likely that those in power will have less margin to manoeuvre in attempts to intervene and restrict the freedom of the internet.

In particular, the campaign over a referendum vote on 12 June 2011 has proved to the public and to the parties that control over traditional media is not enough to manipulate an entire country and to hide the truth.

The impact of the internet revolution on politics is beginning to be felt in Italy. The role of social networks and the use of mobile phones in support of campaigns are already well established. Opposition parties are now trying to use the same social media model to counter the control Berlusconi and his political allies have over traditional media in Italy: twelve million internet connections against five of the country's TV networks! It will be interesting to see over the next months how this conflict will evolve and who will win in the end.

Action steps

Due to the current situation in the country, in order to produce real effects, actions need to intervene simultaneously on various fronts and tackle several problems at the same time.

The low rate of internet penetration, together with the legislative attempts to limit online freedom of expression, will continue to threaten online pluralism. Because of this, action steps in the field of enabling online freedom of expression and online access to information should be focused on tackling the issues hindering internet development:

Infrastructure

- Policy makers should push to eliminate the digital divide by introducing different technological standards in order to spread broadband and wireless coverage.

Legislation

- Internet actors need a legal framework for the internet that is not just an extension of traditional press regulations.
- Freedom of expression should be considered a fundamental value embodied in the open and transparent management of the infrastructure of the internet.

Education

- ICT and media literacy initiatives should be encouraged, in order to improve e-knowledge amongst the Italian population.

Concerning the specific problems posed by the "gag law", possible actions could consist of:

- Monitoring the progression of the proposal in parliament
- Updating information on campaign sites
- Spreading the news amongst global networks
- Educating Italian citizens about the importance of freedom of expression on the internet and not only in the traditional media (this still represents the main focus of public attention). ■

JAMAICA

SAVING A PRIZED JAMAICAN WILDERNESS: COMBINING INTERNET PROTESTS WITH LOCAL ACTIVISM

Telecommunications Policy and Management Programme, University of the West Indies
Hopeton S. Dunn
myspot.mona.uwi.edu/msb/biblio

Introduction

The Cockpit Country region in northwestern Jamaica has immense historical and environmental importance. Sparsely populated by rural farmers, it is regarded by geographers as:

> [T]he largest remaining intact primary wet limestone forest in Jamaica, and is the home to what is likely to be the only viable population of the globally endangered Giant Swallowtail Butterfly. Many of Jamaica's threatened birds are found there, including the endangered Jamaican Blackbird, and it is the habitat for 95% of Jamaica's endemic Black-billed Parrot population.[1]

Its vast and varied vegetative cover is considered to have significant medicinal importance. Additionally, the Cockpit area replenishes the aquifers of major rivers such as the Black River, Great River, Martha Brae, Montego River and Hector's River. These rivers supply water to at least three of Jamaica's fourteen parishes.

Against that background, this Jamaica country report outlines and explains the role of the internet, alongside other traditional media forms, in the advocacy and resistance of Jamaican lobbyists opposed to the government's granting of licences for bauxite prospecting in the Cockpit Country region.

Policy and political context

Though still in need of updating, Jamaica's policy frameworks governing the information and communications technology (ICT) sector and the environment are steadily reaching global standards. In 2010, the government launched its new ICT policy, which takes into account relatively new developments in ICTs and digital convergence. There is a Telecommunications Act (2000), an Access to Information Act (2002), the Electronic Transactions Act (2007), Cybercrimes Act (2010), and a Copyright Act (1993), all which occur in a context of ample freedom of expression guaranteed by the Constitution. The main legislation underpinning environmental regulation is the Natural Resources Conservation Authority Act (1991), which forms the basis for the establishment of the Natural Resources Conservation Authority (NRCA). In terms of the actual enforcement of the NRCA Act, the National Environmental Planning Agency (NEPA) has the lead responsibility.

Among the varying functions of the NRCA is to advise the minister on "matters of general policy relating to the management, development, conservation and care of the environment."[2] Additionally, Section 5 of the NRCA Act grants the minister power over the NRCA. This ostensibly compromises the autonomy and impartiality of the NRCA. If this is so, then in instances where the government authorises economic or social activity that may be deemed to have a deleterious impact on the environment, civil society and activists may have to intervene in the public interest, since the NRCA can be overruled by the minister. The central challenge, however, concerns balancing the need for environmental protection and the need for economic development and expansion, which is the main prerogative of the political directorate.

Internet activism and human rights

In December 2006, the Jamaican public was informed that the minister of agriculture had granted a prospecting licence to the mining company Alcoa. This news was not of itself unusual, excepting that the particular prospecting licence would permit Alcoa to explore for bauxite in the Cockpit Country, that area of significant national and international environmental significance so treasured by both historians and environmentalists.

Professor Michael Day, an international expert on geomorphology, is quoted as saying:

> The Cockpit Country is the international type-example of cockpit karst landscape, and is recognised world-wide as a unique and invaluable natural heritage. In addition to its iconic landscape status, it has great biological

1 www.cockpitcountry.org/factsheet.html

2 Natural Resources Conservation Authority Act of 1991, p. 4. www.nepa.gov.jm/legal/nrca_act_Ipart1.htm

> significance and plays a critical role in maintaining regional groundwater supplies and river discharges. It is probably the only near-pristine karst system remaining in the Caribbean. Additionally, the Cockpit Country has historical and cultural value as a hearth of resistance to colonial occupation.[3]

Beyond just the environmental ramifications, it was felt that the government's unilateral action violated the procedural rights of Jamaicans to be consulted and to be fully engaged in the process of determining whether the Cockpit Country area should be mined for bauxite. These rights are entrenched and guaranteed in the Universal Declaration of Human Rights (UDHR) and the Aarhus Convention on Access to Information, Public Participation in Decision-Making and Access to Justice in Environmental Matters. The UDHR, while not explicitly outlining specific environmental rights, has successfully established reasonable indicators of the link between human and environmental rights when it states in Article 25: "Everyone has the right to a standard of living adequate for the health and well-being of himself and of his family, including food, clothing, housing and medical care and necessary social services." The term "including" must be qualified, since it suggests that the reference is not an exhaustive listing of all factors that could reasonably be construed as being critical to the adequacy of an individuals' health and well-being, and could be further expanded to include the natural environment.

Despite Jamaica not being a signatory or party to the Aarhus Convention, the provisions of the convention bear direct relevance to the issue at hand. In Article 7, which deals with "Public Participation Concerning Plans, Programmes and Policies Relating to the Environment", the convention states:

> Each Party shall make appropriate practical and/or other provisions for the public to participate during the presentation of plans and programmes relating to the environment, within a transparent and fair framework, having provided the necessary information to the public. (...) To the extent appropriate, each Party shall endeavour to provide opportunities for public participation in preparation of policies relating to the environment.[4]

Clearly, given the environmental and historical significance and worth of the Cockpit Country to the material well-being of Jamaicans, they had a procedural right to be consulted in the process of evaluating Alcoa's application for the prospecting licence. Civil society and environmental activists were therefore forthright in their demonstration and refutation of the government's position. And, through this protest and advocacy, they succeeded in forcing the government to withdraw the prospecting licence and establish a process for consultation and wider stakeholder participation. But how and in what ways were the internet and other media crucial to the success of the campaign to save the Jamaican Cockpit wilderness?

Democratising access and the amplification of grassroots voices

Since its emergence less than two decades ago, the internet has given rise to a form of bottom-up grassroots politics among environmental advocates and concerned citizens globally, including in Jamaica and in the diaspora. This grassroots politics is characterised by direct participation, self-organising and community action. For instance, a "Cockpit Country.Org" website was launched which contained a "Save the Cockpit Country" online petition. The website was used as a central repository of information about the Cockpit Country, and contained documents such as letters to various stakeholders and press releases.[5] Other mainstream media were used, such as newspaper articles and letters to the editor, but the new global media networks extended the reach of such local print inputs and helped overcome the circulation bottlenecks involved in only relying on traditional media forms. The internet was able to galvanise, in a more systematic and widespread way, support from a disparate number of individuals and groups in support of preserving the Cockpit Country. For instance, in the online petition, there were comments from locally based individuals but also Jamaicans and others living outside of the country, in such faraway countries as the Netherlands and Poland.

Clearly, unlike other traditional media platforms, the internet is proving and has proven to be among the most effective media to influence public policy and to also assert people's right to be consulted on issues with an impact on their material well-being, ecosystems and historical heritage.

Additionally, the Cockpit Country petition and advocacy campaign lend support to the notion of

3 Cited in a letter from Wendy Lee to NRCA Chairman James Rawle, 2 November 2006. www.jamaicancaves.org/NJCA_Cockpit-Country_Concerns.pdf

4 Aarhus Convention on Access to Information, Public Participation in Decision-Making and Access to Justice in Environmental Matters (1998) www.unece.org/env/pp

5 www.cockpitcountry.org

the emerging "global citizen": an individual who believes that by virtue of our global ecological interconnectedness, one has the "right" to comment and influence policy and decisions concerning the environment in foreign jurisdictions when they may have implications for the entire global ecological system. An example here in the context of the Cockpit Country story is the concern that many natural scientists have about the continued existence of the Giant Swallowtail butterfly, the largest in the western hemisphere. This butterfly can be found only in two parts of the world. It is for this reason that many natural scientists in the Western hemisphere are also opposed to any form of mining in the Cockpit region. Clearly, these concerns and the articulation of them transcend just the concerns of native Jamaicans, to that of the global citizen, and these global expressions of concern were enabled by use of the internet.

Presence and prominence

Faced with limited resources, the leading activists against mining in the Cockpit Country resorted to low-cost internet campaigns that provided a presence among their respective publics: other international environmental advocates, governments, civil society and ordinary Jamaicans, both in the country and in the diaspora. In addition to the online activism, the internet was also used to post material about the groups' offline activities, such as community consultation sessions, and scanned hardcopy petitions by residents of the area against the proposed mining activities. Uploading these offline activities online was found to embolden others elsewhere in Jamaica to join in the process and to lobby the government against giving the go ahead for the start of mining in the Cockpit Country region.

Public education and environmentalism

By far one of the most critical ways in which the internet has been used in the struggle for human rights in the Cockpit Country mining episode is the level of public education about the need for environmental conservation it enabled. The main advocacy website, for instance, contains copious amounts of information about environmental organisations and their work as well as key information about the Cockpit Country and the need for its preservation. A large number of Jamaicans and others who have visited the website have been exposed to the information about the critical need to preserve the natural environment, and in particular the Jamaican Cockpit Country.

Conclusions

Through this instance and others, the internet is being confirmed as a key tool in mobilising public support for environmental, political and ethical causes. Through what are often called the "social networks", activists have been able to go well beyond the social to make them political and advocacy channels that belie their innocuous designation. It is these channels on the internet that in recent times facilitated a successful uprising in Tunisia and Egypt, and which continue to be used where available to mobilise not just local but global public opinion and support for specific causes. They have helped to bring about transparency in many locales by virtue of ordinary citizens digitally capturing events and activities that are illegal or contrary to the tenets of the UDHR.

In more general terms, the main way in which we see the internet helping in securing human rights is through the empowerment of citizens to lobby for their procedural rights to be engaged and included in policy discussions about issues that bear direct relevance to their history and livelihoods. At the same time this global information channel can be used by governments to better consult their constituents on varying policy decisions, once access to the internet is available to wide segments of the population.

However, despite the potential of the internet in enabling both substantive and procedural rights of citizens in Jamaica, and elsewhere, certain critical access limitations remain. Digital divides persist between those Jamaicans living within the country and those residing in the global industrial countries. Similarly, there is a persistent divide between those Jamaicans who live in urban centres and those who reside in the poor rural communities bordering the Cockpit Country. A 2011 study of Jamaican ICT indicators suggested that while individual internet access in all locations was 42%, only 16% of Jamaican households currently have access to the internet. The study also showed that there was an 18% differential in internet access in favour of those individuals who live in urban centres over rural Jamaican residents.[6]

The internet was therefore useful in the Cockpit Country struggle, but mainly through its use by elite lobbyists and advocates, linking this new medium with traditional channels and information and advocacy methods. Any repeat of the mining scenario

6 Dunn, H., Williams, R., Thomas, M. and Brown, A. (2011) *Caribbean Broadband and ICT Indicators Survey*, Telecommunications Policy and Management Programme, University of the West Indies, Jamaica.

in the Cockpit Country should see ordinary citizens being able to use new media in their own online environmental campaign. But whether this happens or not will depend on strategic measures implemented to improve rural ICT access in Jamaica. In the meantime, the victory over Alcoa and the government of Jamaica remains a notable one, facilitated through use of the internet by those citizens with access to this technology.

Action steps

The advocacy campaign to save the Cockpit Country in Jamaica has thrown up some key action steps that must be taken by ICT and environmental activist networks. Some of these include:

- Intensifying the lobby against any future attempts to re-impose a mining licence for transnational companies that would decimate prized historical and environmental resources.
- Intensifying public education around both media literacy and environmental advocacy among all sectors of the society.
- Internet-based environmental and ICT activists must continue to develop innovative ways to achieve similar levels of influence using both traditional and new media forms; this may mean engaging more intensively in community activities and struggles and showcasing these online.
- Public, private and civic measures to increase effective access to the internet by residents of rural Jamaica, including those in the Cockpit Country region.
- The potential of ICTs, in particular the internet, should be further explored for other beneficial uses and applications besides campaigning through a partnership between environmental activists, government and the community.
- Together with the community, alternative sources of economic survival and growth for residents of the Cockpit Country region should be explored. ■

JAPAN

IN THE AFTERMATH OF THE TSUNAMI

Institute for InfoSocionomics, Tama University and information Support pro bono Platform (iSPP)
Izumi Aizu
www.ni.tama.ac.jp and www.ispp.jp

Introduction

The story that comes to my mind is, naturally, the things we are facing right now: the earthquake, tsunami and their consequences, including but not limited to the nuclear power station failure. This report tracks the role of the internet and other communications services during the disaster.

Earthquake, tsunami and nuclear power station damage

On 11 March 2011 at 14:46 p.m., an unprecedented earthquake hit the eastern half of Japan. In less than ten minutes, the first waves of a tsunami arrived on a scale that no one in Japan ever dreamed of. The magnitude of the earthquake was first said to be 8.4 and then changed into 9.0 on the Richter scale, the largest in the recorded history of Japan and the fourth highest in the world.

The maximum reach of the tsunami was more than 40 metres above sea level – at least three to four times higher than most experts had anticipated. Successive waves of seawater washed away almost everything within one to six kilometres from the coastline, affecting over 30 cities and towns in six prefectures, spanning more than 500 kilometres along the coastline. As of 5 August, the death toll had reached 16,050-plus, and the number of missing more than 7,780. A total of more than 23,800 people were killed in the end, the highest loss from any disaster since World War II in Japan.

The tsunami also hit the Fukushima Daiichi nuclear power station and destroyed the regular and emergency cooling systems. On 12 and 13 March, explosions occurred at three of the four units due to the high temperature of the reactor's core, and a huge amount of nuclear contaminants were released into the air. More than 200,000 citizens inside a 30-kilometre radius from the nuclear station evacuated with bare minimum belongings, hoping to return within a few days. They were still in shelters and temporary houses or staying with friends and relatives after four months.

Preparation was less than needed

Japan is well known as the land of natural disasters, not only for earthquakes and tsunamis, but also typhoons, landslides and volcanic eruptions. All these happen frequently in any part of the archipelago. The central and local governments have disaster management divisions, armed with heavy equipment and conducting regular exercises. We thought we were prepared. Unfortunately, that was not the case this time.

To be fair, almost no one expected that an earthquake of this scale and magnitude would occur. There were predictions and warnings of a large earthquake within the next 30 years, but most expected less than 8.0 on the Richter scale. The Kobe earthquake in 1995, which killed more than 6,400 citizens, had a magnitude of 7.3. Simply put, the preparation was far less than needed.

The role of the internet and ICTs for disaster relief

Information plays a critical role in organising rescue, relief and reconstruction work for all social disasters. The so-called Great East Japan Earthquake was no exception. Yet the very information badly needed by the citizens in devastated areas was not available in the aftermath.

It is perhaps one of the first massive disasters that hit a well-developed country equipped with broadband and 3G mobile networks and other information and communications technology (ICT) infrastructure and services. Many citizens were using the internet and smartphones in addition to the conventional mass media such as TV and radio broadcasting to find information or call for rescue. However, most telephone lines where inaccessible. Given the massive call demand from people immediately after the quake, telephone operators blocked 90% of calls in the most devastated areas – a standard practice to ensure that critical connections, such as those used by emergency services, could be made. However, this also meant that many citizens could not talk to their families and friends for hours, and even days in some areas.

In coastal areas, the tsunami waves destroyed most physical infrastructure – roads and railways, telephone and power lines and radio towers. These areas became "information black holes" and that continued for a week to a month or even longer.

The government rescue team had 1,500 radio and satellite mobile phones and other communication devices. But these did not meet the demand for communication, and many could not be delivered to local governments, whose city halls and buildings had been severely damaged or lost. Many people tried to use Twitter, email via mobile phones, social networks such as Facebook or Mixi (a popular service in Japan) to ask to be rescued, for food, medicines or blankets – and some of these messages reached people outside the affected areas who managed to provide the relief needed in time.

Yet the actual usage of internet and ICTs in the devastated areas was very low. The reconstruction work on communications infrastructure started immediately after the disaster, but the sheer amount of damage placed a heavy burden on the infrastructure providers. The pace of reconstruction was slow compared to the massive demand. There had been little policy coordination framework among ICT players for disaster management despite Japan's frequent exposure to natural disasters.

Many actors started voluntary information-sharing services through the internet. Using Google, Yahoo and Mixi, lists of shelters and missing people, services that matched demand, and data on roads that were passable were set up. Teams went to the affected sites and started to help set up access facilities in shelters or local government offices and schools. Most of this work was ad hoc.

A number of concerned ICT professionals started a voluntary and pro bono information support platform called iSPP, drawing on industry, government and civil society. This multi-stakeholder platform coordinated and complemented official relief work. We asked ourselves, "What can the internet and ICTs do for the victims there?" It was late, but we thought it was never too late.

In early April, a number of iSPP members organised a site visit to three prefectures to find out what kind of information and services were really in need. We spoke with local citizens, government officials and ICT professionals who were all seriously affected by the disaster.

The stories we heard were horrible, to put it lightly, especially in coastal cities. When we arrived there, we lost our voices. We just could not imagine what to say. Then, one finds oneself challenged. You *must* say something. You must act.

After the visits, we identified several areas to organise projects around:

- Provide ICT solutions to recovery works – computers, communication devices and people.
- Build common application programming interfaces (APIs) for informational support.
- Facilitate information matching for relief work (goods and people).
- Coordinate NGOs.
- Support local government – coordinate with prefectural and central governments to restore their ICT services for victims and citizens.
- Conduct a survey of people's informational behaviour (how they use and disseminate information).

To be frank, it was not easy to organise all of this work with limited resources. However, iSPP managed to develop some of the projects.

Homes that were washed away and ended up at the foot of a hill where we stayed at my friend's house. No search and rescue operation had been performed there yet after three weeks, on 3 April 2011.

A large ship landed 700 metres away from the pier (picture taken 3 April 2011). You can see the same ship from a Google Earth photo: 38°54'56.99"N, 141°34'51.10"E

FIGURE 1.

Availability of devices and services before and after the earthquake (%) N = 2,815

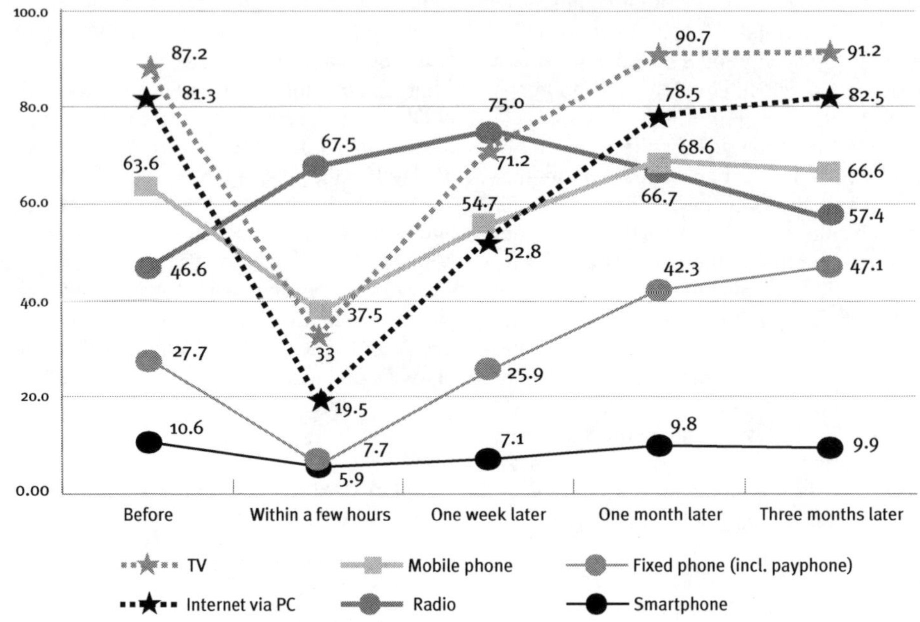

Source: Survey on Information Behaviour, iSPP, July 2011

How did people use ICT services during the severe disaster?

There were mixed reports about the actual use of and demand from people for the internet, mobile phones, Twitter and other social network services. In metropolitan Tokyo and the surroundings, where the earthquake also hit, shutting down most trains in the afternoon and evening, many people used mobile phones and the internet: email, Twitter, Ustream, YouTube, Google and Facebook. These were, we thought, mostly used in the Tokyo area, but not in the heavily damaged and devastated areas of the Tohoku region.

Later, in early April, when we organised a field visit to the Tohoku region, including the cities of Iwaki, Sendai, Natori and Kesen'numa, to see what exactly happened, many people we met told us stories that were different to those we had heard in Tokyo, confirming our expectations. These were some of their comments:

> "None of the digital or analogue media worked at all."

> "Mobile phones were just useless. I tried to call my family members to find out if they were okay. But it didn't connect. When we got through, busy signals were the answers."

> "Eventually we lost battery power. Since the main power lines were totally down for days, we could not recharge the power, and so within a few hours, we lost it."

> "TVs? Come on! When there is no electricity, how can you get to see the TV programmes?"

> "Twitter? Facebook? You are kidding! We were simply not in that mode. Just stunned by the horrible situation; watching the tsunami waves, could not do anything."

To be fair, all the stories, both about what happened in Tokyo and what happened in Tohoku, were largely true. But they were just many tips of a large iceberg, we felt.

A survey on people's information behaviour

Because of this, a survey on people's informational behaviour was carried out by iSPP in July. It was a combination of a web-based online questionnaire, which received 2,815 responses, and personal interviews with 186 interviewees, both conducted with respondents in the devastated areas. The questions were as follows:

- Which tools and media were useful? Which were not?

FIGURE 2.

Information sources people recognised as useful (%) N = 2815

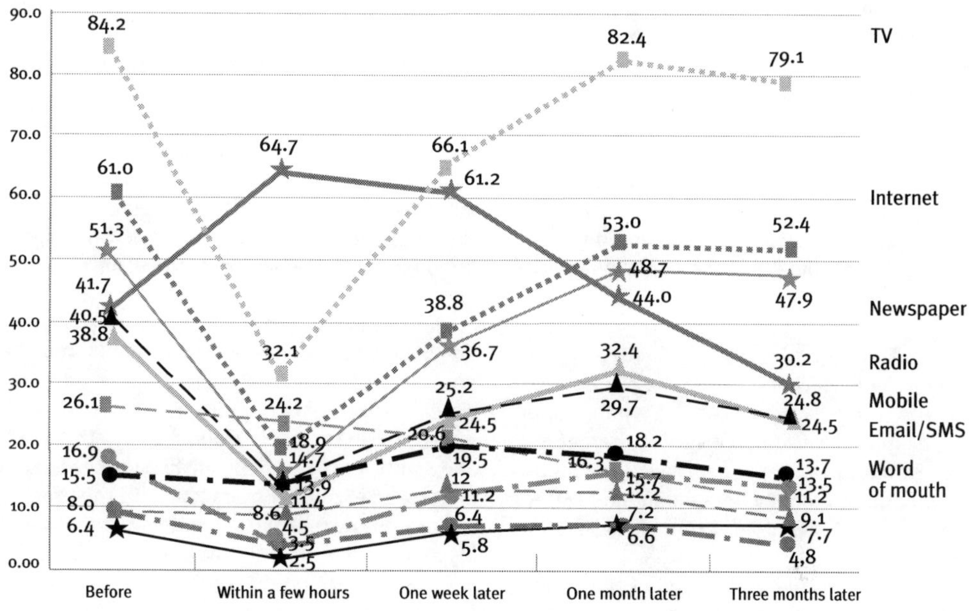

Source: Survey on Information Behaviour, iSPP, July 2011

- Which information resources did affected people rely on?
- Were there any differences given the different locations of the disaster?
- Was internet or Twitter really useful?
- What kind of lessons can we draw from this?

The respondents were residents of three prefectures in the Tohoku region: Iwate, Miyagi and Fukushima. All have coastal areas where the tsunami hit heavily and inland areas where the earthquake hit badly, and people in Iwate especially were also exposed to the danger of the nuclear contamination. There were 5.7 million residents in these three prefectures.

To our knowledge, this was the first attempt at a sizable survey conducted inside the devastated areas in terms of finding out people's informational behaviour.

At the time of writing, we are still processing the data and writing the full report, but some of the early findings from the online survey have been released already. Here is the summary.

Information devices available to affected people

First, we asked which devices were actually available to affected people. According to the 2,815 people who responded to the online survey, a sharp drop is seen in the usage of most communication devices right after the quake: only 37.5% said they could use mobile phones, from 63.6% usage before the earthquake/tsunami hit them. Similarly, 33.4% could watch TV compared to 87.2% before the disaster, and 19.5% could use the internet compared to 81.3% before the event. The only exception was radio – 67.5% of respondents used a radio within a few hours after the quake, an increase of 20 percentage points over regular use.

Up to one week after the earthquake, radio (75.0%) still remained the most available medium, while TVs (71.2%), mobile phones (54.7%) and internet (52.8%) showed good recovery, even though they did not reach the level of availability before the quake.

It is said that up to 72 hours is the most critical period to save the lives of people affected by disasters. Yet as the survey shows, most information channels were not functioning sufficiently during this time. It was extremely difficult to determine the exact degree of damage in the coastal areas, which span 600 kilometres. The police, army and fire and rescue departments all dispatched the first emergency teams, but we knew that the communication lines became more dysfunctional as you approached the affected areas.

It was only in late April, after more than a month, when most major telecommunication operators announced that the repair work on their trunk lines and telephone services was almost done.

The results of this survey corresponded with that: the use of most communication tools and services was recovered between one to three months after the quake.

Useful information sources

Next, we asked which information sources people actually recognised as useful. By information sources, we meant not only TV, radio, internet and telephones, but also newspapers, email and SMS, word of mouth, community notice boards, amateur CB radios, etc. We meant *all* forms of information sources.

Here again we found that 67.4% of the people in the devastated areas responded that radio was most useful within a period of several hours after the quake. This was followed by TV (32.1%) for those who still had a power supply, and then "one-segment" digital broadcast TV (a TV service that can be received from a mobile phone or car navigation devices using butteries). This is a reflection of the fact that electricity was not available to many. Word of mouth was ranked seventh, after newspapers.

Internet services, newspapers, email, mobile phones and fixed-line phones were all under the level of usefulness before the quake.

After a week, TV returned to first place followed by radio, the internet and newspapers.

Action steps

Many people we interviewed emphasised the importance of power supply in an emergency situation. As we have entered the digital age, almost all devices and services are designed to use electric power. But that could become the major source of vulnerability once a large-scale natural disaster hits a technologically advanced society. ICTs can only work when a sufficient supply of electricity is guaranteed.

Of course, super-large-scale natural disasters such as the 9.0 earthquake or a massive tsunami could destroy almost all manmade infrastructure and devices/equipment once it hits land. However, there are always areas outside the devastated areas where people could start to do rescue and relief work. They can bring in resources needed. This time, what we found was a lack of preparedness for organising the rescue work using ICTs.

Though we have benefited much from the use of the latest technologies and services such as Twitter, Facebook, YouTube, to name a few, no well-structured information-sharing mechanisms were ready. At best, it was ad hoc.

Japan is well known for the heavy concentration of all kinds of natural disasters. As I said, it was predicted that at least a 7.5 to 8.0 level earthquake would hit the Tohoku region with 99% probability within 30 years since around 2003. The western and southwest parts of Japan also received a formal alert for an earthquake and tsunami. The Great Kanto Earthquake that hit Tokyo and killed more than 100,000 people, mostly by fire, occurred only 70 years ago. Preparation is the responsibility of policy makers and practitioners using ICTs. And Japan is not the only country subject to such large-scale disasters.

In this regard, we foresee a need for building an international alliance of disaster relief teams. We were told that several international activities were already in place and learned that ICT services for emergency rescue were organised in Thailand and Indonesia in 2004, in Haiti in 2009, and for the recent earthquake in Christchurch, New Zealand this year. We have not teamed up with these efforts in Japan, and because of this we had fallen behind, despite the experiences from the Kobe earthquake and several other disasters in Japan.

Things are never too late. We should start now. ■

JORDAN

NEW MEDIA AND SOCIAL RESISTANCE: MOVING TOWARDS A DIRECT DEMOCRACY

Alarab Alyawm
Yahia Shukkeir
www.alarabalyawm.net

Introduction

The entire world saw the first draft of Egypt's contemporary history being written in Tahrir Square in Cairo. The model for citizen uprising has been appreciated elsewhere, and deserves to be copied, especially in neighbouring Arab countries like Jordan. Hundreds of "cyber tribes" tried on 24 March 2011 to do just that.

Jordanian students had started a protest camp in response to a call on the social networking site Facebook. They chanted pro-reform slogans and called for corrupt officials to be put on trial. They were camped out next to the Interior Circle, or Gamal Abdel Nasser Square – named after the late Egyptian president – in Amman. Many young people met there for the first time. I saw one of them shaking hands with another introducing himself as the "Black Iris", the Jordanian national flower.

But at night, police attempted to disperse the youths, cutting off electricity to the square. Several Jordanian protesters were wounded after "loyalists" of the government attacked their camp as police stood by.

Revolution in Tunisia and Egypt raised hopes for political change in the region, including Jordan; but here the government succeeded in avoiding the results seen in Tunisia and Egypt by managing the transition to democracy.

Policy and political background

During the demonstrations in Jordan, activists used social networks to organise protests and mobilise large numbers of people.

Jordan has a history of persecuting activists and journalists. Fewer press freedoms mean networks such as Twitter or Facebook are viewed not solely as tools for social networking or self-promotion, but as a largely free arena in which to connect, debate and articulate different viewpoints.

The internet gives citizens a huge opportunity to access the other side of stories, and to participate in a counter-public sphere. It also gives people the opportunity to become "citizen journalists" and "newsmakers".

In response to the new media influence, Jordan's government tried to pass new laws to control the new "technology for freedom". In all press freedom indices, Jordan is not free, with one report stating that "[t]he Jordanian media have traditionally been under tight state control."[1]

On 23 June 2011 Jordan's Information Minister Taher Adwan resigned in protest over proposed laws which he said restricted freedom of expression and were a setback to the government's reform plans. "We were working on democratic laws and I was surprised at the drafting of new laws that restrict freedom of expression and lower the ceiling of press freedoms," Odwan told Reuters.[2] Adwan is a well-known novelist and journalist, and after he resigned he was appointed the CEO of the daily newspaper *Alarab Alyawm*.

The role of new technologies in the "Arab Spring"

During the "Arab Spring" all governments in the region were obliged to take note and implement changes to manage the new situation. Some used the old-fashioned model to counter the mass demonstrations, as in Egypt, Syria and Yemen, but for many of these regimes the game was over.

In Jordan the government took a smarter approach compared to neighbouring countries. The decision makers absorbed the anger of the masses in different ways; for instance, by amending the constitution, which was one of the main demands of the demonstrators. The new amendments included the establishment of a constitutional court, and more guarantees of civil rights and liberties.

Young people have succeeded in shaping societal reforms and ensuring that their interests are taken into consideration. The constitutional amendments included the reduction of the minimum age of political candidates to 25 years old. The law of public meetings was also changed to allow people to gather without permission.

One of the main powers of the demonstrators was the use of online social networks. In Jordan, as in many other countries, new media is multiplying,

1 news.bbc.co.uk/2/hi/europe/country_profiles/828763.stm

2 www.guardian.co.uk/world/middle-east-live/2011/jun/21/syria-libya-middle-east-unrest-live

as are the number of satellite TV stations, resulting in a flood of broadcast and web news. Everyone is trying to get a share of the cake.

Blogging is flourishing in Jordan. Many bloggers serve different functions, such as advocating on particular issues or documenting events. Bloggers are potential competitors to traditional media, especially in closed societies.

Jordanian blogger Osama Romoh[3] won first prize in a Bern blogging competition 15 April 2010. Mohammad Omar, one of the early bloggers in Jordan, commented: "It seems that the [role of the] majority of blogs and social networks has turned completely since the 'Arab Spring'. (...) Now it's more about following up on public affairs and politics."[4]

Bater Wardam, one of the early internet activists, said in an article entitled "Electronic Democracy in Jordan"[5] that "maybe the main feature of the websites is that they allow for reader comments," adding that social media "facilitates the dissemination of opinion contrary to the government's."

The new century started with the revolution in new world media. The invention of social networks, starting with Facebook, YouTube and then Twitter, took access to information to a different level. According to the statistics, there are more than 15 million users of Facebook in the Middle East and North Africa (MENA) region and this is increasing rapidly. Today, 27.2 % of Jordanians have access to the internet.[6] In August, the number of Facebook users had grown in the previous five months by 113%, which pushed the number of Facebook users in the country to over one million – over half the number of internet users.[7]

A 2010 survey[8] by Harris Interactive showed that 64% of internet users in Jordan are men and only 33% are women. The number of mobile subscribers[9] in the country stands at 112% of the country's population of six million. In Jordan the mobile plays a more important role than the internet in mobilisation.

These changes in technology have shocked the traditional control exerted by regimes. The "big brother" system has failed to keep up with the rapid changes.

Social networks were intended to be a new form of entertainment and a way of connecting with people. But they were still governed by the idea of design that "people will use your design for something you didn't intend."

A few years of open use of the internet in Jordan resulted in a surge in public conversations and debates. One of the main reasons was the immunity that the internet provided. Government policing forces did not have the technological expertise to be able to identify and thereby censor speakers.

The new revolutions in the region have introduced new leaders such as Wael Ghonim in Egypt, who was working in Google's United Arab Emirates office in Internet City in Dubai. Ghonim became an international figure and energised pro-democracy demonstrations in Egypt. *TIME* magazine[10] added him to its "TIME 100" list of the most influential people of 2011.

The fight for freedom is sweeping across the face of Arab nations as survival in the 21st century makes the old ways impossible. Technology and social networking are giving people an understanding that the world can unite on a global front to support the mass mobilisation efforts of people. Everyone should rise up now in this time of great energy and be free![11]

The protests have used different forms of civil resistance in their sustained campaigns, including strikes and demonstrations. Protesters in Tunisia and Egypt relied on social media such as Facebook, YouTube, Twitter and TwitPic in their early stages to accelerate the pace of social protest. In Jordan there is evidence that social media played a strong role in social resistance.

A member of Youth of March 24,[12] the group that organised the demonstration in the capital Amman using Facebook, told the author that the organisers always take into consideration the worst that the police could do. Because of this they assign some participants the task of documenting everything in the events, especially if police attack demonstrators. This technique was effective on 25 March 2011 when the pro-government gangs attacked the anti-government group, while the police stood by. Youth of March 24 promptly uploaded their visuals on the internet. The images of scores injured during the protests is archived virtually for the future.

There have also been cases of political opportunism. The banned Hizb ut-Tahrir[13] political party took the opportunity of the online space to

3 osamaa.com

4 ammannet.net/blogs/MohammadOmar

5 www.factjo.com/pages/AticleViewPage.aspx?id=1948

6 www.internetworldstats.com/me/jo.htm

7 www.jordanoholic.com/blog/tech/jordan-facebook-statistics-aug2010

8 www.nytimes.com/2011/05/19/world/middleeast/19iht-M19-JORDAN-REFORM.html?_r=1

9 www.jordanews.com/jordan/5103.html

10 www.time.com/time/specials/packages/article/0,28804,2066367_2066369,00.html

11 www.crystalinks.com/2011freedomprotests.html

12 www.facebook.com/shbab.march.24?sk=wall

13 www.hizb-ut-tahrir.org

communicate with people and to promote its ideas on advocating for the Islamic Khilafah state. In the tsunami of demonstrations felt in Jordan, Hizb ut-Tahrir dared to organise public demonstrations. The government was forced not to take action as the demonstrations were peaceful.

Legislative context

Contrary to best practices, in August 2010 Jordan passed the so-called "cyber crimes" law that aims to control internet content. The law primarily regulates security and morality in an electronic communication context. Articles 8 through 10 of the legislation prohibit the use of the internet to download "immoral" materials, including pornography, and using the internet for prostitution or terrorism.

Articles 11 and 12 have been viewed as directly targeting online news media, although the government insists that was not the purpose of the law. Article 11 stipulates a penalty for accessing websites and information systems without a licence – though it does not specify where such licences would be acquired or what such a licensing process would entail. Article 12 provides for the search for and seizure of equipment if they are relevant to cyber crime investigations.

Members of Jordan's online community immediately became concerned that they would have to comply with the registration requirements and rules of liability for journalists and news outlets.

The regulatory framework for news media has been at the centre of a very intense debate over the past ten years, with various regulatory bodies being formed and empowered, merged and restructured, dissolved and then resuscitated.

Jordan is not the only country to regulate access to the internet in this way. Saudi Arabia, Iran and China (which has the so-called "Great Firew all of China") are amongst countries which have introduced laws to restrict access to the internet. "Iran is believed to be worried about the influence of the internet and especially social networking websites, as pro-democracy activists across the Middle East use them to promote and publicise their movements," the *Guardian* reported.[14] However, in passing such a law, Jordan is violating its obligations under international human rights law.

The right to freedom of expression is well established in international law. The two main United Nations human rights instruments – the Universal Declaration on Human Rights (UDHR) and the International Covenant on Civil and Political Rights (ICCPR)[15] – provide in Article 19 of both documents: "Everyone has the right to freedom of opinion and expression; this right includes freedom to hold opinions without interference and to seek, receive and impart information and ideas through any media and regardless of frontiers."

Jordan is also party to the 2004 Arab Charter on Human Rights, which establishes in Article 32 the same guarantees as the abovementioned Article 19. International law also requires states to take positive measures to create a climate in which human rights are genuinely protected and freedom of expression can thrive, including the dissemination of different points of view. The United States Supreme Court has stated that the internet is "the most participatory form of mass speech yet developed."[16]

Revolutions in Tunisia and Egypt, and the "managed democracy" in Jordan, raised hopes for political change north of Jordan. Syrians are organising campaigns in the capital Damascus and other cities, taking inspiration from Egypt, Tunisia and Jordan in using social networking sites to rally their followers and to push for political reforms.

It seems that the new media and information technology have played a vital role in changing the balance of power between government and social resistance movements in the Arab world. Social networking tools such as Twitter, Facebook and YouTube as well as mobile phones have clearly changed the way we communicate with each other across the world. At the same time, repressive regimes are increasingly censoring and monitoring information flows and passing new laws to control the content published by new media.

But governments are losing the battle because cyber-wise young people are more capable of adopting and adapting to the potential of the new weapons compared to the old, ruling elites.

Conclusions

There is an increasing acknowledgment of the link between democracy, human rights, fighting corruption and development, and an awareness that press freedom is not a luxury, but rather a critical factor in social and economic development.

Five centuries ago the invention of printing played a vital role in curbing the church's authority,

14 www.guardian.co.uk/world/2011/jul/13/iran-tightens-online-censorship

15 The ICCPR was incorporated into Jordanian law and published in the Official Gazette twice: in issue No. 4658 on 16 May 2004 and in issue No. 4675 on 16 September 2004 due to errors in wording.

16 www.firstamendmentcenter.org/cyberspeech

and new technologies such as the internet and satellite TV may have the same impact. These new "freedom technologies" will weaken any unfit ideology.

Authoritarian regimes believe they have the right to control the public mind and the content of any media. But new media give a loudspeaker and a platform to the voiceless. They also give the public another account of a story rather than the official governmental tale. In politics new media give political movements, especially in the opposition, an extra-parliamentary opportunity to address the people in a direct democracy.

The radical change in the Arab world is a triumph of new media.

Action steps

In emerging democracies, introducing good laws is the first step to promote an independent, pluralistic and professional media as a fundamental infrastructure of good governance.

It is time to take into consideration the following steps in Jordan:

- New media are part of the information society and offer a huge opportunity to consolidate democracy and to promote development. Governments must not always look at the "half-empty glass" and consider new media a challenge rather than an opportunity.
- Amend existing legislation and develop new laws to ensure that the right to know is secured. This includes passing laws to ensure the right of access to online information.
- Abolish the cyber crimes law and drop any ideas of adopting separate legislation on internet content.
- Improve infrastructure to facilitate internet access.
- Work to reduce the cost of subscribing to the internet. ■

KAZAKHSTAN

MOBILISING ONLINE FOR FREE ELECTIONS

Adil Nurmakov

Introduction

Booming economic development in the mid-2000s in Kazakhstan, fuelled by soaring hydrocarbons prices and increased oil production, arrived after a harsh decade of post-Soviet transition in the country. The rise of middle-class consumerism, slow yet steady growth of salaries for employees of state-funded entities, and massive propaganda proclaiming political stability have neutralised the population's civil consciousness and political participation. The state-secured informal control over civil society through the network of GONGOs (government-organised non-governmental organisations) and use of state social order have left few authoritative NGOs in the field. The financial crisis hit the country in 2007 and highlighted a gap between the rich and the poor, invigorating the society's protest potential, albeit it driven primarily by socially vulnerable groups.

Years of economic well-being in Kazakhstan has led to rapid growth in internet penetration – which keeps on increasing. According to official statistics, the number of subscribers rose from 203,000 in 2004 to 756,500 in 2009;[1] other government sources referred to 4.7 million users online in 2009.[2] Critics say the lack of clarity in methodology used by various agencies to show off their successes leaves a narrow field for quality a nalysis, while excessively high numbers might be a result of counting the same users several times – connected household members, employees having access at work, mobile internet subscribers, etc. The latest official figure was 4.3 million[3] (out of a total population estimated at 16.6 million). Most connections are run by the national internet service provider JSC Kazakhtelecom. A survey conducted by JSC Kazkontent suggests that 37% of its users use social networking sites, 27% prefer forums and 11% host/read blogs.[4]

Political background

Politics is heavily dominated by the presidency and the hidden balancing of interests between various elite groupings. Nursultan Nazarbayev, who is 71, has ruled the country since it gained independence in 1991. Although internationally praised for maintaining interethnic peace and tolerance, the authorities are regularly criticised for their human rights record and electoral practices. Most elections were held ahead of schedule and earned negative assessments from international observer missions. The 2005 presidential election resulted in 91% of votes allegedly going to the incumbent, and the last parliamentary elections in 2007 resulted in a one-party legislature.

The media environment is characterised by stiff government control over both print and broadcast media, either via direct ownership, indirect ownership through national companies or the ruling party, or, more importantly, by restrictive legislation, self-censorship and financial incentives. Opposition and critical voices are effectively excluded from the mainstream media. In these conditions, the internet appears to offer an important space for freer speech. Yet, in 2009, the authorities adopted a set of amendments to various laws that regulate online activities by attaching the status of a mass media outlet to all websites, blogs, forums, etc., and by granting them the prerogative to block web resources whose content runs counter to the national legislation.

The country's Election Law (Chapter 5) does not forbid the use of the internet in campaigns.

Presidential elections 2011

The most recent presidential elections in Kazakhstan were to take place in 2012. In late 2010, a campaign was launched, widely seen as orchestrated by the presidential administration, which sought to extend the authority of the incumbent president until December 2020. The campaigners did not use

1 Statistics Agency of the Republic of Kazakhstan (2010) *Number of Internet Users* www.stat.kz/digital/svyaz/Pages/default.aspx

2 PRIME-TASS (2009) Количество интернет-пользователей в Казахстане превысило 4,7 млн чел. (The number of internet users in Kazakhstan exceeded 4.7 million), 19 October. www.bit.prime-tass.ru/news/show.asp?id=69452&ct=news

3 Novosti-Kazakhstan (2011) Число пользователей интернета в Казахстане достигло 4,3 млн чел. (The number of internet users has reached 4.3 million), 10 January. www.newskaz.ru/society/20110110/1037337.html

4 Kazkontent (2011) Обзор казахстанского Интернет-рынка 2007-2011 (Review of the Kazakhstani internet market 2007-2011), 14 April. kzcontent.kz/rus/kaznet_3/12

web tools at all, completely relying on administrative pressure to collect signatures and on state media propaganda to substantiate the process. The application to conduct a referendum on the issue was approved by the Central Election Commission (CEC), and the campaigners vowed to have more than five million signatures collected in close to a two-week period that included the Christmas and New Year holidays.

The internet community and blogosphere criticised the initiative in various posts and articles, some of them satirical. The opposition – the People's Party "Alga" and the Social Democratic Party "Azat", both unregistered – denounced the referendum, publishing their statements on politically friendly news sites. Unidentified enthusiasts, allegedly associated with the opposition, launched a dedicated website called *elbasy.net* ("no to leader of the nation") to collect signatures in support of Nazarbayev's resignation. According to the website, only 604 signatures arrived in the period between 3 March and 12 May of 2011.[5] Another drive-for-signatures campaign was set up by Bakhytzhan Toregozhina, a leader of the human rights and youth activism group Ar-Rukh-Hak, on a popular Russia-based online petition platform.[6] The drive, aimed against the collection of signatures in support of the referendum, generated around 200 signatures. Apparently the activists had chosen a losing approach for articulating citizen protest by using the internet – against the backdrop of the massive campaign managed by the authorities. As a result, the number of signatories was unconvincing for the public and discrediting for the idea. One more comparatively prominent online action was a remixed and redubbed version of the animated movie *Shrek* satirizing the referendum. It was uploaded to YouTube by an anonymous user, who has never uploaded anything else since. The clip was viewed 1,847 times; only three comments were left.

Support for a referendum was significant and parliament unanimously urged the president to introduce the necessary amendments in the constitution and set a date for the referendum. Although there was no visible protest within the country, international partners were exceptionally critical about the plan by the 2010 Organization for Security and Co-operation in Europe (OSCE) chair country to cancel elections. This forced the government to abandon the idea. The Constitutional Council, to which Nazarbayev had sent the referendum bill after the parliament overpowered his veto, found it illegal. The president agreed and suggested that elections be held. Constitutional amendments allowing the incumbent to announce early elections and a separate law to determine that early presidential elections must be held within two months after the announcement were hastily adopted in just two days. On 4 February, Nazarbayev scheduled the elections for 3 April, leaving virtually no space for election campaigning. The opposition was clearly unprepared. "Azat" conditioned its participation with unrealistic demands for the liberalisation of legislation, and stated it would tour the country and monitor elections. No newsworthy actions followed these promises.

The registered candidates who were allowed to run for the presidency included Nursultan Nazarbayev, Zhambyl Akhmetbekov of the Communist People's Party, Ghani Kassymov of the Patriots Party and green activist Mels Yeleussizov. The parties of Akhmetbekov and Kassymov are trying to position themselves as a sort of opposition, but in fact both are phantom organisations, designed to be satellites of the ruling party. There is no political party behind Yeleussizov, who heads the Environmentalist Union "Tabigat", which does not usually get involved in politics. Kassymov and Yeleussizov had already been presidential candidates in 1999 and 2005 respectively. It was, as a result, widely believed that all candidates in the 2011 elections, except the incumbent president, were booked to act as supporting characters for Nazarbayev's re-election.

The way candidates ran their campaigns supported this assumption. Nazarbayev publicly refused to get involved in campaigning. His competitors sufficed with several paid-for and free (i.e. guaranteed by the election law) publications and TV appearances and some outdoor ads. The campaign was covered very quietly in the media, with no ads aired on TV. In this regard, what appeared to be a sudden desire by the candidates to use social media in their campaigns was not a deliberate intent to reach out for prospective supporters, but seen as a cost-saving way to make it appear as if pre-election agitation was taking place.

Akhmetbekov publicly announced[7] that he would aggressively use new media for self-promotion, but his representation in social networks was the weakest one of all. None of the candidates launched a blog as a more solid and consistent communication medium, and none of them used

5 www.elbasy.net

6 www.onlinepetition.ru/ref2010/petition.html

7 Kazakhstan Today (2011) КНПК намерена использовать для агитации социальные сети (KNPK intends to use social networks for agitation), 3 March. www.kt.kz/?lang=rus&uin=1133168488&chapter=1153533938

Twitter. Clearly there was not much they could have written about on these platforms. Facebook was the main campaigning channel used, which basically came down to a "friending" of random users. The Facebook pages failed to provide information on political agendas, to deliver emotional messages to the readers, or even respond to the comments on their pages, which were abandoned immediately after the elections.

There were two noteworthy web-based movements addressing the issue of participation. One of them pushed for voters to take part in the elections in an unconventional way. Alisher Yelikbayev, one of Kazakhstan's top bloggers, backed the call for participation, but since there was effectively no choice to be made between the candidates – and no option to vote "against all" candidates, as had been possible with previous ballot papers – he thought voters should spoil the ballot.[8] His rationale for doing so was that, on the one hand, this would show people's readiness to vote if there were normal elections, and, on the other hand, the action would use up ballot papers so that they could not be used for fraud and ballot-stuffing.

On the opposite side was a call to boycott the elections, a campaign championed by "Alga", both online and offline. As party chairman Vladimir Kozlov said, its idea was "to boycott the elections that had been discredited."[9] The movement's online front included the creation of dedicated groups and communities on social networking sites. Project coordinators set up pages on numerous social networks, including Facebook and the Russian-based MoiMir and Vkontakte. This multiple online presence was probably a failure, as even the most popular communities had few members (around 400 or less), with members signing on to more than one group. The campaign was accompanied by videos, which included computer graphics, satirically remixed popular movies and other content advocating for the boycott. "Alga's" channel on YouTube has 138 subscribers, several of them accounts set up by the party's regional branches. The most popular video of the whole campaign, redubbed *Lord of the Rings* footage, gathered 4,300 views. The only evidence of the campaign's impact was the CEC chair's remark that it was "destructive, provocative and insulting for voters."[10] This response, however, was more likely caused by comments in the party's traditional media, and the distribution of printed leaflets.

Preliminary results of the elections were announced on the day after voting, and the day after that the final results were made public. According to the official data, voter turnout was 89.98%. The incumbent president reportedly received 95.55% of the votes.[11]

Conclusions

Disillusionment with politics, coupled with the relative well-being of the population, makes it a challenging task for any activist to campaign, especially on the web, given that access is currently not affordable to many in Kazakhstan. In this regard, it is hard to measure the effectiveness of the campaigns held during the 2011 presidential elections. The fact that elections were neither free nor fair depreciates official data on turnout and voter numbers, further complicating attempts to trace campaign results. The boycott campaign was even harder to measure, as many people – despite the official reports of high voter turnout – opted to stay at home not because they supported the cause, but due to a general lack of interest and absence of political struggle.

Politicians who took up social networking on the eve of the elections were following a fashion, but showed little expertise and commitment in running their accounts on the social networking sites. Moreover, the candidates were not actually opposing each other or the incumbent, so it is quite natural that people showed little or no interest in their campaigns.

Few members of the established opposition – although typically excluded in traditional media coverage – showed a desire to seek new media tools to get their messages across. Awkward attempts to employ online media tools ended up with the uncreative duplication of traditional communication methods that appeared not to appeal to an online audience. There is no understanding that social media bear the potential to recruit new, younger members and sympathisers.

At the same time, it needs to be said that new media are starting to penetrate political life and, notably, government officials are taking the lead in setting up online channels in an attempt to get in touch with the population. For instance, some members of parliament and public figures have actively taken to social networks, but tend to

8 Interview with Alisher Yelikbayev (Almaty), 10 May 2011.

9 Interview with Vladimir Kozlov (Almaty), 10 May 2011.

10 Novosti-Kazakhstan (2011) ЦИК призывает граждан не поддаваться призывам бойкотировать выборы. ИА Новости-Казахстан (CEC urges citizens not to follow the calls for boycott of elections), 16 March. www.newskaz.ru/politics/20110316/1242461.html

11 Tengri News (2011) Нурсултан Назарбаев набрал 95,55% голосов на выборах президента Казахстана (Nursultan Nazarbayev won 95.55% of the votes in the Kazakhstan presidential elections), 5 April. tengrinews.kz/vibori/183437

avoid expression of a principled stand or coverage of sensitive issues. At the same time, not all of them respond to comments or get involved in discussions, making many of them again a case of one-way communication. Still, the prime minister's Twitter account is often cited in the news.

There are areas in which social media have repeatedly made a difference. Most importantly, this has been the case when it comes to awareness campaigns (which have included the dissemination of crucial information not covered or insufficiently covered by the mainstream media), and charity campaigns. Experts believe that the efficacy of the latter is explained by the people's readiness for immediate action towards the good, involving no interaction with the authorities. The dead-end nature of political participation in the country rarely produces civil action, except in the expression of virtual sympathy online.

Action steps

- Advocate for the general affordability of access to the internet.
- Promote the computer literacy of the population.
- Encourage the use of social networking websites that have activism-ready functionality, rather than entertainment-centred architecture.
- Train political activists, civil society and opinion leaders on the basics of online communication, starting with Skype (since it offers easy collaborative communication). They also need to be trained on the effective use of social media with the focus on building trust and sustainable communication channels, dedicated and responsible communication practices, and incorporating multimedia into their work.
- Training should be supplemented by reviews of the best innovative communications practices and seminars that encourage creativity in order to avoid the mechanical copying of learned methods.
- Awareness, advocacy or promotional campaigns staged online should be tools for action (preferably offline action).
- New media should be used to raise international awareness and to keep foreign stakeholders (NGOs, media, politicians, etc.) informed.
- Recruiting virtual followers on social networking sites should not be random, but based on an analysis of users. Interventions should be targeted at specific groups and communities, etc.
- Learn by doing; evaluate activities; distinguish between the reasons for error and success. ■

Once Geminated (a seeing)

Kamaria Muntu*

*for Prossy Kakooza and those who struggle to love***

Say this like a prayer
the same waters that part us
fill us with floodlight
and the womb-flow ages in the eddies
and the contentious headlines bleed
fetid rains of sectarian violence
wrapped around soiled diapers
and other articles of the seeming non-dead
We live and breathe as one
and because of our Blackness
our sex
we are hated

I once stood on a city roof watching birds and children
above and below take the day with their lightness
thinking myself to be one less hatred away from human than you
even as the ugly-eyed clawed the tedium of my undernourished bones
I was a lover of men

While you batik touched, plum crushed
were stripped naked and paraded through public streets
corpsed in the defecation of rapists and torturers/
Transatlantic traffickers forging war's endless obscenities –

          a long neck gourd breaks
          and scarred centuries roll out in shrieks
the usual stars become jagged and dim
as they push your voice into underground crotches
and my own songs darken an omen of moons

Illegal for a woman to love a woman in your land
Criminal for a woman to be poor and unloved in mine
We will no longer field the night resembling shadowed death
Fear embattles, engages arms
Veils are blown apart by strong winds of our own making
We fall and stand together against their noise

---

* Kamaria Muntu is a poet, writer and activist currently living in London.

** Prossy Kakooza fled her homeland upon threat of death after being found in bed with her same-sex lover, which is illegal in Uganda. The 26-year-old woman and her partner were taken naked to the police station where Prossy was raped and tortured.

KENYA

PERCEPTIONS AND MISCONCEPTIONS: THE ROLE OF NEW AND TRADITIONAL MEDIA IN KENYA'S POST-ELECTION VIOLENCE (2007)

Kenya ICT Action Network (KICTANet)
Alice Munyua

Introduction

Kenya has a mosaic of 42 ethnic communities, and although it is frequently cited as a model for political stability and economic development in Africa, the extent of violence experienced after the elections in 2007 was unprecedented. The violence left about 1,300 Kenyans dead and about 500,000 people displaced.

Elections in Kenya have been associated with violence for almost two decades; but in 2007 the tensions escalated as mobile phones and the internet became additional means used for political discussions that took on an ethnic dimension and a political bias on a scale that had not been experienced before. This high level of violence set back Kenya's democratic progress gained after multiparty politics was introduced in 1991.

The post-electoral ethnic violence ended after local and international pressure and extensive international mediation efforts under the leadership of former UN Secretary-General Kofi Annan. The government and the opposition agreed to form a grand coalition, which has entered its last lap before the general elections due next year.

A 2008 UN High Commissioner for Human Rights report notes that that while "irregularities in the election process were the primary trigger of the violence, a number of underlying causes – including discrimination, poverty, inequalities and disenfranchisement – fuelled the crisis." The violence in 2007 must also be looked at in the context of the contested nature of land resettlement schemes following Kenya's independence, and the associated political violence.[1]

Although the role of media and social media is believed to have been significant enough to impact on the levels of violence (both positively and negatively), it was not the defining factor. Hate speech in Kenya was not the responsibility of media alone – on previous occasions it has emanated directly from politicians and government offices. Government propaganda and ineffective dialogue can have a key – even if unintentional – role in encouraging polarisation, exacerbating tensions and escalating violence during an election period.

In addition, the use of media to spread violence and encourage a particular ideology is not new to Kenya. Politics has been used to polarise for decades, and various actors in the political arena have stoked this division, using the media to their political advantage.

The media in general, and local language radio stations in particular, undoubtedly played a role in hyping the election in a manner that contributed to the tensions that became the background to the violence. Local stations often broadcasted uncensored statements made by politicians on their campaign trails that amounted to hate speech and helped to fuel tensions. Mobile phone short message service (SMS) and the internet (email, mailing lists, websites and blogs) were also used to propagate hate speech and incite acts of violence in both the pre-election and post-election period. There has been too little discussion on what constitutes hate speech when it comes to online, SMS and broadcast content, or how governments should address the challenge when it occurs. The best antidote to prevent the spread and influence of genocidal information is to have more positive and analytical information.

Policy and political background

The three sources of press and freedom of information laws in Kenya include the new Constitution of Kenya, the Statutory Law, and the Common Law. The Constitution of Kenya, the supreme law, guarantees the right to freedom of expression. Article 35 also guarantees access to reliable information:

> (1) Every citizen has the right of access to (a) information held by the State; and (b) information held by another person and required for the exercise or protection of any right or fundamental freedom. (2) Every person has the right to the correction or deletion of untrue or misleading information that affects the person. (3) The State shall publish and publicize any important information affecting the nation.

1 Anderson, D. and Lochery, E. (2008) Violence and Exodus in Kenya's Rift Valley, 2008: Predictable or Preventable?, *Journal of East African Studies*, 2 (2).

While the Constitution ensures that the freedom and independence of electronic, print and all other types of media are guaranteed, it does not extend to address issues of ethnic incitement, hate speech, incitement to violence, propaganda for war, incitement to cause harm or content that is discriminatory or amounts to the vilification of others. However, Chapter Four of the Bill of Rights in the Constitution states that the right to freedom of expression does not give anyone a right to use hate speech.

The Constitution provides for the right to access information held by the state and information held by another person required for the exercise or protection of any right or fundamental freedom. The values and principles of the right to state-held information include transparency and the provision to the public of timely, accurate information. The government has made huge steps in implementing this aspect of the Constitution, having launched an open data portal in July 2011, making Kenya the first African country to release government data to the public through a single online platform. The portal aggregates government-held information on budget spending, allocation of funds for constituency development, parliamentary proceedings and other detailed statistics on service delivery and demographics.

The Constitution also guarantees that the state shall not exercise control over or interfere with any person engaged in broadcasting, the production or circulation of any publication or the dissemination of information by any medium, or penalise any person for any opinion or view or the content of any broadcast, publication or information disseminated.

Kenya has a plural, sophisticated and robust mass media and communications sector that serves the various competing political, social, economic, cultural and technological needs of diverse interest groups. The key independent print media are the Nation Media Group, the Standard Group, People Limited, and the Times Media Group. Nairobi hosts approximately 120 foreign correspondents representing 100 media organisations. There is no government-owned or controlled newspaper.

In addition, Kenya has several hundred FM radio stations, broadcasting in Swahili or in local languages. Radio has a wide reach in Kenya, especially in rural areas. Some major international broadcasters, including the British Broadcasting Corporation (BBC), Voice of America (VOA) and Radio France International (RFI), rebroadcast their programming in Kenya.

Meanwhile, a Communications Commission of Kenya (CCK) report stating quarterly statistics for October to December 2010 notes that mobile subscriptions have grown from 22.3 million to 24.96 million. Overall teledensity is 64.2%. The number of SMS text messages recorded was 665 million. The total number of internet subscriptions increased from 3.2 million to 4.7 million by end of December 2010. The number of internet users is estimated at 10.2 million.[2]

Identifying the challenge: The responsibility of new and traditional media

Information and communications technologies (ICTs) did not necessarily alter the rumours and stereotypes about different ethnic groups that have been propagated for decades in Kenya. Rumours and stereotypes became central in much of the violence, and technology only speeded up the ways in which these messages penetrated communities and mobilised individuals and groups for action against each other.[3]

Kenya's post-election violence demonstrated the effects that new technology can have. Despite a history of violence associated with elections, these were the first elections where mobile phones and access to vernacular radio stations were widely available. Mobile phones and media (including social media) can play the roles of mirroring events and providing an important opportunity for reflection and insight into political dynamics. They can analyse the level of dialogue, the polarisation, and progress towards reconciliation, including possible avenues for the peaceful resolution of disputes.

However, media institutions regarded as being locked into the power structure acted largely in line with the dominant political ideology of institutions. The media merely amplified institutional viewpoints, drawing on tribalised political views and assumptions as the natural perspective, rather than providing alternatives views. The media were polarised and co-opted during election and post-election violence, and ownership tended to influence the kind of partisanship a media house would adopt.

The government imposed a ban on live broadcasting on 30 December 2008 largely because of the perception that the media had failed to responsibly manage broadcasting during the initial hours of post-election violence. This was presented as a temporary measure to stop vernacular FM stations hijacked by politicians from continuing to incite hatred. The government had also considered closing down the SMS messaging system that was being used to send hate messages. In an interview with

2 www.cck.go.ke

3 Anderson and Lochery (2008) op. cit.

the *Daily Nation*, Safaricom CEO Michael Joseph is said to have persuaded the government to instead allow providers to send messages of calm and peace provided by the service providers themselves, which they did. However, while Kenya did not have a law to prosecute hate speech, the names of individuals believed to have used SMS text messages to promote mob violence were forwarded to the government and Parliament began to consider reviewing legislation to create a new law against hate speech.

Following the initial shock of the eruption of violence, in line with mobile service providers such as Safaricom and Celtel, the media and social networks began to put out calls for Kenyans to shun violence and keep the peace. Journalists were urged to adhere to ethical standards. Many stations began to consistently devote their airtime to promoting non-violence and peace building and supported the mediation process by calling for an urgent settlement of the crisis. The mainstream media provided live coverage of the signing of the power-sharing pact and have continued to monitor and highlight the negotiation of long-term challenges, such as creating national dialogue and fostering reconciliation.

Many Kenyans had also begun to use digital tools to voice their concerns and challenge the mainstream media and government reports, raising local citizen journalism to another level. Kenyan blogs and virtual networks like KICTANet, KE-users, Skunkworks and iHaveNoTribe, among others, became a critical part of the information flow in the country, reacting to the initial ban on live broadcasts. Ushahidi combined mobile phones and the internet to crowdsource information on human rights violations during the post-election violence. Broadcasters began to read entries from influential bloggers over the airwaves, helping them reach 95% of Kenyans.

In these cases, the media, internet and mobile phones acted as enablers providing a positive role in mediating divergent perspectives, and creating a national vision of reconciliation; a space for dialogue that helped to reduce polarisation and supported transitional justice processes.

One of the impacts of the post-election conflict was the move by government to create policy legislation and regulation to address the lack of perceived self-regulation. Several policies were developed or reviewed including the Information and Communication Master Plan (2008), the National ICT Policy (2008) and Freedom of Information Policy (2008), and the Kenya Information and Communications Act, which established the Broadcasting Content Advisory Council launched in 2010. The council is meant to advise the CCK board in the regulation of broadcast content; but it does not provide direction on online and user-generated content.

The Kenyan media are passionate proponents of self-regulation, but no practical implementation mechanisms have been agreed upon. While the media council launched a code of conduct in 2005 for print, television and radio journalists, it lacks enforcement mechanisms. In addition, there is a challenge on developing mechanisms to legislate and regulate hate speech and good taste as a standard upon which a broadcaster can be held criminally liable. The media have argued that Kenya's culturally diverse society does not have a universal value of what is good or hateful, and therefore the discretion of the editor, guided by professional ethics and the existing laws on public nuisance and morality, are adequate.

Bitange Ndemo, the permanent secretary in the Ministry of Information and Communications, argues that freedom to communicate should be moderated by the values that we hold as a society, because managing hate speech through legislation in the absence of a value system would not solve the problems. He further states that it is not in the government interest to, for example, consider censuring internet-related content. He notes that Kenya needs to deal with more deeply seated problems, which include inequalities and poverty, among others. However, he also notes that there is a need to implement broadcast regulations and the broadcast code of conduct before the next elections in 2012 to avoid more violence.[4]

In relation to the internet, as mentioned, Kenya has not yet addressed issues of online and user-generated hate speech, defamation and incitement among others in the legal and regulatory frameworks currently in operation. The new Constitution provides for data protection and privacy, but it does not specify the kind of data that should be protected. With the current technological advancements, geo-location software enables the identification of internet service providers (ISPs) used by an individual and could undermine fundamental rights of freedom of expression and the protection of carriers against content carried over their networks by third parties. Solutions must therefore be found to protect not only ISPs, but also other intermediaries, like mobile service providers and online service providers such as search engines, among others. A code of conduct for intermediaries may be required as well as a regulatory regime that places certain

4 KICTANet mailing list discussions: www.kictanet.or.ke

levels of responsibilities on them, but it needs to protect them as a platform for expression in order to promote an open and free online culture.

Conclusions

Kenya's election violence revealed the role of media, social media and mobile telephones in fostering the spread of violence; but equally it showed their role in spreading peace-related messages and offering a space for reconciliation.

While forms of social media can be important catalysts for political and social mobilisation, and can be used to exacerbate violence or promote peace, they are not the defining factor. However, the unpredictable nature of new technology affects how media policy and regulation in situations of civil unrest are approached. There are therefore very real concerns about elections making violent conflict more likely and how media liberalisation impacts on this.

Post-election media policies need to be addressed prior to elections, which would include policies on introducing restrictions on live broadcasts of violence, to shutting down radio stations, the internet or SMS services in the case of evidence of incitement to violence.

Events around the world indicate that issues of post-election conflict and violence and their relationship to media, social networks and SMS are relevant. Avoiding both pre- and post-election violence also depends on the legitimacy of institutional processes and trust among citizens. If this is not present, close attention needs to be given to media structures, political allegiances and their performance during election periods.

The International Criminal Court has summoned six Kenyans, one of them the chief executive of KASS Radio, to The Hague on charges of crimes against humanity for their alleged roles in the post-election violence. This sets a precedent for the prosecution of others in the future for their role as media in violence.

Action steps

- Multi-stakeholder discussions are necessary, including at the Internet Governance Forum, about the appropriate response to media of all types being used to incite hatred and violence.
- Empirical research to inform policy discussions in the area of intermediary liability needs to be conducted in order to contribute to the development of an appropriate regulatory model to govern intermediaries as common carrier networks.
- Advocacy for policies that protect intermediaries as a platform for freedom of expression is necessary.
- There is a need to advocate for national values that respect human life and diversity. ■

KOREA, REPUBLIC OF

SOUTH KOREA'S 2008 CANDLELIGHT DEMONSTRATIONS AND DIGITAL RIGHTS

Korean Progressive Network Jinbonet
Yeo-Kyung Chang
www.jinbo.net

Introduction

South Korea's internet penetration reached 77.8% in 2010, with 81.6% of households connected. Considering the country's media environment, where the general public's access to mainstream media is somewhat limited, the internet is a critical medium for expression for ordinary citizens.

However, administrative authorities have screened internet content since 1995 and controlled it by threatening criminal punishment, including for cyber defamation. Furthermore, the resident registration number system adopted by the military dictators of the country's past is still used, including for online verification, allowing easier tracking of users by investigative authorities.

Despite this, citizens have used the internet creatively, in particular to proactively organise social resistance and mass demonstrations, as evidenced by the mass candlelight demonstrations that erupted in South Korea during 2008, following plans to import beef from the United States (US) potentially contaminated with mad cow disease.

Policy and political background

After liberation from Japanese occupation in 1945, the Republic of Korea –more commonly known as South Korea – went through a number of military dictatorships, which eventually ended with the 1987 pro-democracy uprising. Since then, democratic institutions, including direct presidential election, have been reinstated or newly introduced, the Constitutional Court system being one such case.

The 1997 presidential election saw the first peaceful change of government when the opposition leader, Kim Dae-Jung, became president. The government changed again in the most recent presidential election in 2007, when Lee Myung-Bak, candidate from the conservative Grand National Party (GNP), was elected. During the April 2008 general elections, the GNP won a majority of seats in the National Assembly.

Beginning 2 May 2008, mass demonstrations took place daily after the government announced plans to import the US beef into the country. Most participants joined the rallies in the evenings after work or school, peacefully holding candles – which is why the rallies were given the name "candlelight demonstrations". From the seventeenth candlelight demonstration on 24 May, participants started street marches, at which point the police started suppressing and arresting participants.

Many people were angered by the police violence, broadcasted live on the internet, and the demonstrations grew larger. According to prosecutor and police statistics, a total of 932,000 people participated in the demonstrations, at least 3,609 people were arrested for demonstrating illegally at night, and at least 1,270 were prosecuted. The demonstrations peaked in June, but dwindled after 15 August due to mass arrests and prosecutions.

The use of the internet

Before candlelight demonstrations were successfully organised, people had discussed the risks of US beef online on popular discussion sites such as Agora and in online communities such as AntiMB. A teenager using the pseudonym "Andante" triggered a debate after demanding the impeachment of President Lee Myung-Bak. Diverse analytical articles, images parodying the authorities, as well as user-created content were posted. There was even a suggestion to include the words "[Myung-Bak Out]" before all posts to freeboards, while others printed banners supporting the demonstrations that could be hung in homes. Voluntary donations and campaigns on various issues to do with the beef imports were organised, and some online communities raised funds to place advertisements in newspapers.

It was then that "offline" gatherings with candles every evening in Cheonggye Plaza were proposed, and those who agreed to this idea started to voluntarily participate in the rallies. In the beginning, the most energetic participants were young people who had spent the entire day at school and used the internet and mobile short messaging service (SMS) to organise their friends and debate various issues. Later, all sorts of online communities of interest – including fashion, cooking, baseball, photography, cars, and mothers with kids groups – started discussing ways to participate in the rallies. Participation was voluntary and fun; debates took place collectively and activities were collaborative.

Once the candlelight demonstrations started, citizens came up with novel action ideas every day. Participants exchanged information on how to counter the media and the police, and even what to do when arrested. "Netizens" showed support by using the same candlelight image on their instant messengers and blogs, while politicians criticising the demonstrations were mocked by being donated KRW 18 (around USD 0.02) each (in Korean, the pronunciation of "eighteen" is also a swearword.) Actions such as simultaneously searching for the phrase "Democracy is Dead" on search engines were organised – increasing the hit count for the search and prominence of the search terms on the search engines – and flash games criticising the president were created. Websites of the ruling party and the president were either hacked or servers brought down by mass simultaneous access.

The fact that a boycott campaign was initiated against those who advertised in news outlets criticised for distorted reporting of the demonstrations is notable. Names of daily newspaper advertisers, their phone numbers, website addresses and other information were collected and posted on the internet every day by volunteers, encouraging others to participate in the boycott and share their experiences. Large numbers participated, to the extent that companies' websites and phone lines were paralysed. When prosecutors started their investigations, as a protest, many participated in a collective action targeting the website of the Prosecutors' Office by "turning themselves in" online for participating in the boycott. On the other hand, support and subscription campaigns were organised for media outlets that were favourable to the demonstrations. These actions arose from the netizens' critical perspective of the mainstream media.

Until the police suppression started, the candlelight demonstrations were mainly peaceful. Citizens voluntarily and publicly voiced their opinion on issues, and created stickers and leaflets to share their ideas. Citizens, online and offline, communicated with one another using digital media, including mobile phones. During all-night demonstrations, citizens used internet freeboards to raise impromptu funds to buy and distribute equipment needed on the streets, including raincoats to protect protestors from police water cannons, and drinks and snacks. Many used personal cameras and camcorders to share images from the streets, using their laptops to access internet live streaming sites like Afreeca. Videos of the protests were uploaded as they were unfolding. Progressive political parties and the internet media, such as Color TV, also started live internet reporting. When live internet streams by digital media became more pervasive, officers ordered riot police to avoid being filmed when beating demonstrators, which was then publicised and harshly criticised.

As police suppression became more violent, citizens became more proactive, debating countermeasures online. People publicised police violence through various internet sites and media, and continued to stream the movements of demonstrators live through the internet. When barricades made of containers were set up by the authorities around the presidential office, there were heated debates on whether or not to cross the line. The momentum and public sentiment on the issue were such that in some communities, citizens continued to hold candlelight demonstrations regularly for over a year.

Violation of freedom of expression

The government response towards the candlelight demonstrations was a violation of freedom of expression. Just after the demonstrations started, the Prosecutors' Office held an emergency meeting and announced that it would investigate what it called "false internet rumours about mad cow disease". It also criminally prosecuted teenagers proposing a student strike against US beef, on grounds of "false communication". Internet users who had raised suspicions about possible rape, manslaughter or desertion by riot police were also subject to criminal prosecution for "false communication". It was only in December 2010 that the Constitutional Court ruled that this clause in the legislation was unconstitutional.

Internet café managers who had participated in the rallies were also indicted or had their homes and offices searched. In particular, those who ran media boycott campaigns were subject to stronger measures, including travel bans and arrest and search warrants. They were prosecuted and found guilty in the first and second instances, and are now undergoing trial at the Supreme Court.

Investigative authorities clearly abused criminal procedures by, for example, issuing a subpoena to an internet user who had joked during the demonstrations about hiring an assassin to kill the president, or arresting those who had disclosed the names of shop owners who had filed suits against demonstrators for compensation. In July 2008, netizens who had been sued for defamation by a police chief whose name was disclosed during an online debate, and was criticised as a result, were acquitted by the Supreme Court. In May 2009, the police filed criminal and civil suits for defamation against a former riot policeman. He had posted online songs ridiculing the riot police's suppression of protests and then tried to make an album of those songs. The police also filed a provisional deposition against the album. However, he was acquitted by both the prosecutors and the court.

The Korea Communications Standards Commission (KCSC), formed by the incumbent administration to screen the internet, was strongly criticised for biased deliberation at the time of the candlelight demonstrations. In May 2008, the KCSC issued a "recommendation to restrain exaggeration and to refine speech" because some internet users had degraded the president by calling him "2MB"[1] or a "wicked person". In July 2008, the commission deemed internet posts boycotting newspaper advertisers to be illegal and decided to delete those posts. During the same month, the police requested KCSC to delete 199 posts criticising the president and government, some of which were deleted. In June 2009, the KCSC decided to delete a photo where a police officer beating citizens at the May Day and first candlelight demonstration anniversary rallies had been named, on grounds of violation of privacy rights.

After the candlelight demonstrations, the government, convinced that the internet was the source of mobilisation, has tried to further regulate the internet. South Korea has been implementing a Real Name Identification System (RNIS) since 2004 – a user can only post online after real-name verification using the user's resident registration number. The RNIS was supposed to be implemented during specific periods such as an election or on 30 major websites only. However, in 2009, the government revised the enforcement ordinance to increase target websites to more than 150. An additional revision to further expand the number of sites is at the moment pending in the National Assembly. In April 2009, Google Korea announced it would refuse the RNIS and disabled upload services to users with "Korea" as the country setting. The RNIS has led many South Korean internet users to seek "cyber asylum" by moving their email or blog accounts from RNIS-required Korean sites to non-Korean services like Google. As of 2009, domain owners who do not use their real name will not be able to access domain name services.

1 "2MB" has two meanings. One is the initials of President Lee Myung-Bak ("2" and "Lee" are pronounced the same in Korean, so 2MB sounds like Lee MB). The other insinuates that President Lee Myung-Bak is not very intelligent, because the memory capacity of his brain is only 2 megabytes (2 MB).

The government has also proposed a revision to fine an internet service provider (ISP) that does not respond to a request to implement temporary measures of deleting or blocking access to information for up to 30 days, and to mandate ISPs to illegally screen internet content. The aim is to strengthen control over the internet through ISPs. Ruling party lawmakers have also tabled a bill to introduce stronger punishment for cyber slander compared to punishment under the penal code, as well as to allow investigation to be initiated without the filing of a complaint. There are concerns that these internet regulations violate freedom of speech and expression as well as lead to a chilling effect whereby internet users will start censoring themselves.

Invasion of privacy

The compulsory RNIS obligates ISPs to retain personal information of users and cooperate with investigations by police or prosecutors. However, investigative authorities have abused this system since they can obtain the name, resident registration number and home address of users without a court order. The investigation of users' personal information held by ISPs increased from 71,024 cases in 2006 to 93,691 in 2007, and more rapidly in 2008 – the time of candlelight demonstrations – to 119,280. Tracking internet protocol (IP) addresses requires a court order. However, provisions are not strictly applied. The recorded number of cases of the submission of IP addresses to investigative authorities was 41,681 in 2006, 41,584 in 2007, and then rapidly increased to 46,667 in 2008.

Furthermore, the police have started running an exclusive internet search system through which they can strengthen monitoring of particular sites or particular search words. The government and the ruling party have also tabled a bill to obligate ISPs to install screening devices and to retain log data, thereby strengthening control over communication.

Conclusion

The internet played a vital role in the candlelight demonstrations, and helped to mobilise ordinary citizens. Through the internet and mobile communications network, citizens debated various social issues, voiced their opinion and organised actions. The internet offers a way for individuals lacking social and economic resources to make themselves heard and empowered.

However, in the wake of the 2008 protests, investigative authorities have formally targeted citizens for their use of the internet, while censorship, tracking and surveillance of internet users has also increased. These trends are a great concern since they can constrain citizens' social participation and social movements through the net.

Action steps

Information and communications technologies (ICTs) have become more prevalent and widely used by citizens to organise social resistance and mass rallies.

In order to promote participation, citizens must be guaranteed online space to collectively debate and converge. However, many governments have recently adopted technologies and policies to regulate and keep surveillance over the internet – and they are benchmarking one another. Therefore, the following countermeasures are recommended not only for South Korea, but equally for elsewhere around the world:

- Formal accusations against internet posts should be minimised. Criminal punishment for false communication or defamation should be abolished. Criticism against heads of state, police or other public figures must be free.
- Administrative deliberation or censorship, in which the government arbitrarily screens internet content, should be abolished. ISPs should not be subject to arbitrary content regulation.
- Provisions allowing only users with verified real names to write posts should be abolished, since the freedom of anonymous speech as well as privacy of internet users are infringed.
- Strict court procedures must be applied when investigative authorities are being provided with information that can be used to track and maintain surveillance over internet users. User information should not be retained at the convenience of investigative authorities. ■

KYRGYZSTAN

THE ROLE OF SOCIAL NETWORKS IN KYRGYZSTAN DURING ETHNIC TENSIONS IN 2010

Civil Initiative on Internet Policy (CIIP)
Tattu Mambetallieva
www.gipi.kg

Kyrgyzstan has experienced two revolutions over the past ten years – the second as recent as April last year. In both cases the situation was aggravated by a clampdown on the media, as well as on the internet. In March 2005, two of the leading internet service providers (ISPs) were targeted by unknown attackers. A series of emails from hackers sent to the providers insisted that they block two Kyrgyzstani news websites, www.msn.kg and www.respublica.kg. Similar letters were sent to a popular regional news site, www.centralasia.ru, demanding that it stop publishing information about the situation in Kyrgyzstan. Mass denial-of-service (DOS) attacks were also launched on sites in Kyrgyzstan. In order to stop the attacks, the network operator had to turn the internet off completely for a day. It was then that Kyrgyzstan was not accessible to the outside world, at least via the internet. The March 2005 coup soon followed.

A similar situation was repeated in 2010, before the April coup. Access to the sites www.fergana.ru, www.centrasia.ru and Web Radio Liberty and to the popular web forum www.dieselforum.kg was blocked. Media outlets placing information in the internet were persecuted – a sign of the times that led to the sudden change of government.

The internet in times of crisis

Although internet penetration is still comparatively low, the growth of internet users in Kyrgyzstan has not slowed. Various surveys offer different figures for the number of users in the country, but all of them concur that the main category of users is young people and that 70% of users are concentrated in central cities.[1]

The set up of the internet infrastructure in Kyrgyzstan means that access to international websites is expensive, while accessing websites and hosting with a .kg domain inside the country is completely free once you have an account with an ISP. This divide has existed from the beginning of the development of the internet in the country, and civil society activists periodically campaign for the cost of international bandwidth to be reduced. However, it is exactly this kind of division of traffic that has made local social networks the most popular social networking sites when compared to Facebook and Twitter, amongst others.

Even the Russian-language social networks that enjoyed enormous popularity in the early days of their birth, such as Odnoklassniki and Vkontakte, rapidly lost their ratings after the appearance of local Kyrgyz social networks. Twitter does not have a large following in Kyrgyzstan. At least initially, Twitter could not be used via mobile phones in the country, but now there are about 100 registered users. About 25,000 Facebook users were registered, most of them Kyrgyz citizens living outside the country. In contrast, the most popular local social network sites account for more than 250,000 users.

Because the main users of the internet in Kyrgyzstan are the youth, the most popular local social networking sites focus on entertainment. Therefore, civic participation in social networks during the events of the April 2010 coup was not apparent.

However, the situation changed in early June of that year when the ethnic conflict in the south occurred. During this period, many people died and it was impossible to achieve political stability for a long time. It was then that different kinds of online content, including videos, photos and articles – much of it amounting to rumour mongering – appeared on various social networking sites, fanning the flames of ethnic conflict. In response, volunteers began countering the misinformation using Skype.

Using Skype for civic networking

When you look at the different stories dealing with the role of social networks during the revolutions, coups and natural disasters in different countries, the creativity of internet users is striking.

This impact is not always positive. The 2010 events in our country, worsened by social issues that led to ethnic tensions, were fuelled by the spreading of false rumours. These included photographs of dead people that could not be verified, and claims that the drinking water in Bishkek, the capital of Kyrgyzstan, was poisoned, and that there had been various militia attacks on civilians.

1 www.gipi.kg/archives/1073

For a long time the interim government could not establish control in the south of the country, making it impossible for it to respond to and refute the rumours.

In order to avoid panic among the population, an urgent mobilisation of volunteers, journalists and grassroots communicators took place in an effort to inform the public about the real situation. It all started spontaneously and randomly. One non-governmental organisation began a Skype conversation with organisations, friends and employees who were in different parts of the capital.

Initially the group acted as a kind of grassroots civic network, with each of the participants recording what he or she saw on the ground, documenting how looters were breaking into shops and setting fire to buildings. This information was promptly reported to a group of people who had volunteered to protect shops and homes from looters. Information was also passed on to the media.

Then the forum started to grow, turning its attention to the other regions of the country, where looting was also happening – and it was able to act as a way of verifying information that was being spread online.

When someone heard rumours, he or she simply logged on to Skype and asked whether anyone could confirm them. This method proved to be incredibly effective, because participants represented a reliable and geographically distributed network. People could add colleagues to a chat group if they happened to be at a location where rumours were spreading, and this would help confirm the real facts on the ground.

The group became very popular. On one night about 2,000 people had joined the chat. Eleven forum chats on Skype were connected by several key users able to organise the conversations and exchange information. The group reached its peak and was no longer able to add new members. Skype chat was full of people sending and receiving information in real time. The forum then moved to a web platform (www.inkg.info) to continue circulating real-time information across the country. The site was called "Checked: not rumours".

Skype chat also played a crucial role in the distribution of humanitarian aid to the south, where a significant number of people were affected by fires and widespread clashes between ethnic groups. Rumours persisted, and included tales about poisoned humanitarian supplies and attacks along the state border. One Skype-chat member called the minister of defence to clarify information about the attacks on the state border – only to find that they were not true.

During the complications that resulted from interethnic friction in the south of the country, social networks included a number of videos and pictures of dead people. However, it was not possible to establish the nationalities or ethnicity of the corpses in the photographs and videos – even while ethnic groups were using the images as calls to action. Because of these images circulated on the internet, ethnic tensions were exacerbated. In response, the Skype group voted online for the removal of the pictures and videos from websites, which resulted in many of them being deleted by administrators of the social networks.

Working with foreign social networks was more complicated, and involved a greater number of internet users outside Kyrgyzstan. Foreign internet users could not fully understand the complexity of the situation. This is why few based outside of the country limited the mass distribution of the different videos, articles and photographs.

As the ethnic conflict became more politicised, this was reflected on the internet. The war of information between the different parties began, with both sides spreading rumours and misinformation. In the south access to the internet was not widespread, which meant that the information needed to be checked via SMS text messages, and with the help of friends. Because of this it took some time to refute the rumours in these areas.

It is still difficult to establish the facts surrounding the role of the internet and the spreading of rumours during the conflict. Different commissions have tried to determine who the perpetrators were and to reconstruct the events. As a result, the commissions, both local and international, have come to different conclusions, which at times contradict each other. But what is clear is that the Skype network demonstrated the effectiveness of using the internet to verify rumours and speculation in times of crises.

Conclusion

During the 2010 coup and subsequent ethnic conflict in Kyrgyzstan, social networks played an effective role in stabilising the situation in the country. On the other hand, they complicated the process of reconciliation between ethnic groups. The main reason for this is the uneven development of infrastructure. Where the internet was available, there was a high likelihood of obtaining reliable information; but there was an information vacuum where internet access was limited. Television and newspapers failed to keep people properly informed. Because of this, access to the internet should be a primary goal of any state. Despite various attempts to control it, it should remain decentralised and self-regulating, a situation which is more likely to guarantee the security of citizens.

However, there remain challenges. With the freedom to access and disseminate information comes responsibility. Given the recent past, the new government has refused to control the mass media, and the internet has offered a broad guarantee of freedom to disseminate information. Twenty new print publications were launched, and more than seven new media outlets started on the internet within five months of the new government coming to power.

But, apparently, the media were not ready for this kind of freedom, which has led to the widespread proliferation of false information. Especially in remote regions of the country, news websites began to disseminate information without checking its validity.[2]

Actions steps

The possibility of broadband access has been discussed for the past five years in Kyrgyzstan, but no real steps have been taken. The process is delayed by the fact that operators do not want to develop their networks in the outlying regions, since it does not pay. The government is always trying to increase the costs of operating in the country, introducing new fees and obligations for those that want to offer services in remote regions.

Broadband access should be a priority for our country because it provides a solution to social problems and solves the problem of information security in general. To achieve this it is necessary to reform the regulatory process in telecommunications services, as well as to ensure the independence of the regulator. This would offer stability for businesses, and boost infrastructural development. Social networks should strengthen themselves through self-regulation. This would mean encouraging users to be responsible for the accuracy of the information disseminated on the internet.

It is also necessary to popularise the idea of the internet as a way to access information, including using mobile phones. Training is necessary. After the events of April and June 2010, civil society activists urgently pushed for measures that would allow Twitter to be used in Kyrgyzstan. Once this was achieved, they travelled to all of the regions in the country to conduct training in the use of Twitter. In 2011 the number of Twitter users in the country had increased ten-fold. ■

2 kg.akipress.org/news:405371 and bektour.com/2011/08/10/kak-mozhno-zastavit-akipress-i-kabar-rasskazat-o-sobytii-kotorogo-nikogda-ne-bylo

LEBANON

BROADBAND AS A HUMAN RIGHT IN LEBANON

Mireille Raad

Introduction

As one of the few countries in the Middle East enjoying a relative degree of freedom of speech on the internet,[1] but suffering from an unbearably slow connection, the installation of a high-capacity submarine internet cable called IMEWE[2] could not have come soon enough.

According to Net Index,[3] Lebanon ranks as the fifth slowest country in the world with an average speed of 0.59 Mbps per user. The entire international bandwidth for the country is only 2.5 Gbps. This low bandwidth creates overbooking and does not allow a committed download rate. End-users are instead provided with a "best effort" connection, limited by a fair usage policy of 3Gb/month.

Prices are unreasonably high (see Table 1). Internet service providers (ISPs) pay a 1,200% [4] tax rate. There is no law to organise infrastructure or duct sharing, so each ISP has the additional cost of providing connectivity to end-users. The direct impact is that users in remote areas do not have internet access or have to rely on the monopoly of local, illegal "internet cable" providers.

In other words, a typical Lebanese user pays high fees for very slow internet and does not actually get what he/she paid for due to the high number of users sharing the low international bandwidth.

Cadmus and Berytar/Aletar are the two fibre-optic cables tasked with keeping Lebanon connected to the world, and both are more than sixteen years old. There is no internal fibre backbone connecting all the different cities. An internet exchange point[5] was recently launched in Beirut, but it cannot service more than 20% of the market.[6]

Services like 3G are still not available to internet users in Lebanon, even though they were commercially introduced ten years ago. There is a kind of monopoly established by Ogero, a state-owned operator, which controls an 80% market share, while the other twenty ISPs combined have only 20%.

Economic and legislative context

With the internet situation being so desperate, one might believe that all troubles would have disappeared after a 3.84 Tbps cable reached Lebanese shores. Lebanon can use 120 Gbps of this cable, a sizeable increase from the current 2.5 Gbps. However, due to political bickering, legislative fights, the absence of a cabinet for long durations, and corruption, this cable remains inactive.

The Lebanese economy is suffering from a crushing USD 60-billion debt. The debt/GDP ratio is approximately 150.7%.[7] According to a study by the World Bank, internet penetration can affect the Lebanese economy in the following ways:

- 1.38% GDP increase per year for every 10% increase in internet penetration
- 0.25% increase in jobs for every 1 percentage point increase in penetration
- USD 90 million per year for every 10% increase.[8]

In July 2002, the Lebanese Telecommunication Act[9] was set to create three main players in the telecom sector:

- The Ministry of Telecommunications
- Telecom Regulatory Authority (TRA)
- Liban Telecom

The ministry sets the visions and strategic goals for the telecom sector, the TRA conducts research and develops roadmaps to achieve those goals, and Liban Telecom was to be the implementer. However, Liban Telecom was not formed for political reasons. Instead the ministry outsourced all the operations to Ogero (Organisme de Gestion et d'Exploitation de l'ex Radio Orient), which was established in

1 opennet.net/research/profiles/lebanon

2 IMEWE is an internet submarine cable with 3.84 Tbps capacity; Lebanon benefits from 120 Gbps. imewecable.com

3 www.netindex.com

4 ISPs buy the international internet feed (E1s) from the Ministry of Telecommunications at USD 2,700 + USD 800 local loop – while the cost for the ministry is USD 300.

5 An internet exchange point is a place where ISPs interconnect to create a local loop.

6 Ogero, a state-owned operator, controls an 80% market share and refuses to connect to the Beirut Internet Exchange (BIX), so the BIX cannot service more than 20% of the users.

7 CIA World Factbook: goo.gl/25k3v

8 www.infodev.org/en/Article.454.html

9 The Lebanese Telecommunication Act is available at: www.ontornet.org/sources/TelecommunicationsLaw.pdf

TABLE 1.

Price and service comparison

Service packages available in Lebanon		Typical triple-play service packages	
Residential			
Download	0.25 Mbps	Download	8 Mbps
Upload	0.064 Mbps	Upload	4 Mbps
Poor quality cable TV		100+ video channels including High Definition	
Very low usage of fixed voice services (mobile prices not included and VoIP is banned)		Unlimited VoIP	
USD 55/month		USD 40/month	
Business			
Download	2 Mbps	Download	10 Mbps
Upload	2 Mbps	Upload	10 Mbps
No video conferencing, VoIP is banned		High-speed internet access via video conference, 100+ video channels including High Definition, unlimited VoIP calls	
USD 4,000/month		USD 500/month	

1972. Ogero is 100% owned by the state and acts under the supervision of the minister.[10]

Instead of collaboration, the three institutions have launched many lawsuits against each other, and there have been numerous media scandals.

Campaigning for broadband

13 December 2010 was the expected launch date for the 13,000-kilometre IMEWE cable that runs between India and France, providing Lebanon with 120 Gbps international bandwidth. Eager Lebanese internet users were excitedly waiting – but instead, the IMEWE consortium, which controls the supply, cancelled the launch because of a dispute between the Telecoms Ministry headed by Charbel Nahas and Ogero.

Minister Nahas had sent a letter to the IMEWE consortium to inform them of the ministry's decision to deprive Ogero of its responsibilities on the IMEWE project, including the launching event. Nahas complained that Ogero informed him about the event only ten days in advance, and that Ogero did not provide regular reports about project progress.[11]

On the other hand, Ogero criticised the minister of telecommunications for wanting to deprive the body of its privileges. It said that the IMEWE consortium gave Ogero the authorisation to prepare for the launch event because of the company's professionalism and high credibility. Ogero also expressed its surprise at the ministry's decision to isolate it instead of rewarding it for its efforts and claimed it had been sending reports about the project progress.

After signing a Broadband Manifesto[12] launched by the IT sector in previous years with no response from Lebanese authorities, frustrated Lebanese users launched three online campaigns to raise awareness and share updates about the IMEWE cable, and to exert pressure for its activation.

The three campaigns are:

- Flip the Switch
- Lebanese Want Fast Internet
- OntorNet (Arabic dialect for "wait for the internet")

All three campaigns used social media as their launching platform to reach their target audience. Local and international media, both traditional and new media, took an interest in the story and the efforts of the activists.

The social media strategy used included:

- Flip the Switch: Facebook group[13] and blog[14]
- Lebanese Want Fast Internet: Facebook page[15] and Facebook ads
- OntorNet: viral video campaign,[16] Facebook page,[17] Twitter community,[18] offline workshops, blog[19] with online presentation and infographics.

10 www.ogero.gov.lb/Published/EN/profile.html

11 www.yalibnan.com/2010/12/14/imewe-cable-launches-its-commercial-operation

12 www.facebook.com/group.php?gid=16011607127

13 www.facebook.com/groups/fliptheswitch

14 fliptheswitch.info

15 www.facebook.com/fastlebanon

16 www.youtube.com/user/ontornet

17 www.facebook.com/OntorNet

18 twitter.com/#!/search?q=%23ontornet

19 blog.ontornet.org

Due to the mounting pressure, and in response to the buzz created on the subject, two different telecom ministers and TRA personnel met with representatives from the Flip the Switch and OntorNet campaigns. OntorNet relied on the online community to crowdsource questions, live-tweeted during the meetings to get live feedback. It released audio recordings of the meetings to allow for more transparency and to hold the people in charge responsible for their statements and promises.

Following these campaigns, there was more awareness of the reasons behind the struggling telecom sector and the communication between the telecom minister and online community became direct. As a result, ministerial plans for broadband in Lebanon became more transparent. Those plans include the launch of 3G services by the end of September 2011 and activation of 10 Gbps out of the 120 Gbps of the IMEWE cable.

Social and political impact

The above story suggests the importance of good and affordable internet connectivity, and its huge social and financial impact. With the Arab Spring and revolutions being shared online, activists in Lebanon are feeling helpless not being able to broadcast their opinions and take on events that directly affect their own country.

For example, during the events that started on 25 January in Egypt, with Egyptians suffering from censorship and internet blackouts, activists in Lebanon who happened to have friends and contacts living a few hours away in Cairo could not use Tor[20] to relay traffic for fellow activists or upload videos and footage they got hold of. Pushing content online was hard, and generating/translating Arabic content that proved to be crucial was near impossible.

This showed the Lebanese that they are actually suffering from a subtle and worse form of censorship.

Business impact

The business impact is reflected in lost opportunities for innovation, creativity, entrepreneurship ideas and services. E-commerce and online businesses have problems running their operations from Lebanon, and have great difficulty getting their users to rely on the web as their favourite way of shopping and doing things.

The country is also suffering a brain drain of highly educated people seeking to further their careers, often in neighbouring countries like the United Arab Emirates (UAE), which happens to have a 98% internet penetration rate.

Since information and communications technologies (ICTs) are involved in every single business process, a bad ICT sector weakens the whole economy, and causes a great loss in business productivity due to the wasting of thousands of hours or the inability to make use of some services.

Lebanon is also missing out on chances for social inclusion for poor and remote areas. Better access to information, e-education and e-government are greatly needed.

Conclusion

ICTs are powerful tools to disseminate information and trigger change. Access to the internet is becoming a human right, not merely an "accident". However, censorship can happen in many forms: censoring content, implementing black lists, bad internet connectivity, and, eventually, pulling the internet "kill switch".

One of the most dangerous aspects of control over the internet is the government monopoly over the expensive fibre-optic networks, licences and infrastructure. In Lebanon the government was late in investing in infrastructure, which set the country ten years back in time in terms of tech.

Another conclusion we can draw is that, sadly, Moore's Law does not apply to legal innovation: the disparities between technology and legislation are likely to become even greater, and we need an increasingly tech-savvy judiciary to be able to have a deep understanding of the issues at stake, and write laws that are not too rigid or too easy to break.

Action steps

The following action steps are suggested for ICT activists in Lebanon. Hopefully they will also prove in handy for others:

- **Lobby for a local Internet Governance Forum** It is crucial for members of civil society, companies and lawmakers to get together at least once a year and discuss ICT challenges and issues. Even if no formal decisions come out of such meetings, it is important to have the discussion and bring people together from different backgrounds and sectors.
- **Create groups and collectives around digital challenges** Technical innovation moves too fast and tends to be complex by default. It is important to have hacker spaces, groups and collectives of geeks and non-tech people alike to raise awareness, share knowledge and pioneer

20 www.torproject.org

the use of technology in innovative projects with social impact. These groups help in the capacity building of new skills that are not being taught in formal education yet, and become crucial to having a leading country in the ICT field.

- **Get decision makers involved with social media** Luring decision makers into actual involvement with social media can be a powerful tool for communication and creating pressure. However, due to the usually huge amount of followers, many assign a PR company to handle their accounts.
- **Beware of "slacktivism"** It is easy to get fooled into a false "feel good" sense about social issues without actually achieving measurable and concrete effects. Raising awareness should not turn into ranting out on social media or spamming.
- **Learn to go anonymous** Article 19 of the United Nations International Covenant on Civil and Political Rights[21] states, "Everyone shall have the right to hold opinions without interference," and "Everyone shall have the right to freedom of expression; this right shall include freedom to seek, receive and impart information and ideas of all kinds, regardless of frontiers, either orally, in writing or in print, in the form of art, or through any other media of his choice." A quick look on the internet will tell you that billions of dollars are spent on monitoring and censoring tools around the world, and that governments and intelligence agencies are information hungry. Activists should never shy away from learning the tech skills that will allow them to protect their inalienable human right to privacy and freedom of expression.

21 secure.wikimedia.org/wikipedia/en/wiki/International_Covenant_on_Civil_and_Political_Rights

MEXICO

SOCIAL NETWORKS AND THE "WAR ON DRUGS"

LaNeta
Olinca Marino
www.laneta.apc.org

Introduction

There have been at least 10,000 minors orphaned, 120,000 persons displaced, and 23,000 young people recruited by organised crime over the course of the current presidential administration in Mexico, in power since 2006.[1] More than 30 mayors have also been assassinated since President Felipe Calderón declared a war on drug trafficking in December 2006, with results that to date have been catastrophic. Although there are no official statistics regarding how many civilians have been murdered since 2006, the *Zeta*, a weekly paper in Tijuana, has documented 50,490 executions throughout the country between December 2006 and May 2011.[2]

As in any war, the general population is very vulnerable. Both assassins and members of the armed forces have been killed. The army has violated civil rights during its raids and roadblocks.[3] Drug cartels use the bodies of their victims to frighten and intimidate their opponents and to send warnings. Reports say 1,226 of the people who have died in the crossfire or in direct attacks between December 2006 and December 2010 are children and teenagers.[4]

The violence that is part of this war does not only affect Mexicans: 10,000 kidnappings of migrants have been registered. In April 2011, a common grave with the bodies of 72 migrants was found in the northern Mexican state of Tamaulipas, and similar cases have occurred regularly elsewhere. Recently, some Central Americans denounced the fact that they were "sold" by agents from the National Migration Institute to the organised crime group Los Zetas.[5] These crimes can be categorised as crimes against humanity.

Information and action against violence

According to the organisations Article 19 and CENCOS (National Centre for Social Communication), more information and better quality information is urgently needed:

> Society needs to know the origin and nature of this violence, without delay. To this end, the people dedicated to disseminating information and opinions regarding the violence should have the minimum guarantees for their security afforded by the state. In the case of falling victim to intimidation, they should be provided with the necessary protection to safeguard their physical integrity and that of their families, so that they can exercise their right to justice.[6]

Despite statements like these, some university professors who carry out research on drug trafficking and organised crime have disappeared, been murdered or have emigrated to other countries where their security can be guaranteed.[7] Journalists who work in Mexico work in one of the most dangerous places in the Americas.[8] According to Article 19 and CENCOS, in 2010 alone, 129 journalists and people in the field of communications media were attacked. The attacks upon female journalists and communicators also include threats to their families.[9] In the first quarter of the 2011, eleven journalists were murdered.[10]

For this reason, some newspapers have changed their idea of journalism in order to carry on reporting in the face of the violence, threats, kidnappings and murders. An example is *El Diario Vanguardia*, based in the northern state of Coahuila, which was able to create a community of 30,000

1 www.eluniversal.com.mx/primera/37103.html

2 www.zetatijuana.com/2011/07/11/50-mil-ejecuciones

3 President Felipe Calderón refuses to withdraw the army from the streets even though this is a repeated demand from the country's citizens, and even though international bodies have called on Mexico to stop using the army for functions that should be carried out by the police forces (such as the United Nations Working Group on Enforced or Involuntary Disappearances, in its Preliminary Report of March 2011).

4 contralinea.info/archivo-revista/index.php/2011/03/22/1-mil-226-ninos-asesinados-en-la-guerra-de-calderon

5 www.jornada.unam.mx/2011/05/10/politica/007n1pol

6 Article 19 and CENCOS (2011) *Violencia en México y el derecho a la información 2010*, Article 19 Oficina para México y Centroamérica and CENCOS, Mexico City, p. 7.

7 www.lajornadadeoriente.com.mx/2011/01/13/puebla/ofa14.php

8 www.criterioonline.com.ar/mas/internacionales/48568-otro-periodista-fue-asesinado-en-mexico

9 Article 19 and CENCOS (2011) op. cit.

10 knightcenter.utexas.edu/es/blog/reportera-policial-es-septima-periodista-asesinada-en-mexico-en-2011

Facebook users and 12,000 Twitter followers to call upon authorities to provide timely and real-time information about the situation. In response to the pressure, the police in the state capital opened a Twitter account (@policiasaltillo). According to the digital publication *El periodismo digital*, the Twitter account created "a way to receive information about what is happening in the city in real time, even though this information is not often included in the newspapers the next day due to the risks."[11] In another example, also in the state of Coahuila, the attorney general has provided information about recent cases of violence using his Twitter and Facebook accounts.[12]

In this way, social networks have started to appear in different states of Mexico as sources of real-time information. In February 2010, for example, in Torreón, Coahuila, the first alerts about a shooting incident were sent out on Twitter. Similar cases have occurred in the states of Jalisco, Zacatecas and Durango. In Veracruz, Nayarit and San Luis Potosí, social networks were used to warn about kidnappings and extortion.[13] In the states of Chihuahua, Tamaulipas, Sinaloa, Guerrero, Morelos, Coahuila, Nuevo León and the Federal District, alerts about situations of violence circulated on social networks. In the Federal District, users also circulated the phone numbers of kidnappers and extortionists.[14]

Paradoxically, the internet has also become a tool used by drug cartels.[15] Narco mails and narco videos targeting rival criminal organisations, as well as authorities and civil society, have proliferated.[16] CNN reports that "videos supposedly sent by cartels show kidnap victims gagged and bound and being tortured at the time of being murdered."[17] According to a Mexican newspaper, "among all of the media that drug lords have at their reach to attract followers, social networks seem to have become one of their main vehicles for communication."[18] This has led some politicians to call for greater regulation on certain digital tools in the country.[19]

While the Mexican population is feeling vulnerable and afraid on a daily basis, it has also participated in different initiatives to say "No more bloodshed". Mexicans have used many different kinds of media to remain united against the war. The internet and mobile phones have been important allies to different sectors of the population, allowing them to exchange information about drug cartel violence and to protect local communities in dangerous situations. Digital media have also served as a channel for the collective expression of civic discontent, and to mobilise citizens.[20]

As part of this general violence, the murders of women in Ciudad Juárez, Chihuahua and in other states of Mexico continue. At least 10,000 women and girls have been violently murdered over the last ten years. Most of these cases are not brought before the courts.[21] Because of this, the families of victims and organisations working in solidarity with them mobilise on the internet. Many initiatives are very active online, such as *Nuestras Hijas de Regreso a Casa* (Bring Our Daughters Home)[22] or *Justicia para Nuestras Hijas* (Justice for Our Daughters), which has a blog,[23] a Twitter account,[24] a Facebook site,[25] a channel on YouTube[26] and a channel on Picasa with a photo gallery of the victims.[27]

A national map was created identifying the sites of crimes on the website *Ciudadanía por la Paz y Justicia en México*[28] (Citizens for Peace and Justice in Mexico), which also encourages civic action. This is a public space. Every event or message sent by SMS, Twitter (#mapaMX #nosoncifras) or with an online form is pre-approved and published by a group of volunteers. For security reasons, personal information related to the authors of the published information is removed. This initiative is based in Cuernavaca, Morelos.[29]

Other social media sites include:

- *Por favor no más sangre* (Please, no more bloodshed): This is a campaign that seeks to end the bloodshed of innocent people caused by the war on drug trafficking.[30]

---

11 www.elperiodismodigital.org/2011/04/periodistas-optan-por-redes-sociales-ante-violencia-en-mexico

12 www.eluniversal.com.mx/estados/79948.html

13 Ibid.

14 Ibid.

15 www.eluniversal.com.mx/primera/36666.html

16 noticias.aollatino.com/2010/12/03/narco-redes-sociales

17 mexico.cnn.com/nacional/2010/03/08/residentes-de-la-frontera-usan-internet-para-combatir-al-crimen-organizado

18 noticias.aollatino.com/2010/12/03/narco-redes-sociales

19 www.eluniversal.com.mx/primera/36666.html

20 Vega, A.F. and Merino, J. (2011) *Ciudadanos.mx: Twitter y el cambio político en México*, Debolsillo, Mexico City.

21 www.eluniversal.com.mx/notas/530233.html

22 www.mujeresdejuarez.org

23 justiciaparanuestrashijas.blogspot.com

24 @JPNH01

25 www.facebook.com/pages/Justicia-Para-Nuestras-Hijas

26 www.youtube.com/jpnh01

27 picasaweb.google.com/justiciaparanuestrashijas

28 pazyjusticia.crowdmap.com

29 www.facebook.com/pages/Red-por-la-Paz-y-la-Justicia/210655688946361; redporlapazyjusticia.org; witter.com/#!/redpazyjusticia

30 es-es.facebook.com/pages/Por-favor-no-más-sangre/184308684920918

- *Contingente Monterrey* (The Monterrey Contingent): These citizens promote creative actions for peace. Their Facebook site reads: "We will meet on the second Sunday of every month on the Esplanade of the Heroes of Monterrey until THERE ARE NO MORE MISSING PERSONS OR INNOCENT DEATHS!"[31]
- *Poesía para nuestros muertos* (Poetry for our dead): An initiative launched by a collective that invites action because "every Mexican has rights and we should fight for our DIGNITY, for PEACE and for JUSTICE to be a basic value in our country."[32]
- "*Menos Días Aquí*" (Fewer Days Here): A project run by volunteers with a blog that records a weekly count of the dead. "We count the number of deaths caused by violence in Mexico. In this way, we keep our dead alive."[33]
- *Balacera MTY* (Shooting in Monterrey): This offers timely and useful information shared by civilians to help avoid situations of risk. *Balacera MTY* is also active on Twitter.[34]

On Twitter, we also find:

- *#ContingenteMX:* Digital action for peace supporting human rights.
- *#Sinviolencia:* Reports and warns of crime.
- *#Tienennombre:* Names victims of violence in Mexico. Emphasises that victims are not statistics – they have names.
- *#BalaceraGDL:* Keeps people informed of shootings and news about security issues in Guadalajara.
- *#noviolenciamx:* Encourages action against violence.
- *#tuitcallejero:* This initiative (which translates as "streettweet") invites people to write a comment with 140 characters or less on a piece of paper and post it somewhere where passersby can read it. It invites people who find the notes to take pictures of them and to post them on their blogs as a way of disseminating the message.[35]

Mexicans demand: "No more bloodshed!"

One of the first campaigns in Mexico using new media was the campaign launched by the famous cartoonist Eduardo del Río (who calls himself RIUS), together with other cartoonists, journalists and intellectuals, as a form of protest against the wave of violence. The idea was to create civic consciousness in spaces where each person can express his or her discontent using social networks. Twitter and Facebook users changed their profile photo to an image of the word "No", which included a drop of blood, to support the movement. Within the first 48 hours of the campaign, 2,155 cybernauts showed their support on Facebook.[36] #NoMasSangre was among Twitter's trending topics for several weeks.[37]

The *Movimiento por la Paz con Justicia y Dignidad* (Movement for Peace with Justice and Dignity) is an important initiative in Mexico. Poet and journalist Javier Sicilia has driven this movement in the wake of the murder of seven youths, including his son, in the state of Morelos in April 2011. To date the movement has organised a series of marches, amongst other activities. The Civic Caravan for Peace with Justice and Dignity, also known as the "Caravan of Consolation", is of particular importance to the movement. It began its journey from Cuernavaca on 4 June from Cuernavaca, travelling through several of the cities hardest hit by violence in Mexico, and heading towards Ciudad Juárez. The caravan travelled over 3,000 kilometres. On Twitter, the hashtag #marchanacional became a trending topic for weeks.[38]

Hundreds of testimonies and demands for the federal government to end the war have been gathered at national marches. Dozens of harrowing testimonies and calls for the state's strategy to change have been launched. One speaker at one of the first *Movimiento por la Paz* marches stated: "These 40,000 deaths[39] belong to us all, they are our dead. There can be no distinction between the deaths of drug dealers, assassins, soldiers and citizens."[40]

Local marches – often spontaneous – have been convened with the help of the internet. This was

31 es-es.facebook.com/ContingenteMty
32 www.facebook.com/poesiaparanuestrosmuertos
33 menosdiasaqui.blogspot.com
34 www.facebook.com/pages/BalaceraMTY; twitter.com/#!/BalaceraMTY
35 quelleguelapaz.blogspot.com/2011/07/tuitcallejero-invitacion-oficial.html
36 www.pueblaonline.com.mx/en_boca_de/?tag=facebook&paged=2
37 dixo.com/2011/01/no-mas-sangre.php
38 www.milenio.com/cdb/doc/noticias2011/434f5cc48739b1e6f2b64e6cf230cc24
39 At the beginning of the mobilisation, in April 2011, the estimated number of deaths was 40,000; in July 2011, the weekly magazine *Zeta* reported an estimated total of 50,000.
40 homozapping.com.mx/2011/04

the case in Ciudad Juárez where a peace protest following a visit to the city by President Calderón was organised through social networking.[41] A similar protest happened in Guadalajara within hours of several violent incidents by criminals. Approximately 700 people spontaneously responded to the call for action put out by young people on social networks.[42]

Groups of Mexicans and sympathisers from the Americas, Asia and Europe have created the *Red Global por la Paz en México* (Global Network for Peace in Mexico).[43] They have organised many different initiatives across the world, some using information and communications technologies (ICTs), including the following: a virtual demonstration with pro-peace images organised in Seoul called "*Sí a la Paz*" (Yes to Peace); "1,000 Cranes for Peace in Mexico", an initiative in Tokyo which dedicated 1,000 origami cranes to heal Mexico; "Ephemeral Ciudad Juárez", set up at the foot of the Eiffel Tower, and consisting of a clothesline pegged with empty envelopes addressed to President Calderón with the names of victims of violence in Mexico as the senders; and "No More Bloodshed", a conference organised in Corcovado de Rio in Brazil, which called for a review of international policies on drug use and drug trafficking.[44]

Action steps

The importance of the internet can be felt in a society constantly threatened by violence. In the case of the "war on drugs" in Mexico, ICTs can be a valuable way to:

- Guarantee citizens' right to monitor cases involving victims of the war.
- Facilitate the participation of citizen groups in providing coverage of the judicial processes brought by the victims of violence.
- Support meetings of those who have been victims in the war.
- Promote ways for citizen representation, such as referendums.
- Monitor and follow up on government security initiatives.
- Promote education and culture instead of violence.

In general, the internet can be used to support the participation of citizens and their mobilisation in efforts aimed at changing the state strategy in combating crime in the country.

More than ever the rights to access to information, free expression and the protection of personal data are critical in Mexico. The protection of journalists must also be guaranteed. Mexican society has much still to do.

41 mexico.cnn.com/nacional/2010/03/08/residentes-de-la-frontera-usan-internet-para-combatir-al-crimen-organizado

42 www.eluniversal.com.mx/estados/79948.html

43 www.redglobalpazmexico.com

44 exteriorpactonacional.blogspot.com

MOROCCO

THE INTERNET REVOLUTION IN THE ARAB REGION PAVES THE WAY TO DEMOCRACY

DiploFoundation
Hanane Boujemi
www.diplomacy.edu

Introduction

2011 marks a significant turning point in the history of the Arab region following the uprising of people against their government leaders. Many reasons triggered this unprecedented wave of rage that toppled established regimes in Tunisia and Egypt, and resulted in the 20 February protests in Morocco.

Corruption, oppression, mediocre standards of living, poverty, inequality and abuse of power constituted the perfect formula for the Arab world revolt. The internet was one of the main channels that mobilised people to unite and fight for their civil rights. Not only did the internet help the masses join forces to air their concerns and legitimate demands, it also proved to be an effective tool to change government policies in the Arab region, and helped in paving the way towards more transparent and democratic processes in the Arab world.

The role of the internet and social networks in the uprising in Morocco

Morocco is one of the countries in the Arab region where the uprising took place in various forms. Street demonstrations throughout major cities of the country called for a change in the decision-making circles and condemned the practices of some public figures who, according to demonstrators, managed to accumulate wealth at the expense of the ordinary citizen and abused their power while serving the country. The internet in general – and social media and networks specifically – helped activists to generate consensus across the various segments of society to express their concerns and opinions about the pressing issues Morocco is facing.

Due to the sharp increase of internet penetration in Morocco,[1] the internet has become an effective tool to harness social solidarity. Online platforms such as blogs, Facebook, YouTube and Twitter are now widely used amongst the youngest generation in Morocco and also played a significant role as a communication channel in the uprising. Protesters used these platforms to achieve widespread consensus for their demands; they also used social media channels to keep both the general public and official authorities updated with what was happening on the ground. Multimedia material was strongly present in reporting on street demonstrations and it can be described as vital to ensuring the credibility of information disseminated. Amongst the many challenges protesters were facing to get their voices heard was the scepticism of the public about their real intentions, especially since the mainstream media depicted them as a threat to the kingdom's stability.

Citizen media gave another dimension to social resistance events in Morocco. Websites like hibapress.com and hespress.com were instantly updated with news video feeds and pictures of the demonstrations. The material gained the respect and credit of readers who were out of the loop, but also generated criticism from people against the uprising. Some articles posted triggered scepticism about the sources of information circulated, especially if they meant to criticise the 20 February Movement or one of its figures. Some commentators on the articles posted even referred to the Moroccan secret services, alleging that they were spoon-feeding the websites, reinforcing the notion of information manipulation.

Another example of citizen media that emerged following the recent uprising events in Morocco is mamfakinch.com. The name "mamfakinch" was coined from the raw Moroccan Arabic dialect to mean: "We're not going to give up." It was established by a group of blogger activists. Its mission consists of pushing for more social and economic reforms. It also defends the right to access information and freedom of expression as inherent human rights of the common citizen.

The internet definitely transformed the perception of information during the protests in Morocco. No significant credit was given to the public or state media due to its legacy of being fully supportive of the government's agenda. Social and citizen media bridged the gap and reached out to the common citizen, allowing more space for freedom of expression.

But, to restate a central complaint, to what extent can the information it provided be judged credible?

1 www.internetworldstats.com/af/ma.htm

The impact of social media on freedom of expression

Social networks and citizen media contributed to the idea of freedom of expression in Morocco during the uprising. Facebook groups and YouTube channels were created to gather opinions of people sharing the same concerns or the same political affiliation. The accessibility and ease of use of internet social tools such as Facebook encouraged some police officers and soldiers to create their own online groups to reveal their working conditions and treatment by their superiors. It was the first time that police and soldiers in Morocco opened up about the kinds of conditions they faced, knowing that the military and public service code prohibit them from protesting against the regime or disclosing details of any sort to the media.

It is not clear whether they were aware that using social media breached their code of conduct, or what impact they were hoping to have. Reports on some social media websites appeared at a later stage claiming that the people who organised the Facebook groups or posted videos on YouTube were tracked down and arrested. However, despite these sorts of negative outcomes, it has to be said that in general social media tools have no doubt helped in improving the status of freedom of expression in different segments of society.

A brief reading of the Moroccan Constitution: The legal context for freedom of expression

Freedom of speech and expression is one of the pillars of a democratic society. The internet and the media in Morocco are relatively free, and people are also entitled to demonstrate and express their views freely. In fact, street demonstrations are not alien as a form of protest in Morocco. The parliament square in the capital city Rabat has witnessed protests by unemployed qualified graduates, including doctors and bachelor's degree holders, for decades.

The current Moroccan Constitution[2] deals broadly with the notion of different freedoms. One of them is freedom of expression. Article 9, which was amended in 1996, states that the constitution shall guarantee all citizens the following:

- Freedom of movement through, and of settlement in, all parts of the kingdom
- Freedom of opinion, and of expression in all its forms
- Freedom of association and the freedom to belong to any union or political group.

However, Article 41 of the amended 2003 Press Code[3] stipulates that journalists and publishers can face financial penalties and risk imprisonment if they violate restrictions on defamation, or publish critical content related to three sensitive topics: the monarchy, territorial integrity (i.e. the calls for independence in the Western Sahara), and Islam. The Press Code emphasises that threats to public order can be considered one of the criteria for censorship. Given these limits, newspapers are reluctant to be openly critical of government policies, and journalists are still not free to express an objective point of view, particularly on the sensitive topics.

Since there is no law in Morocco that limits or regulates freedom of expression on the internet in general, the constitutional articles related to freedom of expression apply. This explains why some bloggers were arrested in the past for criticising state policy or the king.

The 20 February Movement in Morocco

Morocco joined the wave of uprisings in the Arab region, inspired by the Jasmine Revolution in Tunisia and the 25 January Revolution in Egypt. A group of young Moroccan activists called for a day of street demonstrations nationally on 20 February 2011 – the date giving the movement its name.

The movement managed to get support from cyber activists, traditional lefties, Islamists and twenty human rights organisations, including the Moroccan Association of Human Rights and Amnesty Morocco.[4] Their main demands focused on introducing a new democratic constitution; an effective parliamentary monarchy and the separation of government branches (legislative, executive and judicial); language rights for Berber speakers; and the release of all political prisoners.

The main channel used to mobilise the Moroccan population was the internet. 20 February activists created a Facebook group, a YouTube channel and a Twitter account to discuss the issues at stake, mainly related to political and social reform. These attracted thousands of participants and supporters all over the country, as well as worldwide. The Facebook group was the main point of reference for all the movement members coordinating their activities on the ground. It included the movement's official releases and supported group discussions. YouTube was used to broadcast videos from the street protests and to get feedback from members of the movement as events unfolded, and Twitter

2 Chapter One of General Provisions and Basic Principles of the Constitution, adopted September 1996.

3 Article 41 of the Moroccan Press Code, 2003 edition.

4 www.thenation.com/blog/158670/arab-uprisings-what-february-20-protests-tell-us-about-morocco

helped with real-time updates on demonstrations across the country. Other internet channels and websites were also used to report on the events, in particular CrowdVoice[5] and Global Voices.[6]

Besides using these channels to synchronise the movement's branch activities and logistics across Morocco, they were critical in creating awareness amongst the public. YouTube hosted promotional videos[7] produced by the movement featuring citizens from diverse backgrounds explaining their motives for joining the protests. In response to this, YouTube was flooded with personal videos of people explaining their point of view about the situation in Morocco, including the current regime, and also expressing their support for – or refusal to support – the 20 February Movement's call for protests.

Even though the 20 February Movement in Morocco represents only a small minority of people calling for change, and has faced fierce criticism from supporters of the regime, who constitute the majority of the population, its achievements to date can be considered a phenomenal contribution to the democratic process in Morocco. A new amended constitution which takes into consideration some of the movement's demands has been approved. The government has also decided on a wage increase for public sector employees with immediate effect.

Conclusion and recommendations

The uprising in Morocco created a social media frenzy. The use of Facebook, for instance, increased sharply in the first semester of 2011, reaching more than three million subscribers with a population penetration rate of 11.23%.[8] Social media were a vital enabler of much-needed social discourse on taboo topics, and proved to be a successful tool to reach all sections of society.

Unlike Tunisia and Egypt, access to the internet in Morocco was not shut down by the government to silence the uprising, which can be considered a breakthrough for freedom of expression in the Arab region. The government opted for leaving the internet free and accessible for people to express their views – even while there are allegations that it tried to manipulate the content through its secret services.

However, the achievements of the protests so far ought to be attributed to the efforts of the people leading the protest movement, who believed that the time had come to initiate constitutional, social and economic reforms that will benefit the unprivileged. The role of the internet and social media in the Moroccan uprising was that of providing an interactive medium to host real-time debate and to discuss people's demands. This proves that the existing channels of discourse between the state and citizens, including governmental and non-governmental entities, political parties and associations, failed to fulfil the needs of the common citizen who took refuge in the social and citizen media channels to lead a radical change of the idea of the state-citizen relationship. This relationship was based on a top-down approach to decision making when it came to state policies – while the internet helped to make these decisions evolve around the citizens' needs.

Compared to other countries in the Arab region, Morocco enjoys a relatively stable political environment, but still needs to work vigorously towards having a true democratic regime. The internet can have a positive impact on a participatory process that works towards a democratic society where the rule of law, equal opportunities, and an improved standard of living are achieved.

Action steps

The decision-making process in Morocco can be inclusive if the government engages in the current dialogue with its citizens, of which the internet is the main driving force. The mechanisms of how policies are implemented should be altered to reflect the needs of citizens: adopting a bottom-up approach would be the ultimate way to secure a democratic society that recognises the role of people in shaping policies.

The Moroccan state could use the internet as a way to communicate with people by:

- Setting up official online open forums on government websites to host discussions where people can comment on state strategies and policies.
- Launching capacity-building programmes to raise awareness about the role of the internet in initiating a bottom-up approach to decision making.
- Endorsing the use of new technologies by citizens and providing the necessary financial support to deploy the necessary infrastructure.
- Introducing new policies to guarantee the right to access to information.
- Guaranteeing online freedom of expression as a right.
- Reinforcing the notion of open access to data and open government.
- Using ICTs to harness transparency and accountability. ■

5 crowdvoice.org/protesters-demand-reform-in-morocco
6 globalvoicesonline.org/-/world/middle-east-north-africa/morocco
7 www.youtube.com/watch?v=Sof6FSB7gxQ
8 www.socialbakers.com/facebook-statistics/morocco#chart-intervals

MOZAMBIQUE

ICTS AND THE SEPTEMBER STREET PROTESTS IN MAPUTO

Polly Gaster

Introduction

On 1 September 2010 many inhabitants of Mozambique's capital city, Maputo, and the satellite city Matola, were unable to get to work. The main routes into the centre of town had been closed by demonstrators protesting against recent rises in the cost of living. The police tried to quell the protests, at some points using live bullets, resulting in violent confrontations.

The government reacted initially by proclaiming its "irreversible" position on the price rises, but backtracked within a week as further demonstrations were threatened. The events in Mozambique cannot be called a "Facebook revolution", in today's fashionable terminology, but various information and communications technologies (ICTs) played significant roles. Recognition of this provoked a government reaction, with implications for the future freedom of ICT-based communications, while the pattern of ICT usage illustrated the gap between the protesters on the street and civil society organisations.

Legal framework

Mozambique's first multiparty Constitution of 1990 and its 2004 revision[1] guarantee freedom of expression, association and the press. They also explicitly state that the "exercise of freedom of expression (...) and the exercise of the right to information shall not be limited by censorship." The Constitution and the 1991 Press Law[2] are recognised to have played a successful role in promoting press freedom, pluralism of ideas and media diversity.[3] While this legal framework generally meets international standards, there are gaps and curtailments which are the object of lobbying and campaigns, for example limitations on access to information,[4] and the existence of repressive legislation that is in contradiction with the Press Law.

The Telecommunications Law of 2004[5] set out to liberalise the sector, aiming to end the Mozambique Telecommunications Company (TDM) monopoly on landlines and infrastructure by 2007 (this has not yet happened) and encourage private sector value-added services. The Mozambique National Communications Institute (INCM) is the telecoms regulator, but is subordinated to the Ministry of Transport and Communications rather than an independent body.

ICT policy and practice

The government approved a National ICT Policy in 2000,[6] which specifically states that "the State recognises and protects the right of citizens to have access to information and to knowledge spread by ICTs" and adopts the principle of universal access. Internet service providers are not subject to specific licensing, but need to be formally registered with the INCM.

There is no legislation curbing freedom of expression on the internet, and no experience prior to 1 September 2010 of either restrictions (blocking, filtering or otherwise censoring) on access to sites, or arrests or libel cases specifically related to material published on the internet.[7]

Internet access is available via broadband, wireless or mobile phone in Maputo and all ten provincial capitals, and an increasing number of towns in the country's 128 districts. As in other African countries, more and more citizens are turning to the two mobile phone networks (MCel and Vodacom) for internet access, in addition to voice and SMS use, as mobile internet access is more widely available, cheaper and often more reliable. Around six million of Mozambique's 20 million inhabitants now own mobile phones.

1 Assembly of the Republic (2004) *Constituição da República de Moçambique*, Boletim da República I Série nº 51, Maputo, 22 December, Art 48.

2 Assembly of the Republic (1991) *Lei 18/91*, BR I Série nº 32, Maputo, 10 August.

3 MISA-Mozambique (forthcoming 2011) *Assessing Media Development in Mozambique: A study based on UNESCO's Media Development Indicators*, UNESCO Communication and Information Sector, Paris.

4 A draft law on Access to Information designed to rectify this weakness was produced by MISA-Mozambique in a participatory process and submitted to the Assembly in 2005, but has not yet been debated.

5 Assembly of the Republic (2004) *Law 8/2004*, BR I Série nº 29, Maputo, 21 July.

6 Council of Ministers(2000) *Resolution 28/2000*, BR I Série nº 49, 3º Supplement, Maputo, 12 December.

7 MISA-Mozambique (forthcoming 2011) op. cit.

Increasing poverty

A recent study for the World Food Programme on urban poverty[8] showed that the cost of living rose sharply from October 2008 to October 2010. The cost of a basic food basket for a household of five went up by 41% to 3,974 MT/month,[9] while in 2010 the official minimum wage for the formal sectors ranged from 1,500 to 2,700 MT.[10]

The study sample of 1,199 households in Maputo and Matola showed that transport and energy (for lighting and cooking) were the main regular expenses in addition to food. It also provided some striking demographic data, for example:

- 68% of the sample were in the age groups covering 0-29 years.
- Of the 28% of young people (18-29) in the households surveyed, 7% had never been to school, 43% were not working, while the majority of the 57% who earned some income were in the informal sector.
- The number of unemployed heads of household had risen from 4.7% in 2008 to 12% in 2010.
- The main income sources were salaries (42%, down from 60% in 2008), casual labour (30%) and petty trade (17%).

The government had been implementing a policy of strategic subsidies to hold down the costs of such vital items as fuel (including paraffin and cooking gas), electricity, bus fares and bread. Elections took place in late 2009, and six months later the re-elected government started trying to reduce or eliminate these subsidies. So on top of all the general price rises, the final straw was a series of badly coordinated announcements informing the public of specific rises in water, electricity and bread as from 1 September.

The riots[11]

On Wednesday 1 September protesters in Maputo and Matola tried to bring the cities to a halt by blocking the main roads in and out of town with junk and burning tires. Passing vehicles were stoned and some vandalised, and the main bus terminals were also targeted. Some of the symbols of discontent were also attacked and destroyed or looted, such as electricity company offices, buses, grocery stores and a petrol station. Police used tear gas, rubber bullets and in some cases live ammunition to prevent the demonstrators from marching into the city and to try to clear the roads.[12]

The protesters' strategy was successful and the cities did effectively close down. Those who had got to work or school started walking home, and there was almost no traffic. Though the next day was quieter, with more sporadic rioting in specific locations, there was still no public transport and residents opted to stay at home. By 3 September most of the roads had been cleared and traffic – including some buses – was increasing, but most workplaces, schools, shops and banks remained closed. There was a heavy police presence, and just a few short-lived attempts to set up new street barricades. By the end of the three days of protests, there was a total death toll of thirteen in Maputo and Matola, with 154 injured having received medical treatment, some for gunshot wounds.[13] A total of 256 people had been arrested, mostly in Maputo and Matola.[14]

Over the weekend rumours began to circulate, primarily via SMS, of further demonstrations being planned for the following Monday (6 September). However, no demonstrations took place.

The role of ICTs

Many citizens had advance warning that something was going to happen on 1 September through SMS text messages circulated by mobile phone from unnamed sources, notwithstanding police statements to the contrary. It also became obvious on the day that the level of coordination achieved among many different sites must also have been relying on mobile phone. There was no sign of public mobilisation via internet or Facebook, which is not surprising given that the demonstrators clearly came from the poorer residential areas, where internet access and internet-enabled phones are still rare.

Most of the Mozambican press provided full coverage of the events, and the radio and independent

8 Geography Department, Eduardo Mondlane University (2010) *Estudo de Vulnerabilidade Urbana nas Cidades de Maputo e Matola*, EMU/WFP, Maputo.

9 Food basket designed by the Ministry of Health, price calculations made by the Ministry of Planning and Development.

10 Ministries of Finance and Labour (2010) *Diploma Ministerial 103/10*, BR I Série Nº 24, Maputo. 16 June.

11 The data in this section is based on daily English-language newscasts from the Mozambique News Agency (AIM), Maputo, 1-7 September 2010.

12 A report on police tactics and behaviour found that they had believed their own propaganda and no planning had been done for policing protests. The Rapid Intervention Force had not been put on alert, and the regular police force had to cope with little guidance. The police sent to the trouble areas were just coming off their shifts, tired and hungry and badly equipped, while most of the new shift was unable to get to work for two days. This is thought to be one of the main reasons why the riots got out of hand and there were so many casualties. Centre for Public Integrity (2010) *Policia sem preparação, mal equipada e corrupta*, CIP, Maputo (September).

13 Press announcement by the Minister of Health, 6 September 2010.

14 Attorney-General Augusto Paulino in his annual statement to Parliament, 27 April 2011. 178 people were sentenced to prison terms ranging from three days to two years, 64 were acquitted and the other fourteen are still awaiting trial.

television companies made an effort to provide real-time news. However, in addition to the text messages flying around the city between families and friends swopping updates and advice, the internet came into its own as a place for sharing information, aggregating and re-disseminating news, and promoting comment and discussion.

Some Facebook pages, in particular that of the popular free newspaper *@Verdade* (Truth),[15] provided immediate space for citizen reporting on places where there was trouble, or roads had been blocked, amongst other updates. This was an extremely useful source of immediate information from multiple sources and locations. *@Verdade* also ran an Ushahidi-based crowd reporting tool and made some use of Twitter, but the Facebook site was by far the most accessible and important.

Sites also opened themselves up for comment and discussion, throughout both the immediate crisis and the government responses. *Diário de um Sociólogo,*[16] *Reflectindo sobre Moçambique,*[17] the Mozambique Sociology Association[18] and others published a range of contributions on their blogs. They also republished newspaper articles and commentaries, press communiqués and statements from government and civil society, and cross-published reflections from other sites. Videos appearing on YouTube[19] illustrated different aspects of the riots, from police action to looting, and in turn provoked more commentary.

In other words, social media provided space for many voices and opinions to be heard, while the television and radio stations tended to rely on the same pool of analysts (mostly male, mostly journalists or academics) for their studio debates and news programmes.

Government response

Denunciation and backtracking

The first official reactions came from the police, affirming that the demonstrations were illegal because prior permission had not been sought in terms of the law – which was true. This was followed by government ministers on the one hand defending economic policies and the need for price rises and on the other accusing the demonstrators of being "adventurists and bandits". The cabinet spokesman said that the price rises were "irreversible".[20]

However, a mere five days later, following a cabinet meeting on 7 September, the irreversible was reversed. A communiqué was issued announcing a subsidy to maintain the price of bread, cancelling the electricity price rise for social tariff consumers, and reducing the water price rise for the same group, maintaining the tax benefits for tomatoes, potatoes, onions and eggs, and reducing the price of low-grade rice.[21]

Control of communications

One of the most serious aspects of the government response was its move to limit free communication.

On 6 September, when more demonstrations were anticipated, most mobile phone users throughout the country found it impossible to send text messages. The two operators, MCel and Vodacom, both announced that there had been a breakdown and they were working to restore services. Suspicions of interference were unsurprisingly rife, but both the minister of Transport and Communications and INCM publicly denied involvement or knowledge of a government instruction.[22] On 10 September the *Mediafax* daily newspaper claimed the operators had received a letter from the regulator ordering them to close down the SMS service, and on 17 September the weekly *Savana* newspaper published an article carrying a confirmation from Vodacom South Africa and a facsimile of the letter, dated 6 September.[23]

In a separate incident, *@Verdade*'s mobile phone accounts went offline before the general shutdown, as did its website (which was quickly mirrored and made available again via other routes).[24]

SMS services were fully restored on 8 September, followed by an SMS "battle" between messages supporting the government and others strongly critical.

The government's next step was to accelerate the introduction of a ministerial diploma approving a new regulation on the registration of SIM cards.[25] SIM card registration had been under discussion in Mozambique, as in other countries, for some time, but the astonishing feature of this particular diploma was that it defined a time limit of only two months from the date of its publication for all users to register, after which their numbers would be

15 www.facebook.com/jornal.averdade#!/jornal.averdade?sk=wall

16 oficinadesociologia.blogspot.com

17 comunidademocambicana.blogspot.com

18 sociologia-mocambicana.blogspot.com/2010/10/no-olho-do-furacao.html

19 For example: www.youtube.com/watch?v=s2YqY3Quwhk&NR=1

20 AIM, 1-7 September 2010.

21 Council of Ministers Secretariat (2010) Press release, Council of Ministers, Maputo, 7 September.

22 AIM newscast, 8 September 2010.

23 Savana (2010) Grupo Vodacom confirma ordem de bloqueio, *Savana*, 17 September.

24 Interview with Erik Charas, editor of *@Verdade*, Maputo, 2 August 2011.

25 Ministry of Transport and Communications(2010) *Diploma Ministerial 153/2010*, MTC, Maputo, 10 September.

blocked. At the same time, as *Mediafax* reported on 30 September, the ministry rather unconvincingly denied that the timing of the new regulation had anything to do with the riots.

Unsurprisingly, though the deadline provoked large-scale anxiety and long queues, it proved impossible to register everyone in time, and 7 January 2011 was announced as the new cut-off date. That date came and went in silence from government bodies, and there has been no further official announcement since then. Meanwhile, the Centre for Public Integrity denounced the diploma as being "incoherent, illegal and anti-constitutional", calling for it to be revoked.[26]

Communications via internet – email services, blogs, social media – continued throughout and after the crisis period with no interference. In a way this underlines the social split between users: the young people on the streets using mobile phones and the better-off members of the public, commentators and so on using the net to talk about it. In that sense the government's priorities were logical.

Conclusions

The first obvious conclusion from the above sequence of events is that anybody who wants real change should get out onto the street and make life difficult for the government of the day. Civil society organisations had been publishing studies, surveys and reports showing the implications of rising prices for the poor, and warning of the increasing anger of ordinary people, but the government did not want to listen – the 1 September riots brought an immediate response, in the short term, a victory.

The government's handling of the issues did not win it any credibility: its initial policies followed by constantly changing positions displayed both weakness and a sad lack of understanding or awareness of the very real problems of the urban poor. Having met all the demands so quickly, it makes a violent reaction to future price rises or other unpopular policies more likely. Government attempts to clamp down on or limit mobile communications and the right to freedom or expression through ICTs were also signs of policy being made on the hoof, but no less serious for that. Perhaps for the first time it felt seriously challenged, and its immediate resort to illegality in this area is a worrying precedent.

This report has used words such as "protests", "demonstrations" and "riots" more or less interchangeably throughout, and the events of 1 September showed elements of all three. Certainly there were no clear demands formulated, no visible leadership, and no sign of evolution into a more formal social movement. Established civil society organisations were totally marginalised, though some issued their own statements *post hoc*. However, although the middle classes and inhabitants of the city centre were not on the streets demonstrating, there were clear signs of common cause, since the rising cost of living and the growth in corruption are now affecting everyone but the elite groups. It remains to be seen whether converging (though still very differentiated) interests can be converted into common strategies or new forms of social organisation that are more broadly based.

Within this context, the potential of ICTs in Mozambique as tools for organisation, coordination and expression for civil society in the broad sense is now evident. While mobile phone communications still predominate, the social media networks have a growing influence as a substitute or alternative to dialogue through more formal channels and the information provided by traditional media. They are currently acting primarily as information brokers and opinion formers rather than as mobilisers, but while this is in itself a useful function it could easily become more interventional the next time there is a social crisis, as lessons have undoubtedly been learned by all sides.

Action steps

- Establish a civil society coalition for digital inclusion to lobby for large-scale internet access through mobile phones, wireless and pricing systems and keep a watch on government ICT policies to ensure equality of access, freedom of communication, open data and access to information.
- Campaign for a fully independent telecoms and ICT regulator.
- Promote channels for communication and exchanges between the "formal" and "informal" sections of civil society through social media networks.
- Develop strategies for enabling civil society organisations to integrate better use of ICTs into their work and promote training and use among their own constituencies. ▪

26 Centre for Public Integrity (2010) *Observatório de Direito N° 1: Sobre o Registo de Cartões SIM*, CIP, Maputo (November).

NEPAL

WAITING FOR THE NEPAL SPRING

Panos South Asia
Kishor Pradhan
www.panossouthasia.org

Backstage

The tiny, mountainous, newly formed Federal Democratic Republic of Nepal,[1] with a population of about 30 million, was removed from a list of the countries with the worst record of censoring the internet in the 2009 report published by Reporters Without Borders.[2] Just four years earlier, with the persistence of political insurgency and instability after the royal regime had taken over power in the country in February 2005, the national communication systems and services – fixed telephone lines, mobile telephone service, radios and televisions, as well as the internet – were blacked out for seven days. The reason cited was the need to contain the volatile political situation.

When the censorship and clampdown on the media continued for several months after February 2005, the sporadic existence of online citizen journalism publications in Nepal found their due recognition and prominence. During the royal clampdown citizen journalism websites like *Mero Sansar*,[3] started informally by a group of journalists after becoming disenchanted with a mainstream paper, became recognised as an independent source of information and a means to uphold freedom of expression.

The royal coup in Nepal in 2005[4] was the turning point in the history of internet use in the country, sparking the flame of widespread use of blogs and social networking sites that supported civil society resistance. But it was only in 2006 when networking tools like Facebook, Skype and LinkedIn became popular in Nepal. In recent years, this has resulted in a number of spontaneous activist groups emerging online that have been instrumental in civil protest and resistance.

Policy background

The Right to Information Act (2006) guarantees each Nepali citizen the right to demand and receive information on any matter of public importance, except when sharing that information is considered not in the national interest. Though a new constitution for Nepal is still being prepared, the incumbent constitution guarantees freedom of speech and freedom of expression. Nepal as a state is also a signatory to the Universal Declaration of Human Rights and its Article 19 on the right to freedom of opinion and expression.

The country's first legislation on the internet can be found in the Nepal Information Technology (IT) Act (2000). This law was later revised and named the Electronic Transaction Act (2008), which regulates the degree to which the internet can be exploited in Nepal for business or civil purposes. The Electronic Transaction Act also comes close to being a cyber law in Nepal. Besides upholding the legitimacy of electronic document transactions and economic transactions like online banking and online payment, it contains clauses that regulate the content that can be posted on the web. And, of course, penalties, both in terms of monetary fines or imprisonment in the event of violating the regulations, are included.

However, 2010 was not a good year for internet freedom in Nepal. The authorities persistently clamped down on internet service providers (ISPs) by forming a special central investigation bureau that grilled the ISPs on the misuse of the internet by their clientele. Voice over internet protocol (VoIP) is also not yet legal in Nepal, though public internet centres use it illegally. The authorities argued that due to the illegal use of the internet to make telephone calls, the national telecom authority was losing billions of rupees every year. The authorities were also of the view that the internet and VoIP were being illegally used for criminal activities, making it impossible for them to trace these activities. At the same time, the authorities argued that what it considered anti-social content was being published online.

1 Previously a kingdom, Nepal was declared a republic in late May 2008 by the elected Constituent Assembly. Nepal currently has a presidential system of multiparty democracy.

2 en.rsf.org

3 www.mysansar.com "My Sansar" in English translates as "My Universe".

4 For further information on the royal coup visit: www.crisisgroup.org/en/regions/asia/south-asia/nepal/B036-nepal-responding-to-the-royal-coup.aspx

Recently the authorities issued a regulation that one can use the internet or internet telephones in public internet cafés only after registering using an identity document.

Social activism online

Despite these restrictions, online social activism has had some effect in Nepal. In 2011, one of the English dailies in Nepal ran this news headline on 7 May: "Facebook brings hundreds to street."[5] The report said: "There were no organisers, nor were there the leaders. But hundreds of citizens assembled at Maitighar Mandala at 3.00 pm today, just less than a hundred yards from the administrative headquarters Singha Durbar to press for the promulgation of the constitution on time." (sic)

The protests took place just a few weeks before the deadline of 28 May 2011 that had been set for the promulgation of the new constitution. Interestingly, the newspaper reported that banners carried by protestors read, "You have already taken full wages, give us constitution", but no names of organisations who had called for the protests were seen. The campaign was reportedly called "We Are All Nepalis for Change". It was discussed by a dozen people at a gathering a week earlier that then turned into a Facebook campaign, ultimately culminating in the street protests.

The protests were followed by several other Facebook activist campaigns, including "Nepal Unites".[6] Its Facebook page states: "Nepal Unites is a social movement that began on Facebook where frustrated Nepali youths united to speak up and stand up against the current government demanding a timely constitution, and co-operation from the government." It goes on further to say that "Nepal Unites is a social media revolution" that shows the "global concern and strength of youth (...) in building a better and prosperous Nepal." Finally it states, "We are an informal group of concerned Nepali citizens that came together to raise our voice."

Nepal Unites has organised various social and political campaigns, including in countries like the United Kingdom and others where the Nepali diaspora can be found. A BBC TV journalist reported that Nepal Unites protest marches and campaigns have heralded the start of Facebook activism in Nepal. Another Facebook campaign by Nepal Unites was reported by Yahoo news: "Thousands of young Nepalese have united behind a new Facebook campaign to stop paying the country's battling politicians if they cannot produce a new constitution by the May 28 deadline."[7]

The deadline for promulgating the new constitution in Nepal expired on 28 May, and it has been extended by another three months. Nepal Unites continues to organise campaigns on other issues of public interest and importance, such as corruption and unnecessary foreign travel by politicians.

If one compares what is happening in Nepal as far as Facebook or social media activism is concerned to the impact of social media activism in countries like Egypt, the argument can be made that while Nepal Unites has been likened to a social movement, it has not necessarily had that level of impact. This may largely be due to the number of internet users in the country, and the number of those who use social networking tools.

According to Internet World Stats,[8] the number of Facebook users in Nepal as of June 2011 was 1,072,999 – just over 3.5% of the total population of about 30 million people in Nepal. Egypt, on the other hand, is one of the top internet countries in Africa. A little over 20 million people – or around 25% of the total population – have access to the internet and use Facebook. This suggests that the impact of social media activism can be realised when the number of internet users in a country is significant.

While this may hypothetically be the case, I recall that when twelve Nepali migrant workers were killed by an Iraqi militant group in 2004 and the video footage of the killings was posted on the internet, the immediate impact of this was felt. There were riots in Kathmandu, with tyres burned, and many of the labour companies that arranged work for migrant Nepalese were attacked, ransacked and burnt. In 2004 the number of internet users or those who could access the video footage of the Nepalese killed in Iraq was definitely less than what it is today. In that case, the videos were downloaded and burnt on CDs, spreading the images like wild fire. The immediate impact of the videos was so intense and emotive to sections of the Nepalese people that they resorted to violence to express their discontent. With persistent rioting, the government had to impose a curfew in Kathmandu and several other cities. They also had to offer to compensate the families of the victims killed in Iraq.

If somebody were to ask me today if Nepal's "internet generation" is ready to bring about change, my answer would be no. I used to call them the

5 www.thehimalayantimes.com/fullNews.php?headline=Facebook+brings+hundreds+to+streets&NewsID=287061

6 nepalunites.org

7 my.news.yahoo.com/facebook-group-vents-anger-nepals-leaders-025816239.html

8 www.internetworldstats.com/asia.htm

"chat generation" at some point in my quest to understand new media and their impact in our societies and on governance. But nowadays, like others, I call them the "Facebook generation" or rather the "social media generation". When internet penetration has increased by several fold in Nepal, and the population who are children now are youths, then maybe I would say yes, the "internet generation" is ready to bring about the desired change Nepalese people in general have always aspired to.

The social movements incited by social media activism, or for that matter Facebook activism, have not yet been able to really make a dent in the existing political situation in countries like Nepal. However, it cannot be ruled out. Facebook activism is gaining momentum in Nepal, and it is likely to have a multiplier effect that can catalyse the change and bring about a "Nepal Spring".

Not yet concluded...

Social media activism has been gaining ground since May this year in Nepal. It has definitely paved the way for building social resistance, mostly amongst the youth, which has organised several social campaigns pushing for the constitution to be promulgated in Nepal, and fighting against corruption, amongst other things.

Nepal Unites does not consider itself a formal organisation, but a group that started spontaneously because of its concern over the issue of the new constitution and with peace in Nepal. For these sorts of spontaneous associations, their independence is important. While their impact can also be felt in the diaspora, the exact extent of this impact is not yet clear.

Perhaps when the volume of social media activism increases and the right critical mass is created there will be a tangible impact on change in Nepal. While a Nepal Spring is yet to take place as a result of social media activism, there is ample room to wait and watch with loads of optimism to keep buoyant our sense of anticipation.

Action steps

The following action steps can be suggested:

- There is a need for more effective awareness on the potential use of social media activism in social resistance and protest.
- Capacity needs to be developed in civil rights activist groups so that they can use social media tools.
- Social media activists should link up with civil rights activist organisations to make their activities more effective.
- According to the data available, more than 35% of the Nepalese population uses mobile phones. These need to be integrated into activist campaigns using new media. ■

THE NETHERLANDS

A PRIVACY DISASTER? RFID CARDS FOR PUBLIC TRANSPORT IN THE NETHERLANDS

Institute for Information Law
Frederik Zuiderveen Borgesius
www.ivir.nl

Introduction

The ever-growing use of networked computers and databases makes life considerably easier. However, this also makes it easier to keep an eye on citizens. The average Dutch person is registered on 250 to 500 databases.[1] Is the Netherlands "sleepwalking into a surveillance society"?[2] Four years ago, a Big Brother Award was granted to the Dutch citizen: "He is the biggest threat to privacy according to the jury. Due to indifference – 'I have nothing to hide' – and lack of interest in what happens to their personal data, citizens share responsibility for the disappearance of privacy in the Netherlands."[3] This report deals with an example of a database system that threatens privacy: the new electronic payment system for Dutch public transport. The reaction that this system has provoked shows that Dutch citizens seem to be slowly waking up.

Database systems in the Netherlands

A recent report by the Rathenau Institute identifies three recurring problems regarding the introduction of database systems. First, there is often insufficient attention to security and privacy at the design phase. Second, frequently databases are designed with primarily the interests of the company or the state organisation in mind, overlooking the interests of the individual. Third, policy makers often have high expectations of the benefits of databases, which may not always be realistic.[4] A related problem is that sometimes people are not offered a choice on whether or not to participate in a system.[5] All these points are relevant for the OV-Chipcard system.

The OV-Chipcard is a card to pay for public transport services in the Netherlands, comparable with the Oyster card in London and the Octopus card in Hong Kong. Travellers can store credit on the OV-Chipcard, and pay for trips by checking in and checking out of public transport by holding the card against a card reader. One of the primary reasons to launch the OV-Chipcard project was to obtain insight into the use of public transport lines in order to improve efficiency.[6] The OV-Chipcard is supposed to replace all older public transport cards, and in some cities this is already the case.

The OV-Chipcard is RFID-equipped. RFID is short for "radio frequency identification", which is a technology that enables reading and storing information on RFID chips from a distance. RFID chips can be used in objects, such as entrance tags for buildings or library books, and may replace the ubiquitous barcode in the near future. RFID chips can also be inserted into living beings. A famous example is the Dutch discotheque Baja Beachclub, where certain customers had RFID chips implanted that enabled them to pay for their drinks by holding their arm close to an RFID reader.[7] The use of RFID chips in public transport cards and the subsequent storage of data gives us an early glimpse of what it means to live in the "Internet of Things".[8]

Is the Dutch travel card a privacy disaster?

Since the start of the project, the OV-Chipcard system has been plagued with problems. For example, in 2008 researchers found several flaws in the security of the card: it is possible to clone the card and to restore travel credit. Bart Jacobs, professor at the Digital Security Group of the University of Nijmegen, calls the

1 Schermer, B.W. and Wagemans, T. (2009) *Onze digitale schaduw. Een verkennend onderzoek naar het aantal databases waarin de gemiddelde Nederlander geregistreerd staat* (Our digital shadow. An exploratory study on the number of databases in which the average citizen is registered), Considerati, Amsterdam.

2 Richard Thomas, the English Information Commissioner, quoted in Ford, R. (2004) Beware rise of Big Brother state, warns data watchdog, *The Times*, 16 August.

3 www.bigbrotherawards.nl/index_uk.html

4 Munnichs, G. et al. (2010) *Databases. Over ICT-beloftes, informatiehonger en digitale autonomie* (Databases. About ICT promises, data hunger and digital autonomy), Rathenau Institute, The Hague, p. 26-27. www.rathenau.nl/en.html

5 Van 't Hof, C. et al.(2010) *Check in/check uit. Digitalisering van de openbare ruimte* (Check in/check out. Digitization of the public space), NAI, Rotterdam.

6 Vaststelling van de begrotingsstaten van het Ministerie van Verkeer en Waterstaat (XII) voor het jaar 2005 (Adoption of the budget of the Ministry of Transport (XII) for the year 2005), Parliament 2004-2005, 29 800 Chapter XII, Nr. 2, p. 126.

7 European Technology Assessment Group (2007) *RFID and Identity Management in Everyday Life*, Scientific Technology Options Assessment, Brussels, p. 41-42.

8 International Telecommunication Union (2005) *ITU Internet Reports 2005: The Internet of Things*, ITU, Geneva. www.itu.int

OV-Chipcard "technically (...) a nightmare" and a "privacy disaster".[9] He highlights five problems.[10]

First, the OV-Chipcard uses an old kind of RFID chip with poor security, which can be read by anybody using a card reader bought for only ten euro. The RFID chip will show its unique number to any card reader, which makes it possible to recognise and track persons carrying a card. Second, the card is an "open wallet": it is possible to change the contents on the card, unbeknownst to the person carrying the card. It is also possible to read the five last travels from a card.[11] Third, the transaction data of the card (for example, the location where someone gets on and off a bus and the exact times) are processed in a centralised database. "The former East German Stasi would have been jealous of such a database," according to Jacobs. Fourth, the OV-Chipcard is an identity-based system, while before the OV-Chipcard was implemented, one only had to show a ticket (this was an attribute). Jacobs poses the question: "Is it really necessary to tell who you are when you enter a bus? Do we want such a society?"[12] Lastly, although anonymous prepaid cards are available, they are very impractical. Unlike with personalised cards, it is not possible to make use of discount programmes. Most machines accept only coins, not paper money, to store credit on the card (they also accept bankcards, but that would break the anonymity of the process). Jacobs calls the anonymous cards "a sad joke" and concludes: "Privacy is the last thing the designers of the OV-chip system cared about – in sharp contrast with the principle of privacy by design."[13] The privacy and security issues do not end here. In 2010 the website of one of the participating public transport companies exposed the personal data of over 100,000 people,[14] and in 2011 different software packages to hack the cards were distributed on the internet.[15]

The risk of function creep

The creation of large databases always entails the risk of function creep. When data are collected for one purpose, new purposes to make use of those data usually present themselves soon. The OV-Chipcard system is no exception. For example, public transport companies want to use individual travel patterns for direct marketing purposes.[16] One could imagine the scenario that if one travels to Amsterdam, a coupon for a reduction at the local hamburger shop is offered, and if one often travels by first class, a coupon for a more expensive restaurant is offered.[17]

Now that the system is in use in a large part of the Netherlands, function creep has already started. On one occasion, the police asked a public transport company for a list with all identification numbers of the OV-Chipcards used at fare gates of two metro stations during a certain period. The police asked for the name, address, zip code, city of residence and any available photographs of the users. After initially refusing to provide the photographs, the public transport company provided all requested information to the police. It did, however, file a complaint with the court, arguing that the police should have obtained a written authorisation from the examining magistrate in order to demand the photographs. After much litigation, the Dutch Supreme Court confirmed that in this case, demanding the photographs without an authorisation was not in accordance with the law. In short, the Supreme Court held that photographs can contain sensitive personal data, namely data regarding race, which the police could only demand with a written authorisation.[18]

Not surprisingly, the OV-Chipcard project was met with some criticism, for example from Bits of Freedom. This is a Dutch digital rights organisation focusing on privacy and communications freedom in the digital age. Together with a large number of volunteers, the organisation strives to influence policy, for example, by organising campaigns and providing advice. Every year Bits of Freedom organises the Big Brother Awards, and gives an award to individuals, companies, government agencies and proposals that are most threatening to privacy. The public can suggest parties for nominations, and can vote which party should be granted the public award. Bits of Freedom has been following the developments around the OV-Chipcard from the beginning. The company holding the central database with travel data, Trans Link Systems, was nominated in 2003 and 2005. The Dutch railway company was granted a Big Brother Award in 2007 for its role in the OV-Chipcard. In 2011 Trans Link Systems had

9 Jacobs, B. (2010) Architecture Is Politics: Security and Privacy Issues in Transport and Beyond, in Gutwirth, S. et al. (eds) *Data Protection in a Profiled World*, Springer, Dordrecht, p. 292-293.

10 Ibid., p. 292.

11 Ibid., p. 293.

12 Ibid., p. 294.

13 Ibid., p. 294 (internal footnote omitted).

14 Zenger, R. (2010) Datalek: gegevens 168.000 reizigers gelekt via OV chipkaart website (Data breach: data from 168,000 passengers leaked through OV-Chipcard website), *Bits of Freedom*, 18 May. www.bof.nl

15 de Winter, B. (2011) Onzichtbare OV-chiphack vrij beschikbaar (Invisible OV-chip hack is freely available), *Webwereld*, 14 February. www.webwereld.nl

16 OV-Chipcard FAQ: www.ov-chipkaart.nl/faq/?n=64

17 Jacobs (2010) op. cit., p. 293.

18 Hoge Raad (Supreme Court Netherlands), 23 March 2010, *LJN* BK6331.

the dubious honour of winning both a jury award and the public award.

Student action against travel cards

Protests have not been limited to coverage on blogs, websites and traditional media. In early 2010 a group of students became worried and lodged a complaint with the Dutch Data Protection Authority.[19] Most Dutch students are eligible for a state-funded study grant, which includes the right to a card for public transport. The card offers free travel during the week, and discounted travel on the weekend (or vice versa if a student chooses so). An OV-Chipcard for students is personal and the RFID chip contains *inter alia* a unique number, the date of birth, the amount of credit loaded on the card, and the last ten transactions. A picture and the name of the student is printed on the card, but not stored on the RFID chip. When a student checks in and checks out of public transport, the data being processed include: the number of the card, the location where the student checks in, the date and exact time, the credit stored on the card and the credit used for the trip.

In their complaint to the Data Protection Authority the students argued first that on days on which they are eligible for free travel, there is no need to check in and check out. According to the students, it must be possible to open the gates of a metro station without registering a student checking in. Because of this their detailed travel data should not be collected. Second, the public transport companies stored the data – which were not sufficiently anonymised – for seven years in the central database. The students said that this was disproportionate. In addition, the students complained about the lack of transparency about what happens to the processed data. They also questioned whether the database with personal and travel data is sufficiently secured against data breaches and attacks from hackers. In short, the students doubted whether the companies complied with Dutch privacy regulation.[20]

The Data Protection Authority, which had been critical about the OV-Chipcard system from the beginning, started an investigation. In late 2010 the Authority published a scathing report about Trans Link Systems and three of the participating public transport companies. Two public transport companies and Trans Link Systems were found to store the data for a disproportionate period. (After the investigation Trans Link Systems changed the seven-year retention period to two years.) All three companies were found to process data in breach of privacy regulations.[21]

The Authority said that the Dutch railway company provided insufficient information to students. As the students are eligible for free travel during the week, there is no need to register the students checking in or out when they travel by train. However, the railway company fails to adequately inform students that they are not required to check in and out. Moreover, the general information provided by the railway company (such as posters in the stations and messages announced on the train) implies that everybody is required to check in and to check out. Therefore, the railway company did not have legitimate grounds to store and process the students' travel data. In short, each of the investigated companies was in breach of requirements of Dutch privacy regulation. The companies agreed to implement shorter retention periods. However, in July 2011 the Authority found that the railway company was still not informing students sufficiently. If the railway company still fails to inform students by the end of 2011, it has to pay penalties up to a maximum of 375,000 euro.[22]

Influence of citizens

In summary, the OV-Chipcard system is an example of how *not* to design a database system; privacy was clearly an afterthought during the design phase. Because of projects like this, the Dutch Data Protection Authority warns that the Netherlands might be turning into a "glass society".[23] However, there is some (very cautious) reason for optimism. Although the Dutch public seemed to be sleepwalking, a new trend seems to be emerging. Citizens and civil rights organisations make their voices heard more and more, for example on blogs and on social media. Mainstream media have started to report on these protests; sometimes they even make the evening television news.

In some cases, protests against the introduction of poorly designed database systems have influenced policy makers. In 2011 several government plans were adapted, largely because of privacy concerns. A government plan to store four fingerprints of each citizen in a database has been halted after

19 For an overview of the complaint see: www.clinic.nl/wiki/index.php?title=Handhavingsverzoek_studenten_OV-chipkaart

20 Wet bescherming persoonsgegevens (Dutch Data Protection Act).

21 CBP (2010) OV-bedrijven bewaren gegevens reisgedrag in strijd met de wet (Public transport companies store travel data in breach of the law), 9 December. www.cbpweb.nl

22 CBP (2011) CBP dwingt invoering bewaartermijnen reisgegevens af via dwangsom (Data Protection Authority ensures retention periods of travel data are shortened, under threat of penalties, 26 July. www.cbpweb.nl

23 Kohnstamm, J. and Dubbeld, L. (2007) Glazen samenleving in zicht' (Glass society in sight), *Nederlands Juristenblad*, 2007, p. 2369-2375.

civil rights organisations protested for years.[24] The Dutch senate voted against a law implementing national electronic infrastructure through which doctors could exchange patients' medical data, because of insufficient security and privacy safeguards.[25] A plan to introduce compulsory "smart" electricity meters that automatically send a message to the electricity company every fifteen minutes has been adapted as well, as electricity use can reveal much about your life such as your daily habits and rhythm. People are no longer required to have a smart meter installed.[26] So protests can eventually influence policy makers. However, it is important to protest at an early stage. Although protests seem to have some influence on the OV-Chipcard system now, it does not seem plausible that its main characteristics will be changed.

Action steps

- Try to convince policy makers who decide about new database systems to pay attention to privacy by design and to strengthen the position of the individual, for example, by making data processing more transparent. Tell them data should only be used for the original purpose.
- Make your voice heard at an early stage. Protest during the design phase when privacy-threatening systems are planned. Prevention is better than damage control at a later stage.
- The most important advice is to the Dutch public: do not embarrass yourself by winning another Big Brother Award. In other words, do not sleepwalk!

24 Letter of the Minister of Justice to the Parliament, 26 April 2011.

25 State press release, Eerste Kamer stemt tegen landelijk elektronisch patiëntendossier (Senate votes against national electronic patient record), 5 April 2011. www.rijksoverheid.nl

26 State press release, Slimme meter kan snel ingevoerd (Smart meter can be introduced soon), 22 February 2011. www.rijksoverheid.nl

NEW ZEALAND

COPYRIGHT CONUNDRUMS

Jordan Carter Ltd. Internet Consulting
Jordan Carter
about.me/jordantcarter

Introduction

Copyright law does not sound, on the face of it, the most likely area of policy to generate examples of social resistance. Yet since the introduction in 2007 of legislation updating copyright law, a diverse but high-profile campaign has developed in response to efforts by successive New Zealand governments to introduce a new penalty for residential copyright infringement. That penalty is disconnection: the prospect that a citizen caught infringing copyright via the internet might see their access to the network brought to an end.

The campaign was successful insofar as at the time of writing, disconnection had not been implemented in New Zealand. A small but determined campaign spawned new organisations, new forms of resistance to legislative change, and the widespread use of the internet to catalyse citizen action against changes that people did not support.

Suspicion remains that, under continuing pressure from the United States (US) – revealed on WikiLeaks[1] – renewed attempts will be made to bring disconnection into effect (for instance, during the negotiation of the Trans Pacific Partnership Agreement). Its presence today in the New Zealand legislation presents a low barrier should a future government seek to introduce it.

This report explores the background to the disconnection proposals, the efforts governments have made to pursue them, and the response that has developed.

Policy background

There are two parts to the background story of copyright reform that matter to this case: the international and the local context.

On the global scale there have been efforts since the mid-1990s to create new, tighter norms for the protection of intellectual property. The global baseline is the TRIPS Agreement,[2] part of the World Trade Organization (WTO) framework adopted in 1995. All WTO members including New Zealand are committed to its minimum levels of intellectual property (IP) protection. Broadly speaking, developed countries have been advocating stronger IP law since TRIPS, while developing countries have seen the TRIPS baseline as the appropriate level of IP protection.

In New Zealand these global debates have affected copyright law reform. The country is broadly seen as having an effective and high-quality IP law regime. The Copyright Act 1994 underwent a lengthy review starting in 2001, to (among other things) ensure the legislation was fit for the digital age. Changes were introduced into the Parliament in 2007 and passed in 2008, some of which added new "permitted acts" for citizens (e.g. format shifting of music from CD to computer equipment became lawful), but which also included the famed "section 92A" which forms the core of this case.

The rise, fall and rise of disconnection in New Zealand law

The focus of the case is on the efforts made in New Zealand to draw internet intermediaries into a role of protecting the rights of copyright holders.

Until the introduction of amendments to the Copyright Act in 2007, internet intermediaries such as internet service providers (ISPs) had been regarded as conduits for information their customers sought. As with the telephone or postal networks, carriers had no responsibility for the content: that lay with the sender or receiver, in line with relevant laws.

Arguments to push internet intermediaries into a role in enforcing copyright rely on this idea: they are uniquely well positioned to be able to monitor the information their customers are accessing, and have a responsibility to do so. Failing this, they should be responsive to the surveillance done by rights holders, and take action against their customers when copyright infringement occurs.

1 Trans-Pacific Partnership Digest (2010) Wikileaks cables show NZ doubts, US Pressure on TPP, 20 December. www.tppdigest.org/index.php?option=com_content&view=article&id=276%3Awikileaks-cables-show-nz-doubts-us-pressure-on-tpp&catid=1%3Alatest-news&Itemid=1

2 Agreement on Trade-Related Aspects of Intellectual Property Rights.

The 2007 amendments, passed by Parliament in 2008, made use of a series of safe-harbour frameworks to bring intermediaries into the fold. As initially drafted, three specific safe harbours were created. The first was a general protection for an ISP in the common carrier mould, the second a protection against liability for hosted material if it was taken down on becoming aware of it, and the third was an exemption for material cached in the course of the routine operation of the ISP.

All three provisions were reliant on what became section 92A of the Copyright Act. The language of the draft legislation, first introduced in 2007, was as follows:

> **92A Limitations on liability in sections 92B to 92D apply only to qualifying Internet service provider**
> The limitations on liability in sections 92B to 92D apply only in respect of an Internet service provider that has adopted and reasonably implemented a policy that provides for termination, in appropriate circumstances, of the accounts of repeat infringers.[3]

As finally passed in 2008, the legislation specified that this clause would only come into effect on a nominated date. When Parliament's Commerce Select Committee reviewed the draft legislation, it recommended that the clause be deleted because:

> [T]he standard terms and conditions of agreements between an Internet service provider and its customers usually allow for the termination of accounts of people using the services for illegal activity. Moreover, new section 92C already requires an Internet service provider to delete infringing material or prevent access to it as soon as possible after becoming aware of it.[4]

Internet rights advocates celebrated. However, in April 2008, with no public notice or further consultation, the government reintroduced the clause by means of a Supplementary Order Paper, and this clause was passed into law:

> **92A Internet service provider must have policy for terminating accounts of repeat infringers**
>
> (1) An Internet service provider must adopt and reasonably implement a policy that provides for termination, in appropriate circumstances, of the account with that Internet service provider of a repeat infringer.
>
> (2) In subsection (1), **repeat infringer** means a person who repeatedly infringes the copyright in a work by using 1 or more of the Internet services of the Internet service provider to do a restricted act without the consent of the copyright owner.[5]

In this way Parliament gave no guidance as to who would count as a repeat infringer, what sort of infringement would be included, who would judge that infringement had occurred, and what the practical effects of termination should be for the subscribers of a particular ISP.

Dubbed "guilt on accusation" by opponents, and seizing on comments by the minister steering the legislation through Parliament that access to the internet should be considered a human right,[6] a community campaign grew – described in more depth below. Meanwhile, ISPs organised through the Telecommunications Carriers Forum negotiated with rights holder organisations in an attempt to implement the legislation despite the problems created by the drafting used.[7]

These negotiations did not succeed, and while they were underway a general election led to a change of government in November 2008. During the election and after, there were deferrals of the commencement of section 92A (from October 2008 to February 2009[8] and then to March 2009),[9] to try and leave time for the ISP-rights holder negotiations to succeed. Ultimately, however, they failed, and community opposition built to a crescendo.

The main focus of the opposition was around a campaign called #blackout[10] – the hashtag was extensively used by opponents of the law on Facebook and on Twitter, and users of both social networks replaced their avatars with simple black squares. This campaign achieved significant media coverage in the lead-up to the intended commencement date, and was catalysed at the annual KiwiFoo camp, held north of Auckland in February 2009.

Faced with widespread opposition, the newly appointed minister responsible for the legislation

3 Copyright (New Technologies and Performers Rights) Amendment Bill 2007, as introduced by the Government of New Zealand.

4 Commentary, Copyright (New Technologies and Performers Rights) Amendment Bill 2007, as reported by the Commerce Select Committee, p. 7.

5 Section 92A of the Copyright Act 1994 as at January 2011, as inserted by section 53 of the Copyright (New Technologies) Amendment Act 2008.

6 Bell, S. (2008) Internet access a human right, minister says, *Computerworld*, 3 September. computerworld.co.nz/news.nsf/news/6DC929097F31FF8ECC2574B8006D45D8

7 tcf.org.nz/content/98c471de-49ff-4a9e-abb4-49f4b3eee201.html

8 Media release by Hon. Judith Tizard of 3 October 2008. beehive.govt.nz/release/copyright-new-technologies-amendment-comes-force

9 Comments by the prime minister at a media conference, as reported by the Creative Freedom Foundation, 23 February 2009. creativefreedom.org.nz/story.html?id=170

10 See, for example, the article on Wikipedia regarding the campaign: en.wikipedia.org/wiki/New_Zealand_Internet_Blackout

announced[11] that it would be scrapped days before commencement at the end of March. A paper outlining a new proposal for dealing with infringing file sharing was developed by officials and experts, and released to the public in July 2009.[12]

This new framework set up a notice-based system, designed to tackle the major concerns the community had with the previous government's efforts: in particular, the absence of any decisions on infringement on the part of the justice system before penalties were imposed, and the strong and growing community view that the penalty of account termination or suspension was not a proportionate remedy to infringing file sharing.

ISPs would be required to pass notices on to their subscribers when lodged with them by rights holders or their representatives. Three types of notices were required, which ISPs would send based on the record of infringement in preceding weeks and months. After a final notice was sent, rights holders would have the option of taking a case before a (revised and expanded) Copyright Tribunal, which would have the ability to impose a financial penalty on repeat infringers of up to NZD 15,000.

This regime was carefully and vigorously scrutinised in parliamentary debate through 2010, including through select committee hearings which (replicating the 2007 debates) saw rights holder interests arguing that copyright infringing file sharing was causing them significant damage and required a strong legislative response. Community advocates again argued that nobody had presented evidence of economic harm to rights holders of a scale that justified such a policy.

One outcome of the select committee process was that draft clauses to include account suspension (for a period of up to six months, and on the decision of the District Court, and only at the same point or after enough infringement had occurred to allow rights holders to instigate proceedings in the Copyright Tribunal) were not directly implemented. Instead such a power was included, but only to become accessible if the government introduced it into regulation.

Another area that attracted considerable controversy – the inclusion of a new strict liability on account holders for any activity conducted on their internet accounts – was not removed during parliamentary scrutiny, despite widespread fears that this could have a chilling effect on provision of public Wi-Fi services, or create difficulties for large providers such as universities and libraries.[13]

The remaining details of the new regime were outlined in regulations published in July 2011,[14] which included the fees that rights holders would have to pay ISPs to process each notice. In consultations on the regulations, rights holders sought a very low fee,[15] arguing that the education role that notices play would be maximised. ISPs argued[16] that processing notices had real costs and that these should be met. The government set the fee at NZD 25, and when the regime commences on 1 September 2011 it will quickly become apparent what effect this fee has on the flow of notices – and on the arguments parties bring to a review, due six months later, as to whether the fee has been set at an acceptable level.

These proposals were and remain controversial in New Zealand. They have spawned the creation of several organisations dedicated to a different point of view: the Creative Freedom Foundation (CFF),[17] providing a voice for artists who are technologically literate, and TechLiberty,[18] aimed at protecting people's rights in the digital age, are two with the highest profile.

There has been an increase in community knowledge and organisation around the idea that people's rights may be at risk from policy making that does not take the fact of the internet's existence into account. While this community may not be terribly large, it has proved its ability to create significant interest, and apply significant pressure to governments.

The debate around whether access to the internet itself should be considered a right continues – the minister pursuing the copyright reform agenda, Simon Power, acknowledged this debate at a forum organised by InternetNZ and the NZ Human Rights Commission to discuss the internet's effect on human rights norms and laws.[19] Parliament was

11 Media release by Hon. Simon Power of 23 March 2009. beehive.govt.nz/release/government-amend-section-92a

12 Media release by Hon. Simon Power of 14 July 2009. beehive.govt.nz/release/section-92a-proposal-released-consultation

13 Moya, J. (2011) New Zealand's "Three-Strikes" to End Public WiFi?, *ZeroPaid*, 18 April. www.zeropaid.com/news/93137/new-zealands-three-strikes-to-end-public-wi-fi

14 Available on the website of the Ministry of Economic Development at: www.med.govt.nz/upload/Copyright-Infringing-File-Sharing-Regulations-2011.pdf

15 Submission from APRA on the regulatory consultation document, available at: www.med.govt.nz/upload/77298/Australasian%20Performing%20Right%20Associations.pdf

16 Submission from the TCF on the regulatory consultation document, available at: www.med.govt.nz/upload/77298/Telecommunications%20Carriers%20Forum.pdf

17 www.cff.org.nz

18 www.techliberty.org.nz

19 Liddicoat, J. (2010) *Report on Human Rights and Internet Round Table*. www.hrc.co.nz/hrc_new/hrc/cms/files/documents/26-Aug-2010_11-10-14_HR_and_the_Internet_Roundtable_Jul_10.html

littered with reference to the internet as a right by opponents of the new legislation. Some media took the same line.

Conclusions

In New Zealand's case, the emergence of an informed community active on copyright and intellectual property law issues – largely organised through the internet itself – has had a real effect on policy.

If no such community had emerged – and without the options available for propagating its message through the internet, it would not have done – New Zealand would now have copyright legislation that allowed for people's internet accounts to be suspended due to infringing file sharing of copyright material.

The international context continues to evolve, with the US pursuing very significant changes to IP law in negotiations for a Trans Pacific Partnership Agreement (TPP) among nine countries including New Zealand. Such changes, if included in the final agreement, will lead this community to oppose ratification of the TPP by New Zealand.

With ongoing global pressure for tighter IP laws, these issues are likely to remain visible in trade negotiations, and the profile they now have in New Zealand will continue. Activists have used the open internet to fight changes that threaten its existence, and have succeeded: there is no doubt they will use it again, hoping for similar outcomes.

New Zealand's government has taken note. Conversations with negotiating officials indicate the government now uses the community response against the attempt to implement section 92A reforms as a sort of shield, ready to be deployed where other governments ask for dramatic changes to the intellectual property framework. They have used this argument along with another: that the lack of evidence justifying tighter laws means there is little valid reason to implement them.

In that sense, the New Zealand government and the activists are on the same side. Yet the government faces other economic interests for whom the prospects of a TPP – or of another ambition of New Zealand foreign policy, a bilateral free trade agreement with the US – are highly desirable, and who have a louder voice in the public sphere and around the cabinet table.

Action steps

- Use the internet – particularly communities connected through online social networks – to visibly challenge policies you oppose.
- Find robust evidence to back your case, and/or highlight the lack of such evidence backing your opponents' case.
- Work with mainstream media to amplify the message beyond the online community into mainline political and policy debate.
- Create open learning communities where new suggestions are positively received and are adopted where they show potential.
- Use "meatspace" (real-life) gatherings of activists to generate momentum, build personal networks and coordinate action. Social networks online amplify and expand momentum but they do not necessarily instigate it.
- Educate politicians and officials who make policy on information and communications technology (ICT) issues. Many of the mistakes in the New Zealand legislation emerged because those making decisions did not understand the terrain they were working in.
- Attack and undermine "us versus them" frames, and divide those who are on the other side where you can. For instance, in the New Zealand debate, the emergence of CFF was vital to undo claims that all artists sought tougher copyright legislation. ■

NIGERIA

IMPACT OF THE WIKILEAKS CABLES ON NIGERIA: TRANSPARENCY IN GOVERNANCE AND FORUMS FOR CITIZEN VOICE

Fantsuam Foundation
John Dada and Bidi Bala
www.fantsuam.org

Introduction

On 30 November 2010, news broke that there were 4,598 sensitive diplomatic discussions involving the United States (US) Embassy in Nigeria among some 251,287 items released by the online whistle blower WikiLeaks.[1]

The Nigerian government is not usually forthcoming when it comes to sharing information, ostensibly in the interest of national security. Investigative journalism is still in its early stages of development in the country; whistle blowing is a dangerous undertaking and has little or no constitutional protection. This, in part, explains the chequered history of the Freedom of Information Bill, which was designed to make some information more readily available to the governed.

While WikiLeaks claimed that "the cables show the extent of US spying on its allies and the UN; turning a blind eye to corruption and human rights abuse in 'client states'" and White House press secretary Robert Gibbs labelled the WikiLeaks a "reckless and dangerous action," in Nigeria the cables were recognised as one of the most authentic and accurate accounts of the history of Nigeria's governance in one of the most difficult periods of its existence as a nation. And, inadvertently, they helped to confirm the credibility of a home-grown whistle-blowing site, Sahara Reporters, which was established in 1996[2] and has been championing the right to information and challenging government secrecy in Nigeria.

Policy and political background

The period of ill health and eventual death of President Umaru Yar'adua on 5 May 2010[3] was one of high political tension. The legislature and judiciary were unable or unwilling to create an enabling environment for a smooth transition of power from an ailing president to his vice president, Goodluck Jonathan. The public was largely in the dark regarding the power tussle at that time. In the absence of credible information from the various organs of government, the public relied on the usually robust online information sources and news from the diaspora community of Nigerians for rumours, updates and analysis. It was the online newspaper *The Next*[4] that had access to the full WikiLeaks cables on Nigeria, and began their serialisation from 30 March 2010.

Description and analysis of key events

Yar'Adua, who was terminally ill, left the country in November 2009 for medical treatment in Saudi Arabia. The ailing president was "smuggled" back to Nigeria, in the dead of the night, from a Saudi intensive care unit, amidst unprecedented security. The state of his health was shrouded in secrecy, and neither the vice president nor the Senate had first-hand information about his health. The vice president had not been sworn in as acting president, and some bizarre constitutional duties were still being ascribed to the (comatose) president.

What happened during those dark days of governance in Nigeria? Who was or was not in charge? It took WikiLeaks to shed some light on these issues.

The fortuitous, unforeseen ascendancy of a member of the minority tribes in Nigeria to the foremost position in the Nigerian political landscape created disequilibrium in the polity. Jonathan hails from one of the riverine communities that is producing over 90% of Nigeria's oil wealth. His humble background and apparently low political ambitions made him an unlikely candidate for a job that had been the monopoly of a powerful northern political circle. Jonathan's administrative inexperience and lack of confidence was vividly portrayed in WikiLeaks:[5] the US ambassador's team in Abuja and Lagos went to lengths to guide him on how to take the reins of power from a cabal that had surrounded the ailing President Yar'adua. The cables reported how the US ambassador, Robin Sanders, also

1 cablegate.wikileaks.org

2 www.nairaland.com/nigeria/topic-707677.0.html

3 234next.com/csp/cms/sites/Next/Home/5564878-146/umaru_yaradua_is_dead__.csp

4 234next.com/csp/cms/sites/Next/Home/5681720-146/the_complete_wikileaks_cables_on_nigeria.csp

5 saharareporters.com/news-page/wikileaks-cable-nigeria-i-lack-administrative-experience-jonathan-tells-us-ambassador

provided the strategy to get rid of the incumbent chairman of the Independent National Electoral Commission (INEC), Maurice Iwu, who had supervised one of Nigeria's most discredited elections in 2007.

For three months while the president was in a Jeddah hospital, a group of four – comprising his wife, chief security officer, aide-de-camp and chief economic advisor – virtually held the president hostage. They prevented even the vice president from visiting him and there was no constitutional instrument that enabled the vice president to take over the reins of power. The group maintained a public façade of a president who was recuperating, even providing a BBC voice interview and making claims that the president had signed a legislative bill. WikiLeaks confirmed a nation's fears: that the president was indeed comatose all this while.

The constitutional path for a resolution of the political impasse that had paralyzed the nation required that two thirds of the 42-member Federal Executive Council (FEC) declare that the ailing president was "physically incapacitated and mentally unfit" to rule the country. This would pave the way for Jonathan to be sworn in as the legitimate acting president and take the reins of government. But the political dynamics, collusions, party patronages, pecuniary interests and affinities of members of the FEC made such a face-saving action impossible. Efforts were made by former heads of state to persuade the ailing president's surrogates and family members to secure a formal resignation from the president, but to no avail. The nation teetered on the brink of civil breakdown and military takeover. It was almost a relief when Yar'adua died in May 2010 and Jonathan was swiftly sworn in as president.[6]

Some of the major allegations contained in the WikiLeaks included:

- There was a fear of impending military takeover of government.
- The late president's wife, Turai Yar'adua, and the attorney general and chief security officer were receiving large bribes for various oil-related and contract activities.[7]
- The group that kept the president incommunicado also had "nefarious plans" towards Vice President Jonathan.[8]
- The Nigerian Police botched investigations into the murder of Chief Legal Officer of Nigeria Bola Ige.[9]
- The government was involved in assisting kidnappers to collect ransom.[10]
- The speaker of the Nigerian House of Representatives, Dimeji Bankole, claimed that Supreme Court judges took bribes to validate Yar'adua's election.[11]
- The US government had little confidence in the leadership, independence and transparency of Nigeria's anti-corruption czar, Farida Waziri.[12]
- Yar'adua handed over the running of the country to Yayale Ahmed, the secretary to the government,[13] effectively sidelining the vice president.

The polity was heated during the last few months of Yar'adua's life, largely due to the refusal or inability of his surrogates to permit non-family and non-partisan members of government to have access to him. There was no effective flow of information from the Presidency regarding the state of the president's health, and the statutory body that could rescue the situation, the FEC, remained paralysed.

The public had to rely on news leaks as released by Sahara Reporters: in fact Sahara Reporters and its volunteer whistle blowers were the first to alert the nation to the president's terminal illness. Yar'adua's team strenuously denied many of the Sahara Reporters claims. WikiLeaks provided confirmation of many of these leaks and allowed Nigerians to know more about the details of the political intrigues that attended Yar'adua's last days.

Government responses to WikiLeaks have been lame and unconvincing. Its denials are all the more suspect because WikiLeaks merely confirmed earlier revelations by Sahara Reporters.

A recent international judicial pronouncement provided additional support of the authenticity of the WikiLeaks documents and Sahara Reporters allegations, specifically in the case of Anglo-Dutch oil giant Shell. On 3 August 2011 the United Nations (UN) indicted Shell for 30 years of oil spillage and environmental degradation of the Nigerian Niger

6 www.guardian.co.uk/world/2010/dec/08/wikileaks-cables-nigeria-president-death

7 news2.onlinenigeria.com/headlines/61271-wikileaks-on-nigeria-turai-aondoaaka-tanimu-took-millions-in-bribes.html

8 news2.onlinenigeria.com/headlines/61271-wikileaks-on-nigeria-turai-aondoaaka-tanimu-took-millions-in-bribes.html

9 234next.com/csp/cms/sites/Next/Home/5684203-146/story.csp

10 234next.com/csp/cms/sites/Next/Home/5682079-146/story.csp

11 234next.com/csp/cms/sites/Next/News/National/5681699-146/story.csp

12 234next.com/csp/cms/sites/Next/Home/5681717-146/wikileaks_cable_supreme_court_bribe_.csp

13 234next.com/csp/cms/sites/Next/Home/5681904-146/story.csp

Delta.[14] The extent of the infiltration of government machinery by Shell[15] was such that environmental campaigners could only get justice when they took their case to British courts. WikiLeaks had already detailed the vice grip that Shell had on the Nigerian government, and how it exploited its political channels to make any successful prosecution for its environmental negligence impossible.[16] Shell's activities had been extensively reported by Sahara Reporters, but the company's overbearing control and access to government channels ensured that few measures were taken to rein the oil giant in.

Conclusions

Nigeria's own internet-based whistle blower, Sahara Reporters, is a year older than WikiLeaks and its emphasis has been consistently on exposing corruption in Nigeria and Africa. Although there was an attempt by a national daily to undermine the impact of Sahara Reporters by conferring an award[17] on WikiLeaks, the role of Sahara Reporters in defending the right of people to know has not been surpassed by any other news channel in Nigeria. It has been consistent in its revelations of the Nigerian government's abuse of power, and the abuse of power by individuals in government.

Whistle blowing and exposure of corruption within government circles has been one of the longstanding features of Sahara Reporters.[18] Sahara Reporters is written by unpaid citizen reporters, making it more reflective of civil society views. The release of the WikiLeaks documents contributed significantly to the credibility of Sahara Reporters. The WikiLeaks documents on Nigeria have heightened the confidence of Nigerians in the Sahara Reporters, and anecdotal evidence indicates that this online newspaper has become a must-read for Nigerian politicians.

Sahara Reporters uses the internet to reach millions of readers, and it has been nicknamed Africa's WikiLeaks.[19] It effectively uses "citizen reporters" who work with risk-taking whistle blowers to ensure a free flow of information to citizens. The use of information and communications technologies (ICTs) has empowered the civil population to expose human rights abuses and high-level corruption, and it has enabled an unprecedented level of freedom of expression for citizen reporters.

Action steps

In May 2011, after eleven years of struggle, the Nigerian government passed the Freedom of Information Bill into law.[20] The implementation of this law will have teething problems; there will be initial resistance, the result of entrenched ways of information hoarding. Individuals who have been less than candid while in government may try to obstruct access to information needed to bring them to justice. WikiLeaks and Sahara Reporters need to be relied on to ensure an empowered and informed citizenry.

In order to ensure that Sahara Reporters continues its citizen reporting, it is important to:

- Address the high cost of internet access so that Sahara Reporters can become accessible to more citizens. The retail cost for broadband in particular needs to be lowered.
- Enforce the rights of Omoyele Sowore, the editor of Sahara Reporters, to safe unencumbered passage whenever he chooses to return to or visit Nigeria. ■

14 www.iol.co.za/news/africa/un-slams-shell-for-nigeria-pollution-1.1112312

15 english.aljazeera.net/video/africa/2010/12/201012101525432657.html

16 www.guardian.co.uk/business/2010/dec/08/wikileaks-cables-shell-nigeria-spying

17 saharareporters.com/column/nigeria%E2%80%99s-citizen-reporters-sonala-olumhense

18 saharareporters.com

19 wikilinksnews.com/wikileaks-news/nigeria-saharareporters-africas-wikileaks-global-voices-online

20 www.foicoalition.org

OCCUPIED PALESTINIAN TERRITORY

USING THE INTERNET FOR POLICY INCLUSION

Applied Information Management (AIM)
Sam Bahour*
www.aim-palestine.com

Introduction

The critical nature of the telecommunications sector, globally, regionally and within any specific country, has been the focus of many economic development experts. Palestine and the surrounding region are not excluded from the seriousness involved in ensuring that proper and affordable telecommunications services are deployed. Customers expect the growing complexity inherent in the world of telecommunications to be completely transparent and not to interfere for even a split second with the quality of services being provided, despite the content being communicated over the networks – a daunting task in a region where autocratic, police state regimes thrive.

This enormous task assumes, first and foremost, that all citizens of a country are within reach of the provision of telecommunications services, as individuals, households and organisations. A fact of the matter is that as the role and importance of telecommunications grows, the social and political consequences that the least-developed countries face, such as a widening digital divide between the global North and global South or between the rich and poor, are a serious matter for the world community given that the ramifications of such divides impact far beyond the borders of any single state. While the telecommunications sector is leading the privatisation effort in most countries, the ball is easily lost between profit-only-oriented private operators, marginalised public sector administrations and the lack of enforceable regulations – at least in the Middle East.

Working towards transparent and free policy discussions

Addressing this dynamic of how to deal with developing an information and communications and technology (ICT) sector – namely how to contribute to, and hold accountable, the policy-making mechanisms – was the impetus for technology activists in the Palestinian technology sector to organise what has become a thriving online venue called the Information Technology Special Interest Group, better known as ITSIG.

ITSIG is a simple, subscription-based, electronic mailing list that was established by a handful of Palestinians who returned to Palestine in the early 1990s to contribute to building the information technology sector. As a virtual discussion group, it has no legal status. The list has no commercial interests whatsoever – something ITSIG is proud of as we witness the rapid consumerism engulfing our nascent marketplace. ITSIG is possibly the first and only, effective and free Palestinian discussion forum available in Palestine, and has proven itself a beacon of virtual freedom of speech.

The emerging state of Palestine, similar to many least-developed countries, entered the realm of telecommunications under the assumption that it would be able to leap-frog into an industry that is developing at a rapid pace. Reality – if based on the Palestine example so far – has shown that countries with historically poor infrastructure are prone to make the same mistakes and live the same growing pains as those markets that are now well developed. While the developing world falls into the same potholes that developed countries have hit during their development, thousands of communities are missing a window of opportunity to catch up with the rest of the world, while they wait hoping that the needed infrastructure will allow them to become producers – and not merely consumers – in the world of information technology.

The development of participatory-based national economic and social policies has not been the strong point of the region's nation-states. A lack of public due diligence creates a downward momentum in the need to understand problems in full and create scenarios supported by professional analysis. Telecommunications is a long-term project for any country and is inherently related to the issue of national security. Since security in the developing world is frequently inordinately sensitive to a country's political stability, the issue of future-oriented progressive policy development in the sector often falls victim to "larger" political concerns.

* Sam Bahour is one of three moderators of ITSIG and can be reached at sbahour@palnet.com. This report represents only Sam's opinion and not that of the moderators or ITSIG.

Another complicating factor is that the lack of freedom of speech, press and assembly in the region causes slower development of services, since customer feedback for demand of new services is rarely articulated in a transparent and obvious way. In Palestine, specifically, this was caused due to the Israeli military occupation that outlawed the use of faxes or modems through the 1980s, let alone allowing those under occupation to participate in how the sector's infrastructure was being developed. However, similar instances arose in just about every other state in the region, causing self-imposed delays in the country's IT technical and human resource development.

Bottom line, be it due to foreign military occupation or governments that are non-representative of their peoples, it is only a matter of time before technology is employed to bypass the restrictions placed on participatory policy making. For Palestine, a prime example was the establishment of ITSIG in the early 1990s.

The ITSIG online forum is dedicated to information technology in Palestine in the broadest sense. It did not take long before it was clear in the sector that ITSIG provided the only true free and open venue for stakeholders of the ICT community to participate in every aspect of the development of the ICT sector in Palestine.

The objectives of the group are:

- To raise ICT awareness in the Palestinian community
- To bridge the geographic gap between ICT professionals in Palestine and in the diaspora and promote transfer of know-how
- To educate and engage policy makers in ICT-related issues and developments, locally, regionally and internationally
- To provide a venue for due diligence on policy and strategy related to ICTs in Palestine
- To create awareness of local, regional and global development of telecommunications and infrastructure, ICT services (e.g. banking, marketing, telemedicine, industry, public services, etc.), technical ICT issues, legal and regulatory frameworks, and standards
- To promote ICT regulation/deregulation and policies to protect citizen and consumer rights, privacy and accessibility
- To contribute to human resource development and education.

Over the last two decades or so, several hundred subscribers have been privy to a wide range of free and open discussions, sometimes technical, sometimes humorous and many times heated. The mailing list is part and parcel of the policy making in the sector – albeit an informal contributor. From ministers to CEOs, new graduates and diaspora professionals, the diversity of the subscriber base is impressive, with conversations educated and informed. Today the group has over 1,000 active subscribers, which is impressive given the small size of Palestine and its ICT sector.

Although the group has three moderators who keep its nuts and bolts in operation, the discussion posts are unmoderated, meaning any subscriber can post a message which is immediately emailed to all group subscribers. More recently, an associated ITSIG group was also created on the LinkedIn professional online social networking service following the same policy of being unmoderated.

ITSIG is not open to the public; only subscribers are able to make direct postings to the group. One may subscribe to the group at mail.itsig.org/maillist/subscribe.html. After moderators verify that the request was made by a real person, the system will automatically add you to the list of subscribers, and then you can post to the group by emailing general@itsig.org.

The group has publicly available and documented rules governing acceptable behaviour or etiquette. For the most part, subscribers remain within the boundaries of these rules without the need for guidance or moderation, which attests to the professionalism of the subscriber base and the mature level of discussion.

At times, given the volatile political situation we live in, the group is used to disseminate broader political or economic news. The group's etiquette allows for this as long as it is not abused and the non-IT messages are marked in the subject line with "(Non-IT)" in order for subscribers to ignore these if desired.

Hosting for ITSIG was historically donated by a national internet service provider (ISP) and the procurement of equipment made possible through a private sector donation. Group moderators recently moved hosting to an independent location and have automated the subscription process due to the growing administrative burden that accompanied the success of the group.

Over the years, a few powerful players, sometimes government officials and at other times corporate players, have threatened to take legal action against ITSIG. The host of the ITSIG servers was also threatened at times. Other incidents, following heated policy discussions or corporate accountability debates, found some participants receiving death threats. Speculation is that behind many of these threats were the very entrenched economic interests which reach into the political echelons in the country, and which could not fathom that there exists an open platform where their actions could be critiqued unedited. In a sector that is unhealthily wealthy this should be expected and the safeguard to sustaining the platform is the integrity of the subscribers.

Once all was said and done, however, all of these negative reactions fizzled out and it was proven in practice that the conscious decision to keep the technology more low-tech than high-tech, and the organisational setup loose and volunteer-based, rather than a legal entity, safeguarded the forum to the benefit of sector development.

Stakeholders in the ICT sector are virtually everyone, even those who do not have access to telecommunications services – for the lack of interaction with telecommunications is very real grounds for further backwardness and economic repression. In a region which is hyper-centralised, both in government and business, using technology to open the doors of development is key.

Key lessons

Two key lessons in the experience of ITSIG are that:

- Deployment of technology tools does not necessarily mean adding complexity. ITSIG, by design, remains to this day a simple mailing list and has proven that this is sufficient to concretely contribute to policy and other discussions.
- Deployment of technology, as we are seeing and reading about across the Middle East, is not a new phenomenon when used to force the downfall of governments, albeit refreshing when this happens; prior to the internet, faxes were the new weapon on the block, and before that, television, and before that, radio, and before that, the printing press, etc. Using technological platforms connects sector stakeholders and moves society from being observers to being actively involved and informed.

In light of this, it may be worthwhile to note major categories of stakeholders in any sector, and a few of their characteristics:

Users Individuals and businesses; geographically dispersed; difficult to collectively leverage their interests; increasingly demanding needs based either on technological developments or successful commercial marketing techniques.

Suppliers/operators Profit-oriented; competing globally for foreign investment; little incentive to introduce latest technology; shrewd business practices (vs. static government practices); short-term strategy; lack of national interest component in their planning; weak or no sense of social justice.

Governments Unable to keep pace with technology; lack of funds to invest; lack of management required to compete in a global market; motivated by short-term gains.

Bringing these stakeholders into a unified strategy and securing all of their justified interests may be the most difficult aspect of all. Nevertheless, these stakeholders are always present in every country, so finding a framework to bring harmony is a must. Opening up the discussions around policy issues is a perfect starting point. ITSIG did just that for Palestine's ICT sector.

Action steps

- Empower civil society organisations or even motivated groups of individuals on how to employ cost-effective technology.
- Palestine's diverse and fragmented population, due to its political reality, showed the value of using technology to link physically separated parts of a population; this is key to bringing the maximum number of vested interest parties into a policy discussion.
- ITSIG's flexibility to allow both English and Arabic to be used allows for language to be less of a barrier for those knowing only Arabic. It is imperative that the region's discussions be in its own language if the discussion is not to become an elitists' silo.
- Stakeholder clusters, be it a country's ICT sector, education sector, healthcare sector or any other sector or sub-sector, should be active participants in the discussion of their sector's development.
- The region's issues are too similar to limit the discussion to individual countries. Because of this cross-border venues linked by the use of technology should be sought out. ■

PAKISTAN

FIGHTING FOR HUMAN RIGHTS IN BALOCHISTAN ONLINE

Bytes for All Pakistan
Shahzad Ahmad and Nighat Dad
www.bytesforall.pk

Introduction

Sprawling, mineral-rich Balochistan is the largest province of Pakistan and constitutes approximately 44% of the country's total land mass. The official population estimate of Balochistan was approximately 6.51 million as per the 1998 census.[1] Bordering Afghanistan and Iran, the province is however the least developed on all possible socioeconomic indicators. It has Pakistan's weakest growth record, worst infrastructure, greatest water crisis, and weakest fiscal base. Poor economic performance over the years has lead to poor living standards and a high poverty rate. Access to information and communications technologies (ICTs) is low and parts of the province have the weakest state institutions. Decades of under-investment have earned Balochistan a reputation of being a backward region riddled with conflicts, distant from Pakistan's economic hubs, with a life burdened by the toils of the fields and rangelands and tribal disputes, rather than a hub of activity surrounding world-class mining explorations, modern trade links, sustainable agriculture and boasting an empowered community.

Over the last decade, Balochistan has been locked down under a state of information quarantine due to an ongoing military operation against Baloch nationalists – called insurgents by the military and media in Pakistan. Newspaper reports from Balochistan are buried quietly on the inside pages, cloaked in euphemisms or, quite often, not published at all.[2] Amnesty International reports that the disappearance, illegal detention, torture and extra-judicial killings of journalists, lawyers, students and political activists have increased rapidly throughout Balochistan in recent months, with an almost total blackout on these gruesome incidents by the Pakistani media.[3] Due to the information blackout and the national media neglecting coverage of Balochistan issues, the role of the internet in advocacy against human rights abuses and as a tool of social resistance has become very popular.

Separatist identity

Baloch nationalists claim that the Baloch people, an ethno-linguistic group mainly found in Pakistan, Iran and Afghanistan, are a different nation – the reason for their demand for a separate state – whereas Pakistan's government strongly takes this demand as a threat to "national security".[4]

In recent years many Baloch voices raising the issue of Baloch nationalism have been permanently silenced. The result has been 8,000 missing persons[5] and countless bullet-riddled bodies; thousands of people have "disappeared"[6] since the nationalist movement began to expand. In 2006, the Human Rights Commission of Pakistan (HRCP) issued a 340-page report stating that a large number of persons – a number growing at an "alarming rate" – have been picked up by intelligence agencies and taken for detention in secret locations.[7] Relatives never get an explanation of why someone is taken, but the families of the missing persons strongly believe that intelligence agencies and the army are involved in the detention of the Baloch nationalist leaders.[8]

Cognisant of the fact that the power of mainstream media helps form public opinion, the government does all it can to ensure that there is no major exposure of the incidents happening in Balochistan. No doubt journalists are also concerned for their physical safety. Yet the main obstacle to general

1 The official website of Government of Balochistan: www.balochistan.gov.pk/index.php?option=com_content&task=category&sectionid=4&id=42&Itemid=486

2 Walsh, D. (2001) Pakistan's secret dirty war, *The Guardian*, 9 July. www.guardian.co.uk/world/2011/mar/29/balochistan-pakistans-secret-dirty-war

3 Tatchell, P. (2011) Pakistan: Secret, dirty killings in Balochistan, *Daily Times*, 9 July. www.dailytimes.com.pk/default.asp?page=2011%5C07%5C09%5Cstory_9-7-2011_pg7_24

4 en.wikipedia.org/wiki/Balochistan_conflict

5 Fisk, R. (2010) Into the terrifying world of Pakistan's 'disappeared', *The Independent*, 18 March. www.independent.co.uk/opinion/commentators/fisk/robert-fisk-into-the-terrifying-world-of-pakistans-disappeared-1923153.html

6 en.wikipedia.org/wiki/Missing_persons_%28Pakistan%29

7 Asian Human Rights Commission (2006) *Pakistan: The Human Rights Situation in 2006*. material.ahrchk.net/hrreport/2006/Pakistan2006.pdf

8 Asian Human Rights Commission (2011) Army officers acknowledged that a disappeared person was in their custody but the courts failed to recover him, *AHRC News*, 25 January. www.humanrights.asia/news/ahrc-news/AHRC-STM-014-2011

awareness comes from the mainstream media's compliance with the state's twin policies of collective silence about state-perpetrated acts against ordinary Baloch people, and of glossing over the intensity of the acrimony that has arisen in the Baloch people against the Pakistani state and its ruling elite.[9]

A growing number of literate individuals in Balochistan and the diaspora have realised that it is no use relying on mainstream media to put across their point of view – nor is there any point complaining about the lack of coverage of Baloch issues in the national media. Instead, they have increasingly started using the internet as an open and (relatively) unsuppressed means of communication. Technology has given them the means to take matters into their own hands, taking control of the telling of their own narrative and bypassing the mainstream media, whose primary loyalty seems to be a misguided determination to defend what they are told is the "national interest", rather than seeking out the truth.[10]

Despite the fact that Balochistan is Pakistan's least-developed province, with a low population and an even lower literacy rate, it has amazingly become home to the most successful use of the internet as a tool for advocacy, driving social and political discourse for human rights and democracy.

We have witnessed the emergence of a substantial number of online Baloch newspapers, blogs and video-sharing channels in the last couple of years. With the spread of the internet in every district of Balochistan (further facilitated by the spread of mobile phones), the Baloch nationalist movement experienced an unprecedented change and activists started communicating via the internet to a far greater extent.

In 2006, the government took advantage of a Supreme Court ruling which called for the blocking of all blasphemous internet content accessible in Pakistan. This ruling was seized on as the excuse for a crackdown on Baloch websites[11] by a government that was already furious about the use of the internet by political activists in the region. The government blocked several Baloch websites[12] using its controls over the internet and the Pakistan Telecommunication Authority, which turned out to be the worst predator of internet rights in Pakistan.[13]

Social media services such as Twitter, Facebook and YouTube now supplement existing national and international news channels like CNN, BBC and Fox News in an era of new citizen journalism and activism. Both Twitter and Facebook, for example, have been playing a vital role in forming public opinion at the local level as well. These days we find numerous Baloch activists publishing information about the real picture of atrocities committed by government agencies and the army in their region; the activists' primary tool is, increasingly, social media.

While activists have been posting shocking videos of army human rights violations in Balochistan on YouTube and elsewhere, when these are uploaded they are quickly blocked by the Pakistan Telecommunication Authority, as it is within their policy framework to immediately remove content that is deemed abusive of the Pakistani army or against the "national interest". In 2010, some particularly graphic videos of human rights abuses were circulated on the internet. In one such video, filmed on a mobile phone camera, Pakistani soldiers are seen brutally killing a number of teenage boys and prisoners.[14] Foreign media[15] picked up the story and spread it all over the world. The Pakistani army's response was to deny the authenticity of the video and claim that it was faked by militants.[16] But one local told Human Rights Watch: "On February 16, 2010, the army shot all four dead in the area of the Grid Station in the town. We heard the shots that killed these individuals."[17]

As a result of the rise and visibility of the Pakistani army's human rights violations communicated through online videos, the United States (US) State Department and Pentagon decided to cut aid to a half dozen Pakistani army units believed to have killed civilians and unarmed prisoners in different parts of the country, including Balochistan.[18]

Another recent video which has damaged the country's reputation – once again at the international level – was the killing of five Chechen women

9 Arshed, N. (2011) Cautious and selective, *The News*, 6 June. www.jang.com.pk/thenews/jun2011-weekly/nos-12-06-2011/spr.htm#3

10 Unrepresented Nations and Peoples Organization (2011) Balochistan: Little Coverage in Mainstream Media, 24 June. www.unpo.org/article/12798

11 en.wikipedia.org/wiki/Internet_censorship_in_Pakistan

12 Pakistan banned websites in country, 10 August 2006. www.frihost.com/forums/vt-48590.html

13 Pakistan 451 (2006) PTA letter blocking websites, 25 April. pakistan451.wordpress.com/2006/04/27/pta-letter-blocking-websites-april-25-06

14 Perlez, J. (2010) Video Hints at Executions by Pakistanis, *The New York Times*, 29 September. www.nytimes.com/2010/09/30/world/asia/30pstan.html

15 FRANCE 24 Web News (2010) An online video accusing the Pakistan army of extrajudicial killings, 13 October. www.youtube.com/watch?v=oPto_4NXnUA&feature=fvwrel

16 Al Jazeera and agencies (2010) Pakistan army to investigate video, *Al Jazeera*, 8 October. english.aljazeera.net/news/asia/2010/10/20101087424786823.html

17 Human Rights Watch (2010) Pakistan: Extrajudicial Executions by Army in Swat, 16 July. www.hrw.org/en/news/2010/07/16/pakistan-extrajudicial-executions-army-swat

18 Schmitt, E. and Sanger, D. (2010) Pakistani Troops Linked to Abuses Will Lose Aid, *The New York Times*, 21 October. www.nytimes.com/2010/10/22/world/asia/22policy.html?_r=1&scp=1&sq=pakistan%20aid&st=cse

by officers at the Balochistan border. Video footage captured by local residents showed that unarmed foreign nationals were shot over and over again as they lay on the ground pleading for help. Contrary to initial claims by the police and border control officers, there were no suicide jackets in the vehicle and no other explosive items were found.[19] Another report revealed that the shooting happened after the Chechen women turned down a demand for sexual favours by the police and border control officers.[20] One of the women killed was seven months pregnant.[21] When the government failed to take any action regarding the killings, Pakistan's Supreme Court had to finally initiate a *suo moto* action.[22]

Gone are the days when the voice of the masses, a populist movement or an uprising could be hushed or silenced by the authorities. The advent of the internet and social media in particular has changed the rules of the game altogether. We have witnessed the recent revolutions in Tunisia, Egypt and the Middle East, where despite government attempts at censorship and information control, news has spread rapidly and directly from the front lines of citizen activism to a worldwide online audience.

The most popular "Balochistan" page on Facebook has a following of thousands of individuals, which by any standard or stretch of the imagination is significant. When one also takes into account the low literacy rate in the province and the volatile law and order situation, such a public display of opposition against the repression is all the more remarkable. Baloch youths and political activists/workers have formed several Facebook groups and pages, where they share pictures of the missing Baloch people.

Now it takes no time to upload the photos of the so-called "killed and dumped" for a worldwide audience on Facebook, while newspapers still refuse to publish and circulate pictures of slain Balochistan activists.[23] Ironically, they fear the retribution of the state, when these images are already available online. The great strength of social media is that they provide an instant, self-organising medium in which young, lively and outspoken political activists can immediately report local news and information and publish for a worldwide online cyber community.

Dangerous development

In response to this situation, there has been a disturbing development. Since 2007, the Pakistan Telecommunication Authority has been using the sophisticated technology and services of a company called Narus which has the ability to spy on internet and mobile phone users using deep packet inspection (DPI), which allows them to read content in real time. This company has not only aided repressive regimes like Egypt's (which is known to have attempted a blanket cut-off of all internet communications this year) but also provides its services to other repressive regimes notorious for online censorship, such as Saudi Arabia, Iran, Libya and China.[24]

Even so, Baloch Facebookers and Tweeples have an advantage over a government which is increasingly frightened of adverse international attention on its domestic policies. In today's climate, attempting to restrict freedom of expression in the face of the power of social media is not only technically difficult, it is also bound to be seen and widely reported. For the government, as much as for the individual citizen, the internet offers nowhere to hide.

Action steps

From a Pakistani perspective, it is an established fact that cyberspace is the next big frontier and the war on civil rights will be fought via the internet and using digital tools. This is why it is important for the world community to continue to:

- Support internet freedom in repressive regimes
- Strengthen the capacities of human rights activists working on digital security
- Raise awareness about internet rights and principles among the general public
- Promote the effective participation of women and other marginalised segments of society in the policy processes relating to digital rights
- Inculcate and strengthen the human rights agenda in cyberspace. ■

19 Baloch, S. (2011) Chechen suspects were not wearing suicide vests, police confirm, *The Express Tribune*, 19 May. tribune.com.pk/story/171770/chechen-suspects-were-not-wearing-suicide-vests-police-confirm

20 The Express Tribune (n/d) Chechen women "terrorists" refused sexual advances: PTI (video). tribune.com.pk/multimedia/videos/173812

21 Baloch, S. (2011) Chechen 'terrorist' was pregnant when shot dead, *The Express Tribune*, 20 May. tribune.com.pk/story/172557/chechen-terrorist-was-pregnant-when-shot-dead

22 Baloch, S. (2011) Kharotabad incident: Judicial inquiry into Chechens' killing ordered, *The Express Tribune*, 21 May. tribune.com.pk/story/173082/kharotabad-incident-judicial-inquiry-into-chechens-killing-ordered

23 Akbar, M. S. (2011) Taking social media by storm, *Crisis Balochistan*, 18 June. www.crisisbalochistan.com/secondary_menu/global-issues-development/general-development/taking-social-media-by-storm.html

24 Karr, T. (2011) One U.S. Corporation's Role in Egypt's Brutal Crackdown, *Crisis Balochistan*, 28 January. www.crisisbalochistan.com/secondary_menu/news/how-pakistan-monitors-net-traffic.html

PERU

PUSHING FOR THE PROSECUTION OF HUMAN RIGHTS VIOLATIONS

Red Científica Peruana and CONDESAN
Jorge Bossio, María Campos and Miguel Saravia
www.rcp.net.pe and www.condesan.org

Introduction

Between 1980 and 2000 Peru suffered an internal armed conflict[1] that led to the death of over 69,000 people, besides a large number of indirect victims (e.g. displaced persons, widows, orphans, etc.). According to the final report of the Truth and Reconciliation Commission (TRC),[2] the Sendero Luminoso (Shining Path) rebel group[3] was the main party responsible for the deaths, but the actions of state forces also resulted in the deaths of innocent people.

The Peruvian state used the armed forces to try to quell the armed uprising and the terrorism that came with it. However, in doing this numerous human rights violations were committed. The TRC stated that "the behavior of members of the armed forces not only involved some individual excesses by officers or soldiers, but also entailed generalized and/or systematic practices of human rights violations that constitute crimes against humanity as well as transgressions of the norms of International Humanitarian Law."[4]

The investigation and later prosecution of those responsible began after the fall of the Alberto Fujimori regime. Human rights activists, as well as United Nations (UN) Human Rights Special Rapporteur Martin Scheinin,[5] have pointed out that while many of the trials are still ongoing,[6] they are at risk due the fact that political groups close to the military are lobbying to end the prosecution.

This report refers to the use of social networks by human rights activists to prevent the application of a law – Legislative Decree 1097 (DL 1097) – that would pardon the soldiers being prosecuted for human rights violations in Peru.

Social networks have for some time been used as a platform for activism and alternative media in Peru. However, the number of professionals and institutions registered on them was low until late 2010, when the electoral campaign boosted their use. The case of DL 1097 is special because it represents one of the first times human rights activists have used social media to create awareness of a cause amongst the general population. The success of this campaign has become an incentive for civil society groups and human rights activists to use new technologies in their campaigning.

Policy and political background

On 2 July 2010, during the second term in office of President Alan García (who was implicated in human rights violations during his first term between 1985 and 1990), the Peruvian Congress gave him powers to change the laws concerning individuals being prosecuted for human rights violations. He was given 60 days to enact the changes.

On 1 September, a day before the deadline, the Congress approved a package of decrees presented by the government, among which was DL 1097. This decree mandated that ongoing trials for military and police personnel accused of human rights violations would need to end if they exceeded the period stipulated for the prosecution of regular crimes. This measure went against international treaties signed by the Peruvian government, which stipulate that crimes against humanity do not have a time limit for prosecution.

When the decrees were passed, Peru was immersed in local government electoral campaigns. All the front pages of the main newspapers were filled with news referring to the elections, and the decree was hardly mentioned.

Social networks for human rights advocacy: A chronology of DL 1097's short life

The day after DL 1097 was approved, an NGO called the National Coordinator for Human Rights held a press conference in order to publicly criticise the decree. Realising that this issue was not getting enough public attention, a group of activists also decided to take action, and started a Facebook campaign. These activists were Javier Torres, head of the

1 This report adopts the terminology of the Truth and Reconciliation Commission.

2 For more details see: www.cverdad.org.pe/ingles/ifinal/conclusiones.php

3 For more details see: www.britannica.com/EBchecked/topic/540794/Shining-Path

4 The Geneva Conventions of 1949.

5 www.noticiasser.pe/08/09/2010/nacional/relator-especial-de-las-naciones-unidas-sobre-los-derechos-humanos-concluye-su-m

6 Rivera, C. (2010) El estado del proceso de judicialización de graves violaciones a los derechos humanos en el Perú, *Justicia Viva*, 22 July. www.justiciaviva.org.pe/notihome/notihome01.php?noti=333; see also Burt, J. M. (2010) Los juicios invisibles, *Noticias SER*, 4 August. www.noticiasser.pe/04/08/2010/los-juicios-invisibles

SER association,[7] Félix Reátegui, expert on transitional justice matters, and Eduardo Gonzales, head of the International Centre for Transitional Justice (ICTJ) Truth and Memory programme.

The response was immediate. Nearly 300 intellectuals, artists and politicians, amongst others, signed a petition launched by the activists that was posted on their walls.[8] A further 230 people signed up on Torres' personal Facebook page.

Given the great response to the initiative, the need to create a page entirely devoted to the campaign was urgent. Dánae Rivadereyra, a well-known local blogger and reporter on the news and blog platform Lamula.pe, met with Torres to propose starting a dedicated Facebook page. The intention was to continue with the signature collection process and to channel news and comments referring to the matter. On 4 September, the page called No al Decreto Legislativo 1097[9] (No to Legislative Decree 1097) was created. During the fifteen days of activism, which ended in the decree being withdrawn, the page attracted over 4,000 followers.

The traditional media also started to provide more coverage of the issue. There were not enough headlines, but there was a certain general interest growing in newspapers, radio and TV shows as the subject gained importance on Facebook and on blogs.

On 9 September, as part of the strategy to annul the decree, activists used the Facebook page to call for a sit-in in front of the Palace of Justice the next day. The turnout was not as strong as expected: around 300 people signed up to attend the event, but only around 100 showed up.

However, according to Torres, the use of social networks had already managed to get the media's attention and the collaboration of more personalities. Thanks to their support, on 12 September the organisers of the Facebook campaign published a statement objecting to DL 1097, which included supporters' signatures, in a national newspaper.[10]

In the meantime, Rafael Rey, the defence minister and, ironically, one of the promoters of the decree, came out on TV and radio shows declaring that the government did not seek the immunity of human rights violators and that he was "glad of having been available to bring reason [to the situation] and to concretise the will of the Peruvian government."[11]

However, the ruling party was starting to experience internal conflict in Congress. On 10 September Luis Gonzáles Posada, a ruling party congressman, declared on one of the most important radio news channels that "there is a great incompatibility in perspectives, a position that Minister Rey is going to have to explain. Yesterday I heard the prime minister saying the government was not consulted."[12]

On 13 September, Mario Vargas Llosa, head of the Memory Museum project (which commemorates the victims of the conflict), publicly resigned from his position, declaring that the reason for his resignation was "the recent DL 1097 that (...) constitutes a thinly disguised amnesty to benefit a large number of people linked to the dictatorship and sentenced (...) for crimes against humanity." He called for "this ignoble decree" to be abolished.[13]

On the same day, President Alan García sent an urgent request to the Congress to annul the decree. On 14 September, only thirteen days after it had been approved, DL 1097 was annulled with 90 votes in favour and one against.

After that, the activists continued their campaign, trying to get other anti-civil rights decrees annulled.[14] However, they did not succeed in keeping the public's attention and the Facebook campaign was a failure. Those decrees are still in force today.

Not a revolution

This was not a revolution. No regime fell. What happened in the first half of September 2010 was an attempt by civil society activists to use social networks as an alternative media channel for campaigning. The campaign's aim was to generate awareness on an issue that, otherwise, would have passed by unnoticed.

As we can see, the role that social networks played in the campaign was mixed. According to Torres, social media boosted the impact of the campaign, which otherwise would only have involved a small group of activists. For him, Facebook served as a tool to raise public awareness. However, Reátegui says that "the direct impact of social networks in the annulment of the decree was insignificant." He believes they only echoed issues that emerged in other media spaces.

It is important to say that the use of social networks had a narrow reach in Peru. Just 34.8% of the Peruvian population has access to the internet: 50.4% in the capital city, 38.4% in urban areas and 9.9% in rural areas. Most of the users are young and

7 Servicios Educativos Rurales: www.ser.org.pe

8 For a complete list see: www.facebook.com/note.php?note_id=425696859262

9 www.facebook.com/pages/NO-al-Decreto-Legislativo-1097/144408128929046

10 www.larepublica.pe/pagina_impreso.php?pub=larepublica&anho=2010&mes=09&dia=12&pid=1&sec=15&pag=11

11 www.larepublica.pe/07-09-2010/rafael-rey-niega-que-polemico-dl-1097-busque-impunidad-de-violadores-de-ddhh

12 www.rpp.com.pe/2010-09-11-gonzales-posada-sobre-dl-1097-rafael-rey-tendra-que-dar-explicaciones-noticia_294419.html

13 www.scribd.com/doc/37361078/Carta-de-renuncia-de-Mario-Vargas-Llosa

14 Such as DL 1095 which authorises military intervention and the use of force to deal with social demonstrations.

with high levels of education (82.1% of the population with college, technical institute or university degrees are internet users, while only 2% of the population with no more than primary education access the internet).[15] In urban areas, only 35% of internet users are on Facebook.[16]

As noted by Castells, "Not every person in the world participates in the networks (...). But everybody is affected by the processes that take place in global networks."[17] Although the author is referring to the global "network society", the principle is applicable to the case at hand. Exclusion from digital networks is a product of the social structures of society.[18] Internet and social network users in Peru represent a privileged sector of society, which has greater capacity to apply political pressure.

The reason why media are considered a "fourth estate" is because they have the capability to exert pressure on the government by generating public opinion. Traditionally, public opinion was measured through surveys or by the evidence of mobilisation. The feelings expressed during daily conversations could not be measured because they were fleeting. This does not happen anymore. Social networks offer tangible evidence of how the population is processing certain information. In the Peruvian case, while they did not have great mobilising power in terms of numbers, the political role of social networks was to capture a sense of public discontent that proved powerful. They let the government know how people felt, albeit not through demonstrations in the streets.

Conclusions

Facebook played two roles during the campaign against DL 1097. The first was as an alternative means of information dissemination due to the traditional media's concentration on electoral news. This created awareness amongst the general population. Second, it was used as a tool for the expression of public opinion.

While the surreptitious manner in which DL 1097 was approved helped provoke a strong public reaction, the use of Facebook allowed the activists to respond quickly to the decree.

However, the commitment to the cause did not manage to transcend the social networks. As mentioned before, the attempt to translate the Facebook support into a public demonstration – through a sit-in in front of the Palace of Justice – failed. This could be because the issue had already been taken up by the mass media, and political personalities had already spoken out against the decree. That is, there was a feeling that the matter had been adopted by actors who had more influence over the government than Facebook users. The consensus that was generated around the need to annul DL 1097 (except for the position of its main defender, Defence Minister Rafael Rey) diminished the necessity to be committed beyond the social networks.

Finally, the commitment to human rights was intense – even though the intensity was circumscribed to the networks. However, it was short lived and focused on a particular issue. This is seen in the failure to campaign against another decree, DL 1095 (which sought to authorise military intervention against social demonstrations).

We would like to end this report with an extract from our interview with Félix Reátegui:

> The bottom line, for me, is that these social networks, at least among us [Peruvians], have for now a reactive character rather than a preventive one, and that, in any case, they still do not have the capacity to be "translated" into popular demonstrations. In other places in the world where social networks have had shocking effects [...] what has happened is that the net is little more than a "coordination platform" for collective action... A government is not afraid of the net *per se*, but of the people who come out into the streets, who have been coordinated using the net.

Action steps

- In the Peruvian context, where social mobilisation is very rare amongst the middle and upper classes, social networks are a good way to express opinions and generate pressure on governments. However, they have to be used with moderation for campaigning. People seem to lose interest very quickly.
- Human rights movements should focus on a particular case in order to generate support using social networks. A long campaign should be thought of in terms of a series of time-separated causes.
- It is, of course, very important to engage social networks, so that users can share issues with their contacts.
- Finally, it is important to engage the traditional media in social media campaigns, using press releases and holding media briefings. ■

15 Instituto Nacional de Estadística e Informática (2011) *Las Tecnologías de la Información y Comunicación en los Hogares. Trimestre: Octubre, Noviembre, Diciembre 2010.*

16 Pontificia Universidad Católica del Perú (2010) *Encuesta de Opinión, Junio 2010.*

17 Castells, M. (2009) *Comunicación y Poder*, Alianza Editorial S.A., Madrid, p. 51.

18 Ibid., p. 52.

ROMANIA

MOBILISING FOR AN OPEN eROMANIA

StrawberryNet Foundation
Rozália Klára Bakó
www.sbnet.ro

Introduction

Information and communications technologies (ICTs) are key tools for economic and social inclusion, but the rural and elderly population have scarce access to advanced ICT infrastructure and few skills to use the technology in Romania.[1] The younger generation's digital skills[2] are also low, a study has shown.[3] Under these circumstances, it is crucial that the government takes a lead role in reducing the digital divide. Does it meet such an expectation, given that a digital culture accessible to all is critical for promoting human rights? And to what extent is a digital culture critical for human rights? This report[4] considers the case of the eRomania programme, aimed at bringing Romanian citizens online.

The recent economic crisis had a moderate impact on the ICT sector in Romania, with a 5% decrease in its turnover between 2009 and 2010. However, many ICT businesses – mostly small and medium sized – went bankrupt: 3,140 companies in 2009 and 4,870 in 2010.[5] At the same time, the crisis had a strong impact on the population's quality of life: 38% of Romanians barely reached a minimal income level in 2009.[6] Romania's 21.4 million inhabitants[7] – nearly half of them living in rural areas – are struggling to survive the economic downturn. Public sector salaries were cut by 25% in June 2010.

An overall assessment of Romania's network readiness[8] for 2010-2011 has shown *stagnation* compared to previous years' evaluations. The country ranked 65th out of 138 after aggregating the three criteria for measurement: environment,[9] readiness[10] and usage[11] of ICTs. While the *infrastructure* component scored higher (45th of 138), *readiness* – including quality of education and training, tariffs for ICT services, and governmental visions and attitudes concerning information technology – pulled Romania down to the lower half of the world ranking.[12] It is not a surprisingly poor score if we only look at the apologetic governmental statements on ICTs. With a 13.7% broadband penetration rate in 2010[13] Romania ranked 27th of 27 among European Union (EU) countries and 41st of 138 countries in the world.[14] Meanwhile, a media scandal broke out after USD 120 million (EUR 84 million) in EU funds were blocked by Brussels in June 2010 because Romanian authorities intended to divert them from broadband infrastructural development towards the controversial eRomania project.[15] In 2010, the EU's ICT strategy[16] restated the objective of bringing basic broadband to all Europeans by 2013.

1 Tufă, L. (2010) Diviziunea digitală. Accesul şi utilizarea internetului în România, comparativ cu ţările Uniunii Europene, *Calitatea vieţii*, 21 (1-2), p. 71-86. www.revistacalitateavietii.ro/2010/CV-1-2-2010/05.pdf

2 In terms of media literacy and digital content creation.

3 Preoteasa, M., Comanescu, I., Avădani, I. and Vasilache, A. (2010) *Mapping Digital Media: Romania*, Open Society Foundations, p. 11. www.soros.org/initiatives/media/articles_publications/publications/mapping-digital-media-romania-20110501/mapping-digital-media-romania-20110501.pdf

4 Compiled through desk research, key informant interviews and participant observation at: www.eurodig.org/romania

5 Ghitulescu, R. (2011) Studiu IT&C: industria TI&C 2009-2010. Bilantul anilor de criza, *Marketwatch.ro*, 27 May. www.marketwatch.ro/articol/7717/STUDIU_ITC_Industria_TIC_2009-2010_Bilantul_anilor_de_criza

6 TNS CSOP Romania (2009) *Impactul crizei economice*, TNS Social si politic, August 2009, p. 21. www.csop.ro/fck_fisiere/file/Panelul_efectele_crizei_asupra_populatiei.pdf

7 According to official statistics: www.insse.ro/cms/files%5Cpublicatii%5CRomania%20in%20cifre%202010.pdf

8 World Economic Forum (WEF)(2011) *The Global Information Technology Report 2010-2011*, p. 267. www3.weforum.org/docs/WEF_GITR_Report_2011.pdf

9 Including market environment, political and regulatory environment, and infrastructure environment.

10 Individual, business and governmental level of readiness.

11 Individual, business and governmental level of usage.

12 Ranked 76th of 138 countries. WEF (2011) Op. cit., p. 267.

13 Eurostat (2010) *Broadband penetration rate*. epp.eurostat.ec.europa.eu/tgm/table.do?tab=table&init=1&language=en&pcode=tsiir150&plugin=1

14 WEF (2011) op. cit., p. 371.

15 Vasilache, A. (2011) Portalul eRomania si Programul national de reforma 2011-2013: Haos privind data finalizarii si scopul acestui proiect. Domeniile de internet eromania.ro si e-romania.ro sunt in proprietatea unor firme, *Hotnews*, 3 May. economie.hotnews.ro/stiri-telecom-7437500-fonduri-europene-84-milioane-euro-pentru-internet-broadband-fix-vor-transferate-catre-proiectul-romania-ministerul-comunicatiilor-acuzat-deturnare-fonduri.htm

16 European Commission (2010) *A Digital Agenda for Europe*, Brussels, 19 May, p. 19.

Policy and political background

Digital inclusion has been a high priority on the Romanian ICT Ministry's agenda since 2004, and is still present in the authorities' official statements[17] and actions. An important step in facilitating equal access to ICT infrastructure is the 200 Euro Programme, launched in 2004 and operational since 2005,[18] in partnership with the Ministry of Education. The programme helps Romania's low-income families purchase computers for school-going children and for university students, assisted by governmental financial aid. A total of 198,248 pupils and students benefited[19] from the 200 Euro Programme between 2005 and 2011.[20]

Tangible results concerning digital inclusion in the country have also been achieved by the Knowledge Economy Project (2006-2010). Romanian authorities contracted a World Bank loan of USD 60 million and, adding USD 9.4 million[21] to the budget, helped disconnected communities get internet access, and supported small business e-development and local content creation.[22] This effort was awarded the European Commission's e-Inclusion medal in 2008 in the Geographical Inclusion section.[23] Other projects, such as Biblionet,[24] are also worth mentioning.

Romania's EU membership since 2007 has opened access to the so-called "structural funds", aimed at resolving structural imbalances between countries, regions and social groups across the EU. As highlighted in the 2008 Global Information Society Watch (GISWatch) country report,[25] the Romanian government has declared its commitment to ICT development by planning to allocate USD 550 million of EU funds to stimulating ICT use, electronic services and the e-economy. EU funding in general is a controversial issue in Romania due to the poor financial management of the authorities, often attracting criticism from Brussels. As mentioned, in June 2010 the EU blocked the USD 120 million allocated initially for broadband infrastructural development in rural areas because the Romanian Ministry of Communications and Information Society intended to redirect the money towards the eRomania portal.[26]

The eRomania case: A portal, a project or a strategy?

A media scandal around the eRomania programme[27] was sparked in March 2010 when Romanian authorities announced the intention to spend a total of USD 718 million (EUR 500 million) on the eRomania portal and its implementation strategy. The amount was considered too large for a poorly prepared and presented initiative, with little public consultation involved. Mainstream media and the blogosphere reacted instantly. Former chair of the Parliamentary Commission for ICTs, Varujan Pambuccian, declared his surprise that authorities were tendering a project before planning it properly. "What is eRomania? A site? A portal? A Romanian Wikipedia built from the taxpayers' money?" media representatives asked.[28] Public anger was expressed in articles and online videos entitled "More expensive than Avatar"[29] or "eRomania, a governmental site for 500 million Euro".[30] The key question journalists asked was: What do taxpayers get for such an amount of money? As one publication put it: "The short answer, according to the ICT Ministry's plan, is an IBM Blue Gene supercomputer, a unique database and 300 electronic services by the end of 2011."[31] In June 2011 the eRomania portal was still not operational (the site has been "under construction" for two years)[32] and media criticism is continuing.[33]

17 Ministerul Comunicatiior si Societatii Informationale (2011) Combaterea decalajului digital, alfabetizarea digitală şi accesul la serviciile de e-Guvernare sunt prioritare pentru MCSI, Comunicat de presă, 17 May. www.mcsi.ro/Minister/Comunicate-de-presa/Combaterea-decalajului-digital,-alfabetizarii-digi

18 euro200.edu.ro/

19 Case studies conducted in central Romania's rural regions show the importance of the 200 Euro Programme. Gagyi, J. (2010) Új média: egy erdélyi vizsgálat, *Reconect*, 2 (2), p. 95. reconect.org/issue/nr-2-2010

20 Calculated from yearly reports available at: euro200.edu.ro

21 www.ecomunitate.ro/proiect

22 The Knowledge Economy Project was targeted at 255 disconnected rural and small town communities across Romania.

23 A total of 37 medals have been awarded for the best of 469 projects from 34 European countries. www.citizensonline.org.uk/e-inclusionawards/media/display?contentId=5238

24 www.biblionet.ro

25 Bakó, R. (2008) Romania, in Finlay, A. (ed) *Global Information Society Watch*, Association for Progressive Communications, p. 167. www.giswatch.org/country-report/2008/romania

26 economie.hotnews.ro/stiri-telecom-8301752-solutia-pentru-deblocarea-84-milioane-euro-pentru-internet-broadband-zonele-sarace-din-romania-prezentata-comisiei-europene-saptamana-viitoare.htm?cfadac=

27 The tag "programme" is given by this report. Media discourses call eRomania a "project" or a "portal", while government officials tag it a "strategy".

28 Raileanu, S. (2010) Ce este eRomânia? Ce vom primi în schimbul a 500 de milioane de euro?, *Money.ro*, 16 April. www.money.ro/ce-este-eromania-ce-vom-primi-in-schimbul-a-500-de-milioane-de-euro-1_551461.html

29 www.dstanca.ro/2010/atentie-la-eromania.html

30 www.zf.ro/business-hi-tech/eromania-un-site-al-statului-de-500-mil-euro-cred-ca-mai-mult-va-costa-coordonarea-lui-ce-spun-cei-care-fac-site-uri-cu-1-milion-de-euro-5754271

31 www.money.ro/ce-este-eromania-ce-vom-primi-in-schimbul-a-500-de-milioane-de-euro-1_551461.html

32 Screenshotted in a blog (www.tashy.ro), available at: i34.tinypic.com/24vp4k9.jpg

33 economie.hotnews.ro/stiri-telecom-8581597-portalul-eromania-programul-national-reforma-2011-2013-haos-privind-data-finalizarii-scopul-acestui-proiect.htm

On 14 April 2010, the Association for Technology and Internet initiated an online petition[34] calling for an open eRomania project – a protest broadly publicised by Romanian open source forums,[35] mainstream media[36] and blogs.[37] The Manifesto for an Open eRomania Project was signed by 200 NGOs, open source activists, bloggers and ICT business leaders. The petition – an open letter addressed to Minister of Communications and Information Society Gabriel Sandu – pleaded for an open and transparent eRomania project based on open access, open standards and technological neutrality:

> Manifesto for an Open eRomania Project[38]
>
> An initiative supporting seven principles of an open eRomania:
>
> 1. Open access to all the content created through the project, and making it available on the internet.
> 2. Publishing all the public data from activities financed with public money in an open content format.
> 3. Reusing content already existing on the internet (including the content created by public institutions).
> 4. Use of open formats and open standards for the eRomania project.
> 5. Publishing all the computer programs created through the project using public money on a specialised website and under free licences.
> 6. Compliance with accessibility standards.
> 7. Implementing projects needed for public services and ensuring that they do not compete with the private sector.

Meanwhile, a public meeting was held on 30 April 2010 by the Association for Technology and Internet and the Council of Europe Office in Romania, in partnership with StrawberryNet Foundation, to address the topic of open e-government.[39] State Secretary of the Ministry of Communications and Information Society Andrei Săvulescu was invited to answer questions addressed by ICT stakeholders[40] related to the controversial eRomania initiative. Multiple issues were raised by ICT experts concerning the governmental vision, aims, action plan and technical solutions involved in such a costly programme. The government representative was not prepared to address the wide palette of concrete and targeted questions, but rather tried to temper the discontent and criticism of workshop participants related to the level of transparency and feasibility of the eRomania strategy.

Both the workshop and media inquiries have shown the poor level of communicating[41] this initiative to stakeholders and to the public at large. eRomania's six components have not been clearly presented and explained, but rather simply listed for the benefit of journalists:[42]

> eRomania 1: information portal and access point to eRomania platform
>
> eRomania 2: information and local services for 3,300 localities
>
> eRomania 3: standardisation of documents
>
> eRomania 4: ensuring information flow
>
> eRomania 5: Ghiseul.ro tax e-payment system
>
> eRomania 6: search engine in a unique database.

By June 2011, the eRomania 5 online payment service Ghiseul.ro had been implemented, as a pilot project that had started up in March 2011 – but with major security breaches. Detected and popularised by bloggers, the security issues were then hyped by the mainstream media[43] and corrected soon after. As for the initial eRomania web page launched in June 2009, it can only be found in the web archive, in three versions: the first one[44] was changed very quickly due to criticism[45] of its dysfunctionality; the second[46] and the third[47] versions – explaining that the website features serve only to show the portal concept – have also been withdrawn by the Ministry of Communications and Information Society. As mentioned, the web page www.romania.gov.ro is "under construction", and has been so since June 2009 and up to the time of writing.[48] However, the data centre of the eRomania 2 component was

34 www.apti.ro/proiect-deschis-eRomania

35 forum.ubuntu.softwareliber.ro/viewtopic.php?id=8761

36 economie.hotnews.ro/stiri-telecom-7087154-manifest-pentru-utilizare-deschisa-resurselor-din-proiectul-eromania-estimat-circa-500-milioane-euro.htm

37 www.manafu.ro/2010/03/manifest-pentru-un-proiect-deschis-eromania

38 English translation from: nicubunu.blogspot.com/2010/03/manifest-pentru-un-proiect-deschis.html

39 Organised as a workshop, part of the Eurodig 2010 Programme. www.eurodig.org/romania

40 Civil society organisation representatives, open source community members, programmers, ICT business players.

41 observator.a1.ro/eveniment/Interviu-incendiar-cu-Andrei-Savulescu-director-iT_6903.html

42 www.money.ro/ce-este-eromania-ce-vom-primi-in-schimbul-a-500-de-milioane-de-euro-1_551461.html

43 stirileprotv.ro/stiri/social/ghiseul-ro-fara-secrete-pentru-bloggerii-romani-au-depistat-cateva-erori.html

44 web.archive.org/web/20090617080900/http://www.romania.gov.ro

45 www.jurnalul.ro/jurnalul-national/jurnalul-national/guvernul-face-economii-sa-bage-romania-pe-net-536575.html

46 web.archive.org/web/20090620065946/http://www.romania.gov.ro

47 web.archive.org/web/20090626232532/http://www.romania.gov.ro

48 Screenshotted by a blogger on 6 June 2010, in June 2011 it looks the same: i34.tinypic.com/24vp4k9.jpg

already functional in June 2011 – the work of a large Romanian ICT company.[49]

Under media and civil society pressure, authorities still send unclear messages concerning an initiative meant to bring citizens online. Are the high expenses justified? Is it a properly designed programme and will it impact significantly on the digital divide in the country, with only 36.82% of households[50] connected to broadband internet in December 2010? Analysing the eRomania strategy might help to give an answer.

The government's Decision No. 195 on 9 March 2010 concerning the eRomania strategy[51] established the key principles, objectives and steps of the programme.[52] The strategy, aimed at developing a fair and efficient e-government[53] and planned to be implemented during 2010-2013, highlights three main components: firstly, e-government services, aimed at increasing the quality of interaction between citizens and government; secondly, integration with the broader concept of "Digital Romania" related to enhancing citizen participation and trust; and thirdly, a continuous alignment to innovative technologies. The main services to be implemented are those monitored by the EU, relating to income tax payment, job searches, social security, the renewal of personal documents, car registration, e-health and e-environment.

What is wrong with the eRomania initiative? Bogdan Manolea, an ICT policy expert, explains:

> Although at first sight the programme looks all right, it has two main problems. On the one hand, it reinvents the wheel by paying for services that are already developed; on the other hand, it creates a closed project that seems to be competing with the business sector. For the objective "access to legislative information", there are already four databases created with public funding.[54]

49 economie.hotnews.ro/stiri-telecom-8985407-video-cheltuieli-publice-ministerul-comunicatiilor-sute-mii-euro-intr-centru-date-care-gazduiasca-sisteme-eromania-eacademie.htm

50 ANCOM (2010) *Piata de comunicatii electronice din România,* Autoritatea Natională pentru Administrare si Reglementare în Comunicatii, Raport de date statistice 1 iulie-31 decembrie 2010, p.57.

51 www.avocatnet.ro/UserFiles/articleFiles/strategia_nationala_04281549.html

52 There is no link from the Ministry of Communications and Information Society to the eRomania strategy on 23 June 2011.

53 According to a United Nations 2010 survey, Romania ranks 47th of 183 countries for e-government services. United Nations (2010) *E-Government Survey 2010: Leveraging e-government at a time of financial and economic crisis,* p.114. unpan1.un.org/intradoc/groups/public/documents/UN-DPADM/UNPAN038853.pdf

54 Manolea, B. (2010) E-governmentul meu! Sau unde se duce 1/2 miliard de euro?, *Drept si internet – noutati & opinii*, 16 March. legi-internet.ro/blogs/index.php/2010/03/16/egovernment-romania-eromania1-lipsa-continut-deschis#c14959%29

As for the portal aimed at providing information about Romanian localities (eRomania 2), why pay for a second Wikipedia-like site from the taxpayers' money? Why "a pharaonic digitalisation project that doesn't even work"?[55] Last, but not least, the programme has been developed and launched with little public consultation involved, and communicated unprofessionally.

Conclusions

Romania is committed to closing the digital gap and the eRomania programme is an ambitious initiative with the intention of bringing citizens online. Its core service provision is in line with the EU's Digital Agenda, and with international e-government standards concerning the transition from an online presence to transactional and connected governance.

However, when it comes to content and financial matters, the eRomania strategy shows that the authorities' approach to designing and implementing ICT policy lacks clarity, fairness and stakeholders' involvement. The result is a largely contested *patchwork* of overbudgeted projects, poorly managed and communicated.

The Manifesto for an Open e-Romania Project was the first civil society public protest on ICT policy matters. It mobilised 200 NGO leaders, bloggers and open source activists. Even if the governmental machinery is moving on in promoting its own initiatives and interest groups, mainstream media and civil society actors are more and more vocal in advocating for proper information and consultation in public ICT matters.

Action steps

Lessons learned by ICT activists from the eRomania case are manifold:

- Mobilising small groups in a larger stream makes a protest more visible to the media and to the public at large.
- Civil society actors should be more proactive in participating in ICT policy making and advocating for digital rights.
- A connected, fair and inclusive information society for all should be the common goal of government, business and civil society actors. As Tim Berners-Lee put it, "competitive disclosure"[56] is necessary for an open internet: the public's right to know overwrites the authorities' reflex for secrecy. ■

55 Radescu, A. (2010) Guvernul face economii să bage România pe net!, *Jurnalul National*, 22 February. www.jurnalul.ro/jurnalul-national/jurnalul-national/guvernul-face-economii-sa-bage-romania-pe-net-536575.html

56 www.telegraph.co.uk/technology/news/7052785/Data.gov.uk-Sir-Tim-Berners-Lee-QandA.html

RWANDA

BALANCING FREEDOM OF EXPRESSION: THE NEED FOR LIMITATIONS AND RESPONSIBILITIES

Media High Council
Emmanuel Habumuremyi
www.mhc.gov.rw

Introduction

The inevitable freedom of expression that the internet brings is still a matter of discussion in Rwanda, where the place and function of the mass media in general have been complex and critical, quite often even central. The media, previously seen as perpetrators of propaganda for violence, preachers of hatred, instruments of repression and silencing, are now expected to be brokers of peace, healers of wounds, advocates for freedom and justice and, above all, partners in national reconstruction and development and democratic governance of the country. The advent of the internet in Rwanda has had a mixed impact on this function.

The internet has raised new ethical and control issues due to the growing number of new technologies. A new trend amongst some local media is to have a presence on the internet besides print and broadcast news items. The sharing of content on Facebook,[1] Twitter and other social media on current issues is becoming a culture amongst journalists. The main reason for this trend is the growing number of mobile subscribers which has reached 4,125,033 people with a penetration rate of 38%.[2] This goes hand in hand with a media sector that is undergoing transformation in terms of the legal and institutional framework.

The issue of content published on the internet by some local media websites is being criticised by local leaders and the general public who are seeing the media as working with "enemies of the state".[3] Online content from two local media houses has already been blocked in Rwanda. While this impacts negatively on freedom of expression and opinion, a lack of professional and public standards in internet use has also had a negative impact on news production. However, as this report argues, improving media ethics in the age of the internet is not simply a case of journalistic standards, but also involves the willingness on the part of the state to engage the media.

Policy and political background

The value and importance of media freedom is articulated in Rwandan laws and is endorsed and promoted in international and regional legal instruments that the Rwandan government has endorsed: Article 19 of the UN Universal Declaration of Human Rights of 1948, the International Covenant on Civil and Political Rights, the African Charter on Human and Peoples' Rights, the European Convention on Human Rights, and the American Convention on Human Rights.

Following these commitments, Article 34 of the 2003 Rwandan Constitution[4] stipulates: "Freedom of [the] press and freedom of information are recognised and guaranteed by the State." The constitution further requires the adoption of laws that determine the conditions for exercising this freedom.

The media law,[5] particularly Article 16, states: "Freedom of the media and freedom to receive information are authorised and recognised by the State. Such freedom shall be applicable in accordance with legal provisions." According to the same media law, censorship is prohibited. The media law also provides the right for individuals and organisations to establish media enterprises and describes necessary requirements.

In April 2011, a Rwandan government cabinet meeting approved a broadcasting policy which was considered critical to the migration from analogue to digital broadcasting.[6] The policy discourages concentration of ownership of print and electronic media,[7] so as to promote a diversity of views and freedom of expression.

Access to information is also guaranteed in the constitution. The Access to Information Bill is now

1 www.facebook.com/groups/abanyamakuru

2 RURA (2011) Mobile Subscribers as of July 2011. www.rura.gov.rw/index.php?option=com_content&view=article&id=278&Itemid=237

3 www.cpj.org/2010/12/rwandan-adviser-must-retract-accusation-against-ed.php

4 www.amategeko.net/display_rubrique.php?Information_ID=1434&Parent_ID=30694645&type=public&Langue_ID=An

5 www.mhc.gov.rw/fileadmin/templates/PdfDocuments/Laws/Media_Law_brief.pdf

6 allafrica.com/stories/201104290013.html

7 MINICT (2011) Rwanda Broadcasting Policy, Kigali.

tabled before parliament for consideration and approval. It is widely believed that if this bill is approved, it will be a breakthrough for the right to access information in Rwanda.[8]

On 1 June 2011 the government of Rwanda adopted a new media policy which aims at strengthening media self-regulation and reducing statutory regulation. This was adopted by a cabinet meeting on 30 March 2011. The purpose of the policy was to allow media practitioners to regulate themselves by holding each other accountable *vis-à-vis* professional standards. The process is voluntary and based on a code of ethics. Its merit is that it promotes professionalism and builds a more respected media industry.

The Media High Council's (MHC)[9] new mandate focuses on advocating for media freedom, capacity building in the media sector, and ensuring that the environment is conducive for media development. At the moment, MHC has an online platform for media practitioners to report any violation committed against them.[10]

Rwanda has big plans for the internet and its place in the future development of the country. At present, barely 4.8%[11] of the population is online using ADSL or accessing the fibre optic backbone. On a more positive note, Rwandan authorities are reportedly pushing officials to get online and use the popular social media networks.[12]

When looking at the media sector, apart from easy access to the internet everywhere in the city of Kigali and urban and rural areas via mobile phones, media houses offer internet access and computer training to practicing journalists. The MHC has also started the Rwanda Press Centre,[13] which is equipped with a considerable number of computers fully connected to wireless broadband (WiBro) internet. These computers are accessed free of charge by practicing journalists. This is manifested by an increasing number of blogs, and an increase in the numbers of newspapers and broadcasts accessed online.

Changing communication habits...

Despite the limited number of internet users in Rwanda, the authorities are at least starting to use the internet to communicate with the population either through mobile phones, institutional websites, or social media such as Twitter and Facebook. At the same time, "opponents" of the government are using the same channels to tarnish and weaken the official leaders' political agenda and the development efforts by the government, while sharing their opinions on Rwandan history which are in many cases opposed to the government's policy and strategies to eradicate the causes of conflicts that led to the 1994 genocide against Tutsis.

International organisations also play a big role either in advocating for more freedom of expression in Rwanda or in perpetuating "confusion" on the real status of media freedom in Rwanda. Reports on media freedom violations in Rwanda by the Committee to Protect Journalists (CPJ)[14] and Reporters without Borders (RSF) from 1994 to 2010 concerned mainly two newspapers: *Umuseso* and *Umuvugizi.* RSF says that the two newspapers "have long been two of the regime's biggest bugbears."[15] However, the MHC has responded to these reports by saying: "It is unfortunate that organisations that claim to be internationally reputable and credible can base their conclusions on sentiments and hearsay rather than facts and evidence in the name of defence of media freedom."[16] For MHC the allegations made by these watchdogs are "deliberately intended at misleading the international community, diverting them from the real problem of unprofessional practices in the Rwandan media."

The Rwandan media's ability to take a central position as the fourth estate appears a distant goal. Based on the discussion during a national dialogue on media development in Rwanda held in November 2010, it was mentioned that "it is a common knowledge that many media outlets of this country are run like briefcase companies. Some operate from makeshift newsrooms with hardly any business plans and without a vision for the future. Most private media outlets are unable to hire and retain journalists and pay all remunerations."[17] The organisers of the dialogue felt that this was the cause of all unethical practices that come with journalism: blackmail, which is common, extortion, and a concentration on coverage of conferences and seminars where journalists will receive per diems. Such practices of course put the profession's credibility in deficit as it fails to attract qualified and experienced

8 Various interviews, December 2010-March 2011, Kigali.

9 www.amategeko.net/display_rubrique.php?ActDo=ShowArt&Information_ID=2872&Parent_ID=30704083&type=public&Langue_ID=An&rubID=30704203

10 www.mhc.gov.rw/case

11 Statistics from www.rura.gov.rw

12 kigaliwire.com/2011/03/17/rwanda-prepares-to-tweet

13 www.rwandapresscentre.org

14 www.cpj.org/2011/02/attacks-on-the-press-2010-rwanda.php

15 en.rsf.org/rwanda-paul-kagame-03-05-2010,37198.html

16 MHC (2010) Response to RSF and CPJ on Umuvugizi and Umuseso Suspension. fesmedia.org/african-media-news/detail/datum/2010/04/22/rwanda-mhc-responds-to-rsf-and-cpj-on-umuvugizi-and-umuseso-suspension-opinion

17 MHC (2010) Concept note on the National Dialogue on Media Development.

TABLE 1.

Mobile subscribers as of July 2011

Operators	Active subscribers		Mobile penetration rate	
	June	July	June	July
MTN Rwanda	2,793,788	2,824,874		
Tigo Rwanda	1,116,598	1,300,159		
TOTAL	3,910,386	4,125,033	36.5%	38.4%

Source: Rwanda Utilities Regulatory Agency (RURA)

graduates mindful of ethics and who would serve as role models to new entrants.

The print sector is the most vulnerable of all. As if a shortage of daily newspapers and low levels of print copies were not bad enough, the newspaper distribution systems remain weak. The haphazard distribution systems reflect the low capacity of the country's press which serves only Kigali City and other urban areas.

Difficulties of access to information in public offices are a potential source of self-censorship, or, alternatively, the publication of rumours or one-sided stories. This is also caused by the practice of many senior government officials to shun the media whenever invited to debate or to react to media stories. All this points to serious challenges for a free media and affects media practice development.

The fact that libel and slander are still considered criminal as opposed to civil offences in media law and, worse still, punishable by a prison sentence, is seen by many practitioners as a serious impediment to the media's role in fighting corruption and abuse of office.

Looking at the newly published Media Sector Assessment in Rwanda (June 2011), the difficulties faced by the local media to access some senior government officials for interviews as compared to the foreign/international media, and the segregation between state media and some private media, with the former getting preferential treatment, point to an unhealthy relationship between media and government.

In this context, online media is flourishing. In Rwanda, many people are exchanging information through the use of internet, and many people access the internet through their mobile phones.

An emerging number of news websites are becoming popular and being considered as a free space to express citizen opinions on political and socioeconomic matters. Among the popular sites are Igihe,[18] Umuseke[19] and Igitondo,[20] which provide a free space for public comments. This is different to the *New Times*[21] – an online version of a pro-government newspaper – and the Rwanda Bureau of Information and Broadcasting (Orinfor)[22] websites, which offer one-way communication without instant feedback.

Another set of websites consists of government-critical websites owned by some recognised media houses in Rwanda or based outside of the country. In this regard, Tom Rhodes from CPJ has asserted: "Even though there are four internet service providers in Rwanda, the government keeps a close, cozy relationship with them allowing them to censor independent news sites such as *Umusingi* and occasionally *Umuvugizi*."[23] This can give the impression that the private media sector in Rwanda is under repression and that the government is aggressive towards what watchdog organisations call "independent" media in Rwanda.

Controversial and different views exist. Some people see the government's efforts to put in place infrastructure and promote the use of the internet as progress towards changing the country's socioeconomic situation, which is a positive sign for a developing country, while others see the use of the internet as "a new way for Rwandans to discuss their ethnic affiliations." Others see it as a tool for politicians' propaganda.

In the meantime, Facebook is helping people publish detailed information about their lives. Users expect some of these details to be public and others to be kept private. They argue, reasonably, that adult users should be free to publish information about their lives if they choose to do so. But lately many users have come to doubt Facebook's commitment to privacy.[24]

Rwandan President Paul Kagame is very active on Twitter. During the East African Internet

18 www.igihe .com

19 www.umuseke.com

20 www.igitondo.com

21 www.newtimes.co.rw

22 www.orinfor.gov.rw

23 Rhodes, T. (2011) The Internet in East Africa: An aid or a weapon?, *Committee to Protect Journalists*, 17 June. www.cpj.org/blog/2011/06/the-internet-in-east-africa-an-aid-or-a-weapon.php

24 roomfordebate.blogs.nytimes.com/2010/05/25/should-government-take-on-facebook

Governance Forum held in Kigali in August 2011, Senator Wellars Gasamagera stated that the president does not mind using social networks to respond openly to issues relating to the current state of governance in the country. Kagame was recently featured on YouTube's[25] Worldview, answering questions about Rwanda and life after the genocide. His presence here, in addition to his monthly press conference with cabinet ministers, contributes to access to information for journalists, and makes the leaders accountable and responsive to citizens. However, there is a need to measure the impact of these interventions in solving people's problems.

Conclusion

In Rwanda, the use of the internet is growing because of the government's policy on infrastructure rollout. But despite the considerable number of internet connection points all over the country, there is still an information vacuum in Rwanda. Access and literacy are all for the privileged few – even electricity is still a problem in rural areas. The internet's impact on news standards is also mixed. Few local media publications enrich the far corners of the country. Many of them plagiarise information available on the internet. A large number of news items mix personal opinion with factual information – often a result of the lack of access to state information. As the Rwandan president has shown, this can to some extent be remedied using social media. The credibility of anonymous authors remains an issue. According to Tom Ndahiro, a Rwandan civil society activist, "the internet has empowered bigots and increased the anonymous sources of deleterious discourse. Before and slightly after the genocide Rwandans only received information through print media and radios."[26] In Rwanda, there is a tendency towards not recognising professional journalism standards such as accuracy, fair balance and responsibility where the news is often biased – both on and offline.

Action steps

- More space for debates between media and government officials is needed so that there is common agreement on issues of freedom of expression, access to information, privacy, legal frameworks, and the need for public awareness.
- The youth and children should be proactively involved in discussions to prepare them for the responsible use of the internet in the future.
- Baseline research on internet use is needed in the country. This should consider the issue of freedom of expression in conjunction with other rights.
- Clear instructions should be put in place to guide people on what to do when websites are blocked by internet service providers. ■

25 www.youtube.com/watch?v=hGbbKo5nbJM

26 Ndahiro, T. (2010) Media watchdogs in a post-genocide Rwanda: A Caveat, *Friends of Evil*, 30 November. friendsofevil.wordpress.com/2010/11/30/media-watchdogs-in-a-post-genocide-rwanda-a-caveat

SAUDI ARABIA

SOCIAL NETWORKING AND THE WOMEN WHO AREN'T ALLOWED TO DRIVE CARS

Saudi Arabian Strategic Internet Consultancy (SASIc)
Rafid Fatani
www.SASIconsult.com

Introduction

In November 2010 a revolution began in the federal state of Tunisia. Revolutionary fervour soon spread throughout the Arab world, as political uprisings were ignited by a hope to emulate Tunisians' newly found freedom from oppression. The reign of tyrannical regimes, synonymous with the Arab world, was to be challenged. Perhaps surprisingly, the catalyst for this change was neither a political figure, nor an army of soldiers, but ordinary citizens armed with a new instrument of power: the internet, and Web 2.0.

In the midst of these developments, the western region of Saudi Arabia (in particular, Jeddah) suffered major floods, leading to widespread devastation and the loss of many lives. Victims of these tragic events blamed the government. They claimed that corruption within both government and private industry exacerbated the scale of the devastation.

Substantial funding for drainage infrastructure in the region had been set aside in 2009, but the planned projects did not materialise. In response to the catastrophic events that unfolded, the authorities in Jeddah said they did not have the capacity to prevent the floods, or to properly help those affected.

These sorts of incidents, combined with a high unemployment rate, created discontent amongst the public. The revolutionary contagion in North Africa looked certain to spread to Saudi Arabia. Some 40% of the population is under fourteen years of age, and unemployment hovers at persistently high levels. Consequently, the country did not escape radical protest, and political demands could not be circumvented. Ultimately, however, the "revolutionary fever" never quite gathered the momentum needed to seriously endanger the political landscape. During March 2011, an anonymous group called for a public protest to voice opposition to the political regime. In response, the Saudi Arabian authorities clamped down, violating the rights to freedom of expression.

Simmering change...

What could have been the Saudi Arabian revolution continues to simmer. Dissidents and reformists have found a use for new media. Facebook, YouTube, Twitter and online forums have become the new medium through which an agenda for change is being formulated. The ease in reaching the masses in relative freedom and anonymity afforded by digital media has bolstered the willingness for open discussion, largely free from fear of persecution.

The Saudi Arabian government was quick to realise the risk posed by such open and unchecked discussions, and proceeded to publish new regulatory restrictions for digital media, including blogs. The new rules, effective since January 2011, encourage all users to register officially with the government, and strictly prohibit criticism of Islam and all statements thought to compromise public order.

The new legislation sparked an outburst of criticism online. A petition was signed by over 6,000 Saudi Arabian citizens and sent to King Abdullah Bin Abdul-Aziz requesting the implementation of a constitutional monarchy. While the petition received no direct response from the King, the act of defiance catalysed a move to push for economic, social and political changes in Saudi Arabia. In late June 2011, a draft was leaked of a new anti-terrorism law that would allow the authorities to prosecute peaceful dissent as a terrorist crime, in partial response to the online demonstrations. This law, if enacted, would allow extended detention without charge or trial.[1]

On 18 March 2011 King Abdullah commended Saudi Arabians for their loyalty in the wake of the weeks of unrest, before issuing eighteen royal decrees stipulating the introduction of a national minimum wage and unemployment benefits. The nation has maintained its highly conservative attitude throughout the uprisings in North Africa. As a consequence of a new decree designed to further control religious dialogue, the government has pointedly issued official warnings, and ordered the closure of numerous websites and satellite television shows. The aim is to subvert the influence of fatwas[2] issued by clerics not sponsored by the state.

1 Questioning the integrity of the King or the Crown Prince would carry a minimum prison sentence of ten years under this new act.

2 en.wikipedia.org/wiki/Fatw%C4%81

Extremists online...

The growing presence, relevance and consequence of digital media and social networking have been further recognised within religious power circles. In an attempt to pre-empt further uprisings in response to censorship, Saudi Arabian clerics looked to use social media as a medium for influence and coercion. Sites such as Twitter, Facebook and YouTube have been used, attracting thousands of fans, dousing the fire of revolution.

The active and dynamic use of Twitter has been utilised to disseminate the perspective of a conservative Saudi majority and religious scholars, in this case with reference to the permissibility of women driving cars. Egotistical and extreme religious-orthodox "scholars" such as Al-Ahmad maintain their own Facebook fan pages and use their online presence to revile any call for open discussion on reforming the role of female rights in the country.

Nevertheless, internet-based initiatives continue to serve as a useful instrument for political pressure. A simple campaign was created, calling for the human rights of Saudi Arabian women to be upheld. As a result, 17 June 2011 saw more than 29 Saudi Arabian women drive their cars in protest against the kingdom's de facto ban on female driving.

The story of Manal al-Sharif

Women in Saudi Arabia have had limited freedom of movement for a long time. In practice they are not allowed to drive motor vehicles (period), nor are they allowed to leave Saudi Arabia without consent from their male guardian – and in some cases, a woman's son is her guardian.

In 1990, 47 brave Saudi Arabian women from Riyadh's intelligentsia were arrested, dismissed from their jobs, and banned from travelling after staging a defiant protest. Disgust at the unwritten "law of convention" prohibiting women from driving was carefully surfaced publicly as the women drove in a convoy of fourteen cars into the capital. Despite the consequences for the women in 1990, defiance was rekindled in the wake of the Arab world revolutionary uprisings in 2011. This time, the protest had global reach, as images and videos of women driving through Saudi Arabia were posted on Facebook and Twitter.

One of these women, Wajeha al-Huwaider, cofounded the Association for the Protection and Defense of Women's Rights in Saudi Arabia in 2007 with Fawzia al-Uyouni, another women's rights activist. Together they created a petition that was signed by 1,100 Saudis and sent to King Abdullah asking for women to be allowed to drive. The petition was not officially responded to, yet Huwaider did not waver. On International Women's Day 2008, she filmed herself driving and received international media attention after the video was posted on YouTube. Yet again, the Saudi government did not react.

In 2011, inspired by the Arab Spring, a group of Saudi activists started a campaign on Facebook called "Teach me how to drive so I can protect myself",[3] as well as under the hash tag #Women2Drive[4] on Twitter, in an attempt to raise the issue publicly once more. In a matter of days, over 12,000 signatories showed their support on the Facebook campaign page. One of the founders of the page, Manal al-Sharif, drove her car in Khobar, one of the prominent cities in the Eastern Province, with Huwaider filming the protest. She posted the video on YouTube and Facebook, saying in the video: "This is a volunteer campaign to help the girls of this country [learn to drive]. At least for times of emergency, God forbid. What if whoever is driving them has a heart attack?"

She had also invited all women in Saudi Arabia to start driving on 17 June. After posting the video, she was detained by the religious police on 21 May, and released six hours later. Two days later, around 600,000 people had watched the video.

The response this campaign had created worried the authorities and they arrested her again on 22 May, causing international news agencies to focus the world's attention on the issue. Her lawyer Adnan al-Saleh said that she was charged with "inciting women to drive" and "rallying public opinion". In reaction to al-Sharif's arrest, several Saudi women published videos of themselves driving over the next few days. In response, the authorities stated that al-Sharif would remain in detention until 5 June 2011, according to lawyer Waleed Aboul Khair.

Different news organisations attributed the long duration of al-Sharif's detention to the Saudi authorities' fear of protest movements in Saudi Arabia generally. *The National*, a government-owned English-language daily newspaper published in Abu Dhabi, said al-Sharif had written a letter to King Abdullah and that 4,500 Saudis had signed an online petition to the King. The article described "an outpouring of indignation and disbelief by both Saudis and critics abroad that Ms al-Sharif was jailed for something that is not a moral or criminal offence."[5]

3 www.facebook.com/pages/Teach-me-how-to-drive-so-I-can-protect-myself/132205866854879

4 See Twitter hashtag #Women2Drive for photos, videos, and commentary.

5 www.thenational.ae/news/worldwide/middle-east/saudi-woman-driver-released-from-jail-after-nine-days

On 30 May al-Sharif was freed, under conditions that included bail, returning for questioning if requested, not talking to the media and not driving.

Can social media help Saudi Arabian women drive?

While not a reflection of the general public's perspective, there has been vocal opposition to the protests by conservative groups. An anti-driving group on Facebook has called for "real men" to physically attack those women choosing to drive. Female activists were dubbed "Westernised whores" on Twitter. It is clear that the far-reaching immediacy of social media is now recognised by both the orthodox conservatives and revolutionary activists.

Those in defence of the right of women to drive argue that widespread support of the issue is immaterial; instead it should be considered an issue of constitutional morality, a matter of individual rights.

While positive, statements by the social media activist Eman Al Nafjan such as "We need to do it again" are somewhat misguided. Protests that endanger the well-being of women should not be considered an event – rather a means to an end. The campaign should remain active and ongoing supporters should build momentum in order to galvanise change.

Social media have given voice to the masses, and inspired young, forward-thinking progressive Saudi Arabians to ambitiously chase their aspirations. Many appealed to United States (US) Secretary of State Hillary Clinton to emphasise her support for the issue. In response, she openly praised the actions of protesters, while stressing that their actions were not motivated by outsiders.

There remains a new sense of hope for constitutional reform in Saudi Arabia. The relative conservatism and diplomacy of the kingdom's media have been circumvented through access to the internet. People from all over the world have contributed to the "Honk for Saudi Women" viral campaign.

It has become apparent that times are changing, that the rules of engagement are now relevant to the 21st century, but that the question still remains as to whether social media can help change legislation in practice.

Thoughts towards action steps

This discussion represents only a small part of a complex and evolving debate over the role of virtual and civil freedoms in Saudi Arabia. At the same time, online censorship reflects draconian laws in the "offline" world. The fact that Manal al-Sharif's campaign was kept alive by her supporters online, even after it was deleted from various social media channels, shows the dramatic impact social media have in Saudi society. As seen in previous cases, today's socially engaged audience likes to discuss things; and once an incident goes viral, there is not much government censorship can do in terms of controlling what follows. Uploading al-Sharif's video on YouTube empowered her cause in a smart way that enabled the message to impact on internet users directly.

Although the 17 June movement saw several women drive around the country, it will be interesting to see how much additional support and attention the #Women2Drive social media movement will draw in the coming months. According to raw data, the male population, especially on Twitter, has been very active in discussions on the issue. However, as the campaign continues to gather support, more and more women tweet about their successful driving experiences in Saudi Arabia. As the momentum continues to build, we can expect to see an increase in the number of women using social media to make their voices heard.

The Saudi social media scene has been exceptionally active in the last few months following the Arab Spring. This has created an anti-autocratic movement amongst the Saudi youth to voice their concerns, knowing that the Saudi government can do little to censor dialogue. While the government needs to introduce laws on privacy and individual rights, online as well as offline, young activists all over the kingdom are engaging in dialogue with the Saudi youth through social media and people are becoming more aware of the political and social changes in the region.

We have yet to reach the peak of the social media phenomenon, as there is so much more to expect from the tech-savvy youth of Saudi Arabia. Governmental perspectives have yet to become a central part of the debate. The potential of technologies to contribute to broader dialogue using Web 2.0 tools can be felt – and the youth are now more capable and qualified to identify their liberty and rights. It is now time for the government to choose, either to be part of the debate, or part of the problem. ■

SPAIN

THE INTERNET IN A NEW AGE OF DIGITAL ACTIVISM

Pangea and BarcelonaTech (UPC)
Leandro Navarro
pangea.org and upc.edu

Introduction

Several important events in Spain in the last year illustrate how intertwined and influential the internet has become in the life of citizens, human rights and democracy. These events include an online discussion on freedom of access to content, given a new law limiting web links and peer-to-peer (P2P) downloads of copyrighted content; an online debate around the international Anti-Counterfeiting Trade Agreement (ACTA); a discussion on equality legislation with risks for content censorship on the internet; and the highly visible 15 May (15M) social movement,[1] which has a strong internet presence. All of these show how the internet has acquired a central role, not only as an enabler for access to knowledge and supporting freedom of expression, but also as an effective tool for *collective* expression and social activism and action – and its influence on the political and policy agenda is beginning to be felt.

Given these events as background, this report has been compiled from the responses to questionnaires circulated to three internet and human rights organisations: X.net,[2] Asociación de Internautas (Internauts Association),[3] and Partit Pirata de Catalunya (Pirate Party of Catalonia).[4] In particular, we wanted to find out how they felt about the role of the internet in a new age of digital activism.

Policy and political background

The Spanish legal system is underpinned by European Union (European Parliament) directives.

The Spanish Constitution also takes into account what it calls Popular Legislative Initiatives (ILPs) that allow grassroots initiatives to submit petitions to be discussed by the Spanish parliament, or the parliaments of autonomous communities. However, this mechanism is seldom used, with a few exceptions (e.g. a recent ILP to ban bullfighting in Catalonia due to animal abuse and killing was discussed and approved as a law by the Catalan parliament),[5] and proposals are usually discarded in the parliamentary process.

Privacy, data protection and data retention are mentioned in the Spanish Constitution and covered by the Data Protection Law (LOPD, 1999), which complies with the European Directive 95/46 CE, the E-Commerce Law (LSSI, 2002) – implementing Directive 2000/31/CE, and partially Directive 98/27/CE – and Law 56/2007, dealing with the promotion of the information society.

Freedom of expression on the internet was recently challenged by the so-called "Sinde Law", which contains a controversial clause that would allow blocking websites with content or links infringing copyright. However, this clause has not yet been implemented to our knowledge. Another potential challenge to freedom of expression on the internet is the proposed law on equality and non-discrimination (popularly know as the "Pajín Law") that might fine websites when content (including comments from visitors) could constitute direct or indirect discrimination.

The role of the internet in citizen participation

The recent year in particular has been marked by online activist initiatives. In many instances this has been the result of tensions between business interests and social movements supporting human rights. These tensions are evident at the national and global level. One of these local events was the 15M movement. Many people participated in the 15M gatherings, demonstrations and camps that happened all over Spain. The movement used internet sites and tools to inform and promote the active participation of citizens who felt the political and economic system was abusing democracy.

For example, protest statements included ones like "Europe for the citizens and not for the banks". The movement developed a manifesto calling for an end to the privileges of politicians, an end to unemployment, the right to housing and good quality

1 en.wikipedia.org/wiki/2011_Spanish_protests
2 whois--x.net
3 www.internautas.org
4 pirata.cat
5 en.wikipedia.org/wiki/Ban_on_bullfighting_in_Catalonia

public services, the need to control banks, a tax on wealth and speculative capital movements, the guarantee of citizen freedoms and participatory democracy, and a reduction of military spending.

The internet is playing a key role in complementing these sorts of activities, and has been used to collect and disseminate information, discuss and prioritise ideas, build consensus, and produce documents and manifestos about how the political and economic system could be regenerated.

When respondents were asked how effective the internet was in collecting representative opinions of Spanish citizens, the replies highlighted the key importance of extending internet access to more people; the fact that the internet is an interactive medium that is democratising participation in politics; the role of internet communities and thematic threads (including on Twitter) as a way for collective debate to occur; and the proliferation of voices, which stands in contrast to the presence of single perspectives from the so-called "popes" of the net.

Regarding the effectiveness of tools for collective participation and collective decision making on the internet, replies highlighted the importance of tools for the collaborative editing of documents (pads), knowledge sharing (wikis), email lists (with educated users following netiquette) or websites combining these with other specific web campaigning applications – for example, the "Todos contra el canon"[6] (Everyone against the levy) campaign against the private copying levy. Decision-making tools based on voting securely online were also mentioned (e.g. IdeaTorrent, Helios Voting).

Organisations, informal groups or campaigns taking an active role or representing the internet community on issues of human rights and the internet were also identified by respondents. Apart from the organisations surveyed themselves, the Spanish Association of Small and Medium Informatics and New Tech Companies,[7] Hacktivistas, Red-SOStenible.net, the Oxcars, and the campaigns "Democracia Real YA" (Real Democracy NOW), FC-Forum.net, "Todos contra el canon", and "No les votes"[8] (Don't vote for them) were mentioned.

Respondents shared the opinion that the established political world effectively ignores critical internet issues, as events over the past year show to a different degree. For this reason the power of the internet to aggregate ideas and opinions usually surprises them. The reasons behind this general lack of interest in the internet include the idea that traditional political parties and the public administration do not fully understand the internet or are not able to incorporate its potential for a new way of interacting into their work, and that political parties are based on a model that precludes close interaction with citizens. It is illustrative to see that political parties during political campaigns tend to hire advertising companies to create "an active presence" on social media sites – but after that they return to their websites that largely offer a one-way flow of information without any kind of support for "participatory democracy" or organised interaction with citizens.

Even more worrying is that ideas from citizens expressed and collectively formulated online can be perceived as challenging the established political order. This resistance to change affects politics and social progress negatively.

The net effect is that the political world ignores most initiatives or ideas coming through spontaneous or less formal groups that use the internet as a means to build or make visible proposals without going through the formal structures of political parties. They are usually perceived as manipulated ideas coming from a non-representative minority. There are a few exceptions of initiatives born on the internet with a real impact, sometimes forced by the use of established structures such as judicial decisions or petitions.

Regarding how internet rights should be considered in the Spanish social and legal environment, the following issues were highlighted by respondents as relevant given the tensions between internet policies, economic and business interests, human rights and democracy:

- The internet should be considered a basic tool for communication, creation and innovation that supports citizen participation. Its neutrality and freedom should be preserved.
- Privacy, data protection and security are challenged by specific issues such as terrorism and the protection of intellectual property. This presents a dangerous move towards an Orwellian society. While security is necessary, it should not be at the expense of civil liberties. National laws and the European directives should be reformulated accordingly. Transparency in mechanisms for security and protection and their application is required from the government.
- While the internet has helped to make government decision making more transparent, it also allows for personal data to be accumulated. Citizens need to be empowered so that they have more control over how they are being tracked.

6 www.todoscontraelcanon.com

7 www.apemit.org

8 www.nolesvotes.com

- Participation: ICTs enable the more democratic and direct participation of citizens. There is no need to call for expensive and time-consuming referendums to know the opinion of citizens, as there are internet-based tools that can be used to poll citizens on topics that affect them.
- Universal broadband: Apart from the well-known arguments in favour of universal access, there is also a growth in the provision of public services in the public administration in general. Services such as health or education are being delivered over the internet. In this way the net becomes a means for citizen service and social participation and access to the internet becomes a growing human rights concern.
- Network neutrality: From the perspective of fundamental human rights this is equivalent to the principle of equality and non-discrimination of network users, and its defence is essential for the internet to be a basic tool for communication for everyone.
- Author rights (intellectual property): Technology changes require new business models. The digital private copying levy is unsustainable and a new equilibrium must be restored between author rights and the collective right of access to culture. As the European Directive 2000/31/CE suggests, there is a need to "agree upon codes of conduct." Events such as FCForum or the Oxcars have helped the creative sector to see the social function of cultural production as a service to the community, as opposed to the industrial model imposed by large multinational media industries.

Action steps

There are several key topics of common interest for ICT activists in Spain and Europe:

- An obvious direction is strengthening coordination among multiple organisations in Spain to work in common directions. That is already happening in most campaigns and occurs through personal or organisational links. This type of coordination is also relevant to organisations in other countries of the EU or with pan-European organisations such as the European Digital Rights Initiative (EDRI) (Pangea and X.net are already members).
- Widening the political representation of the "internet world" implies working towards including more citizens in the digital world. Strategies for "universal service" or "broadband for all", timidly discussed at the national or European level (e.g. Digital Agenda 2020), or community networking initiatives such as Guifi.net, are ways to enable the internet as a tool for participation and e-democracy. As has been said: "The internet is not just another TV."[9] An accessible, affordable, universal and content-neutral internet with open knowledge and open services is essential in the battle for civil rights in the 21st century. This requires supporting regulations: a national law, a European directive.
- Network neutrality: Its defence is essential to avoid the internet ending up under the control of just a few. Net neutrality requires the development of supporting regulations.
- Independent internet media and services: This highlights the importance of choosing commercially independent and community-owned internet services and applications (i.e. run by non-profit social movements, such as the Wikimedia foundation) over those with commercial interests (e.g. Facebook, Twitter). New models of cultural production have a key social role in facilitating access to rich and diverse content for communities.
- Visibility on the street: ICT activism and political activities on the internet should have a strong presence "on the street" and a real impact in the political arena. But the way to go is through complementing internet initiatives with activities on the ground, rather than working from the other way around (e.g. in the way that traditional political campaigns typically have a weak internet presence).
- ICT activism, "bottom-up politics", and citizen participation using the internet are already strong in Spain, as clearly shown by the 15M movement. These sorts of movements have been successful in developing manifestos following a bottom-up and participatory process, and have been successful in attracting the attention of both citizens and the traditional media (press, TV). The challenge now is to be heard effectively by political parties and governmental structures – a task that is very difficult given that the political voice is coming from an unconventional source. ■

9 internetnoseraotratv.net/en

SWEDEN

WIKILEAKS IN SWEDEN: A NOTE ON LOCAL SOURCE PROTECTION IN A GLOBAL ONLINE WORLD

Association for Progressive Communications (APC)
Henrik Almström
www.apc.org

Introduction

While the internet has enabled almost limitless possibilities to publish and disseminate large quantities of data, and opened up whistle-blowing opportunities in numerous contexts, the case of WikiLeaks has shown that protection of sources has become a critical issue.

Soon after it was established in 2007, WikiLeaks moved its content to Swedish and Belgian servers to enjoy the strong legal protection of free speech that these countries provide.

WikiLeaks was not the only whistle-blowing site around, but it had slowly built up confidence in the internet community through strong encryption technology and security routines. Together with some very extraordinary leaks during 2010, the site developed into the most well-known global whistle-blowing site in the world.

Since its inception, WikiLeaks has created major controversies, whether through making information publically available, or being blocked from credit card donations, or through accusations of sexual crimes against its founder, Julian Assange.

This report focuses on WikiLeaks' presence in Sweden, and what WikiLeaks may have achieved or not achieved through this. The rape allegations against Assange and the issue of his extradition to Sweden have deliberately not been dealt with. For one, the situation has the potential to cloud the issue of the function of WikiLeaks and fundamental civil rights. Some might argue that the accusations are part of attempts by the Swedish state in collusion with the United States (US) authorities to continue to discredit WikiLeaks, and to deny its potential as a powerful human rights tool. Others may argue that Assange, by using WikiLeaks as leverage to avoid personal legal proceedings, is jeopardising the future of WikiLeaks. How the controversy fits into the scenario is currently open to speculation only.

Policy and political background

Freedom of expression has a long history in Sweden, and the first law protecting free speech dates back to 1766. In addition to the right for any individual to express oneself freely there is strong and comprehensive protection for the press through two constitutional laws, the Freedom of the Press Act SFS 1949:105 and the Fundamental Law on Freedom of Expression SFS 1991:1469.

The legislation, which establishes protection from interference from the government and other state bodies, is detailed and describes a number of requirements to qualify for protection. These relate to how, in which form, to what purpose and through what media the material is being published, but do not relate to the actual content of the publication. For example, commercial advertising does not qualify because of its commercial purpose and, similarly, private email does not qualify because it is not intended to be published publicly.

The main requirements for protection of internet content are:[1]

- That the material is provided upon specific request from a user (i.e. not through using automatic website pop-ups).
- That the website appears as a uniform product (e.g. it should have a coherent design and cannot be a mass of unformatted or unedited data or text simply put online).
- That the website content cannot be altered or changed by anyone other than the editorial staff running the website.

If these requirements are fulfilled, the editor may file for a so-called "Certificate of No Legal Impediment to Publication", which certifies that the website and its content, as well as the editorial staff and their sources, are protected through:[2]

- Source protection – sources have the right to stay anonymous and it is a criminal offence for editorial staff to reveal any information about the source.
- Inquiry protection – no public authority or other public body may inquire into the identity of the source.[3]

1 The Fundamental Law on Freedom of Expression, Article 9, Chapter 1.
2 The Fundamental Law on Freedom of Expression, Chapter 2.
3 The Fundamental Law on Freedom of Expression, Article 4, Chapter 2.

- Prohibition of censoring[4] – any scrutiny of content prior to publication or similar act of censoring from a public authority or other public body is prohibited.

However, a Certificate of No Legal Impediment to Publication not only entails protection, it also means responsibilities: it requires the appointment of a named responsible editor who is liable for all content on the website. This is only in relation to an exclusive and limited list of criminal offences, which can only be prosecuted by the Chancellor of Justice in accordance with the rules laid down in the Freedom of the Press Act.[5]

The principles behind the constitutional protection can be compared to that of a boxing ring. Boxers enter the ring knowing that in the ring certain rules apply, protecting them from illegal actions; but they are at the same time subject to certain physical risks that are allowed by the same rules that protect them in the first place. The risk of taking on the liability of being a responsible editor is something the editor would have to accept to be able to enjoy the benefits of source protection, inquiry protection and prohibition of censoring.

It is, however, important to understand that the protection of sources only relates to the protection of anonymous sources, and not the protection of a whistle blower as such. If an anonymous source is revealed, the protection for the individual is very limited. The Swedish legislation does not provide any protection from retaliatory actions taken by, for example, private companies or foreign governments. It is therefore critical to protect the anonymity of the source in the first place, particularly in the case of international leaks, where the source may come from a country with poor rule of law, and therefore may face arbitrary retaliation from the state.

The benefits of legal uncertainty...

Being a whistle-blowing site, WikiLeaks is critically dependent on sources for information, and on the protection of these sources. One of WikiLeaks' strong advantages, which has contributed to the success of the site, is its reputation of being able to keep its sources completely anonymous.

WikiLeaks source protection is primarily technical, with a sophisticated and partly secret system where individuals can file information in a "dropbox". This first step is important as it avoids any face-to-face interaction between the source and WikiLeaks. While traditional journalists often have to build up trust with sources to develop a story, the drop-box system enables leaking at anytime by anyone, without a relationship being developed between two individuals.

After the drop-box system, multiple servers in different countries create a complex system of information flow that makes it virtually impossible for any individual within the WikiLeaks organisation to identify a source without collaborating with numerous other colleagues in the organisation. This way WikiLeaks has ensured technical measures as well as organisational structures and staff routines to protect the sources.

When looking for strong legal protection, the step to Sweden was not a long one; already early in the history of WikiLeaks, the organisation had put many of its servers in Sweden with help from companies with a background in the Swedish file-sharing site Pirate Bay.

As described above, the Swedish legal protection offered to sources is strong – as long as the leak is kept anonymous. Locating its servers in Sweden also means that any foreign government that would be interested in investigating a leak, or in tracing the information back to a possible leak, or even taking measures to prevent the publication of a particular leak, would have to take legal measures in Sweden. Generally this would not be possible without collaboration with Swedish public authorities. Any such collaboration would mean that Swedish public authority officials would be guilty of violating the law, which is punishable by a fine or imprisonment for up to one year.[6] They could also face being fired. Of course, it does happen that Swedish public authority officials violate the freedom of the press laws, but generally the laws are well known and well respected, and cases of violations are brought to court in accordance with the special procedures set forth in the Freedom of the Press Act.[7] This means that foreign governments or other actors would be left to take measures against WikiLeaks entirely on their own, without support from Swedish public authorities.

With this protection in sight, WikiLeaks decided to apply for the Certificate of No Legal Impediment to Publication in accordance with the Fundamental Law on Freedom of Expression.[8] Appearing to comply with the requirements for the certificate, this was a natural step to enjoy strong legal protection. An important factor here was that WikiLeaks, in spite of its name, is not a wiki: its content is not

4 The Fundamental Law on Freedom of Expression, Article 3, Chapter 1.

5 The Fundamental Law on Freedom of Expression, Article 1, Chapter 7, with reference to Freedom of the Press Act, Article 1-4, Chapter 9.

6 The Fundamental Law on Freedom of Expression, Article 5, Chapter 2.

7 The Fundamental Law on Freedom of Expression, Article 1, Chapter 7, with reference to Freedom of the Press Act, Article 1-4, Chapter 9.

8 The Fundamental Law on Freedom of Expression, Article 4, Chapter 2.

user-generated. All content is submitted or leaked through the drop-box system, but then, as a second step, published by the WikiLeaks organisation. This level of gatekeeping means that it functions more like a traditional media outlet.

For WikiLeaks to receive the certificate, the organisation needed to appoint a responsible editor, and this editor needed to be accountable in Sweden, which means the editor would need to be a Swedish citizen or have valid Swedish residence and a work permit. Assange was appointed responsible editor and applied for Swedish residence and a work permit at the Swedish Migration Board.

The application for residence and work permit was, however, denied and WikiLeaks did not qualify for the Certificate of No Legal Impediment to Publication. The reason behind the decision by the Swedish Migration Board is not available as the board's decisions are not public. At the time of writing, the grounds for the decision of the Swedish Migration Board have to the best of my knowledge not been leaked by the Board, nor by Assange himself.

Being denied the certificate means that WikiLeaks did not become expressly protected by the Swedish constitution. But since the website may comply with the requirements for protection, the site may still be considered protected, as the legislation provides for automatic protection in some cases, including for some mass media organisations.[9] This second type of protection, which includes the same protection as the "regular" protection, automatically applies and is in force without any form of prior registration or application process. Whether WikiLeaks should be considered protected or not, under the automatic protection for mass media organisations, currently remains unclear.

The denial of the application is, of course, a setback for WikiLeaks. However, the fact that WikiLeaks *may* enjoy protection without the Certificate of No Legal Impediment to Publication is an uncertainty that in itself is a protection from interference from any inquiry, scrutiny or censoring from a Swedish public authority. The uncertainty is likely to deter most Swedish public authorities and their employees from investigating leaks and sources, as well as trying to interfere with what is being published, as the individual conducting the search or action faces the risk of criminal charges. As a result, the uncertainty may still work in WikiLeaks' favour.

Conclusions

Even if Assange was given a work permit, enabling WikiLeaks to be granted the Certificate of No Legal Impediment to Publication, would this then have been something valuable for WikiLeaks?

Clear legal protection often implies being subsumed into a legal system, a system which might not be adapted to all the needs of WikiLeaks. The Swedish system for the protection of the press is aimed at traditional printed newspapers, with adjustments that cater for online supplements to newspapers and, more recently, to online databases.[10] Instead of publishing traditionally edited articles, original documents are published on WikiLeaks after a somewhat limited fact check. This model of mass media might not fit perfectly well in a system which requires a single responsible editor, which is the main requirement for enjoying full protection in Sweden.

Instead, the legal uncertainty of WikiLeaks, which is currently the case, may work in WikiLeaks' favour.

Action steps

The process of WikiLeaks' endeavours to enable safe and secure leaking is an ongoing story which is the case for anyone dealing with the publication of sensitive content online. In the case of WikiLeaks the outcome is unclear, with more questions than answers. However, some conclusions can be drawn:

- Source protection, legal as well as technical, must build upon strict procedures and routines.
- Legal source protection should always be combined with technical protection and vice versa.
- Legal source protection is normally not the same as whistle-blower protection. Even under Sweden's legal protection, an individual source who is revealed would only enjoy very limited protection, particularly in an international context.
- Strong legal protection might not always be the best option – stronger technical measures that protect the anonymity of sources, including mirroring servers in different parts of the world, may prove more effective. ■

9 The Fundamental Law on Freedom of Expression, Article 9, Chapter 1.

10 The Fundamental Law on Freedom of Expression, Article 1, Chapter 1.

SWITZERLAND

SURVEILLANCE AND SECURITY MANIA VIOLATING BASIC RIGHTS

Comunica-ch
Wolf Ludwig
www.comunica-ch.net

Introduction

Switzerland is generally not perceived as a country conflicting with international human rights standards. According to United Nations (UN) reports and other specialised human rights sources, basic rights like freedom of speech and association and the right of access to information are normally granted. Problem areas, with obvious deficits and demands for improvement, are the rights of asylum seekers, migrants or religious minorities such as Muslims living in the country.[1] In the 2010 World Press Freedom Index published by Reporters Without Borders, Switzerland again shares first place with a number of Nordic countries: "These six countries set an example in the way they respect journalists and news media and protect them from judicial abuse."[2]

But in the context of digital access rights, Switzerland is still not at the forefront compared to Nordic countries like Finland. And issues of privacy, amongst other concerns, have been raised regarding new surveillance regulations that are part of national security and telecommunication laws. As in other countries, widespread security considerations – mostly referring to terrorist threats or child pornography – are increasingly threatening and undermining the principles of access and openness, as well as civil rights.

Policy and political background

Most attempts to revise legal instruments and laws in Switzerland have been strongly disputed and criticised in the last years. Even if "most internet users are concerned about security," according to a 2010 survey on internet use conducted by the Federal Statistical Office (FSO), the proposed law revisions seem to be inappropriate and do not find approval from civil society organisations and the business sector.[3]

The proposed revision of the Federal Act on Measures for Safeguarding National Security (BWIS)[4] wants to introduce new preventive security measures, but was rejected by Parliament in spring 2009. One of the main concerns is the suggested surveillance of non-public spaces. From a human rights viewpoint, a thorough assessment of legally protected interests as well as of the concept of freedom versus security is needed.[5] The process of revision is still ongoing and will not be completed until the end of 2012.

Another law that is strongly contested is the Revision of the Federal Act on the Surveillance of Post and Telecommunications (BÜPF). The Federal Department of Justice and Police argues that the act "needs to be adapted to new technological developments, including the Internet" and related communication tools.[6] In the BÜPF consultation, from May to September 2010, the official language sounds merely technical, and avoids stating any political implications. Government officials just promise: "Not more but better surveillance."[7]

1 UN Committee on Economic, Social and Cultural Rights, Concluding observations of the Committee on Economic, Social and Cultural Rights, Switzerland, 26 November 2010; UN Human Rights Committee, Concluding observations of the Human Rights Committee, Switzerland, 3 November 2009. www.unhcr.org/refworld/country,,HRC,,CHE,4562d8b62,4afbda552,0.html; Internet should remain as open as possible – UN expert on freedom of expression, Press Releases, Special Rapporteur on freedom of expression, June 2011. www.ohchr.org/en/NewsEvents/Pages/DisplayNews.aspx?NewsID=11108&LangID=E

2 Reporters without Borders (2010) 2010 World Press Freedom Index. www.reporter-ohne-grenzen.de/fileadmin/rte/docs/2010/101019_Europa_GB.pdf

3 Omnibus 2010 Survey on Internet Use conducted by the Federal Statistical Office (FSO), February 2011. www.admin.ch/aktuell/00089/index.html?lang=en&msg-id=37540

4 Please note that English is not an official language of the Swiss Confederation. The legal and other translations provided here are not necessarily "official" translations and therefore have no legal force.

5 Zusatzbotschaft und Entwurf für die Änderung des Bundesgesetzes über Massnahmen zur Wahrung der inneren Sicherheit, press release, October 2010. www.vbs.admin.ch/internet/vbs/de/home/documentation/news/news_detail.35915.nsb.html; Staatsschutz in Lightversion – Wichtige Punkte werden später geregelt, humanrights, Focus Switzerland (Update: 08.11.2010). www.humanrights.ch/de/Schweiz/Inneres/Person/Sicherheit/idart_8257-content.html?zur=827

6 „Ablehnende Stellungnahme zum Entwurf BWIS II", press release, 29 September 2006. www.humanrights.ch/de/Schweiz/Inneres/Person/Sicherheit/idart_4576-content.html

7 Überwachung des Fernmeldeverkehrs an die technische Entwicklung anpassen, Vernehmlassung zur Änderung des BÜPF eröffnet, press release EJPD, 19 May 2010. www.ejpd.admin.ch/content/ejpd/de/home/dokumentation/mi/2010/2010-05-19.html

Broad-scale surveillance widely contested

Over the last years the legal instruments and options to increase state surveillance were systematically extended in Switzerland – by the two legislative revisions mentioned, and through other laws still pending. The official tapping of phone lines and computers, wiretapping of private spaces or the use of other surveillance methods are, according to various civil and human rights organisations and networks, "violating several basic rights granted by the constitution and are not appropriate under rule of law considerations."[8] A spokesperson for the Swiss Pirate Party recently said: "[There] are many little steps that we accept in the name of security. But suddenly we have a surveillance state."[9]

State security forces are permitted to stake out people in public and generally accessible spaces, including using cameras and bugging devices. But the private sphere has been legally protected since the Secret Files Scandal which shocked the public in 1989.[10] Following this, the Federal Court affirmed that measures by security forces interfering in the private sphere needed a judicial writ.[11]

According to the proposed BÜPF law, internet service providers (ISPs) are forced to upgrade their surveillance and storage capacities to completely control broadband internet communication – in real time. This enables a systematic surveillance of any surfing behaviour of internet users in the country. The technology and devices for surveillance upgrades on behalf of state security must be paid for by the service providers themselves. According to some, the cost could amount to anything from half a million to more than one million Swiss francs, depending on the size of the access provider. The usual compensation for these sorts of collaborative efforts and services will not be given under the new law. Observers predict that most of the 650 ISPs in Switzerland will not be able to afford costly upgrades like this and – except for the bigger market players – will have to close down.[12]

8 „Ablehnende Stellungnahme zum Entwurf BWIS II", press release, 29 September 2006. www.humanrights.ch/de/Schweiz/Inneres/Person/Sicherheit/idart_4576-content.html

9 „Überwachungswahn der Beamten in Bern", Tagesanzeiger, 19 August 2010. www.tagesanzeiger.ch/digital/internet/berwachungswahn-der-Beamten-in-Bern/story/12403271

10 Wikipedia, Secret Files Scandal. en.wikipedia.org/wiki/Secret_files_scandal

11 „Unter Druck der Amerikaner", Interview „Der Bund", April 2006. www.humanrights.ch/upload/pdf/060218_bund_staatsschutz_weber.pdf

12 Spitzel im Netz, Handelszeitung, 14 July 2011. www.handelszeitung.ch/unternehmen/spitzel-im-netz

Federal department pushed to explain

In the first round of the usual consultations on new laws[13] between May and September 2010 the proposed BÜPF revisions were harshly criticised by most stakeholders from the business sector and civil society. The strongest concern was raised about the intended installation of Trojan horses on computers of suspects and the lengthening of the current data retention period from six to twelve months. (Under the contested data retention rules, ISPs are obliged to store comprehensive customer data to be delivered to security forces on demand). Another bone of contention is a new broad definition of "access providers", including all sorts of internet-related services. The broad resistance from various parts of society – including the right-wing Swiss Peoples Party (SVP/UDC), usually at the law and order front – caused some delays in the legislative procedure and pushed the Federal Department of Justice and Police into a crisis where they needed to explain their motives. Since the end of the consultation period, almost a year ago, there has been a remarkable silence.

Until recently: in early June 2011, the Federal Department of Justice and Police launched another consultation regarding a part-revision of the Ordinance on the Surveillance of Post and Telecommunications (VÜPF).[14] Observers are surprised that the Ordinance suddenly needs to be revised before the respective federal law (BÜPF) is passed – it normally happens the other way round. One of the official arguments for the hurry is that the Ordinance will allow Switzerland to sign the Council of Europe's Cybercrime Convention at the beginning of 2012. But critics surmise that an accelerated revision of the Ordinance may circumvent the legislative power of the Parliament without creating the required legislative basis for any new surveillance laws. And the recent VÜPF proposal still includes many of the strongly contested measures from the BÜPF: comprehensive state surveillance of internet traffic, lacking limits of monitoring options and areas, as well as too vaguely defined legitimate targets for surveillance (not only very serious crime or terrorism, as some suggest). The protection of privacy has also not been considered properly.[15] This has pushed some in the Swiss media to ask for a "pause for reflection."[16]

13 Vernehmlassungen, Swiss Confederation website. www.admin.ch/dokumentation/gesetz/pc/index.html?lang=de

14 Revision des BÜPF und der VÜPF, Federal Department of Justice and Police website, August 2011. www.ejpd.admin.ch/content/ejpd/de/home/dokumentation/info/2011/2011-08-120.html

15 Spitzel im Netz, Handelszeitung, 14 July 2011. www.handelszeitung.ch/unternehmen/spitzel-im-netz

16 Überwachung, Eine Denkpause ist nötig, Handelszeitung, 14 July 2011 (not available online).

Substantial privacy concerns

In his proposal regarding the BÜPF revision, the Federal Data Protection and Information Commissioner (FDPIC) found fault with the "too openly defined field of application of the law." Furthermore, the FDPIC considers the intended catalogue of criminal offences, in the Code of Criminal Procedure (StPO), as "too comprehensive regarding the placement of Trojan horses on computers and smartphones" because this offers "massive interference with the private life of people concerned." Besides telecommunications, all data on the computer, including private and personal data, can be monitored after the installation of the surveillance programmes. These concerns were not taken into consideration in the BÜPF consultation draft.

The draft law provides access to the information of monitored persons but not for their spouses or communication partners who are not part of the criminal procedure, but were affected by the surveillance and data storage. In his statement the Commissioner further referred to the German Constitutional Court judgement that data retention should be allowed only under certain conditions. In view of this, the planned prolongation of the data retention period to twelve months in Switzerland should be reassessed under aspects of proportionality.[17] According to other official sources, such as the Federal Department of Justice and Police, around 50 internet surveillances have been conducted against criminal organisations (involved in crimes such as blackmailing and money laundering) over the last years.[18] This figure does not offer much evidence for the state's demand for the widespread upgrade of surveillance capacities of Swiss access providers.

The biggest player on the Swiss telecom market, Swisscom and its competitor Sunrise, recently successfully sued the Federal Department of Justice and Police. In its verdict the Federal Administration Court approved the refusal of the two telecom providers to monitor the mobile internet traffic of suspects in police investigations. Costly investments in special devices would be needed for this purpose. And the provisions in law for such forced investments are missing. How the internet may be monitored is also not specified in the draft law nor in the Ordinance. The state ordering the surveillance was therefore judged "unlawful".[19]

Since the revelation of a second Secret Files Scandal in summer 2010, and similar incidents, the confidence of the public in security forces has notably decreased. A Swiss daily paper, under the headline "The Secret Files Scandal – a story of lies and deception", said the recent scandal is "not only a story of over-zealous spies and sluggish controllers but a chronicle of lies and deception – from the secret service up to the Federal Council." Regarding the continuous revision of the Federal Act on Measures for Safeguarding National Security (BWIS), a parliamentarian and member of the Social Democratic Party announced that "our side will only give hand to it [support the new legislation], if strong control mechanisms are granted."[20] Until now security matters are usually ab/used to increase the power and impact of secret and security services and law enforcement agencies.

Conclusions: A question of credibility and proportionality

As in other European countries, state security and cyber crime continue to be raised as worrying issues in the media and in public opinion. Any social or security issue, such as child pornography or paedophilia, the lack of privacy awareness among social networks users, or other current irritations and abuses in the digital age, give ground to the proponents of all sorts of new laws and protections, and to those who argue for more power and control of society by security forces.

Generally, human and civil rights concerns are raised by the usual suspects, such as civil society organisations, trade unions and left-wing parties, and do not find much support in other political circles. In the case of the BÜPF and VÜPF revisions, a broad alliance of different stakeholders in Swiss society has already shown resistance against the new surveillance laws. The row of unusual suspects ranges from access providers, various business associations and the right-wing Swiss People's Party (the Christian Democratic People's Party and the Liberal Party announced themselves indifferent in this matter). Swiss telecom and access providers almost unanimously refuse to be (mis)used as deputy sheriffs for state prosecutions. This broad political concern and alliance offer reason for hope that the planned surveillance act may not be applied.

17 FDPIC proposal on the revision of the BÜPF, 18th Annual Report 2010-11, point 1.4.9, June 2011. www.edoeb.admin.ch/dokumentation/00445/00509/01732/01753/index.html?lang=de

18 Swisscom kritisiert Schnüffelaufträge, Handelszeitung, 13 July 2011. www.handelszeitung.ch/unternehmen/swisscom-kritisiert-schnueffelauftraege

19 Swisscom kritisiert Schnüffelaufträge, Handelszeitung, 13 July 2011. www.handelszeitung.ch/unternehmen/swisscom-kritisiert-schnueffelauftraege

20 Die Fichenaffäre – eine Geschichte von Lug und Trug, Tagesanzeiger, 5 July 2010. www.tagesanzeiger.ch/schweiz/standard/Die-Fichen affaere--eine-Geschichte-von-Lug-und-Trug/story/16223362

The analysis of the Swiss human and civil rights situation in the information society shows that the country may be among the best candidates in terms of freedom of expression and access and openness principles, but that all sorts of security concerns systematically violate basic citizen rights – as in many other European countries where human rights are said to be fundamental and respected.

Action steps

- If the BÜPF should pass the legislative chambers, civil society networks and business associations may consider calling for a referendum to stop this law, in line with the Swiss tradition of direct democracy. The chances for success are not evident, even considering a broader political alliance, but it will prolong the public discourse on state surveillance and security measures undermining fundamental rights.
- Strengthen parliamentarian and public control over any new security and surveillance laws including ordinances.
- Establish an independent national human rights institution that complies with the principles relating to the status of national institutions for the promotion and protection of human rights (Paris Principles and Recommendation 6, UN Committee on Economic, Social and Cultural Rights).
- Provide more human rights education to parliamentarians (in line with Recommendation 21, UN Committee on Economic, Social and Cultural Rights).
- Expunge Article 293 of the Swiss Criminal Code which threatens media and other people with punishment when quoting official sources defined as "confidential" and in doing so contradicts the Federal Open Government Act. ■

Links of stakeholders – civil society and business actors

Humanrights.ch (MERS), Focus Switzerland
www.humanrights.ch/de/Schweiz/Inneres/Person/Sicherheit/index.html

Amnesty International, Swiss section
www.amnesty.ch/en?set_language=en&cl=en

Grundrechte.ch www.grundrechte.ch

Demokratische Juristinnen und Juristen der Schweiz
www.djs-jds.ch

Swiss Privacy Foundation www.privacyfoundation.ch

Digitale Gesellschaft www.digitale-gesellschaft.ch

Digitale Allmend blog.allmend.ch

Swiss Internet User Group (SIUG) www.siug.ch

ICT Switzerland www.ictswitzerland.ch

Information Security Society Switzerland (ISSS)
www.isss.ch

Swiss Telecommunications Association (asut)
www.asut.ch/content/content_renderer.php

TANZANIA

JAMMING THE NEWS: TAKING THE STRUGGLE ONLINE

Collaboration on International ICT Policy for East and Southern Africa (CIPESA)
Lillian Nalwoga
www.cipesa.org

Introduction

Since independence, Tanzania, under the Chama Cha Mapinduzi (CCM) party, has enjoyed political stability and national unity more than other countries in a region wrecked by civil wars. However, the recent elections in October 2010 won by incumbent president Jakaya Kikwete saw CCM's popularity slide from 80.2% in the December 2005 elections[1] to 61.2% of the vote.[2] With this came a worrying intolerance for critical media both online and offline. A number of journalists have been intimidated and harassed by government officials for questioning the government's democratic credentials, while some political and social rallies and demonstrations have been repressed. To fight this new authoritarianism, some Tanzanians, including politicians,[3] have resorted to social media to express their views. However, the government has also been implicated in attempts to block websites and blogs whose content has been perceived as a threat.

To its credit, Tanzania's government has worked to boost the country's internet infrastructure. The national fibre-optic network currently under construction is set to cover all districts in the country by June 2012. Out of the 26 regions and 127 districts in the country, 19 regions and 59 districts have been connected to the network so far.[4] The Tanzania Communications Regulatory Authority (TCRA) reports that by June 2010 there were 4.8 million internet users and 19.5 million telephone subscribers from a population of 43.7 million.[5] Nonetheless, the low literacy levels, low levels of infrastructure rollout beyond major urban centres, and high access and usage costs still bar the wider majority of Tanzanians from the information society.

Policy and political background

At the policy level, the country has laws that seem to improve citizens' rights to information and freedom of expression. However, for the most part the same legislation gives with one hand and takes away with the other. Article 18 of the Tanzanian Constitution guarantees the right to freedom of expression and the right to seek, receive and impart information. But the constitution in semi-autonomous Zanzibar only gives citizens the right to receive information. It gives no rights to seek or impart it. These guarantees are also insufficiently implemented in Tanzanian domestic legislation. This is mainly witnessed in restrictive laws applied by the government that limit freedom of expression.

For example, in the Police Force and Auxiliary Police Act of 2002, Sections 43, 44, 45 and 46 provide a number of subjective unrestricted powers to police officers without laying down objective criteria for issuing stop orders when censoring information. Further, the National Security Act of 1970 gives the government absolute capacity to define what should be disclosed to or withheld from the public, and makes it a punishable offence to in any way investigate, obtain, possess, comment on, pass on or publish any document or information which the government considers to be classified. In addition, the 1976 Newspaper Act sets limitations on what public servants can reveal to the public.

Whereas the Electronic and Postal Communications Act of 2010[6] calls for the observation of the rights to freedom of expression and information, it has come under scrutiny for not being user friendly, as it focuses more on punishing offenders rather than exploring the possibilities and potential in the communications sector.[7]

1 Tanzania 2005 presidential election results: www.eisa.org.za/WEP/tan2005resultsa.html

2 National Electoral Commission: nec.go.tz/pdf/Presidentials.pdf

3 Tungaraza, J. N. (2011) Tanzania: Opposition MP Tweets His Arrest, *Global Voices*, 5 June. globalvoicesonline.org/2011/06/05/tanzania-opposition-mp-tweets-his-arrest

4 Saiboko, A. (2011) Kikwete: Fibre-optic network to cover all districts next year, *Daily News*, 25 May. www.dailynews.co.tz/home/?n=20151&cat=home

5 Tanzania Communications Regulatory Authority (2010) *Report on Internet and Data Services in Tanzania*. tcra.go.tz/display.php?type=headlines&code=46

6 The Electronic and Postal Communications Act was enacted to keep abreast with developments in the electronic communications industry, and provide for a comprehensive regulatory regime for electronic and postal communications services providers.

7 Media Council of Tanzania (2011) *Tanzania: State of the Media Report, 2010*. www.mct.or.tz/mediacouncil/index.php?option=com_phocadownload&view=category&download=27:state-of-the-media-report-2010&id=1:downloads&Itemid=867

Attempts to control social media...

Tanzania has seen an increase in online publishing. In a country where freedom of expression and association are being suppressed, internet users have resorted to searching for information from other media such as the internet. Because of this, the Tanzanian government has been accused of blocking websites and blogs it has perceived as a threat.

One such website is JamiiForums.com, which has become a target for the Tanzanian government. The website publishes and discusses topics ranging from politics and economics to societal issues in Tanzania and beyond. On average, over 20,000 people visit the forums daily and spend at least seventeen minutes browsing at least eleven pages per person. The membership registration increases at a rate of 25% every month. Currently there are about 40,000 registered members.[8] This makes JamiiForums one of the most popular and vibrant websites in Tanzania.

However, on a number of occasions, the forum has come under attack by the government over allegations that it was working to "undermine" the ruling party and the government. In April 2011 the forum's hosts reacted with a press release reassuring their members that the government allegations were intended to threaten and deter the online community from exercising their freedom of speech and association.[9] The forum's hosts have also, on a number of occasions, been interrogated by the authorities over content that irked the government. In a recent British Broadcasting Corporation (BCC) article, it was reported that the government is cloning the JamiiForums website in an attempt to control content produced on that website.[10] Although the government has not come out and admitted this new allegation, it is believed that it is now trying to institute a mechanism through which content on social media sites can be controlled or even censored, as seen in China.[11] Evidence of this is in the proposed Information and Broadcasting Policy 2007, currently under review, which will require everyone wishing to establish blogs or websites to register with the registrar of companies and also get a licence from the TCRA.[12] However, this policy has not been welcomed by media activists, who have proposed a number of recommendations including removal of the proposition on the internet, noting that that the internet cannot be treated in the same manner as radio and television broadcasters.

Print media has not been spared in the government crackdown. Local newspapers have come under constant attack for allegedly publishing articles critical of the government.[13] A crackdown on opposition demonstrations has also seen freedom of expression and association come under attack. Demonstrators have faced resistance from police and government when they have attempted to exercise their rights to protest.[14]

An increase in internet penetration from 5% in 2005 to 11% in June 2010 in Tanzania indicates a gradual increase in internet usage. This increase may be attributed to the proliferation of mobile phones in the country, which allows citizens to access mobile internet anywhere. Political activists, civil society organisations and journalists are using the internet to voice their concerns, and to reach a wide range of citizens. Organisations like Article 19, the Media Council of Tanzania (MCT), the Tanzania Media Women's Association (TAMWA) and Daraja are using online platforms to urge citizens to hold the government accountable.

In cases of biased reporting from government-owned media outlets, they have served as alternative news sources, capturing actual events as they happened. This was the case when it came to the Gongo la Mboto blasts.[15] The blasts killed over 20 people and injured at least 184 in the Dar es Salaam army base, but army officials declined to discuss the cause of the blasts. As a result, netizens captured events of the blasts by uploading and sharing photos of victims.[16] Soon, stories about the blasts were all over the internet providing an opportunity for Tanzanians in the diaspora to follow the events. Tanzanian tweets were able to share

8 JamiiForums, where we dare to talk openly: www.jamiiforums.com/index.php

9 JamiiForums (2011) Tanzania's Ruling Party threatens online social media, *Fikra Pevu*, 19 April. www.fikrapevu.com/habari/political-paranoia-tanzanias-ruling-party-in-fear-of-online-social-media

10 Allen, K. (2011) African jitters over blogs and social media, *BBC News*, 18 June. www.bbc.co.uk/news/world-africa-13786143#story_continues_1

11 Internet censorship in the People's Republic of China: en.wikipedia.org/wiki/Internet_censorship_in_the_People%27s_Republic_of_China

12 The proposed policy seeks to amend the 2003 Information and Broadcasting Policy and aims at, among other things, prohibiting ownership of more than one type of media outlet.

13 Media Council of Tanzania (n.d.) MCT condemns newspaper ban. www.mct.or.tz/index.php?option=com_content&task=view&id=120&Itemid=1

14 AFP (2010) Tanzania police break up demonstration, *News24*, 28 December. www.news24.com/Africa/News/Tanzania-police-break-up-demonstration-20101228

15 Simbadeo (2011) Gongo la Mboto bomb blasts... a glimpse. simbadeo.wordpress.com/2011/02/17/gongo-la-mboto-bomb-blasts-a-glimpse

16 Macha, N. (2011) Tanzania: Netizens comment on bomb explosions at army base, *Global Voices*, 18 February. globalvoicesonline.org/2011/02/18/tanzania-netizens-comment-on-bomb-explosions-at-army-base

information about the possible causes of the blast while calling on the government to investigate. Other netizens felt that the government had learnt nothing from the 2009 Mbagala bomb blasts[17] and that it had failed to fulfil the promises of moving the camp to a non-residential area. One blogger expressed his dissatisfaction, wondering why after two years since the Mbagala blasts, when residents went through the same experience, there was nothing done to prevent its reoccurrence.[18] As the discussions and criticisms developed, netizens demanded the resignation of the minister of defence, a call that was welcomed by the country's opposition, who also called for his immediate resignation.[19] The cause of the bomb blasts has not been established, as such information of a military nature is considered "classified information" by the government. To date only speculations have been made as to the possible causes of the bombs.

Conclusions

As the Tanzanian government continues to limit access to news by jamming and inhibiting independent voices in papers, new internet-based media are enabling citizens to find alternative means of mobilising, publishing, resisting, and accessing information. The relative safety of the online world compared to physical demonstrations and print journalism are all emboldening citizens and civil society groups to take their clamour for better governance into the virtual world. And, without a doubt, the Tanzanian government is listening, and is convinced about the power of internet activism, which is why it has been attempting to block the use of online forums such as JamiiForums.

The government needs to make information accessible to the public, as this will make it more transparent and accountable. A failure to do so will prompt citizens to seek alternative means to exercise their democratic rights, to air their opinions freely and fairly. The mere blocking of communication media and interrogating or persecuting citizens will only make them invent new means to express their concerns. The era of controlling what information should be made available to the public is no more. The public will continue to invent new means to make themselves heard, and at any cost.

Action steps

- Research citizens' perceptions on the use of information and communications technologies (ICTs), especially social media tools for social resistance. ICT activists need to better understand knowledge, attitudes and perceptions in the use of ICTs for social resistance. This will help to understand how best to involve users in exercising their rights to free speech.
- Create awareness about the use and existence of ICT tools for citizen participation.
- In terms of policy advocacy, ICT activists need to engage the government in reviewing policies and laws that seem to negate freedom of expression and access to information. Advocacy campaigns calling for the promotion of affordable access to ICTs will also reduce challenges associated with accessing ICTs, while improving access to information. ■

17 BBC (2009) Deadly blasts rock Tanzanian city, *BBC News*, 29 April 2009. news.bbc.co.uk/2/hi/africa/8024656.stm

18 Bongo Blast (2011) Of Dar bomb blasts and Mbagala lesson that never was, 23 March. symeniah.blogspot.com/2011/03/of-dar-bomb-blasts-and-mbagala-lesson.html

19 Kilyinga, N. (2011) Opposition wants Mwinyi to resign, *Daily News*, 18 February. dailynews.co.tz/bunge/?n=17355

THAILAND

WALLS OF FAME, WITCH HUNTS, AND THE POWER OF THE CROWD...

Thai Netizen Network
Arthit Suriyawongkul
thainetizen.org

Introduction

Better access to information using information and communications technologies (ICTs) results in an optimistic vision of civil society where informed citizens decide rationally, voices of minorities get heard, and individuals collectively move towards democracy. Cases from Thailand in 2010 show another side. Participatory online platforms went against the participatory democratic culture and violated human rights.

A large number of the cases presented here occurred during the massive anti-government protests by the so-called "Red Shirts" in Bangkok and other major cities between March and May 2010, including two crackdowns, which led to at least 92 casualties. Observations, interviews and group discussions were conducted between March 2010 and May 2011. Informants are internet users aged 22 to 35, journalists, scholars and activists, including one key figure of the post-May 2010 Red Shirts movement.

The internet penetration rate in Thailand is 33%. The number of internet users is estimated to be 21.14 million, up 15.5% from a year before. The number of broadband users is 2.47 million, up 22.87% (figures as of October 2010).[1] Facebook accounts number about 9.43 million, with 86.91% registering the Bangkok metropolitan area as the place where they live (as of May 2011).

From 2007 to 2010, 74,686 urls were officially blocked, using the 2007 Computer-related Crime Act,[2] with *lèse majesté* (offending the monarchy) given as the main reason (76.76%); 185 legal cases were filed, with defamation, fraudulent content and *lèse majesté* as the top three offences.[3] There were more urls blocked using other laws (such as the Emergency Decree)[4] or using non-official means.

Policy and political background

After the 1992 Black May[5] crackdown, military popularity dropped drastically. Social movements pushed for a "People's Constitution", which was adopted in 1997. The importance of an independent media was promoted. Media reform legislation was passed, including the reallocation of airwaves, which were to be taken back from the government and military (however, this aspect is still not realised).

In the 2001 and 2005 general elections, the Thai Rak Thai Party, headed by telecoms tycoon Thaksin Shinawatra, won historic landslide victories. However, the government was reportedly involved in activities that inappropriately influenced the media, directly and indirectly, through the Thaksin telecoms conglomerate. Because of this, civil society turned to alternatives, such as the internet.[6] Cable TV, online newspapers, web forums and blogs played a significant role in a 2005-2006 anti-Thaksin campaign, led by the People's Alliance for Democracy (PAD), later known as the "Yellow Shirts".[7]

This resulted in a military coup in 2006. Online blogs and forums opposing the coup emerged. As a result, the 2007 Computer-related Crime Act was the first law passed by the military-appointed legislative assembly, imposing liabilities on intermediaries and creating an atmosphere of fear and self-censorship. Digital media users were arrested in line with the Act, often in conjunction with the *lèse majesté* law. Low-power radio broadcasters were also suppressed.[8]

1 Thai Netizen Network (2010) *Thailand Internet Liberty Report 2010*, Thai Netizen Network, Bangkok. thainetizen.org/node/2640

2 Computer-related Crime Act, BE 2550 (2007), available at: thainetizen.org/node/421

3 iLaw (2010) *Situational Report on Control and Censorship of Online Media through the Use of Laws and the Imposition of Thai State Policies*, iLaw Project, Bangkok. ilaw.or.th/node/632

4 Emergency Decree on Public Administration in Emergency Situation, BE 2548 (2005), available at: en.wikisource.org/wiki/Emergency_Decree_on_Public_Administration_in_Emergency_Situation,_BE_2548_(2005)

5 The 17-20 May 1992 popular protests in Bangkok against the post-coup government and the bloody military crackdown that followed. Up to 200,000 people demonstrated in central Bangkok at the height of the protests.

6 For more details see Daorueng, P. (2004) Thai Civil Society and Government Control: A Cyber Struggle?, in Gan, S. (ed) *Asian Cyberactivism: Freedom of Expression and Media Censorship*, Freidrich Naumann Foundation, Bangkok, p. 406-440.

7 For more information see Chaisukkosol, C. (2010) The Internet & Nonviolent Struggle: The anti-government movement in Thailand 2005-06, *Social Alternatives* (3), September.

8 Wilailert, S. (2010) *Where thinking differently is a crime: Report of community radio intervention during political conflict situation*, Campaign for Popular Media Reform, Bangkok. thainetizen.org/node/2639

Parts of the "anti-coup" movement developed into what is known today as the Red Shirts movement. The movement included the larger United Front for Democracy Against Dictatorship (UDD) and the smaller Red Siam factions.

Campaigning online: From walls of fame to witch hunts...

Early political campaigns on online social network sites aimed at creating campaign identities. For example, in 2008 NoCoup.org ran a "Bored of PAD Mob" campaign, distributing one million stickers offline and asking supporters to use the campaign logo as their hi5 or MSN Messenger avatar.

Twitter was introduced in Thailand in 2008, but it was only in July 2009 that the wider public really got to know about it. At the time, a number of Twitter accounts of figures in Thai politics were entered into a Twitter Wall of Fame competition. Anyone could propose any Twitter account as a candidate for Mr/Ms Twitter, and everybody could vote as many times as they wanted. @Thaksinlive, Thaksin's Twitter account, was also proposed. As a key political figure, anything about him hits the mainstream media. Lots of internet users flocked to vote, either for Thaksin or someone else to push him out of the top position. There was a case of a user who had not used the internet before, but who showed an interest in using Twitter and voting for Thaksin.[9] People mobilised, calling for support and organising strategic votes. In the end, @Thaksinlive came second place. The winner was @peterfacinelli – the account of United States (US) actor Peter Facinelli of *Twilight* fame. @chaturon, the account for a former secretary-general of the Thai Rak Thai party, came third. Fourth to seventh places were all Thais, and many of them could be identified as Red Shirts from their red-coloured avatars.[10] The competition recognised this phenomenon in its analysis of the results: "This was a tough competition because [Facinelli's] fans were taking on a political voting battle with a large section of the population of Thailand expressing support for Thaksin Shinawatra, the exiled Prime Minister."[11]

In 2009, the availability of a Thai-language user interface, and the emergence of social games like FarmVille, contributed to the popularity of Facebook among Thai users. In 2010, politics was a new driver. About 500,000 users joined Facebook in six weeks between two crackdowns.[12] While we cannot say that the political situation was a major contribution to the growth of Thailand's Facebook users, we cannot deny that it drove up the number of posts to Facebook pages. Some people had Facebook accounts long before the protests, but became more active because of them. They posted links to local and international news on the protests and video clips of current and past demonstrations, annotated with their own comments.

Facebook groups and fan pages have been created to show support for political causes. Political campaigning was here again, with at least 70 different avatars created by groups of varying ideologies during different periods of the protests.[13] A very common phrase used in these campaigns was "Confident that over one million Thais...", found in statements like: "Confident that over one million Thais are against the dissolution [of the government]"; "Confident that over one million Thais are so irritated with politics"; and – poking fun at the campaigns – "Confident that over one million Thais can't distinguished between basil and sweet basil".

Some avatars were printed as stickers, and could be seen on public benches and elsewhere. On 18 April 2010, a demonstration of 2,000 "Multicoloured Shirts" took place at the Victory Monument in Bangkok. Most of them were fans of a pro-government Facebook page and members of the group "Civilian Volunteers to Protect the Motherland". They sang the national anthem and the royal anthem, and carried banners with phrases including, "Stop protesting, we want to live our normal life" and "We provide moral support to the troops". They also chanted in unison, "We love the king, we love the country".[14]

This was exactly what many Thais were doing online: posting patriotic songs and speeches to YouTube – including a speech by actor Pongpat Wachirabanjong: "If you hate father,[15] if you no longer love him, then leave. Because this house belongs to the father." Sites expressed frustration with the protests, showing support for the government's crackdown. Many Thais linked the Red Shirts with the anti-monarchy movements.

9 www.ipattt.com/2009/twitter-thaksinlive

10 www.ipattt.com/2009/thaksinlive-peterfacinelli

11 j.mp/ipattt-twitter-world

12 Russell, J. (2010) Politics Drives Record Facebook Growth In Thailand, *Asian Correspondent*, 26 April. asiancorrespondent.com/jon-russell/2010/04/26/politics-driving-record-facebook-growth-in-thailand; Russell, J. (2010) Politics Drives Facebook Membership In Thailand Past 3 Million Mark, *Asian Correspondent*, 21 May. asiancorrespondent.com/jon-russell/2010/05/21/politics-drives-facebook-membership-in-thailand-past-3-million-mark

13 www.fringer.org/?p=475

14 The Nation (2010) Another multicoloured mass rally held at Victory Monument, *The Nation*, 18 April. www.nationmultimedia.com/home/2010/04/18/politics/Another-multicoloured-mass-rally-held-at-Victory-M-30127351.html

15 The word "father" here is interpreted as "the King", the father of all Thais.

What can be called a "digital witch hunt" then emerged, as users began hunting down those who were against the monarchy, spearheaded by online collectives such as the Social Sanction: SS[16] and Rachanorarag[17] Facebook fan pages. The personal data of victims, including their home addresses and phone numbers, were posted online. One person was even physically threatened, as the groups tracked down with reasonable accuracy – within a one-kilometre radius – where she lived (probably using social media), and offered a cash bounty to anyone who would "surprise" her at home.

A more prominent case involved the singer Withawat Thaokhamlue, widely known as "Mark V11", who was participating in the popular Academy Fantasia singing contest. A group called "Confident that over one million Thais are against Mark V11" was created around July 2010, prompted by controversial messages being posted to Withawat's Facebook profile page. The media reported that he had criticised then-Prime Minister Abhisit Vejjajiva,[18] but internet users found that he had also posted a message that read, "Remove the picture that every house has",[19] referring to an image of the current king. Due to public anger, Withawat had to quit the contest and left the country.

The Ministry of Information and Communication Technology operates a 24-hour hotline for reporting "inappropriate websites". In July 2010, the ICT Ministry and the Ministry of Education launched the Internet Scout Capacity Building project, widely known as Cyber Scout, to train students to search websites: "If they find good content about the King's activities, speeches, or his virtue, they will post this content to websites that contain messages that insult the King." It is expected to help build a "King-loving consciousness" amongst the youth.[20] The Cyber Scout group on Dek-D.com[21] shows the king's image in Scout dress very prominently at the top of the page, followed by the words: "The rules of Boy Scouts make it very explicit that 'I will do my best to do my duty to God, the King and my Country.' Therefore, the Boy Scout is part of the Nation and defends the Monarchy."[22] The ministry had spent 1.9 million baht between June and September and will allocate a further 578 million baht to train 100,000 Cyber Scouts in around 1,000 community ICT centres.[23]

As a consequence, a number of Thai users have since changed their behaviour on Facebook to avoid possible attacks. Users have changed their names to pseudonyms, limited their profile visibility, cancelled their accounts, or created new ones that are shared only among close friends with similar political views.

During the March-May 2010 protests and crackdowns, a large number of video clips were posted online by people who were in the field, many taken using mobile phones (sometimes posting these clips was interrupted when mobile phone signals in areas were shut down). Information, including videos, was selectively used and circulated by both sides – pro-Reds and anti-Reds – to support their arguments. At that time, the Centre for the Resolution of Emergency Situations (CRES) had full control over TV stations. Every evening CRES ran a "daily update" programme on TV, in addition to regular breaking news slots during the day. The video clips gradually became the main feature of the updates. A CRES spokesperson curated the clips, giving explanations for each of them. Clips that indicated possible violence by Red Shirts were rerun, often freeze-framed so that violence could be pointed out.[24] Controversial clips were also aired, but with explanations of the "truth" and why rumours were just misunderstandings or were from distorted sources.[25] After the broadcasting of these clips each day, debates erupted on social network sites, together with links to the online video clips that had just been seen on TV.

In October 2010, another set of video clips were shared widely. They were a series of video clips showing Constitutional Court members meeting in a restaurant with a Democrat Party member and discussing the court case involving the dissolution of the Democrat Party.[26] Unlike the CRES clips, there were not shown on television. The government warned that the dissemination of the videos could violate the law. All downloads of the clips were blocked, simply by the government asking internet service providers (ISPs) for their "cooperation". This meant that obtaining a court order to prevent the airing of the video clips was unnecessary. The government has influence over ISPs because it can terminate telecommunication operator licences. Two of the biggest internet

16 www.facebook.com/SocialSanction

17 www.facebook.com/Rachanorarag

18 Pandey, D. (2010) Political battles go online, *Bangkok Post*, 1 August. www.bangkokpost.com/tech/techscoop/188908/political-battles-go-online

19 www.boringdays.net/mark-thaokhamlue-v11

20 www.manager.co.th/Cyberbiz/ViewNews.aspx?NewsID=9530000095980

21 Dek-D.com is the largest student community site. Among all website categories, it ranked fourth in 2009. group.dek-d.com/cyberscout

22 The Village Scouts, under the patronage of the royal family, played a significant role in the massacre of 6 October 1976, in which a large number of left-wing activists and students lost their lives.

23 tewson.com/cyber-scout

24 For example, see: video.mthai.com/player.php?id=6M1274155740M0

25 For example, see: youtu.be/7qKkhC9AEIc (a CRES announcement after the 10 April 2010 crackdown)

26 youtu.be/iP4r-1isXJs; youtu.be/4mDnFau3UUQ; youtu.be/bWQ9xT71sSU; www.youtube.com/ohmygod3009

international gateways for Thailand are also operated by "public companies" which are 100% owned by the government.

Conclusion

Governments now recognise the power of the crowd. With their control of funding, infrastructure and dominant ideology, they have more resources to draw on than political dissidents.

New media have changed the media landscape and modes of news production. Social media and online video clips play important roles in national politics. Nonetheless, traditional media still play a dominant role, setting the public agenda. Without the support of the mainstream media, stories from citizen reporters hardly find their way to a wider public.

Without the decentralisation of content gatekeeping, especially for broadcasting, and decentralised ownership of telecommunications and internet infrastructure, new media, which structurally still depend on traditional media, will have a very limited ability to challenge the status quo in the political sphere.

In the special situation where the power to produce new media meets the very limited freedom to broadcast, people in the street can keep control of the narrative that is fed into public discourse. Ownership of communication infrastructure is crucial. Citizen reporters in times of emergency, like during a crackdown, cannot rely on state-controlled infrastructure.

More capacity and freedom of media production do not automatically mean more freedom to express thoughts in public. More capacity to collaborate and gather information online can be used to harm individual human rights.

Action steps

- Citizen media ownership needs to be campaigned for and realised.
- At a local level, affordable and self-sustained technologies like low-power radio, open source GSM networks, mesh internet networks and mobile power generators need to be explored more by activists. Social activists and journalists need to work more with technologists and "hackers".
- When it comes to media literacy training, do not train only in the use of tools, but also in storytelling.
- There is lots of creativity online: try to connect this with people on the ground. After the crackdowns, Sombat Boonngamanong of Red Sunday (an initiative within the Red Shirts movement) developed a collaborative approach which turned out to be very successful. He posted ideas for gathering in fun and creative ways on Facebook and Twitter, and people then joined the conversations and helped organise the events. As people working online felt more involved and the activities looked fun, they began joining in the "offline" gatherings. This worked both ways – videos and photos of the gatherings were shared on social media sites. This kind of interaction brings more people to the movement. Red Sunday managed to reach 10,000 people on the streets within a few months, even during the state of emergency.[27]
- Finally, foreign governments and international NGOs should review their grants carefully if in the end the grants may be used for counter-democratic movements. This was the case of community IT centres used for Cyber Scout training. ■

27 Fuller, T. and Mydans, S. (2010) Protesters Return to Bangkok Streets, *The New York Times*, 19 September. www.nytimes.com/2010/09/20/world/asia/20thai.html

TUNISIA

THE INTERNET: CATALYSING A LEADERLESS REVOLUTION

Arab World Internet Institute
Khaled Koubaa
www.aw2i.org

Introduction

Since December 2010 Tunisia has experienced an unprecedented and spontaneous wave of protests, fuelled by a persistent lack of freedom of expression, anger over governance corruption issues, and mounting frustration over unemployment and social exclusion. These countrywide protests led to the toppling of the regime and the ousting of Tunisia's second president, Zine El Abidine Ben Ali, on 14 January 2011 after 23 years in power. His departure into exile in Saudi Arabia has not calmed the violence as demonstrations and resistance continue on the streets, and on social networks. The political outlook has been positively impacted by the revolution. An interim president and government have been established, different high commissions responsible for protecting the revolution appointed and various reforms initiated.

This social resistance was buoyed by pictures posted on Facebook, flashed on Twitter and published on blogs and other online forums. This gave the revolution different names: the "Internet Revolution", "Twitter Revolution" or "Jasmine Revolution"; but regardless of the name, Tunisian youth demonstrated the important and critical role that the internet and social media play in struggles for freedom and for human rights today.

Policy and political background

Tunisia has an impressive political history: slavery was abolished in 1848, a Constitution established in 1861, polygamy abolished in 1956, abortion legalised in 1973, a Human Rights League established in 1977. Of the Arab countries, these qualified her as the one nearest to democracy.

The first president, Habib Bourguiba, went to great lengths to build the country by investing in education and health, but without being able to deepen democracy in the country. On 7 November 1987, Zine El Abidine Ben Ali, just nominated prime minister, ousted Bourguiba in a bloodless coup, while promising that there would be "*no* presidency for life".

Ben Ali was the darling of the Western countries and considered the trusted leader who would maintain Tunisia's pro-Western policies and keep the country away from the extremism found in its larger neighbours: Libya and Algeria.

But the reality was different, and Ben Ali began consolidating his rule by restraining the opposition, and taking control of the media and armed forces. In 1999 he organised Tunisia's first multi-candidate presidential election and won it with 99.44% of the vote. A constitutional referendum in 2002 amended the upper age limit for a presidential candidate to 75 years of age, to give him the ability to run for a fifth term in 2009. He won with 89% of the vote.

Under his regime, Tunisia became known as one of the most restrictive countries with a poor human rights record, including the imprisonment of opinion leaders, the surveillance of websites, emails and other internet activities, the restriction of freedom of association, and the harassment and intimidation of cyber activists.

The internet as a catalyst to change...

One of the clearest signs of social resistance in Tunisia was the revolt in Redeyef in 2008, in the mining area of Gafsa in the centre of the country. This was brutally crushed by police, and no news went out other than a few videos published online – on the video platform YouTube, which had already been blocked by authorities. A small number of activists and journalists tried to unveil what happened but they were imprisoned and harassed by Ben Ali's regime.

Cyber activists had already been hard hit by the death in 2005 of Zouhair Yahyaoui, one of the first people to denounce human rights violations on his website TuneZine. Moreover, the release of WikiLeaks cables had made citizens more aware of the corruption of the regime, in particularly Ben Ali's family.

Other incidents also showed signs of brewing social unrest: the death of Abdesselem Trimeche in April 2010 in Monastir, and Chamseddine El Hani in November 2010 in Metlaoui – both immolated themselves. Neither case was covered by the media, other than some information and videos posted on social websites. Similarly, clashes between police and protesters in the southern Tunisian region of Ben Guerdane in August 2010 were lightly reported by the media.

On the morning of 17 December, Mohamed Bouazizi, a 26-year-old vegetable trader, immolated himself after a municipal inspector tried to confiscate his merchandise. That afternoon, Ali Bouazizi – a cousin of Mohamed Bouazizi – uploaded a video on Facebook of the first protest, just in front of the Sidi Bouzid governorate, a few metres from the place where his cousin had immolated himself.

The same day Al Jazeera news downloaded the video of the protest from Facebook and broadcasted it on Al Jazeera Mubasher.

Unlike the Green Revolution in Iran in 2009, Tunisian activists used social media tools effectively by capturing and uploading videos on Facebook and sharing them on Twitter – but the heart of the protests lay in the organised and violent protests in different towns in the country.

Unlike Mubarak, who shut down the internet for five days in Egypt, Ben Ali was counting on his legendary oppressive structure and the self-censorship from his citizens that he was used to dealing with. This structure was – unfortunately for him – not able or prepared to respond to the rapid dissemination of information using new social media.

Cyber activists were the first on the scene, documenting and sharing news of the protests; but by the first week of January, millions of internet users became more and more active, reacting to what was happening each day and night in Kasserine, Thala, Menzel and Bouzaian; and to the very repressive police reaction that they witnessed.

Tunisian citizens were also able to follow information reported by international TV channels (Al Jazeera, France 24, Al Arabiya, etc.), which were broadcasting videos and information reported by normal citizens and activists on the ground. The state-owned TV7 – named after 7 November 1987 when Ben Ali secured power through his putsch – continued to ignore the growing social uprising.

Despite the censorship of almost all video and image-sharing platforms (e.g. YouTube, Dailymotion, Vimeo, Flickr), Tunisian protesters learned quickly how to use proxies, anonymisers and circumvention tools to share information on platforms like Facebook and Twitter – the hashtags #bouazizi and #sidibouzid reached a high-level trend worldwide.

The Tunisian authorities meanwhile tried every means possible to thwart the flow of information, which pushed the New York-based Committee to Protect Journalists to send an open letter to Ben Ali stating: "Regional and international media have reported that numerous local and international news websites covering the street protests were blocked in Tunisia. One report placed your country, along with Saudi Arabia, as the worst in the region regarding Internet censorship. A 2009 CPJ study found Tunisia to be one of the 10 worst countries worldwide to be a blogger, in part for the same reasons."[1]

The Ben Ali regime had also begun to attack activists' Facebook and email accounts. A hidden script injected into popular site login pages had been discovered by cyber activists,[2] and the Electronic Frontier Foundation advised Tunisians to use HTTPS to log in to their accounts, allowing information to be encrypted.[3]

Unfortunately, many online journalists and activists reported that their accounts had been deleted or compromised. Ben Ali's cyber militia used the stolen passwords to delete Facebook groups, pages, videos and accounts.[4]

For those reasons "Anonymous" – an international internet activism group – attacked different official Tunisian websites, including those of the presidency and the government, using distributed denial of service (DDoS) attacks.[5]

El Général, a Tunisian rap singer originally from Sfax in southeastern Tunisia, had been arrested after publishing a rap song online criticising President Ben Ali. His video was to become very popular among young Tunisians and widely circulated online. Other activists were arrested by police in different towns and their computers seized.[6]

Ben Ali gave three speeches, calling the protests and riots "terrorist acts". In his last speech he asked for pardon by declaring his intention not to run as a candidate for a new term in the 2014 elections, and promising to give freedom to the media and put an end to censorship of the internet.

On the night of 13 January, just after this last speech, the Ben Ali regime tried to play catch-up and organise pro-Ben Ali riots using paid militia from his political party RCD. At the same time, activists were intelligent enough to continue resistance on social media sites to spread the call for a big demonstration to be organised the next day.

The protests by then had gained vocal international support. United States Secretary of State

1 www.cpj.org/2011/01/tunisia-must-end-censorship-on-coverage-of-unrest.php

2 www.thetechherald.com/article.php/201101/6651/Tunisian-government-harvesting-usernames-and-passwords

3 www.eff.org/deeplinks/2011/01/eff-calls-immediate-action-defend-tunisian

4 www.wired.com/threatlevel/2011/01/tunisia/2

5 english.aljazeera.net/indepth/features/2011/01/20111614145839362.html

6 en.rsf.org/tunisia-wave-of-arrests-of-bloggers-and-07-01-2011,39238.html

Hillary Clinton declared in a speech during a meeting in Qatar on 13 January: "There's no problem with people peacefully demonstrating and protesting. It's going on in Tunisia right now. We support peaceful protest and the right of assembly."[7]

The 14 January demonstrations came to a head as thousands of people gathered outside the Ministry of Interior, a symbol of the Ben Ali regime's repression. Beginning in the afternoon, while Tunisian TV7 announced a state of emergency "to protect the Tunisian people and their properties," bloggers and cyber activists reported that a special security force had arrested members of the Trabelsi family – the family of Ben Ali's wife – at an airport. Later, TV7 declared that a major announcement to the Tunisian people was to be made soon. Bloggers began to report movements of the presidential airplane and spoke about a coup.

At the end of the day, Tunisian Prime Minister Mohamed Ghannouchi declared in an official statement that Ben Ali had stepped down, and that he had taken over as interim president as allowed by Article 56 of the Tunisian Constitution.

Tunisia began writing a new wave of liberty and tweets stated: "Every Arab leader is watching Tunisia in fear. Every Arab citizen is watching Tunisia in hope and solidarity."[8]

Despite the happiness of Tunisians after this announcement, the first reaction of cyber activists was to continue their hard work. Straight away they called for Ghannouchi to step down and appoint Foued Mebazaa, the president of the Chamber of Deputies, as interim president, drawing on Article 57 and not 56[9] of the Constitution. They felt that Article 56 might give Ben Ali the opportunity to return to Tunisia as president if he wanted to. By 15 January Mebazaa took power as interim president and appointed Ghannouchi as interim prime minister.

Social mobilisation through social media tools to support civil resistance against attacks from the militia continued following Ben Ali's departure. The hashtag #situation reported what happened in each city, warning of sniper locations, asking for blood donations, and even saving lives. A seventeen-year-old Tunisian cyber activist tweeted using his account @BulletSkan: "The army is not responding to calls! There are armed men in our yard! We need help!" – which helped others to warn the army about his situation, a move which saved him.[10]

Protesters, from all parts of the country, remained in the Kasbah in Tunis in front of the prime minister's offices, now to demand that the transitional government resign. The Kasbah sit-in (the first and second)[11] was encouraged and followed by social media. Different groups and pages on Facebook were dedicated to Kasbah. Even a dedicated committee to coordinate citizen media was created by activist participants in the sit-ins to report about their long days and difficult weather conditions.

After this sit-in, Mohamed Ghannouchi announced his resignation as prime minister of the interim government, and the interim president appointed Beji Caid el Sebsi in his place. The interim president then announced that an election would be held for a Constituent Assembly.

Conclusions

Evgeny Morozov, a visiting scholar at Stanford and a Schwartz Fellow at the New America Foundation, asked the following question in his article "First thoughts on Tunisia and the role of the Internet about the uprising": "Would this revolution have happened if there were no Facebook and Twitter?" And his answer was "Yes."[12]

On the other hand, in an official statement about the events in Tunisia, Twitter representative Sean Garrett stated: "We might be able to provide thoughtful analysis after all the events of Tunisia have unfolded. But, right now, along with the rest of the world, we sit back and watch in awe at how people are using Twitter and other platforms to provide on-the-ground perspective at what might become a truly historic moment."[13]

The answer from Tunisian activists to Morozov's question would be, for sure: "No." This is mainly because, as explained above, without social media tools other traditional media such as Al Jazeera would not have been able to report on what happened. International organisations and other countries would not have been able to understand what happened and would not have put more pressure on the Ben Ali regime.

7 www.enduringamerica.com/home/2011/1/13/tunisia-liveblog-concession-or-confrontation.html

8 techcrunch.com/2011/01/16/tunisia-2

9 Article 56 delegates power to the prime minister in case of temporary disability of the president. In this case the president may return. Article 57 gives power to the president of the Chamber of Deputies after an absolute disability of the president and does not allow the president back to office.

10 videos.tf1.fr/infos/lci-est-a-vous/tunisie-twitter-a-sauve-ma-vie-6226394.html

11 There were two Kasbah sit-ins, both between mid-January and the end of February.

12 neteffect.foreignpolicy.com/posts/2011/01/14/first_thoughts_on_tunisia_and_the_role_of_the_internet

13 techcrunch.com/2011/01/14/tunisia

The internet and social media deserve full credit in helping citizens to design their future and make it happen. They catalysed and facilitated the revolution and anarchy that were organised but effectively leaderless.

Protests were in fact spontaneous and citizen-led – not supported by a central decision-making process. In this sense the internet helped to create a "user-generated" revolution, where everyone was participating in a different way in a countrywide revolutionary process. Even after 14 January and after the politicians took over the process of change, social media still supported the resistance with the aim of defining the "new" Tunisia.

Action steps

Today Tunisia has a clear chance to rebuild a new country. Using the internet, citizens are more likely to lead this process. Cyber activists should pay attention to the need for:

- A national broadband plan that ensures access for all in the country. This will help the Tunisian economy become more competitive by creating jobs and supporting entrepreneurship. Social solutions can be enabled by access to faster internet.
- A more open and solid internet governance system is needed, and a decentralised infrastructure that can guarantee freedom of expression. An open and more accountable government is needed. ■

UNITED KINGDOM

CUTTING TO THE CORE: THE ROLE OF SOCIAL MEDIA IN RESISTANCE IN THE UK

Open Rights Group
Javier Ruiz
www.openrightsgroup.org

Introduction

The global crisis in the UK

The financial crisis of 2008 hit the United Kingdom (UK) particularly hard. Besides its own housing bubble, and the vulnerability to commodity prices due to the global character of its economy, Britain had to provide support to a disproportionately large financial sector around the City of London, which was estimated would add £1.5 trillion to the national debt.[1] Although the recession officially ended at the end of 2009, the economy has not recovered sustained growth, and unemployment is on the rise, with fears of a double-dip recession. However, the defining aspect of the crisis in the UK has not been foreclosures, price increases or youth unemployment, but the national debt.

Austerity...

The centre-right coalition government that took power in May 2010 made reducing the national debt its main priority, and quickly embarked on a major austerity programme that it claimed could lead to an irreversible reshaping of the welfare state. The necessity and severity of the cuts are widely debated,[2] and in particular their relationship to bailing out the banking sector.[3] There is also a widespread popular perception of bankers as villains, particularly in relation to the payment of large bonuses, fuelled by the rapid recovery of the sector in contrast to the rest of the economy. There are also fears that these cuts will push the country further into recession.[4]

...and its discontents

Perhaps surprisingly, the government – particularly the Conservative majority in the coalition – has not suffered the expected level of political backlash seen in other countries under strict austerity measures, such as Spain. However, this does not mean that there is no opposition to these policies. The past year has seen an unprecedented intensity of social struggles by students, independent civic networks and trade unions, with the support of a large sector of the population. This past year has also witnessed a major escalation in innovative uses of the internet for social mobilisation, although it remains unclear whether this has reached its full potential for organisation and coordination.

UK Uncut

We have chosen the new phenomenon called UK Uncut as the central story for our report. Although it is not the largest or most sophisticated operation in terms of internet use, overall it is the most innovative.

UK Uncut came to prominence after 70 activists occupied and closed down mobile company Vodafone's flagship store in Central London on 27 October 2010.[5] They had been mobilised on Twitter by the use of the hashtag #ukuncut, prompted by claims that Vodafone had been given an unfair amnesty on £6 billion of unpaid taxes, enough to cover some of the most severe cuts in social welfare. Within three days the protest had gone viral and 30 Vodafone stores had been occupied or picketed around the country.

There are now about 40 local Uncut groups in the UK, regularly organising fortnightly occupations and pickets of high street names associated with tax avoidance, including clothes retailer Topshop, the pharmacist Boots, and the banks HSBC and Barclays. Meanwhile, a spin-off called US Uncut has started across the Atlantic in the United States, with around 100 local participant nodes.

UK Uncut is characteristic of many current political phenomena in rejecting any form of incorporation or legal structure. In itself this is not new, UK Uncut being the latest incarnation of a particular political culture of creative non-violent direct action. Since the mid-1990s these networks have been very active in the UK on environmental issues,

1 www.thisismoney.co.uk/news/article.html?in_article_id=493025&in_page_id=2

2 www.thisismoney.co.uk/credit-crisis

3 www.guardian.co.uk/politics/2009/feb/20/public-debt-gordon-brown

4 www.guardian.co.uk/politics/2011/jun/04/george-osborne-plan-not-working

5 www.ukuncut.org.uk/about/ukuncut

international solidarity, and the so-called anti-globalisation movement. These loose networks are generally composed of organising clusters based on personal acquaintance that coalesce around specific forms of action, rather than ideology. As a result we have seen clusters such as Reclaim the Streets, protest samba bands and a Climate Camp, among many others.

The focus on common action rather than political discourse can be very effective at cutting through complex arguments. Although most of the people in these networks would probably describe themselves as anti-capitalists, UK Uncut has focused on a very simple equation between cuts and tax avoidance. Also, closing down a store in a busy high street has a direct economic effect, albeit small.

Anyone can use the UK Uncut "brand" and call an action, and despite the potential for abuse, the core London organisers have only had to disown a very few fake calls to action.

UK Uncut core communications uses what has become the standard mobilisation toolkit of social media: Twitter, Facebook and a blog. They have large numbers of followers on all platforms – almost 30,000 on Twitter – and take pride in being media savvy. This includes placing tactical articles in progressive newspapers, such as *The Guardian*, and use of short viral YouTube videos.

Despite the strong use of the internet for mobilisation for actions, aspects of the actual planning – secretive by necessity, such as choosing a target – tend to rely on face-to-face personal communication and trust, while organisational continuity is maintained typically in weekly or fortnightly evening meetings in public places.

Winter of discontent 2010-2011

UK Uncut are smart netizens, but they are not alone. These same online tools were also used by students in their ultimately unsuccessful protests against the trebling of university fees to £9,000 per year, in what nevertheless became some of the most challenging demonstrations for the authorities in years. This winter up to 50,000 students took to the streets on three occasions in disdain at their own National Union of Students, seen as weak and too close to the political establishment. Social media, with Twitter tags such as #dayx, brought out much larger numbers of students than expected by both organisers and police.

The opening salvo was the spontaneous mass occupation of the headquarters of the Conservative Party on 10 November 2010, which caused widespread shock and energised the students. This was followed by several increasingly assertive demonstrations accompanied by violent repression as authorities attempted to re-establish control of the situation. For the first time in recent memory, student protests included the more socially and ethnically diverse pupils from secondary education, who unlike their counterparts elsewhere in Europe, are generally not politicised. These protests were broadcasted around the world by satellite channels and weaved across social media. The UK has a disproportionate influence in global culture, as seen with the recent royal wedding of Prince William and Kate Middleton, and the student demos were followed live at homes in the Middle East,[6] together with updates on WikiLeaks' release of US diplomatic cables.

The anti-fees days of action, together with a wave of dozens of high profile campus occupations,[7] have been a significant political epiphany for a whole generation of students, largely outside unions and political parties. This also includes traditional left outfits that had dominated much of the resistance to the Iraq war. These new networks, some of them already active in campaigns against the Gaza war in January 2009, are finding their way into the wider anti-cuts movement, with many students taking part in UK Uncut actions.

At the same time, mainstream labour unions, completely tied up with the Labour Party and traditionally quite reluctant to mobilise, made some unprecedented moves this winter. Several large unions have publicly supported the students and UK Uncut[8] – including mobilising for actions – with some even calling for "non-violent resistance"[9] and a "broad strike movement"[10] against what they see as all-out war on the welfare state.

Part of this rapport was an attempt to harness the online world with a large conference in January 2011 called Netroots UK,[11] which brought together 500 trade unionists, activists and key digital players. This included influential blogs, such as Liberal Conspiracy,[12] and specialist online campaigning organisations 38 Degrees and Avaaz. The presence of US providers of campaigning services and tools, such as Blue State Digital, was a giveaway to its

6 See Solomon, C. and Palmieri, T. (eds) (2011) *Springtime: The New Student Rebellions*, Verso, London.

7 occupations.org.uk/occupations-2010

8 www.unitetheunion.org/news__events/latest_news/unite_backs_uk_uncut_s_banks_a.aspx

9 www.coalitionofresistance.org.uk/2011/06/rail-union-tssa-votes-to-participate-in-non-violent-resistance-activities

10 www.guardian.co.uk/commentisfree/2010/dec/19/unions-students-strike-fight-cuts

11 www.netrootsuk.org

12 liberalconspiracy.org

being inspired by the US initiatives[13] that helped bring Barack Obama to the White House.

The event was broadly perceived in positive terms, but ultimately it did not lead to a progressive digital front in the UK. Clear divisions emerged on a range of issues such as support for the Labour Party, although in the long term more subtle cultural differences may have also played a role. The large mobilisation of trade unions against the cuts on 26 March 2011 saw over 250,000 people in Central London, but in every way it was a traditional left and unions march. On the day, UK Uncut organised a series of theatrical actions independent from the main march, culminating in a mass occupation of luxury retailer, popular tourist destination and alleged tax avoider Fortnum and Mason's, which led to the controversial arrest of 145 people.

The most innovative use of Twitter on the day came from the police, whose @CO11MetPolice account[14] had been tested for the first time during the Climate Camp protests in 2009. Meanwhile, some technical activists have upped the ante and developed their own live mobile information system to enable demonstrators to evade police lines. The Sukey project[15] is a technological breakthrough in a long cat-and-mouse information game between police and protesters in Europe that has seen the development of multiple SMS and web systems, including Indymedia's early experiments with Twitter,[16] and had even led to eight activists being sentenced to long prison terms in Sweden in 2001.[17] The project is still in early stages, but as in previous attempts the critical success factors will be adoption rates and trust by activists.

The anti-cuts demo #march26 was called and organised by unions, but many of the participants in the main march came from other backgrounds. Many of these people travelled to London in trade union TUC[18] buses or by independent means. There were also citizens with disabilities, who are doubly targeted by the cuts in services and reductions of benefits.[19] Of course the students were there, together with lawyers and NGOs protesting cuts in legal aid,[20] and campaigners concerned about radical reforms to the National Health Service. Despite the large and diverse crowd, small side events organised by anarchist networks, punctuated by attacks on banks and luxury shops, grabbed the attention of mainstream media.

Since the cuts were announced in May 2010, innumerable local campaigns have been organised by communities trying to save specific services ranging from children's centres and public libraries to hospitals and parks.[21]

These networks are all organising regular actions and campaigns, including UK Uncut, which seems to have survived the mass arrest of its London core. Several large trade unions also planned a coordinated strike on 30 June 2011, which promised to become the next focal point for the anti-cuts networks.

Organisation

The #march26 demo showed that the current landscape of social struggle in the UK is very rich and diverse, composed of overlapping networks, campaigns and organisations, and UK Uncut is embedded in this mesh. Questions remain, however, on whether this movement will be successful in achieving its aims. Local campaigns, mostly organised around Facebook pages, have little influence on decisions taken by central government, while large demonstrations without continuity are occasional storms any government can cope with. Even some of the most successful national single-issue campaigns, such as those on legal aid and disability, taken in isolation will simply push the cuts elsewhere, notwithstanding the positive contagion effect they may have.

As we saw in relation to Netroots UK, attempts to bring together diverse groups are fraught with difficulties. The leftwing gathering[22] around the union-led Coalition of Resistance[23] seemed to reproduce the model of past experiences, such as the unsuccessful Put People First mobilisation around the London G20 in 2009.[24] Nevertheless, in a departure from the past, they now support non-violent civil disobedience, and even help publicise UK Uncut actions. Proponents of a more grassroots approach believe that a union-led campaign will fail to engage the rest of society affected by austerity policies,[25] but the alternatives have so far failed to materialise.

13 www.netrootsnation.org

14 twitter.com/#!/CO11MetPolice

15 sukey.org

16 www.indymedia.org.uk/en/2007/09/380691.html

17 en.wikipedia.org/wiki/Protests_during_the_EU_summit_in_Gothenburg_2001

18 righttowork.org.uk/2011/01/transport-to-the-tuc-march-for-the-alternative-on-26th-march

19 www.dpac.uk.net/2011/02/light-up-a-map-of-the-uk-online-in-solidarity-with-the-protesters-on-the-streets-on-26-march

20 www.justice-for-all.org.uk/Who-we-are

21 stopthecutscoalition.org

22 www.guardian.co.uk/commentisfree/2010/aug/04/time-to-organise-resistance-now

23 www.coalitionofresistance.org.uk

24 www.putpeoplefirst.org.uk

25 www.guardian.co.uk/commentisfree/2010/aug/09/tony-benns-coalition-resistance-needs-stategic-approach

There are profound differences on the type of organisation needed, with an important sector believing that these decentralised networks fuelled by the internet – UK Uncut, students, etc. – will be enough to generate a new movement with sufficient coordination to reverse the cuts.[26] The success of leaderless network movements in the Middle East and North Africa seemed for a while to vindicate this approach, although this is now tempered by events in several countries such as Syria.

A halfway point is provided by the website False Economy,[27] which provides a very polished portal of information on campaigns, also allowing the publication of new events. There are also several other projects using web tools to allow people to report and map specific cuts.[28] However, there are no spaces for the national coordination of campaign groups, and despite lots of ad hoc communications through backchannels, nobody is publicly discussing a real strategy.

UK Uncut activists claim they would like to have a national meeting of local campaigns, despite the difficulty of not knowing who exactly organises in each city. However, they fear the authorities would use it as an opportunity to clamp down on alleged ringleaders, in another step in the campaign of sustained repression against them.

Action – reaction

After being caught off guard by UK Uncut, the authorities slowly reacted. There had been some minor arrests around the country and isolated use of pepper spray against peaceful protesters in London. However, the mass arrest on 26 March of 145 activists seems to be a turning point designed, albeit unsuccessfully, to incapacitate the organisation. Bail conditions prevent the activists from entering the main shopping area in Central London and all their clothes were taken for forensic examination. In a new frontier for rights and technology, their smartphones were confiscated with all their digital social and political life inside. To achieve this with home computers would have required a special warrant.

The fact that there were almost no other arrests on the day other than for non-violent protests, despite the destruction of property by others, has generated criticisms of the Metropolitan Police's handling of the situation. Some lawyers have said that this is an attack on the fundamental democratic right to protest.[29] Large sectors of the media have falsely portrayed UK Uncut as responsible for the violence, no doubt helped by police Twitter messages such as:

> @CO11MetPoliceMetropolitan Police
> Fortnum and Mason's is surrounded by police as this is a crime scene. Persons responsible will be arrested #ukuncut

The use of Twitter by police has been criticised by several of the people interviewed for this report. There is an impression of lack of accountability, which allows messages out that would be a lot more nuanced in a press conference.

Students have also been treated quite harshly. Prime Minister David Cameron threatened that the "full weight of the law" would fall on students who occupied the Conservative headquarters,[30] with sectors of the media collaborating in publishing "Wanted" photo galleries to help hunt for suspects.[31]

Police handling of further student protests and smaller marches that broke away from union-organised events has generated great controversy. This is particularly due to the widespread use of "kettling", which involves surrounding and corralling protesters for long periods of time without proper access to food, water or sanitation. Critics claim this is a punitive detention designed to put people off from going to demonstrations, rather than preventing breaches of public order. It is also claimed that this containment technique provokes more violence as protesters feel trapped and attempt to break through police lines. Besides kettling, police have been criticised for excessive baton charges and riding horses against groups of schoolchildren.

Separately, police have arrested suspected protest leaders in early morning raids, particularly around the time of the royal wedding[32] – although it is unclear how police intelligence relates to internet surveillance. According to protester support group Green and Black, and lawyer Mike Schwartz from Bindmans, there are no known cases of people being arrested on the basis of evidence collected on social media. However, comments made on Facebook have apparently been brought up in court to

26 See the article on Open Sourcing of Political Activism by Guy Aitchison and Aaron Peters here: felixcohen.co.uk/FightBack

27 falseeconomy.org.uk

28 wherearethecuts.org and anticuts.org.uk

29 www.guardian.co.uk/uk/2011/mar/30/uk-uncut-arrests-protests?CMP=NECNETTXT766

30 www.opendemocracy.net/ourkingdom/guy-aitchison/significance-of-millbank-british-protest-begins

31 www.thisislondon.co.uk/standard-pictures/CCTV+images+of+student+riot+suspects+released-latest.do?id=23379553

32 news.sky.com/skynews/Home/Royal-Wedding/Royal-Wedding-Police-Have-Arrested-20-People-Amid-Fears-Of-A-Plot-To-Disrupt-The-Royal-Wedding/Article/201104415981406

support the case against those arrested for public disorder.

A very controversial incident involving Facebook was the closure of over 50 profile pages of protest groups on the eve of the royal wedding,[33] ostensibly for breaching the terms and conditions of Facebook, which make clear that organisations cannot use personal profiles. Facebook denies any active involvement, claiming that closures are automated if sites are reported. Attempts by Open Rights Group to find out the level of coordination behind the closures have been stonewalled by Facebook. Interestingly, Richard Allan, Facebook EU head of policy, claims that a similar situation happened in Egypt during the protests, which led to them strengthening their processes for migrating from personal profiles to pages suited for organisations. Egyptian activists have partly confirmed this.

Without Facebook's collaboration we will probably never know who reported the offending protest sites, and whether this involved elements of the state. An early attempt by police to close down a website providing students with advice on destroying potential evidence to avoid arrest[34] backfired when it was mirrored WikiLeaks style. Since then the authorities have taken a more conciliatory tone, with, for example, Sukey being invited to friendly talks with police – although this could also be interpreted as letting the activists know they are known.

In an attempt to counter criticisms, the police took the unprecedented step of allowing human rights observers into their control room for the 26 March demo, but they were criticised[35] for the fact that the use of kettling was considered as first resort. In general, the ubiquity of multimedia recording devices and social media has had an effect on police, with several high-profile cases where they have been caught lying red handed.[36] A recent court ruling in April 2011 placed further restrictions on the use of kettling.[37]

In general, the repression of the anti-cuts movement, while fairly harsh for UK standards, is quite targeted and has not reached large sectors of society. However, it shows that the movement has not yet managed to break into politically neutral spaces to dominate the national conversation, win the arguments and de-legitimise any criminalisation. This, for example, has happened in Spain with the build up of the broad and radical democracy and anti-austerity movement, organised around town square occupations. There are further protests and strikes on the horizon.

P.S. And then the riots – looking back at action steps already taken

As this report was being finalised, we witnessed the largest explosion of civil unrest in England in living memory, with five people killed in various incidents and widespread looting and arson. The disturbances started after police in North London shot a black suspect, but quickly spread, first across London and then major cities in England. Although there were no clear political demands, the demographics of those arrested show the majority to be very young and generally unemployed, with 41% living in the top 10% of the poorest areas of the UK.[38]

The aftermath has seen a draconian crackdown that resembles an undeclared state of emergency, admittedly with widespread support from the majority of the population, who after the shock and fear are now in the mood for vengeance. Around 3,000 people have been arrested[39] as police pore over 20,000 hours of closed circuit television (CCTV) footage. Some 100 people have been sent to prison every day since,[40] with courts instructed to "disregard normal sentencing guidelines."[41] As an example, a college student without a criminal record was jailed for six months for the opportunistic theft of a bottle of mineral water.[42] The government is calling for those convicted to be "stripped of benefits,"[43] and the newly launched e-petitions site has seen 216,000 people in support of this measure.[44] Some families where one member has been arrested during the riots are already being evicted from social housing.[45]

In this bonfire of liberal values and civil rights the internet and social media have received special attention. While North London was still in flames, a local parliamentarian unsuccessfully called for shutting down Blackberry Messenger (BBM)

33 wiki.openrightsgroup.org/wiki/FB_takedowns
34 www.fitwatch.org.uk
35 www.bbc.co.uk/news/uk-13109259
36 en.wikipedia.org/wiki/Death_of_Ian_Tomlinson
37 en.wikipedia.org/wiki/Kettling

38 www.alex-singleton.com/?p=507
39 www.guardian.co.uk/news/datablog/2011/aug/09/uk-riots-data-figures
40 www.bloomberg.com/news/2011-08-20/two-murders-among-crimes-in-uk-riots-police.html
41 www.guardian.co.uk/uk/2011/aug/15/riots-magistrates-sentencing
42 www.telegraph.co.uk/news/uknews/crime/8695988/London-riots-Lidl-water-thief-jailed-for-six-months.html
43 www.communitycare.co.uk/blogs/childrens-services-blog/2011/08/strip-convicted-rioters-of-their-benefits-says-ids.html
44 epetitions.direct.gov.uk/petitions/7337
45 www.guardian.co.uk/uk/2011/aug/12/london-riots-wandsworth-council-eviction

service, pointed out as the key tool rioters were using to coordinate.[46] Blackberrys are the most popular smartphone with UK youth, holding a 37% market share,[47] partly due to BBM, their free messaging service. BBM runs on Blackberry's internal network and is scrambled with basic encryption,[48] which makes it more difficult to monitor than the fully transparent Twitter. This has been seen as a threat by several governments around the globe, such as India,[49] although in the UK Blackberry is fully cooperating with authorities.[50]

The prime minister launched a widely condemned attack on social media as part of his speech to Parliament on 11 August.[51] David Cameron initially called for police to be able to shut down social networks, and for rioters to be banned from using social media. In our experience of preferred modes of internet governance in the UK, the government will probably eschew new kill-switch powers for police, and probably propose some self-regulated scheme. Home Secretary Theresa May has announced a meeting with major social media firms Facebook, Twitter and RIM (the company behind Blackberry).[52] It remains to be seen whether social media companies will risk their reputation by agreeing to self-censorship, or the UK government will press with new legislation. A seventeen-year-old has already been banned for twelve months from Facebook by a judge after posting a message saying "I think we should start rioting, it's about time we stopped the authorities pushing us about and ruining this country."[53] Separately, two young men have received four-year prison sentences for setting up calls on Facebook for "riots" in rural areas. In both cases only the police turned up and no violence took place.[54]

Many of the critics of this attack on the internet and social communications point at the valuable role these served in providing timely information, fundraising for victims, and even the coordination of mass clean-up operations.[55] And, some argue, social websites have also been used by police, with their Flickr photo gallery of suspects generating hundreds of identification calls.[56] ■

46 www.theregister.co.uk/2011/08/09/bbm_suspension

47 stakeholders.ofcom.org.uk/market-data-research/market-data/communications-market-reports/cmr11/uk/1.39

48 www.berryreview.com/2010/08/06/faq-blackberry-messenger-pin-messages-are-not-encrypted

49 www.ft.com/cms/s/0/c73f4b10-bf47-11e0-898c-00144feabdc0.html

50 www.guardian.co.uk/technology/2011/aug/09/london-riots-blackberrys-police

51 www.apc.org/en/node/12807

52 socialmediaobservatory.com/social-media-news/facebook-rim-to-meet-with-uk-government-over-proposed-social-media-ban

53 www.bbc.co.uk/news/uk-england-suffolk-14556016

54 www.guardian.co.uk/uk/2011/aug/16/facebook-riot-calls-men-jailed

55 twitter.com/#!/riotcleanup

56 www.flickr.com/photos/metropolitanpolice/sets/72157627267892973

UNITED STATES

DIGITAL YOUTH: SEXUAL DEVELOPMENT AND EXPRESSION, AND THE COMPLICATIONS OF MODERN TECHNOLOGIES

Sex Work Awareness
Melissa Ditmore and Kevicha Echols
www.sexworkawareness.org
and www.infoandthelibrary.org

Introduction

As the internet became rapidly available in parts of the United States (US) in the mid- to late-1990s, parents and conservative groups began to voice their concerns about the freedom of information flow in cyberspace and how children could possibly access information that is considered harmful and/or inappropriate. The real concern was children's exposure to sexually explicit material, in addition to how the unrestricted availability of sexually explicit material could possibly affect persons and interpersonal relationships.

In the US, school and public library computers are required to restrict access to content that is harmful to minors. "Harmful" is vague: it means obscene content, and obscenity is not clearly defined and has been the subject of litigation. Though this harm is not clearly defined or located, what is typically restricted is information about sexuality. In some places this includes sex education materials. There are a range of concerns about the dangers of sexuality and technology. According to Attwood, "The developing focus on children in the way pornography consumption is figured is consistent with a shift in the way moral panics are constructed."[1]

The issues of access to information, particularly sexual information, and how information is restricted pre-date the internet. Information about sexual matters has a history of restriction in the US, including Victorian-era censorship of information about birth control sent through the mail, 20th-century decisions about who could use the birth control pill, and now, discussions about exposure and access to sexual material for school-age children and adolescents via the internet and mobile phones.

Attwood further notes that companies that produce internet filtering software "draw on this figure of the young person in their marketing"[2] and that parents are enticed to protect their children from the luring porn producers. Recent moral panics about the availability of pornography on the internet project the figure of the child victim and cyber porn addict to symbolise the "dangerous" overwhelming wealth of sexual material online coming into the homes of families.[3]

Policy and legislative context

The Children's Internet Protection Act (CIPA) was passed by the US Congress in 2000, and survived several legal challenges, being finally upheld by the Supreme Court in 2003. The law states that schools and libraries receiving federal funding to purchase computers used to access the internet and for related costs for accessing the internet must have:

> ...in place a policy of internet safety for minors that includes the operation of a technology protection measure with respect to any of its computers with internet access that protects access through such computers to visual depictions that are (A)(i)(I) obscene; (II) child pornography, or (III) harmful to minors; (ii) and is enforcing the operation of such technology protection measure during any use of such computers by minors.[4]

CIPA defines the term "minor" as "an individual who has not attained the age of 17."[5] A provision in the CIPA legislation allows for the disabling of filters by adult users under the conditions of "enabling access to bona fide research or other lawful purposes."[6]

While judged to be constitutional, the law is not without its problems. In particular, the definition of "harmful to minors" is similar to obscenity laws, which are subjective in nature and depend on context. CIPA provides this definition:

> **(2) HARMFUL TO MINORS.**—The term "harmful to minors" means any picture, image, graphic image file, or other visual depiction that—

1 Attwood, F. (2007) "Other" or "one of us"?: The porn user in public and academic discourse, *Participations: Journal of Audience and Reception Studies*, 4 (1), p. 5. www.participations.org/Volume%204/Issue%201/4_01_attwood.htm

2 Ibid., p. 5.

3 Ibid.

4 Children's Internet Protection Act, p. 3. ifea.net/cipa.pdf

5 Ibid., p. 5.

6 Ibid., p. 7.

(A) taken as a whole and with respect to minors, appeals to a prurient interest in nudity, sex, or excretion; (B) depicts, describes, or represents, in a patently offensive way with respect to what is suitable for minors, an actual or simulated sexual act or sexual contact, actual or simulated normal or perverted sexual acts, or a lewd exhibition of the genitals; and (C) taken as a whole, lacks serious literary, artistic, political, or scientific value as to minors.[7]

The notion of "harmful to minors" is itself problematic. Judith Levine makes the case that restricting access to information, particularly about sex (the most commonly restricted topic) is what is actually harmful to minors because a lack of information renders them ill-prepared to face sexual experiences.[8]

The negative implications of legislation and surveillance for young people

The rise of the public's use of the internet in the US over the past fifteen years coincides with the erosion of sex education in the US in the past decade.[9] It is not coincidental that laws such as CIPA, which require that minors' access to information be restricted, arose at the same time as efforts to limit sexuality education to abstinence-only programmes, because these restrictions on content in education and in access to information were promoted by similar blocs of social conservatives in the US.

While US youth have less access to information about sexuality in educational institutions, they have incorporated new technology including smartphones and the internet in normal youthful sexual experimentation. For example, these new technologies have been used by youth to make and share photographs of themselves, including images that may be considered pornographic. Freedom of expression is guaranteed by the US Constitution, but people under eighteen years of age are not assumed to be able to consent, thereby creating a situation in which freedom of expression in the form of making and sharing sexual images of oneself could render youth vulnerable to serious criminal charges for making and distributing child pornography – in the form of photographs shared with their peers. What confounds this situation is that states in the US have laws that acknowledge that the age of sexual consent for minors falls between the ages of fourteen and eighteen years.[10]

US adolescents use new technologies in sexual experimentation. This is normal behaviour but involves severe legal and personal risks. Of particular concern is the practice of "sexting": sending and receiving mobile phone messages with sexual content, including photographs taken with camera phones or digital cameras.[11] Media research company The Nielsen Group reported that 77% of US teens own a mobile phone, 83% of teen mobile users use text messaging, and 56% use picture messaging; within a two-year period texting among teens went up 566%, with the average teen sending or receiving an average of 2,899 texts per month.[12] The ease and rapidity with which information can be shared electronically means that any image, once sent, may and probably will be rebroadcast. Moreover, once the content is "out there", containment is impossible.

More seriously, however, possession or distribution of such images may cause young people to fall foul of child pornography laws. One young man in the state of Florida had received some pictures of his girlfriend without any clothes on. At the time he received the pictures he was seventeen years old. When he subsequently broke up with his girlfriend, he unwisely decided to send her pictures to his list of contacts. Just a few days after his eighteenth birthday, he was met by police authorities and arrested and charged with nearly 75 counts of child pornography.[13] In another case in Pennsylvania, three teen girls and three teen boys, fourteen to seventeen years in age, were charged with child pornography because the teen girls had texted nude photos of themselves to the boys.[14] The particular status of child pornography in US law exposes senders and recipients to draconian punishments and to lasting consequences, such as being required to register as a sex offender.[15] Laws designed to protect young

7 Ibid., p. 2

8 Levine, J. (2003) *Harmful to Minors: The Perils of Protecting Children from Sex*, Thunder's Mouth Press, New York.

9 Jones, R. K. and Biddlecom, A. E. (2011) Is the Internet Filling the Sexual Health Information Gap for Teens? An Exploratory Study, *Journal of Health Communication*, 16 (2). dx.doi.org/10.1080/10810730.2010.535112

10 AVERT (2011) Worldwide ages of consent. www.avert.org/age-of-consent.htm

11 CBS/Associated Press (2009) "Sexting" Shockingly Common Among Teens, *CBS News*, 15 January. www.cbsnews.com/stories/2009/01/15/national/main4723161.shtml

12 Nielsen Company (2009) *How Teens Use Media: A Nielsen report on the myths and realities of teen media trends*. blog.nielsen.com/nielsenwire/reports/nielsen_howteensusemedia_june09.pdf

13 Harkins, G. (2011) One-size-fits-all laws for sex offenders miss the mark, *Medill Reports Chicago*, 15 February. news.medill.northwestern.edu/chicago/news.aspx?id=178523

14 Associated Press (2009) Judge Puts "Sexting" Prosecution On Hold, *CBS News*, 30 March. www.cbsnews.com/stories/2009/03/30/national/main4905250.shtml?source=RSSattr=HOME_4905250

15 Feyerick, D. and Steffen, S. (2009) "Sexting" lands teen on sex offender list, *CNN*, 7 April. articles.cnn.com/2009-04-07/justice/sexting.busts_1_phillip-alpert-offender-list-offender-registry?_s=PM:CRIME

people from adult predators can and are used to punish young people for what are best described as youthful indiscretions – and to punish them very severely.

In a survey of teens (13-19 years) and young adults (20-26 years), conducted by the National Campaign to Prevent Teen and Unplanned Pregnancy, 20% of teens and 33% of young adults responded that they have sent or posted nude or semi-nude video and/or photos of themselves. Of these numbers, 22% were teen girls and 36% were young adult women. The majority of respondents who had sent/posted sexually suggestive content or images sent them to a boyfriend or girlfriend; 71% of teen girls and 83% of young adult women reported this. Nearly half of the respondents in the survey reported that it is common for sexually suggestive content and/or nude images to be viewed by people other than the person the original message is intended for.[16] Many adults worry with good reason that young people may not understand the consequences that may arise from sending sexual content and images, even if sent only to someone that they trust.

Accordingly, many adults perceive a growing need to control not merely what information young people may access, but also what information they may transmit. Existing internet filtering software may contain some features related to this. At least one private company offers software applications that enable supervision of mobile phone use.[17] The homepage of the site declares that the software was "developed by parents for parents." A variety of types of supervision are offered, including sexting. The filter for mobile phone sexting claims to be able to detect nudity in images, presumably using techniques similar to those employed by image filtering software. Such techniques may be error prone: for example, most people's genital area is darker than the rest of their skin, and dark skin tone has been marked as nudity by some filters. With such a filter, people with darker skin tone may *always* be tagged as nude and filtered.

The software can also be used to forward questionable messages automatically to a supervisor, intended to be a parent or guardian. This feature is itself subject to potential abuse. Spouses or partners may also make use of the surveillance features of the software, sometimes without benign intent or effects.

In general, any surveillance feature raises the potential for abuse. In one current case, it is alleged that a supervisor working for a Philadelphia school district used software installed on school-mandated laptop computers to spy on children. The software was intended to control use of the computers by children and provide a security mechanism in case of theft. Instead, complainants allege that employees of the school district used the software to surreptitiously take photographs of children in their own bedrooms, a very serious violation of their privacy[18] that could include the surreptitious creation of child pornography.

Conclusion

Policies in the US continue to be developed based on moral panics and fear, including fear of the ways new technology will be used for sexual purposes. Child pornography laws and laws restricting the digital transmission of any sexual images of children can criminalise normal youth behaviour. They live in a digital age where communication does not require face-to-face meeting and the possibilities to experiment sexually are arguably very different to the ways people experienced sexual development and experimentation in the past. Educating rather than criminalising youth may have a far more positive effect on their future. Sexual behaviour documented digitally, including sexting, is inherently vulnerable to exposure. It is simply very easy to share. Minors who experiment sexually with digital media risk being classified as sex offenders if a zealous person who pursues prosecution discovers them. More research in collaboration with parents, educators, librarians, sexologists, and psychologists is necessary – those who can provide insight and experience working with youth and understand their mental capabilities as well as vulnerabilities when using the internet. This will offer more practical considerations for children's internet and mobile phone use and contribute to their growth and development by helping parents work with their children to exercise discernment and critical thinking when faced with controversial or inappropriate sexual materials.

Youth in the US have sexual rights and freedoms which are acknowledged in state laws defining the age of sexual consent and marriage, access to sexual health care such as birth control information and services without a parent, as well as youth sexuality organisations which advocate comprehensive sexuality education for youth through peer education

16 National Campaign to Prevent Teen and Unplanned Pregnancy and Cosmogirl.com (2009) *Sex and Tech: Results from a Survey of Teens and Young Adults.* www.thenationalcampaign.org/sextech/pdf/sextech_summary.pdf

17 www.mykidissafe.com/homepage.php

18 Robbins vs. Lower Merion School District (2010) Court filing, United States District Court for the District of Eastern Pennsylvania.

(many of which are mostly accessible online). As youth become curious about their bodies and sexuality, they may sexually experiment and develop relationships with their peers. However, it is key to understand that youth will express their sexuality using the means of the current time, in this case the internet. The countermeasure of over-restricting access risks limiting the rights of association and expression of young people, and inappropriate supervision of their day-to-day communications.

Action steps

- Share this article with youth and people who work with youth!
- Support efforts to educate youth about sexting and the possible consequences they face, including sharing information directly.
- Provide the space for youth to be learners and teachers about sexting issues. Sexuality websites run by youth provide insights into their issues and concerns, as do sex education programmes run by youth peer educators.
- Include the stories of teens who became registered sex offenders for sexting and explain the possible consequences of forwarding pictures not intended to be shared.
- Advocate on behalf of youth who have been unjustly affected by extreme enforcement of child pornography laws. This can be as simple as emailing legislators and encouraging them and others to limit the use of sex offender registries to people who directly harm others, rather than for youth making and sharing images of themselves.
- Support youth who have been unjustly affected. Support can mean simple kindness in the face of the isolation they have experienced, but also can be more material such as assistance with job searches or placement.
- Join APC's Don't Forward Violence campaign.[19] ▪

19 www.takebackthetech.net/pledge/i-dont-forward-violence

URUGUAY

THE BATTLE AGAINST FORGETTING IN URUGUAY

OBSERVATIC, Universidad de la República
Soledad Morales Ramos
www.observatic.edu.uy/inicio

Introduction

Uruguay is considered a bastion of democracy in the Latin American region, with high levels of support for democracy and the ongoing institutionalisation of democratic practice.

Nevertheless, since the end of the period of dictatorship (1973-1985), one issue remains unsolved: the legal amnesty given to members of the military and police forces who committed human rights violations during that period.

Over the last 26 years, human rights organisations and the Frente Amplio (FA) party (now the ruling party) have been fighting for justice and against amnesty. In 1989, a referendum on the annulment of the amnesty law took place, but it was found that the law was supported by the majority of people. In 2009, citizens were called to vote in a plebiscite on the annulment of the law, but the result was negative once again. Finally, in 2011, another unsuccessful attempt was made to persuade parliament to scrap the law.

Despite the failure of these initiatives, civil society has become a key player leading the ongoing struggle for human rights. In this struggle, the internet has become an important tool for creating awareness.

Policy and political background

Law 15,848 of 1986, commonly known as the "amnesty law", legislates that the state is unable to punish crimes against humanity committed by the military and police during the dictatorship. It also states that these crimes against society can only be investigated with prior authorisation from the Executive of the Judiciary.

The amnesty law was passed in a historical context characterised by fear. In early 1985, after the dictatorship ended and new parliamentary and executive authorities were elected, formal complaints about human rights violations committed during the period 1973-1985 were made.

As a consequence, a state of unrest arose among the armed forces, and its members refused to appear before the courts. At the same time, fear started to grow amongst the new democratic authorities who thought that the military would disregard judiciary decisions, which could ultimately result in a new period of dictatorship.

The government of President Julio María Sanguinetti began negotiations between the government and opposition parties in order to find a legal solution to this matter. As a result, the parliament passed the amnesty law just in time to avoid the military being in contempt of court.

Members of the FA, the ruling party in Uruguay since 2005, had borne the brunt of the persecution during the dictatorship because of their leftist political leaning. Although in its first term of government the FA agreed not to annul the law, it gave the judiciary power to conduct investigations which ended in the imprisonment of several members of the military and civilians. Despite this, the FA did not take a leading role in the campaign to collect signatures supporting the annulment of the law in 2007. As a result, the so-called "YES" campaign launched during the subsequent plebiscite was unsuccessful.

In its second term, the FA promised to overturn the amnesty law and in 2010 started a parliamentary debate. This occurred in a complex political context where ethical discussions about the decision of the governing party to overrule what citizens had decided in the plebiscite took place.

Initiatives against the law

After the law was approved, as mentioned, there were several initiatives to expunge it from the Uruguayan legal system:

- **First referendum** This process began in 1987 with the collection of signatures to call for a referendum. This led to a referendum on 16 April 1989 popularly referred to as the "Green Vote",[1] aimed at repealing the law. This was not successful, although 43% of those who took part in the referendum voted in favour of repealing the law.
  This decision marked the perspective of subsequent governments, which avoided discussing the issue for the next twenty years. However, civil

1 In the referendum there were two ballots to choose from: the "yellow vote" to keep the amnesty law in force, and the "green vote" to repeal it.

society continued to campaign on the issue during the time.

- **Plebiscite on the law's annulment** In 2004, the FA came into government for the first time, and committed to limit the scope of the law. The new administration established criteria to allow certain crimes to be prosecuted. This resulted in various investigations into human rights violations during the dictatorship and the prosecution of those responsible. However, there was little other progress regarding the annulment of the law.[2]

  In September 2007 civil society organisations[3] began a campaign to collect signatures for a partial annulment of the law.[4] Although in December 2007 the FA decided to support the campaign, this support did not come to much: the political party did not support the campaign financially, or in ways that reflected the importance of the debate for the party. Despite this lack of political support, the campaign organised by civil society gathered 340,043 signatures. In a plebiscite held on 25 October 2009, the effort was rejected: 47.98% voted for the annulment but more than 50% of the votes cast were needed to bring about change.

- **Bill interpreting the amnesty law** In 2010, the FA introduced a bill that offered an interpretation of the amnesty law. This stated that certain articles were in violation of the Constitution. After a complex parliamentary process with strong support from civil society, the bill was not approved because it did not garner the necessary majority.

Social resistance online

The fight against the human rights violations committed during the Uruguayan dictatorship has been driven by human rights organisations and relatives of the "disappeared",[5] as well as the FA.

But over the last six years that the FA has been in government, its attitude towards the amnesty law has been moderate. The FA set up criteria that allowed many cases to be investigated and a number of military men and civilians responsible for the crimes were found guilty. Progress was also made in the investigation and search for disappeared persons and, as a result, the remains of several of them were found in military compounds.

Although civil society plays a key role in the struggle against amnesty, the support of the FA has always been significant. However, its low profile during the most recent campaign to collect signatures resulted in a shift in the approach by activists that was clearly felt in 2007 with the introduction of the internet and Web 2.0 tools as key elements of campaigning.

Social and political participation in Uruguay is closely linked to political structures, including the influence of trade unions. This means that participation takes classical forms, such as mass rallies and marches and the use of radio and newspaper as forums for expression and the exchange of ideas.

However, not all followers of a party or organisation are involved in these structures, either by choice or by chance. Many believe that in order to make participation effective, they need specific skills or qualifications, as well as the time.

In this context, people who did not feel the traditional forms of participation were relevant to them began to use the internet and Web 2.0 tools. The new media tools were used in a way which was neither coordinated by nor necessarily linked to a formal organisation.

Web 2.0 tools started to play an important role in citizen participation. Websites, groups on social networking sites like Facebook, online discussions, videos, presentations and articles that addressed the issue of amnesty began appearing on the internet.

In the process of collecting signatures in support of a plebiscite in 2009, Web 2.0 tools had an important role to play in disseminating the objectives of the campaign, which at that point had a minimal presence in the mass media. Videos that encouraged people to sign the call for a plebiscite were uploaded on YouTube (at this stage the FA did not actively participate in the campaign).

Once the signatures were collected, the "YES" campaign started and Web 2.0 played a significant role in the context of a weak response from the mass media. Web 2.0 tools were used in conjunction with marches, rallies, and the printing of stickers and fliers. Again, YouTube played an important and unique role during the campaign.

When the plebiscite was lost, post-plebiscite campaigning began, with Web 2.0 tools forming the centre of those activities. The aim of the campaigning was to create an avenue for people to express

2 Due to political circumstances surrounding the 2004 national elections, the FA promised that the law would not be annulled or repealed. This was part of the political costs of being a leftist political force in the national government for the first time.

3 In particular, the PIT-CNT (the central trade union federation), groups of relatives of the disappeared, the University Students Federation of Uruguay (FEUU), and some of the parties that make up the Frente Amplio, which is a coalition party: the Communist Party of Uruguay (PCU), Nuevo Espacio (NE) and the People's Victory Party (PVP).

4 The aim was to nullify Articles 1, 2, 3 and 4 of the amnesty law. To call a plebiscite it is necessary to collect a number of signatures equal to 10% of those eligible to vote (about 250,000 people).

5 en.wikipedia.org/wiki/Forced_disappearance

their feelings on the loss of the plebiscite. Dozens of Facebook groups criticising the results and calling for people to carry on the struggle were created.

Shortly after this, a move began to push for parliament to annul the law – an advocacy drive which is ongoing. Dozens of Facebook groups were created in support of this, and numerous events have been held with the objective of getting feedback on how events are unfolding, and to continue to push for change.

Conclusions

Despite the failure of the referendum and plebiscite, social networks played an important role in the construction of new means of social and political participation. They increased the participation of citizens who do not normally participate in traditional channels created for political participation.

The use of information and communication technologies (ICTs), especially Web 2.0 tools, has helped the fight for human rights despite the lack of FA support. The tools help consolidate a strategy of resistance and social and political participation. Since the first judicial investigation was approved by the FA government, the internet has played a role in the dissemination of decisions taken by the court, as a way to express the feelings and ideas of citizens, and to continue to demand that action be taken by the governing party.

Web 2.0 tools were used at times when institutions would not support the fight against amnesty, and civil society had little access to the mass media.

Social networks – mainly Facebook and YouTube – were used to circulate the objectives of the struggle, to call for the participation and commitment of thousands of citizens, and to express and exchange views. The struggle has not ended and the internet will have an increasingly important role to play in the social resistance for justice and memory.

Thoughts towards action steps

- In Uruguay, the support of the party system is fundamental to any struggle related to human rights or to any civil society initiative. This is reflected in the lack of support from the FA at the stage of collecting signatures for the plebiscite and during the "YES" campaign, an absence which determined the failure of the initiative.
- Using the internet for social resistance requires the proactive participation of supporters of a cause, who should be encouraged to find ways to participate.
- The use of the internet in social resistance is an important way to get support from people who do not normally participate in traditional forms of political engagement and struggle.
- However, activists should seek ways to link campaigns using new media tools with the potential of traditional media, given that new media typically do not seem to attract people to a cause when they do not already share a point of view. ■

Links to civil society organisations involved in the fight against the amnesty law

Anular la ley de Caducidad de la Pretensión Punitiva del estado en Uruguay
www.causes.com/causes/542971

Campaña por la extradición de Manuel Cordero
www.rel-uita.org/campanias/cordero-2008/formulario.shtml

Comisión Derechos Humanos Aecco
www.facebook.com/#!/profile.php?id=100001107864314

Comisión Derechos Humanos Ceup
www.facebook.com/#!/profile.php?id=100000446391142

Federación Latinoamericana de Asociaciones de Familiares de Detenidos-Desaparecidos (FEDEFAM)
www.desaparecidos.org/fedefam

Hijos Uruguay
hijosuruguay.blogspot.com/
www.facebook.com/profile.php?id=100001714707283

Iguales y punto
igualesypunto.blogspot.com

Madres y familiares de uruguayos detenidos desaparecidos
www.desaparecidos.org.uy/madresyfamiliara.html

Nos sobra una ley – Cine documental
www.nossobraunaley.com

Por la nulidad de la ley de caducidad
www.nulidadleycaducidad.org.uy

Servicio de paz y justicia (SERPAJ)
www.serpaj.org.uy/serpajph

VENEZUELA

REFORM LAWS THAT LIMIT AND CONTROL THE INTERNET AND ELECTRONIC MEDIA IN VENEZUELA: THE IMPACT OF REGULATIONS ON FREEDOM OF EXPRESSION

EsLaRed
Sandra Benítez
www.eslared.org.ve

Introduction

The following report analyses the current status and impact that reforms to legislation by the National Assembly of Venezuela in 2010 have had on freedom of expression and, particularly, the control of media such as the internet, including social networking and instant messaging. This analysis identifies some of the principles behind the reforms set out in the government's strategic plans, given the legal framework of the Venezuelan Constitution which establishes internet access as a policy priority for the development of the state. It refers to reports from international bodies such as the Inter-American Commission on Human Rights[1] and the Inter-American Press Association,[2] debates, treaties and campaigns, among others, that have emerged at the national and international levels expressing different views on the legislative reforms in the country. We have also identified some cases where the application of the laws and the impact they have had on the daily lives of all citizens are evident. Finally, we identified some trends that are emerging in the use of and access to the internet, and defined a series of actions and recommendations on freedom of expression in Venezuela.

Legal framework

The regulatory framework for the telecommunications sector in Venezuela has undergone a series of changes in recent years, among which are strategic legal reforms, such as the Telecommunications Act[3] and the Law on Social Responsibility in Radio, Television and Electronic Media.[4] In particular, reforms in these laws are aimed at extending new powers to regulatory bodies, and responsibilities to new players, such as subscription television channels, electronic media, and the service providers and users who use the internet to disseminate large amounts of content. The aim, in other words, is to regulate the media (including social media) that use the internet as a platform for publication and broadcasting.

In Venezuela there are other laws that seek to control cyber crime and the general use of electronic media, such as the Law on Data Messages and Electronic Signatures[5] and the Special Law on Cyber Crime.[6] These new laws provide an advanced legal framework for innovative transaction mechanisms.

Other aspects of the legal framework have to do with regulations established by presidential decree in which the use and development of the internet are regulated. In particular, Decree No. 825[7] declares the internet a priority for the development of the state. Venezuela is also part of international organisations like the International Telecommunication Union (ITU),[8] among others, that establish regulatory codes at the international level to be adopted by member countries.

Shifts in government policy

It is important to note that amongst Latin American countries, Venezuela has the highest internet penetration, according to official statistics from the National Telecommunications Commission (CONATEL).[9] Registered internet users in the first quarter of 2011 stood at 10,421,557, which represents a penetration of approximately 36%. However, studies estimate that 45% of Venezuelans are internet users.[10] For Venezuelans, while the internet offers access to varied content and to online transactions, it is particularly important as a vehicle to express political dissent.

1 www.cidh.oas.org/DefaultE.htm

2 www.sipiapa.org/v4/index.php?idioma=us

3 Gaceta Oficial Nº 39.610 de la República Bolivariana de Venezuela, Ley Orgánica de Telecomunicaciones, Año 2010. www.conatel.gob.ve/files/leyrs.pdf

4 Gaceta Oficial Nº 39.610 de la República Bolivariana de Venezuela, Ley de Responsabilidad Social, Radio, Televisión y Medios Electrónicos, Año 2010. www.conatel.gob.ve/files/leyrs.pdf

5 Ley de Mensajes de Datos y Firmas Electrónicas, Año 2001. www.tsj.gov.ve/legislacion/dmdfe.htm

6 Ley Especial sobre Delitos Informáticos, Año 2001. www.tsj.gov.ve/legislacion/ledi.htm

7 Decreto presidencial Nº 825, publicado en la Gaceta Oficial Nº 36.955 del 22 de mayo del año 2000. www.cecalc.ula.ve/internetprioritaria/decreto825.html

8 www.itu.int/en/Pages/default.aspx

9 www.conatel.gob.ve/files/Indicadores/indicadores2011/presentacion_a_publicar_I_trim_2011.pdf

10 wiki.cecalc.ula.ve/index.php/Comunicaci%C3%B3n_Digital,_Ciencia_y_Sociedad

For the most part, the increase in the use of the internet has been driven by public policies applied since 2000, which are based on principles established in national plans and presidential decrees. The following are particularly important:

- National Plan for Telecommunications, Information Technology and Postal Services (PNTIySP) 2007-2013:[11] This "recognises communication as a human right and telecommunications and information technology as tools for securing that right."
- Presidential Decree No. 825: This declares access to and use of the internet a priority policy concern, and the internet "an invaluable tool for accessing and disseminating ideas." It states that public administration bodies should include goals that facilitate the use of the internet.

Similarly – although perhaps more ominously – the authorities have stated: "Within the government communication strategies it is necessary to increase the use of social networking as a means of communication. (...) This [can be used as a strategy] against potential disinformation."[12]

Since 2009 the government has announced a series of decrees that contradict the principles stated above. These have caused some concern and even protests in different sectors of Venezuelan society. These are:

- Decree 6449[13] where President Hugo Chávez decreed in 2009 that the use of the internet in the public sector was a luxury and amounted to superfluous spending. The decree stated that all processing of payments for internet services should be authorised in advance by the executive vice president. It was argued that this was based on the need to rationalise public sector spending. This move sparked a series of reactions in civil society.[14] These included advocating nationally and internationally through websites[15] in the interest of proposing new models of internet use. These initiatives resulted in a statement[16] which was presented to the National Assembly and the Ministry of Higher Education. However, it has yet to receive a response from the government. The statement suggests the following actions: a) eliminate the classification of internet use as a luxury expenditure, b) keep the internet as a policy priority, c) develop policies of internet best practices, and d) develop internet applications to optimise public resources and to promote formal education online.

  It is important to note that at the same time the government declared the internet a luxury expenditure, as a step towards reducing public spending, it also invested heavily in National Telephone Company of Venezuela (CANTV) shares, effectively giving it full control of the company. It also acquired a communications satellite at considerable cost and funded the installation of a fibre-optic cable between Venezuela and Cuba.
- The attachment of the Telecommunications Regulatory Agency (CONATEL)[17] to the Executive Vice President's Office in 2010. Here the Inter-American Commission on Human Rights (IACHR) reiterates its concern about the current legal framework in its Annual Report 2010.[18] It argues the importance of the "pursuit of a significant degree of autonomy and independence of the bodies responsible for regulating telecommunications (...) to ensure the highest degree of pluralism and diversity of the communication media in public debate. (...) The guarantees of impartiality and independence (...) [ensure] communication media [are not] controlled by political or economic groups." In its defence the government justifies such a change as follows: "Right now telecommunications is a strategic area for Venezuelan democracy and political stability [and CONATEL] must have a top-level assignment."[19]
- Partial reform of the Telecommunications Law (LOT) and the Law on Social Responsibility in Radio, Television and Electronic Media (RESORTE). These reforms generally expand the powers of CONATEL and extend regulations to new areas (e.g. subscription television services, suppliers and users who use the internet to disseminate mass content).

  Amongst the limitations[20] imposed by RESORTE are expressions or information that "promote hatred or intolerance", "promote anxiety among citizens" and "do not recognise the authorities." These are prohibited, even online. However, these expressions can be extremely difficult to

11 ociweb.mcti.gob.ve/@api/deki/files/71/=pntiysp-2007-2013-CNTI.pdf

12 www.aporrea.org/medios/a98631.html

13 Gaceta Oficial Nº 39.146, Decreto 6.649, Año 2009. www.cecalc.ula.ve/internetprioritaria/documentos/decreto6649.pdf

14 www.cecalc.ula.ve/internetprioritaria/documentos/internetprioritarialista.pdf

15 www.cecalc.ula.ve/internetprioritaria; todosenred.wordpress.com

16 www.cecalc.ula.ve/internetprioritaria/pronunciamiento.html

17 Comisión Nacional de Telecomunicaciones de Venezuela: www.conatel.gob.ve

18 www.cidh.oas.org/annualrep/2010sp/indice2010.htm

19 www.radiomundial.com.ve/yvke/noticia.php?464903

20 Amongst other things, RESORTE: a) extends the possibility of intervening in media content and the internet, and b) increases the number of conditions to operate a national pay television service and content regulation of both subscription television and regular television.

define, leaving users with uncertainty about the scope of their right to freedom of expression and ideas. The law also requires internet service providers to develop mechanisms which would "restrict the dissemination" of these kinds of expressions and establishes the responsibility of service providers for the expressions of others when they do not take measures to restrict such speech at the request of CONATEL. With respect to LOT it says that "telecommunications services are services of public interest," which means that they are subject to restrictions for reasons of public interest established by the Constitution, the law and the agencies under the National Executive (CONATEL).

Given these actions, various positions at the national level to justify the reforms as a way to control and regulate the sector for the benefit of a new model of socialist development have been argued. However, civil society has also expressed concern, arguing that the freedom of expression of citizens may be compromised, violating one of the inescapable duties of a democratic society. According to the IACHR, the risk of such reforms, standards and measures is that they give administrative authorities the freedom to restrict content at their discretion, and this is incompatible with the right to freedom of thought and expression.[21]

Here are a few incidents of note that took place in Venezuela in recent months that show the impact of the reforms: a) there have been reports[22] filed at the Attorney General's Office about the forum Noticiero Digital (Digital News)[23] saying it has been spreading false information issued by third parties; b) there are forums such as Aporrea.org[24] and Chiguire Bipolar[25] which published different types of content, including political, entertainment and religious content, but which may be seen as "intolerant speech"; c) The National Assembly appointed a commission to investigate website administrators "who commit crimes stipulated in the Venezuelan Penal Code and the Constitution, as well as the implementation of sanctions and measures relevant to such illegal acts" and to investigate those "web portals that use the internet inappropriately and unethically as media," among others.[26]

It is important to note that Venezuela is a member of the ITU[27] and that to date it has incorporated into national law all the recommendations of the organisation. International regulations on the internet establish agreements[28] to regulate content carriers only, and not content. That is, the ITU does not encourage rules for filtering content[29] through regulation; this paradigm is one of the main elements of the global agreements concerning the regulation of telecommunications.[30] Given this, through the reforms the government ignores the rules that it helped create.

New trends

- **The trend towards widespread use of the internet versus the tendency to control the internet for political purposes** Users utilise information and communications technologies (ICTs) to do the following: communicate, search for information, send and receive content, socialise, store videos/photos and conduct transactions. Faced with this array of users, the content managed via the internet and social networks transcends national boundaries. This makes content and political views difficult to control, a situation that is risky for the government which responds with efforts to control access to content.
- **The trend towards secrecy and anonymity** A controlled society is a society less informed and less able to express itself. The decline of democratic life implies a negative impact on freedom. Violating freedom of expression results in a society that is afraid to express its diverse opinions. This produces a tendency towards secrecy, anonymity and self-censorship.
- **The trend to establish patterns of control and interference** Four well-defined patterns already exist that disrupt and impact negatively on internet freedom: the blocking of relevant political content, cyber attacks on critical sites, the control of the telecommunications infrastructure, and manipulation of information available online.

21 www.cidh.oas.org/annualrep/2010sp/indice2010.htm

22 www.noticias24.com/actualidad/noticia/147544/chavez-pide-actuar-contra-noticierodigital-por-difundir-el-falso-asesinarto-de-diosdado-cabello; www.elbrollo.com/topic/410687-periodista-de-avila-tv-denuncia-a-noticiero-digital-ante-fiscalia

23 www.noticierodigital.com

24 www.aporrealos.com/forum/viewtopic.php?t=45659

25 www.elchiguirebipolar.net

26 politica.eluniversal.com/2010/03/16/pol_ava_an-investigara-a-adm_16A3597413.shtml

27 The ITU membership includes 192 states, national telecommunications regulators and 700 private companies.

28 ITU agreements deal with access to ICTs, data transmission protocols, management of signals (voice and data) and the formation of networks and connecting users.

29 The ITU does not regulate content, such as the use of language, topics, the protection of minors, etc.

30 deontoscopio.wordpress.com/2010/12/14/sobre-la-pretendida-regulacion-de-internet

Action steps

Here are some actions that could be implemented in Venezuela:

- Enact good practices in the use of resources such as the internet and the electronic media at the national level, through: a) a declaration of social principles and behavioural and operational requirements which recognise the rights and commitments of the different sectors of Venezuelan society; b) implementing good-practice policies for the internet,[31] and c) establishing a national commission for internet use (this commission would be responsible for assessing impacts and discussing and agreeing upon monitoring mechanisms, without disrupting the freedom of content).
- Establish communication policies that strengthen e-government by strengthening channels of communication through social networks and electronic media. This would promote citizen participation and recognise the potential of ICTs in the development process. Similarly, it also creates the conditions to keep users informed on various topics, such as government decisions,[32] reports,[33] state services,[34] and critical safety information.[35]
- Government media: Withdraw Internet Decree 6649 which defines the internet as a luxury expenditure for public institutions, and promote the rational use of ICT resources in public institutions through good practices in the interest of increasing productivity. This means promoting the appropriate use of the internet and social networks in government institutions in order to ensure that services can be properly delivered.
- Public awareness campaigns: Implement educational and information campaigns through social networks and the electronic media so that users know the benefits and risks that the reform laws LOT and RESORTE have on freedom of expression. Citizens also need to be informed of the rights they have in demanding to be heard and to participate politically.
- Evaluate international agreements and responsibilities outlined with established institutions like the ITU, the United Nations and others. Rules that determine the filtering of internet content, social networks and electronic media need to be reconsidered. The relevant government agencies can identify potential conflicts with these agreements and consider adjustments to the reforms. ■

31 buenaspracticasinternet.blogspot.com/2009/05/ideas-para-mejorar-nuestros-enlaces.html

32 www.noticias24.com/actualidad/noticia/157245/analisis-reuters-twitter-devuelve-a-chavez-a-la-realidad-de-venezuela

33 twitter.com/#!/antvvenezuela

34 cubanosusa.com/mundo/noticiasenvideo/856351-mision-chavez-candanga-para-atender-denuncias-por-twitter.html; twitter.com/#!/INAMEH; twitter.com/#!/mpptc; twitter.com/#!/Corpoelect

35 twitter.com/#!/Polibaruta; twitter.com/#!/Polivalcarabobo; twitter.com/#!/POLICIA_CHACAO; twitter.com/#!/IAPMVARGAS

ZAMBIA

ICTS AND THE STRUGGLE FOR SOCIAL CHANGE: THE CASE OF THE BAROTSE UPRISING

CeeJay Multimedia Consultancy
Caesar Jere

Introduction

Human rights, including social and economic rights, have become real and key issues that are being used by political and other interest groups to either support or challenge the continued rule of governments. In Zambia, as the 2011 tripartite elections (to elect the republican president, members of parliament and local councillors) drew closer, political parties, civil society organisations (CSOs), non-governmental organisations (NGOs) and religious organisations highlighted human rights and governance issues on the internet to comment on the performance of the government and ruling party, the Movement for Multiparty Democracy (MMD). Generally, the issues that were in focus related to good governance, corruption, mismanagement of public resources, transparency and accountability.

This report deals with an episode in Western Zambia that raised human rights concerns regarding the behaviour of police who shot dead two unarmed demonstrators and injured several others who were demanding the restoration of the 1964 Barotse Agreement. The incident attracted wide condemnation of the state by many human rights activists who criticised the government, especially after it justified the incident by saying it was necessary to preserve public order and security.

Background

In May 1964, just before Zambia (then Northern Rhodesia) became independent from British colonial rule, the interim government, represented by Kenneth Kaunda as prime minister, the British government and the Barotseland Royal Establishment (BRE) of Western Zambia, signed an agreement which was to recognise the supremacy of the royal establishment through King Lewanika of the Lozi people of Western Zambia. The agreement was to bestow powers on the BRE in the local administration of the area, including prevailing over natural resources such as land and forests. The agreement was to take effect upon Northern Rhodesia's independence, becoming the sovereign state of Zambia in October of the same year. Prior to independence, the Barotseland native government enjoyed special recognition by the colonial administration, as historically it was the first area of contact for British colonisers exploring Northern Rhodesia.[1]

However, to date, the so-called Barotse Agreement has not been implemented. All successive Zambian governments have failed to recognise the agreement. Kaunda, who later became the first Zambian president at independence in October 1964, had his own reasons for not implementing the agreement, possibly for fear of giving too much power to the BRE and provoking other traditional rulers from other parts of the country who could demand similar recognition. Successive governments followed suit.

Zambia has since independence remained a unitary state,[2] avoiding a federal system of government in which power is overly decentralised to local governments. Although the devolution of power from the central government to local authorities has been slowly implemented over the years, there are no serious plans or policy declarations to transfer power to local authorities more than they are seen to deserve, as the central government appears to think that this could weaken its control over local authorities.

The riots

The Barotse riots which happened on 14 January 2011 in Mongu, the capital district of Western Zambia, could probably have been avoided had the government considered calls made by members of the Barotse Patriotic Front (BFP) and some CSOs for it to engage leaders of the BFP and hear their grievances. However, the government was adamant and claimed that it did not recognise leaders of the BFP as representatives of the people of Western Province, apart from the *Litunga* (King) and his royal establishment.

The Litunga himself had kept a low profile and did not publicly support the demands of the BFP which was calling for the secession of the Western Province from the rest of Zambia. The BFP accused

1 The Barotse Agreement of 1964, Her Majesty's Stationary Office, London.

2 The Constitution of Zambia, 1996.

the government of taking the people of Western Province for granted and failing to develop the area compared to other parts of the country. To this effect, the BFP and other Lozi movements advocating for the restoration of the Barotse Agreement – such as the Movement for the Restoration of Barotseland – were wary that the Litunga had been compromised by the state which had allegedly undermined his powers by doing him favours. So they decided to confront the state on their own to demand their rights: the restoration of the Barotse Agreement, or else the secession of the province from the rest of the country.[3]

On the day of the riots, the BPF and the other movements had defied a police warning in which they had refused a permit to hold a meeting demanding the restoration of the Barotse Agreement by the state.

People killed

It was during the protests that two people were killed and several others injured by police shooting. The protesters went on a rampage destroying property, pelting police officers with stones and attempting to set a fuel filling station ablaze. Besides the police shootings, an innocent child was accidentally killed by a stone thrown by rioters. A total of 106 rioters were arrested.[4] A Facebook posting indicated that 125 people were wounded and that police had arrested Maxwell Mututwa, the 92-year-old suspected mastermind of the demonstration.[5]

Widespread concern

The shooting of the rioters raised widespread concern among many people, especially human rights activists. The situation was further aggravated by comments by the republican vice president when he justified the shooting during a session of parliament. He told parliament that "the security agencies acted with restraint and professionally to quell the riot." He further argued that the incident warranted the police use of minimum force against the rioters in order to prevent further loss of life and property.[6] This statement infuriated many people.

Campaign issue

Consequently, many members of the public and CSOs used the Mongu killings as a campaign issue against the government and the ruling MMD in the run-up to the 2011 elections. However, some quarters supported the firm stance taken by the government in maintaining law and order. The internet was among the many communication platforms (apart from newspapers, radio and television) that were used to voice the views of various groups on the incident – and those of the general public – which became largely politicised given the elections that were drawing near in the same year.

For instance, a Catholic priest in charge of the Mongu diocese, Bishop Paul Duffy, incited the people of Western Province to rise up against the government. Duffy alleged that the government had done nothing for them apart from sending police to kill them. He therefore urged the people to vote the MMD out of power.[7]

However, the government and MMD dismissed Duffy's allegations as being based on ignorance. They said there was development taking place in the province and that the government would not tolerate some misguided individuals inciting the majority of people in the province to rebel against the government and cause riots.[8]

Meanwhile, Duffy was supported by some opposition political parties who used the issue of the Barotse Agreement and underdevelopment as campaign weapons to undermine the government's popularity in the area. For instance, Michael Sata, leader of a strong opposition political party, the Patriotic Front (PF), repeatedly stated that he would bring development to the area and restore the Barotse Agreement once elected to power. He also continuously condemned the government for justifying the use of live bullets on demonstrators.

Sata's condemnation of the state in justifying the use of firearms on unarmed demonstrators was echoed by many interest groups and the general public. A prominent legal practitioner, Abraham Mwansa, argued that the rights of the Barotse demonstrators were violated in so many ways. He stated that it was unfortunate that the people accused of being responsible for the Mongu fracas were prosecuted while "no action was taken against the trigger-happy cops who killed some of these totally unarmed and defenceless people."[9] Mwansa's views were supported by CSOs and NGOs such as Transparency International Zambia (TIZ), the

3 allafrica.com/stories/201103040798.html

4 www.lusakatimes.com/2011/01/14/riotous-mongu-separatists-arrested

5 www.facebook.com/topic.php?uid=15877306073&topic=15641&post=90775

6 www.zambianwatchdog.com/?p=11613

7 www.lusakatimes.com/2011/03/09/stop-inciting-people-duffy-told

8 Ibid.

9 maravi.blogspot.com/2011/05/barotse-activists-also-have-human.html

Southern African Centre for Constructive Resolution of Disputes (SACCORD) and the Non-Governmental Organisation Coordinating Committee (NGOCC), among others.

Lawlessness and anarchy

However, some political analysts and CSOs such as the Committee of Citizens and Forum for Leadership Search argued that lawlessness bred anarchy. They asserted that in a lawless society, respect for the law and other people's rights do not matter and they therefore demanded that rules and laws that are formulated should be observed by all citizens to make the process of governance workable. They noted that while the Mongu incident was regrettable, it could however have been avoided had the people heeded the advice of the police and government that the meeting of the Barotse activists was not in the interest of public order as it was likely to yield violence.[10] Other CSOs, such as Leadership in Development, admonished Caritas Catholic church members who had supported the rioters and called for people to remove the ruling MMD by voting for PF.[11]

Notwithstanding such sentiments, it appeared that many people of the Western Province, especially those who felt that their rights had been abused, had expressed disappointment with the government over the way that it handled the Mongu riots, including the subsequent detention of the rioters. Some concerned human rights groups and members of the public also expressed concern over the manner in which the detainees were treated while in detention. For instance, a group of about twenty eminent Zambians, who included a former prime minister, intelligentsia and opposition members of parliament, wrote a petition to the president in which they expressed their "profound misgivings regarding the manner in which the government had handled the trial of those citizens who were arrested in connection with the riots."[12]

It was further observed that the state had denied the detainees their right to health by not providing them with medical treatment at opportune times. As a result, one of the detainees, Mwiya Sihope, had a leg amputated allegedly after contracting an infection while detained in the overcrowded prison. Sihope later died. Another man, Davison Siyoto, whose kneecap was shattered during the police shootings, also had a leg amputated. In addition, a juvenile detainee died after contracting a disease while in prison. The deaths were widely condemned and the blame passed on to the state. The authorities were also questioned over the detention of juveniles with adults as this was an abrogation of the rights of the juveniles who should be detained separately from adults.[13]

The state's insensitivity

Many people in the Western Province were bitter with the state's insensitivity over the deaths and injuries arising from the Mongu riots and called for the removal of the ruling MMD from power. Maxwell Mututwa, the 92-year-old arrested allegedly for being a mastermind of the riot, but later released on account of old age, said that "it's time for President [Rupiah] Banda and his MMD government to vacate office before they commit further bloodshed."[14] And a Mongu businessman, Morris Litula, stated that President Banda will have to answer to the police's shooting of his nephew, Caleb Ng'andu, after he has been voted out of office.[15]

Conclusion

This story demonstrates that the use of information and communications technologies (ICTs) in the diffusion of information related to human rights and social change in Zambia is playing a critical role in informing the public about the happenings that concern the rights of citizens. Notably, the internet has become a reliable tool in reaching out to the public and soliciting the views of citizens about human rights issues that are critical to their well-being. Internet platforms such as blogs, online publications, social media (i.e. Facebook and Twitter), where the different views of citizens on human rights issues can be exchanged and accessed, are playing an increasingly important role in the dissemination of pertinent information on human rights.

However, for social media (such as Facebook) to play a constant and active role in the dissemination and promotion of human rights information in Zambia, there is a need to re-examine the impact of the mainstream media (print, radio, television) on social media. Currently it appears that the mainstream media in Zambia are the major source of information that sets and primes the agenda (be it political, social or economic) that in turn influences the topics of discussion on social media. Once the topical news frames are no longer on the agenda of mainstream media, the social media discussion groups also lose momentum. This should not be the case, as the internet, including social media platforms,

10 allafrica.com/stories/201103040798.html

11 www.facebook.com/pages/Lusaka-Times/129559187092070

12 www.postzambia.com/post-print_article.php?articleId=20024

13 zambia24.com/latest-news/rupiah-must-go-mututwa.html

14 Ibid.

15 www.izambia.co.zm/index

should instead change the tide and aim to become the regular supplier of news for mainstream media.

New media platforms are obviously more potent and versatile. They are capable of generating and processing a wider variety of information within a shorter time compared to traditional media. But as long as the mainstream media continue to dominate and set the agenda for social media, the topics on social media will remain unsustainable and inconclusive. This was the case regarding the events this report examines. There were no sustained and coherent discussions that were posted on social media including Facebook and Twitter.

This report shows how the internet was used to influence the position of members of the public to either support or reject a view affecting their socio-economic and political rights, especially where the government is seen not to respect and uphold such rights. Through the use of ICTs, the public can therefore be persuaded to either side with opposition groups calling for change of government in order to promote these rights, or the public may be induced to understand the government's action which may be perceived as a violation of human rights, as was the case of the Mongu shootings by the police.

Action steps

The right to information is a critical entitlement that should be widely availed to all Zambian citizens, especially those residing in the marginalised rural areas where communication is hampered by various infrastructural factors. The right to information is a key right that makes it possible to access all other rights – be they social, economic or political.

However, while access to mobile telephony has rapidly spread to most rural areas in Zambia, internet access and participation is still low in most rural parts of the country compared to urban areas. It is therefore recommended that for more citizens to participate and understand issues that affect their rights and subsequently their livelihoods, the following should be considered by the government and other relevant stakeholders:

- Roll out ICTs, especially the internet, to rural areas and ensure that broadband reaches many rural communities to enable more people to have access to the internet.
- Design and implement programmes that build capacity among various stakeholders in the regular use of social media platforms in promoting and advocating human rights and social change.
- Implement policy statements in the 2007 ICT policy document that envisages the growth and expansion of ICTs, including the internet, to rural areas and its access at subsidised rates.[16]
- Increase the availability of ICT training at schools in rural areas.
- Waive or reduce taxes for businesses intending to set up internet access points.
- Waive or reduce taxes on ICT equipment intended for use in rural areas. ▪

16 Zambia ICT Policy, 2007